Backbase 4 RIA Development

Create Enterprise-grade Rich Internet Applications using the Backbase Client Framework

Ghica van Emde Boas

Sergey Ilinsky

BIRMINGHAM - MUMBAI

Backbase 4 RIA Development

Copyright © 2009 Packt Publishing

First published: December 2009

Production Reference: 1041209

Published by Packt Publishing Ltd.
32 Lincoln Road
Olton
Birmingham, B27 6PA, UK.

ISBN 978-1-847199-12-6

www.packtpub.com

Cover Image by Vinayak Chittar (vinayak.chittar@gmail.com)

Credits

Authors

Ghica van Emde Boas

Sergey Ilinsky

Reviewers

Deepak Vohra

Jerry Spohn

Peter Svensson

Acquisition Editor

Douglas Paterson

Development Editor

Dilip Venkatesh

Technical Editor

Wilson D'souza

Copy Editor

Ajay Shanker

Indexer

Hemangini Bari

Editorial Team Leader

Abhijeet Deobhakta

Project Team Leader

Priya Mukherji

Project Coordinator

Ashwin Shetty

Proofreader

Lynda Sliwoski

Graphics

Nilesh R. Mohite

Production Coordinator

Adline Swetha Jesuthas

Cover Work

Adline Swetha Jesuthas

About the Authors

Ghica van Emde Boas is an independent IT Consultant. She was employed by IBM in the Netherlands for 30 years as a relational database developer, as an IT Architect, and as a Java developer involved with the largest Java framework ever written—the IBM SanFrancisco Framework. She has been taking part in the development of object-oriented methodologies within IBM. She has been teaching these at IBM's Object Technology University in Belgium and the USA.

Ghica has co-organized several workshops on Generative Model Transformations at OOPSLA (Object-oriented Programming, Systems, Languages, and Applications) conferences, the place where it all happened: objects, design patterns, modeling wars (UML), eXtreme programming, and Agile development. She now specializes in PHP, MySQL, and web application development. She helped write the client framework documentation for Backbase.

Ghica has written two books in Dutch about PHP and MySQL for Pearson Education, and has contributed considerably to the Dutch translation of *"Foundations of Ajax"*, *by Ryan Asleson and Nathaniel T. Schutta, Apress*. While at IBM, Ghica participated in writing two Redbooks and published two articles, one in the IBM Journal of Research and Development and the other in the IBM Systems Journal.

Ghica lives and works in the Netherlands. She is married and has three children. She likes rowing on the Spaarne River.

First of all, I would like to thank Dimitra Retsina, Jouk Pleiter, and Gerbert Kaandorp from Backbase for their enthusiasm about this book-writing project and for supporting me by allowing access to all information about the Backbase framework that I needed.

Sergey Ilinsky deserves my gratitude for his spontaneous offer to be a co-author and for the fierce discussions we had, which were always interesting.

Without the help of the R&D crew at Backbase, this book would contain a lot more errors and fewer examples. Thanks!

The Planning & Scores group at the ROC Eindhoven (a very large school in the Netherlands) helped me by developing widgets that I could use in the sample application, while Geert Broekmans wrote the PHP database framework used in the sample application of the book.

I am truly grateful for the help and useful comments from the reviewers and the staff at Packt Publishing.

Of course writing this book would not have been possible without the ongoing support for my information technology related adventures, from my husband, Peter.

Sergey Ilinsky is a senior UI engineer at Nedstat BV and a Tech Lead for an open source project at Clientside OY. He has worked for Backbase for three years, evangelizing open-standards based software development, while engineering and developing core parts of the Backbase Client Framework.

Having been heavily involved with client-side development since 2003, he became an expert in many standard and proprietary web technologies. He is also a contributor to some of the modern web-related specifications. Sergey can frequently be found on AJAX or client-side technology related forums, or he can be met at international developers' conferences where he occasionally gives talks.

I would like to thank Backbase for the opportunity they gave me to work and improve on this beautiful piece of software—the Backbase Ajax Client Framework—and later for letting me join the project of writing this book.

Thanks to Ghica van Emde Boas, the main writer of the book, who I had the pleasure to work with and who never sent me a third email reminder whenever I delayed my part.

Thanks to the staff of Packt Publishing involved in this book project.

I would like to express special gratitude to my girlfriend, Elena O., for her tolerance and ongoing support.

About the Reviewers

Deepak Vohra is a consultant and a principal member of the NuBean.com software company. Deepak is a Sun Certified Java Programmer and Web Component Developer, and has worked in the fields of XML and Java programming and J2EE for over five years. Deepak is the co-author of the book "*Pro XML Development with Java Technology*", *Apress* and was the technical reviewer for the book *WebLogic: The Definitive Guide*", *O'Reilly*. Deepak was also the technical reviewer for the book "*Ruby Programming for the Absolute Beginner*", *Course Technology PTR* and the technical editor for the book "*Prototype and Scriptaculous in Action*", *Manning Publications*. Deepak is also the author of the books "*JDBC 4.0 and Oracle JDeveloper for J2EE Development*", *Packt Publishing* and "*Processing XML Documents with Oracle JDeveloper 11g*", *Packt Publishing*.

Jerry L. Spohn is a Manager of Development for a medium-sized software development firm in Exton, Pennsylvania. His responsibilities include managing a team of developers and assisting in architecting a large, multilingual, multi-currency loan accounting system, written in COBOL and Java. He is also responsible for maintaining and tracking a system-wide program database documentation web site, for which he uses DotNetNuke as the portal.

Jerry is also the owner of Spohn Software LLC, a small consulting firm that helps small businesses in all aspects of maintaining and improving their business processes. This includes helping with the creation and maintenance of websites, general office productivity issues, and computer procurement. Spohn Software, as a firm, prefers to teach their clients how to solve their own problems internally, rather than require a long-term contract, thereby making the business more productive and profitable in the future.

Jerry currently resides in Fleetwood, Pennsylvania. He enjoys spending time with his two sons, Nicholas and Nolan.

Peter Svensson is a developer, architect, father, and runs his own company—Greener Grass AB. When he's not arranging the Scandinavian Web Developer Conference or managing the Stockholm Google Technology User Group, he develops rich web applications using the Dojo AJAX Toolkit and no Flash whatsoever. He's also the author of *"Learning Dojo"*, *Packt Publishing*.

Thanks to my loving family for supporting my crazy stunts, frequent flights, and benevolent maniacal schemes.

Table of Contents

Preface

This book is about squaring the circles of web applications. It deals with the *Backbase Client Framework*.

Before you put this book away because you think that squaring circles is rather vague and mathematically impossible, let's hasten to say that this book will give you a solid foundation in web application programming using the Backbase Client Framework.

Now, before you again think of putting this book away because you are not sure why you should use the Backbase framework instead of one of the many other JavaScript frameworks or libraries out there, give us a chance to briefly explain what squaring the circles of web applications means and what the Backbase framework has to do with this.

Here is a set of rhetorical questions: Would it not be nice if you have an extensive library of UI widgets that could be used in the same way as HTML? If you could extend HTML with new widgets and components in any way you like? If you could use AJAX almost transparently? If you could bind data retrieved dynamically from a server in flexible ways to any widget, in particular to complex data grids?

Of course, that would be nice for a number of reasons. First of all, XML-based UI definition languages such as HTML have been proven to be a very effective and natural way to lay out web pages. UI designers are familiar with them and have good tools to help them make good designs.

Therefore, the UI designer or the developer who plays this role should be able to define the UI using an XML-based UI definition language directly. It should not be necessary to generate the HTML or UI definition in complex ways using a server scripting language such as PHP or JSP; even worse is constructing the DOM tree to define the UI using JavaScript. This is because it is very hard to predict what the final result on the web page will be from the perspective of the UI designer. Yet, this is a common practice today.

Rich UI widgets will have rich interaction with each other and with a server. For example, to retrieve new data dynamically from a database to be displayed in a table, a drop-down list, or a report, and so on. Common interaction patters involve also submitting form data that can be used for updates on a server.

Creating rich interaction is a programmer's job. On the client side, you will want to use JavaScript and on the server side, you have a choice of options according to your preference or that of your developers. The question is how do you prevent polluting your nice, clean, square-bracketed XML-based UI definition language with the round JavaScript objects that you need to implement the desired behavior?

The answer is the Backbase Client Framework. For details of how this happens and how you really square the circles, we refer to the rest of this book. But let's briefly introduce the framework here: the Backbase Client Framework is a standards-based, server independent, cross-browser framework to create Rich Internet Applications (RIAs).

RIA development is usually associated with either Adobe Flex or Microsoft Silverlight. Although both have similar XML-based UI definition languages, the main difference with the Backbase framework is that they need a plugin to run, whereas the Backbase framework does not because it is developed in JavaScript.

Backbase allows the development of web applications that run within all major browsers, whereas developers are able to use established standards for XHTML, DOM, CSS, XPath, and XSLT, even if the browser used does not support them. The transparent use of AJAX technologies, for example to submit forms or to retrieve updates for data grids, can be taken for granted with the Backbase framework.

This book teaches you how to use the Backbase framework effectively from *Hello Backbase* to complex custom-defined UI components. The book contains a complete overview of all UI libraries available within the Backbase framework and shows examples for each element described. It teaches you how to develop your own widgets, providing a comprehensive overview of the Backbase Tag Definition Language (TDL) and by showing interesting, non-trivial examples.

Significant attention is given to the architectural aspects of designing a web application, showing sample applications using a Model-View-Controller approach.

What this book covers

Here is a summary of the chapter contents:

Chapter 1: *Hello Backbase!*, walks you through the steps to set up your development environment.

The famous *Hello World* is shown in many variations: with only basic JavaScript, a Backbase UI widget together with basic JavaScript, a Backbase Tag Library widget together with the Backbase XML Execution Language, and finally using AJAX communication with a server script.

This chapter teaches you something about XML namespaces.

Chapter 2: *User Interface Development*, provides a closer look at the Backbase UI markup languages and their XML namespaces. We give an overview of the Backbase Tag Library (BTL) and details about the UI layout widgets in BTL.

The proper layout of an application user interface involves styling with CSS. We describe how CSS can interact with the BTL widgets and how you can go about styling in your web application.

Chapter 3: *Writing the Application Logic*, provides more details about the execution logic of a web application. We look at the Backbase programming model and the various APIs it provides. In particular, we look at the Backbase XML Execution Language and at the Command Functions.

We add a few new BTL widgets to our repertoire: the *Info and Notify* widgets.

Chapter 4: *Client-server Communication and Forms*, covers subjects that range from low level details about asynchronous communication between client and server, to high level web application architecture.

We show you the details of *forms* support, including validation options, in the Backbase framework and list the widgets available in this category.

We will start applying the knowledge acquired in these four chapters to design and develop a sample application for a travel blog site, the C3D sample application.

Chapter 5: *Data-bound Widgets*, deals with data binding which is an interaction between a data source, usually residing on a server (for example, a database), and a data observer is usually an object on the client that can map this data to a UI widget.

In this chapter we discuss data binding, the data-bound widgets in the Backbase framework, and how you can make your own widget.

The most powerful data-bound widget in the Backbase framework is the `dataGrid`. With 11 examples, we explore many details of using this grid.

Chapter 6: *More Dynamic Behavior,* talks about:

Behaviors: Generic functionality that you can attach to any Backbase element.

The built-in behaviors, in particular the *drag-and-drop* behavior: how you can influence the dragging of elements and the things you can do when the element is dropped. We also discuss the *resize* behavior with its options.

Command functions to add, remove, or set behaviors dynamically.

The *broadcaster/observer* elements and functions.

Animation with the *Synchronized Multimedia Integration Language* (SMIL).

Chapter 7: *Creating UI Components,* gives a lot of detail about the *Tag Definition Language* (TDL), the most interesting and unique feature of the Backbase framework. We show that you can build powerful UI components using TDL, which promises new ways of doing web application development.

Chapter 8: *Widget Wrap-Up,* covers almost all the remaining BTL widgets and command functions. We will look in detail at *actions, menus,* and *windows.*

Chapter 9: *Debugging, Optimization, and Deployment,* shows that the Backbase tool set, especially the *debugger,* has an advantage over other tools because it works with all browsers. In addition, the Backbase debugger allows you to inspect your Backbase application structure and all custom built widgets easily.

Using the guidelines set forth by the **YSlow** tool, we describe what you can do to optimize a Backbase web application.

We look at deploying the Backbase framework libraries, optimizing the TDL bindings, and using the optimized versions of the bindings delivered with the Backbase package.

Chapter 10: *Framework Comparison,* is a rather theoretical chapter that will show you a way to look at the various JavaScript frameworks available and how to categorize them.

We illustrate with an example the difference in coding style for a pure JavaScript framework as opposed to the Backbase framework using XML for UI layout. We also illustrate how easy it is to integrate other frameworks into the Backbase framework.

Chapter 11: *The Square Web Application*, formulates what a *square web application* is and how to develop one.

This last chapter provides a last look at the C3D travel blog sample application. It shows changes and updates according to the *make it work, make it right, make it fast* principle. The details of uploading an image and of including a Google map are included.

We end the chapter by developing a square puzzle.

What you need for this book

This book includes many examples. All examples are provided in the sample code for this book in an easily operational form. Many examples only require a browser to run. You will need a web development environment, as explained in Chapter 1, to run the examples where server interaction is involved. Later in the book, you will need to set up a database to run the C3D sample application.

Who this book is for

This book is for web developers who want to develop applications using the Backbase Client Framework. It may also be interesting for web developers and web application architects who want to know more about XML-based web application architectures.

Conventions

In this book, you will find a number of styles of text that distinguish between different kinds of information. Here are some examples of these styles, and an explanation of their meaning.

Code words in text are shown as follows: "We can include other contexts through the use of the `include` directive."

A block of code is set as follows:

```
<?xml version="1.0" encoding="UTF-8"?>
<div xmlns="http://www.w3.org/1999/xhtml">
   <p>
      The server says: Hello <strong>John Doe</strong>! - on:
      Friday 30th of May 2008 12:50:43 PM
   </p>
</div>
```

When we wish to draw your attention to a particular part of a code block, the relevant lines or items are set in bold:

```
<div>
  <e:handler
    xmlns:e="http://www.backbase.com/2006/xel"
    event="click" type="text/javascript">
    alert('Backbase says hello!');
  </e:handler>
  Click me
</div>
```

New terms and **important words** are shown in bold. Words that you see on the screen, in menus or dialog boxes for example, appear in the text like this: "clicking the **Next** button moves you to the next screen".

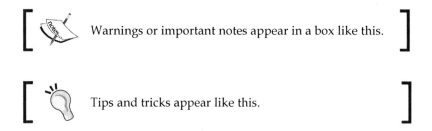

> Warnings or important notes appear in a box like this.

> Tips and tricks appear like this.

Reader feedback

Feedback from our readers is always welcome. Let us know what you think about this book—what you liked or may have disliked. Reader feedback is important for us to develop titles that you really get the most out of.

To send us general feedback, simply send an email to feedback@packtpub.com, and mention the book title via the subject of your message.

If there is a book that you need and would like to see us publish, please send us a note in the **SUGGEST A TITLE** form on www.packtpub.com or email suggest@packtpub.com.

If there is a topic that you have expertise in and you are interested in either writing or contributing to a book on, see our author guide on www.packtpub.com/authors.

Customer support

Now that you are the proud owner of a Packt book, we have a number of things to help you to get the most from your purchase.

Downloading the example code for the book

Visit http://www.packtpub.com/files/code/9126_Code.zip to directly download the example code.

The downloadable files contain instructions on how to use them.

Errata

Although we have taken every care to ensure the accuracy of our content, mistakes do happen. If you find a mistake in one of our books—maybe a mistake in the text or the code—we would be grateful if you would report this to us. By doing so, you can save other readers from frustration, and help us to improve subsequent versions of this book. If you find any errata, please report them by visiting http://www.packtpub.com/support, selecting your book, clicking on the **let us know** link, and entering the details of your errata. Once your errata are verified, your submission will be accepted and the errata added to any list of existing errata. Any existing errata can be viewed by selecting your title from http://www.packtpub.com/support.

Piracy

Piracy of copyright material on the Internet is an ongoing problem across all media. At Packt, we take the protection of our copyright and licenses very seriously. If you come across any illegal copies of our works, in any form, on the Internet, please provide us with the location address or web site name immediately so that we can pursue a remedy.

Please contact us at copyright@packtpub.com with a link to the suspected pirated material.

We appreciate your help in protecting our authors, and our ability to bring you valuable content.

Questions

You can contact us at questions@packtpub.com if you are having a problem with any aspect of the book, and we will do our best to address it.

1
Hello Backbase!

In this chapter, we will say "hello!" to the Backbase Client Framework. We will explain how to download the framework and how to install it. Then, we will discuss how to set up a new application that'll show "Hello World!". At the end of this chapter, we will also show a simple page layout using a Backbase `panelSet` widget. We will expand this page into a client web application in later chapters.

In each chapter, we will cover some background information that will help you understand how the Backbase framework works. In this chapter we will look at the following subjects in more detail:

- What are Backbase, AJAX, and RIA?
- Setting up your development environment, downloading the Backbase Client Framework, and installing it
- The Backbase Explorer
- The Backbase page skeleton that is needed to load the client runtime of the framework
- "Hello Backbase" examples
- Namespaces and how they are used in the Backbase framework
- A basic page with a `panelSet`

What is Backbase?

The **Backbase Client Framework** is a standards based, server independent, cross-browser solution to creating web applications, ranging from traditional to desktop-like. It uses AJAX technologies to easily develop and deploy Rich Internet Applications.

This is a mouthful of a definition. Let's look at the meaning of those terms first:

- Standards based: XHMTL, CSS, XML, and JavaScript are used according to defined standards.

- Server independent: The Backbase Client Framework is server agnostic, as it does not know which server or which server language it is communicating with.

- AJAX: Asynchronous JavaScript and XML is an enabling technology for creating Rich Internet Applications. We will provide an overview in Chapter 4.

- RIA (Rich Internet Applications): This is what you can build using the Backbase Client Framework — web applications that have a rich user interface, and allow a user to interact with the application. In addition to AJAX as a communication enabler, there is also an extensive library with UI widgets available.

In addition to the Client Framework, Backbase offers a set of extensions for the Java environment. It includes a **JavaServer Faces (JSF)** extension, a generic connector for JSP or Struts, and a Data Services extension. These extensions are not discussed in this book.

What can Backbase do for me?

If you are like us and like many web developers, you may have started writing simple HTML when developing web applications. After a while, you may have decided to separate presentation from structure and to give your web pages a better look using CSS. The next thing in your evolution as a web developer would have been making your pages more user friendly and interactive, by creating tool tips, pop-up windows, tab boxes, and by validating forms before submitting. Maybe you did this using little pieces of JavaScript downloaded from the Web or by building your own JavaScript function libraries. On top of this, you may have tried to give your web applications the look and feel of a desktop application by using AJAX, requiring more JavaScript everywhere.

Now, what happened to the source code of your web pages? Again, if you are like us, over time the HTML code became littered with many pieces of JavaScript. It became difficult to see what the structure of the page was, even more so when you tried to generate the HTML code from PHP or JSP or some other server-side scripting language. Perhaps, you found out too that it is really hard to make a web page that will show well in all major browsers.

Would it not be nice if there was...

- A framework that has the tool tips and the tab boxes readily available for you and will allow you to code these widgets as if they were HTML tags?

- A framework that has AJAX support almost transparently built in?

- A framework that allows you to bind data from a database to widgets on your page, such as a data grid with paging, sorting, and more?

- A framework that allows you to extend the provided widgets or build your own widgets, and then use these widgets in exactly the same way as the widgets provided with the framework?

- And finally, a framework that runs in standard browsers without requiring a plugin?

The Backbase Client Framework is such a framework. We will call it Backbase most of the time, which is also the name of the company that built the framework. Backbase can be used freely. There is no difference between the commercial and the community edition, except for the license, which states that you should not deploy it commercially on a server with more than two processors.

This book is intended to make you an expert in using the Backbase framework. We will cover just enough of AJAX, XML, XHTML, namespaces, XPath, CSS, and the Document Object Model (DOM) to make the Backbase framework easier to use, and to understand why Backbase is built like it is. While doing so, we hope that we can increase your knowledge of the core client web technologies and how they relate to each other. With this knowledge, you can evaluate Backbase against other frameworks and decide which one suits your purpose the best.

To round off this introduction, let's summarize the advantages of using the Backbase Client Framework:

- The framework is written in JavaScript. Therefore, it runs on all modern browsers and requires no plugin or prior installation.

- The framework is XML based. This means that you can define your GUIs using XML tags. This is very important for clarity of code and design, and is more familiar to UI developers.

- The widgets that are built-in or that you create are *objects*, in the meaning of being object oriented. This means that you can use object-oriented design methods effectively to design a Backbase application.

- The framework itself is built using a Model-View-Controller (MVC) architecture. You are encouraged to similarly design your applications using MVC.

- The framework is standards based and provides cross-browser functionality. This means that the Backbase framework allows you to use standards, such as DOM 3 events or SMIL that may not be available in all browsers.

- Another transparent feature is the AJAX communication built into several UI widgets. For example, you do not need to create `XMLHttpRequest` objects to submit a form. The framework will do this automatically for you if and when you tell it where the response should go.

- There is an Eclipse IDE plugin available to help with the syntax of UI widgets.

- The framework easily integrates with third-party widgets.

The Backbase Explorer

Let us first take a look at what the Backbase framework contains. On the Developer Network site of Backbase, there is a set of demos that you can view online or download for further inspection. The URL for this site is `http://bdn.backbase.com/client/demos`.

These demos include Sample Application Layouts, a Progressive Enhancement Demo, a Rich Forms Demo, and Coexistence Demos. You can take a look at those and run them online, but according to our opinion, they are only mildly interesting, except for the **Backbase Explorer**.

The Backbase Explorer allows you to view all UI widgets from the **Backbase Tag Library (BTL)**; you can see the source code that is needed to show the example, and you can change the source code to see what happens. For example, if you click on **Windows & Dialogs | window management | windowArea**, you can see something like this:

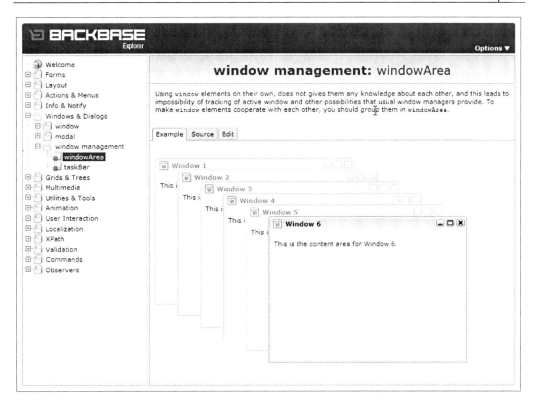

The Backbase Explorer is an interesting and useful application that can be used to learn more about the Backbase framework and about the widgets it offers.

Also, take a look at the **Sample Application Layouts** on the same online demo page. This will give you an idea of the kind of layouts you can easily make using Backbase. We will use a simplified version of one of these as the starting point for the example application that we will be developing throughout the book.

Each of the demos is downloadable and contained in a ZIP file. When unzipped, it can execute immediately on your local PC because the essential parts of the Backbase framework are included with it.

Setting up a web development environment

Before we start looking at the Backbase Client Framework, you may want to consider the setting up of a development environment that you will need to execute the examples provided in the book or to develop your own applications. We assume that you already have experience with web application development. Therefore, we will keep it short.

To try out the application we are developing, you will need a web server, a language environment that you can use to develop the server side of your application, and a browser in which you can execute your application.

The web server and a server scripting language

To serve web pages locally, you need to have a web server installed on your local PC. You can use any web server you like in combination with the Backbase framework. For example, popular web servers are Apache and IIS.

Also, you will need a server scripting language, such as JSP or PHP. Backbase will work with all server languages, therefore the choice is yours. Just remember that Backbase can communicate with any web server and any server scripting language that outputs the right XHTML to the browser.

If you already have a local development environment set up, then that is fine. Keep using it! Otherwise, you could obtain the XAMPP package, which you can download from: www.apachefriends.org. This package is really easy to install and includes Apache, PHP, MySQL, PHPMyAdmin, and more. It is available for several operating systems including various types of Linux, Mac OS, and Windows.

Examples in this book that require communication with a server will mostly use PHP because that is the easiest environment to set up, and also easy to understand, even if you are not familiar with it.

 There exists a JSF version of Backbase framework, which offers tight integration with JavaServer Faces (JSF). We are not discussing the JSF version of the Backbase framework in this book.

The browser

To execute and view the application we are developing, you need a browser. The browser landscape is changing very fast. A year ago, there would have been only one recommendation that we would have made here: use Mozilla Firefox! Not only because it is a good browser, but mainly because of Firebug, the debugging plugin for Firefox. Firebug gives you the ability to edit, debug, and monitor CSS, XHTML, JavaScript, and network traffic live in any web page viewed in the browser. You can find Firebug at `http://www.getfirebug.com`.

Today, there are a lot more browsers that do a good job at implementing web standards and that offer good debugging facilities such as Google Chrome, Safari, and Microsoft Internet Explorer 8.

A handy plugin to use for Microsoft Internet Explorer prior to version 8 is the MSIE Developer Toolbar. It provides a variety of tools for quickly creating, understanding, and troubleshooting web pages in the MSIE browser. Search for Developer Toolbar at `http://www.microsoft.com/downloads/`.

We should specifically mention the **Backbase debugger**. This is a Firebug style debugger that will work across all supported browsers. It will start automatically in the Backbase development environment when something goes wrong. It will help you to debug applications in browsers for which no good tools are available.

Although many examples shown in this book and in the Backbase documentation do not really require communication with a server, you may not be able to execute them locally by typing the file location as URL in the browser because of security restrictions in the browser you are using.

Firefox is an example of such a browser. You can lift this restriction in Firefox by placing a file with the name `user.js` (if it does not exist) in the `defaults/pref` folder of the browser and adding the following line:

`pref("security.fileuri.strict_origin_policy", false);`

If you are a Windows user, you may be able to find this folder here: `C:\Program Files\Mozilla Firefox\defaults\pref`.

Be aware of the security risks you are taking though!

You will need more than one browser to test your application. A considerable percentage of the users of your web application will be using browsers other than the one you chose to develop with, and unfortunately, even Backbase cannot guarantee that your application will look the same in all browsers. At the minimum, you should have Mozilla Firefox and Microsoft Internet Explorer available for testing.

Using an IDE

In addition to a web server, you will need a tool that you can use to edit your application source code. Although any text editor such as Notepad is sufficient, you will be more productive if you use a suitable Integrated Development Environment (IDE). Again, if you already use an IDE that you are comfortable with, please keep using it. Otherwise, we would recommend installing the Eclipse IDE. Eclipse is an open source IDE with many plugins available for specific development tasks. One of those is a Backbase plugin that will help with code completion. This plugin is included in the package when you download the Backbase framework. However, Eclipse can be downloaded from `http://www.eclipse.org`. Be sure to download a version of Eclipse with web development capabilities already included. A plugin that supports PHP, of which there are several available, is useful too.

As an alternative, you could consider **Aptana Studio**, an Eclipse-based IDE that is targeted at AJAX developers. Among many features, it has support for Adobe Air application development. It has many plugins for all kinds of handy development tasks. You can download Aptana as a standalone application or as an Eclipse IDE plugin from `http://www.aptana.com`.

Download the Backbase framework

Your development environment is now set up; therefore, it is time to download Backbase Client Framework from `http://www.backbase.com/download`.

Once you have downloaded the package, which comes as a ZIP file, you can unzip it to a convenient location. The unzipped package should look similar to this:

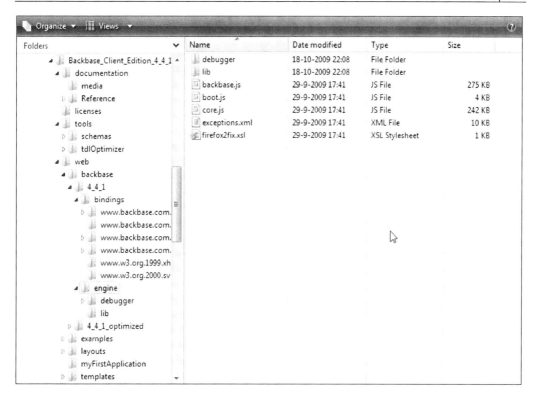

Warning: What we describe here is the structure of the Backbase package as you can find it on the Web at the time of writing. Changes have occurred in the past and may happen again.

In order to use the Backbase framework, your web server must send it to a browser. Therefore, we must copy the framework to a location where the web server can find it. Your web server serves its pages from its document root. Its default location for the document root can be very different depending on the web server you are using and by configuring the web server, you can have multiple roots at almost any location in the file system on the host of your web server.

Let's assume that your development web server is Apache from the XAMPP package and that you have installed it on the C: drive. The default document root is then: `c:\xampp\htdocs`. The easy way to install the Backbase framework is to copy the `backbase` folder found in the `web` folder and paste it as a subfolder of `htdocs`. For the time being, you can delete the `4_4_1_optimized` folder that you just copied. You will need the optimized version of the framework only when you are actually deploying your application on a publicly visible server.

The Backbase page skeleton

There is one more thing we would like to take care of before we really start. It will save a lot of useless book space if we can explain what a typical starter page for the Backbase framework looks like and then forget about it. Of course, the examples that are supplied with this book are all ready to execute and therefore this source code will repeat the skeleton page code where required.

For any Backbase enabled page, you need an HTML file, usually named `index.html`, which looks like this:

```
<!-- -->
<!DOCTYPE html PUBLIC "-//W3C//DTD XHTML 1.0 Strict//EN"
  "http://www.w3.org/TR/xhtml1/DTD/xhtml1-strict.dtd">
<html xmlns="http://www.w3.org/1999/xhtml"
  xmlns:xi="http://www.w3.org/2001/XInclude">
  <head>
  <meta http-equiv="Content-Type"
    content="text/xhtml; charset=UTF-8" />
  <title>The Title of your Application</title>
  <script type="text/javascript"
    src="../../backbase/4_4_1/engine/boot.js" >
  </script>
  </head>
  <body>
     <script type="application/backbase+xml">
       <xi:include
         href="../../backbase/4_4_1/bindings/config.xml">
       </xi:include>
       <!-- YOUR APPLICATION CODE GOES HERE -->
     </script>
  </body>
</html>
```

The version number of the Backbase Client Framework release is specified in the *[version]* folder name (for example, 4_4_1). If your version of the Backbase Client Framework is different from the one shown here, you must adapt the code samples accordingly.

There are some interesting points:

- If you are including third-party libraries or your own JavaScript libraries, you should include them in the `head` section of the HTML document, as usual.

  At the place where it says: `<!-- YOUR APPLICATION CODE GOES HERE -->`, you can put your application code. We will call this a Backbase area. The code that you can put here can be ordinary XHTML, widgets that are provided by Backbase, or widgets that you have built yourself.

  The `<!-- YOUR APPLICATION CODE GOES HERE -->` part is contained within `script` tags with `type="application/backbase+xml"`. The `type` attribute signals the Client Runtime that it should process the contents. The `xml` part of the `type` attribute says that the contents should be proper XML.

- There can be multiple Backbase area's areas. In fact, there can be as many areas as you like. This is convenient if you are converting an older web application to a Backbase application or when you have large chunks of conventional HTML in your application. As the Backbase framework takes some overhead to process this HTML, there is a performance advantage to put code that does not require processing by the Client Runtime outside a Backbase area.

- The code in a Backbase must adhere to XHTML standards and most importantly, all tags must be properly closed. This can be a source of errors if you are converting an older application where for example `<input>` and `<img>` tags are often not closed. Another XHTML violation to watch out for is that attribute values in tags must be enclosed in quotes and all attributes specified must have a value. For example, you should code `selected="selected"` instead of just `selected` in a `select` box.

- The Backbase JavaScript engine in `boot.js` is loaded in the header of the HTML page. It is very important to make sure that you have a proper path specification here. Many times, when you set up a new application, you get an empty page at your first try to see your application. The cause is almost always that your path specification is wrong. If this happens to you, it is convenient to use a tool like Firebug to see what the server returns and why it cannot find the Backbase libraries.

- To use the Backbase widgets, you must include the configuration files, also called **implementation bindings** for the tags:

  ```
  <xi:include href="../../backbase/4_4_1/bindings/config.xml">
  </xi:include>
  ```

- The `config.xml` file contains an additional include for the specific skin you want to use. The default is the **chameleon** skin. As an alternative, you can use the **system** skin. Similar to the earlier point, your path specification must be correct; otherwise your page will most likely stay empty.

- The inclusion of the configuration files is done with the statement: `xi:include`. We make use here of **XInclude**, or XML Inclusions, which is a W3C standard for merging XML files. This facility makes it possible to code your web pages in a more modular way by dividing your code in smaller chunks, which can be combined at runtime. See `http://www.w3.org/TR/xinclude/` for details. Backbase has implemented the XInclude standard in its framework according to the standard and you see it used here to include the configuration files. We will see more of it later in this chapter.

  The HTML tag contains two namespace declarations — `xmlns="http://www.w3.org/1999/xhtml"` and `xmlns:xi="http://www.w3.org/2001/XInclude"`. The XHTML namespace is the default namespace and therefore you do not need to add a prefix in front of the XHTML tags. The XInclude namespace is declared with the `xi` prefix, which you saw used in front of the `include` statement that was used to include the Backbase configuration files. For now, just remember that you need them and that it is important to declare namespaces appropriately in your code. Later in this chapter, there is a section that explains what you really need to know about XML, XHTML, and namespaces. The Backbase Client Framework uses several specific Backbase XML namespaces in addition to providing implementation for several standard ones like the XInclude. We will see some examples in the next section.

The document starts with: `<!-- -->`. This is done to enforce **quirks** mode in the Microsoft Internet Explorer browser. This is a requirement for the Backbase Tag Library widgets to allow box elements to be rendered consistently across browsers.

As we said earlier, the startup `index.html` file is very similar for all applications. All you have to do when you set up a new application is copy the starter skeleton to a proper place in the file system where your server can find it, and adjust the path settings in such a way that the Backbase libraries can be found. Also, give your HTML document the proper title and meta-information in the `head` section.

 From now on, we will usually take for granted that you know how to surround our example code shown in the book with the right skeleton code.

"Hello Backbase" in four variations

In the previous sections, we talked about downloading the Backbase package and about trying out the demos on the Developer Network site of Backbase. We also showed what a Backbase starter page looks like, so finally, we can show real Backbase code.

It is time to say "Hello Backbase!" We will do so by showing typical "Hello World" examples as follows:

- The first example shows a simple alert when you click on the **Click me** text. It serves to make sure that we have the right setup for our applications.

- The second and third examples are a bit more interesting: a balloon from the Backbase Tag Library is shown, with the text that you typed in an input field. The difference between the two is the use of JavaScript or the XML Execution Language, as you will see.

- The fourth example is an AJAX example. It involves communication with a server, which echoes the text typed in, together with a timestamp. The response is added to earlier responses without refreshing the page.

Downloading the example code for the book

Visit `http://www.packtpub.com/files/code/9126_Code.zip` to directly download the example code.

The downloadable files contain instructions on how to use them.

We assume that you have a web development environment set up now and that you have put the Backbase libraries at the right place. We will take a follow-along approach for explaining the "Hello World!" examples, but of course you can also just execute the ready-to-run downloaded source code instead of typing the code yourself.

Start with creating a new folder named `bookApps`, or whatever name you like better. Next, create a subfolder of the `bookApps` folder named `helloWorld`.

Verifying the installation of the Backbase framework

Create an HTML file named `hello1.html` and put this file in the `helloWorld` folder. Copy the skeleton file that we saw in the previous section into `hello1.html`. Remember the following:

- In this file, we made sure that the Backbase Framework Client Runtime will be loaded because of the `<script>` tag in the head section of the HTML document.

- The `<script>` tag in the body section of the HTML document has a type declaration, `application/backbase+xml`, which tells the client runtime to process whatever is contained within the tag.

- The first thing that the client runtime is asked to process is the inclusion of the `config.xml` file, which contains the bindings that define the UI widgets.

The position where `<!-- YOUR APPLICATION CODE GOES HERE -->` is placed tells the runtime that it should process whatever we replace this with.

Namespace declarations are needed for all the namespaces used, in the tag where they are used, or a parent tag within the document.

Replace `<!-- YOUR APPLICATION CODE GOES HERE -->` with the following content:

```
<div>
  <e:handler
    xmlns:e="http://www.backbase.com/2006/xel"
    event="click" type="text/javascript">
    alert('Backbase says hello!');
  </e:handler>
  Click me
</div>
```

To see your first "Hello" example in action, you can either double-click on `hello1.html` in the Windows explorer (if you are running Windows), or, if you have started your local server, you can open a browser and type something like this in the address bar: `http://localhost/bookApps/helloWorld/hello1.html`.

After clicking on the **Click me** text, you should see a result that is similar to what is shown in the following picture:

What if you do not see anything? The most common problem that could be the cause is that the path to `boot.js` or `config.xml` is not correct. If you are running with a server, check that it is running properly, and that it can find your `hello1.html`.

When all is well: Congratulations! The Backbase Client Framework is running successfully.

Let us look at the code:

- The interesting part of the code is the event handler for the `div` element that contains the **Click me** text. The `e:handler` tag is part of the XML Execution Language (XEL), a custom markup language that is provided with the Backbase Client Framework, and that can be used as a replacement for JavaScript in many cases.
- The namespace that we need for using XEL is declared in the `e:handler` tag itself; it could also have been declared in the `<div>` or `<html>` tags.
- Between the start and end `e:handler` tags, you can code either JavaScript, as in this example, or XEL, as we will see in the next "Hello World!" example.

You could have coded the example also as "Hello World" without the Backbase event handler: `<div onclick="alert('Backbase says hello!');">Click me! </div>`. At first sight, this is shorter, so why would we need Backbase for this? Well, usually, you need more in the event handler than just a short alert. In such case, you have two choices: either clutter your page with hard to read JavaScript or create a JavaScript function that you put in the `head` section. Before you know it, you will have many of these functions, which become hard to maintain and organize. In the case of the XEL event handler, you can write well-formatted and well-structured JavaScript code that stays local to the widget where you put the event handler. Of course, you can define more global functionality as well and you will see examples of this in several variations later in the book.

XML namespaces! In this first example, you saw again a new XML namespace, this time for XEL. We already saw the XHTML and the XInclude namespace declaration in the page skeleton; in the next section you will see the Backbase Tag Library, the Commands, and the Forms namespace. Yes, that is a lot of namespaces and we will see a few more in the rest of the book. We promise that you will find out how useful these are and that you will get used to it.

This was a very simple example that made sure the Backbase framework is working right. In the next three examples, we will expand your knowledge by demonstrating a personalized "Hello World", using a tag from the Backbase Tag Library. The last "Hello World" example will demonstrate the AJAX functionality of the Backbase Client Framework by showing a form with one input field, which, when submitted, causes a response to be displayed somewhere in the page without a page refresh.

"Hello World" using a Backbase balloon

This section contains a pair of examples showing how to create a BTL balloon that is filled with custom text.

 The `balloon` widget displays an image similar to that of a dialogue box in a comic book. The balloon can contain text, images, or other widgets. The user can click on the **x** icon in the balloon to close it or the balloon can be displayed for a limited amount of time. The balloon is positioned in relationship to its parent widget.

The `balloon` widget is similar to a `toolTip` because they represent information that becomes available only after an action is performed. Most often, these widgets are used to present contextual information about a widget in your application.

This is not the easiest example for showing a Backbase GUI widget from the Backbase Tag Library. However, we have chosen it because we wanted to show an example that illustrates the power of using pre-built widgets.

The example is done twice, to show that BTL can be coded in two ways, either by using an event handler with JavaScript content, or by using no JavaScript at all. The second version of the example shows the Backbase-specific XML Execution Language (XEL) and Backbase Commands instead of JavaScript. Any combination of these two styles is also possible, as many examples in the Backbase documentation and in this book will show.

Below is a picture of what the result of trying the example will look like:

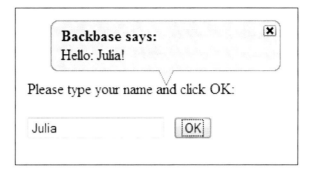

The user will type a name, and after clicking **OK**, the balloon will appear. The user can click on the **x** to close it. Otherwise, it will disappear automatically after a while.

The JavaScript balloon

The first balloon example uses JavaScript in the event handler of the button, similar to the previous example, which had an event handler on the `div` element using the XML Execution Language.

We saw the XEL namespace before. The Backbase Tag Library (BTL) namespace is new; we need it because the balloon widget belongs to it.

Create a file in the `helloWorld` folder that you created in the first tutorial, name it `hello2.html`, and then add a copy of the starter skeleton as content. Make sure that you understand what the contents of the `hello2.html` file represent. Look back if needed.

Because we need more namespace declarations than in the previous example, it is more convenient to add them to the `<html>` tag of the skeleton page:

```
xmlns:b="http://www.backbase.com/2006/btl"
xmlns:e="http://www.backbase.com/2006/xel"
```

Replace the part where it says `<!-- YOUR APPLICATION CODE GOES HERE -->` in the starter page skeleton with the following code:

```
<div style="margin: 80px 0 0 20px; width: 300px;">
   <p> Please type your name and click OK: </p>
   <input id="myInput" type="text" />
   <button style="margin-left: 10px;">
      OK
      <e:handler event="click" type="text/javascript">
```

```
        var oBalloon =
          bb.document.getElementById('myBalloon');
        var oInput =
          bb.document.getElementById('myInput');
        var sValue = bb.getProperty(oInput,'value');
        bb.command.setText(oBalloon,
          'Hello: ' + sValue,'replaceChildren');
        oBalloon.setAttribute('open', 'true');
      </e:handler>
    </button>
    <b:balloon label="Backbase says:"
       id="myBalloon" mode="top-center"
       timeout="10s" width="250px" />
</div>
```

Save your work and type this in the address bar: `http://localhost/bookApps/ helloWorld/hello2.html`. After typing your name in the input field and clicking **OK**, you should see the balloon appear.

Let's examine the code:

- You will see that there are two namespace prefixes present: the `e:` prefix for XML Execution Language that we saw before and the `b:` prefix for the Backbase Tag Library, which contains the balloon widget. We chose this time to add the namespace declarations to the `<html>` tag.

- There is a `b:balloon` widget on the page. Initially, you do not see it because the `open` attribute is `false` by default. We need the event handler on the **OK** button to set the `open` attribute to `true`.

- The balloon will stay visible for 10 seconds after it appears and will be positioned at the top left of its parent widget, the `div` in this case. We specified a margin for the `div`, to give the `b:balloon` enough space.

- The balloon in our code has a label, but no content. We want to build the content of the balloon dynamically, using the value in the input field at the time the **OK** button is clicked.

- The event handler for the click event of the button is specified in the same way as in the "Backbase says hello!" alert example, except that it contains a lot more JavaScript code. Now the usefulness of the XEL event handler becomes more convincing—if you would have placed the code in a single `onclick="..."` line, it would have become rather unreadable. By the way, you can still use your old ways of coding JavaScript if you prefer.

- The bb object that is used in the code is of particular interest. The Backbase Client Runtime creates an additional DOM-like layer that shields you from browser incompatibilities. You can address the Backbase elements on this layer in the same way as the elements in the original DOM layer by using the bb object. The bb object is instantiated when the Client Runtime is loaded.

- In our example, we need to find two elements by ID in the Backbase space. To do so, you should use the bb.document object provided by the Client Runtime, instead of the document object provided by the browser. The variable oBalloon receives a reference to the balloon, by looking up its ID using bb.document.getElementById().

- Although the input widget looks like a normal HTML widget, it is in fact also a Backbase widget because it is placed in the Backbase area. Therefore, we use the bb object again to find it by ID.

- We find the value of what is typed in the input field by using bb.getProperty. The next line requires some explanation: we need to have the text that is displayed in a text node. We create the text node by using the command functions, bb.command.setText.

- Finally, the open attribute is set to true and the balloon will be shown.

We will have more information about the bb object and the commands later in the book. For specific details, the Backbase documentation is a good source, in particular, the Backbase Reference at http://download.backbase.com/docs/client/current/Reference.chm.

You have now seen that the BTL widgets can be used and extended in a straightforward way using JavaScript. The next example looks exactly the same when you try it out, but the event handler now uses XEL instead of JavaScript.

The XEL balloon

As in the previous example, create a file in the helloWorld folder and this time name it hello3.html. Add a copy of the starter skeleton as content and replace <!-- YOUR APPLICATION CODE GOES HERE --> with the following content:

```
<div xmlns:b="http://www.backbase.com/2006/btl"
    xmlns:c="http://www.backbase.com/2006/command"
    xmlns:e="http://www.backbase.com/2006/xel"
    style="margin: 80px 0 0 20px; width: 300px;">
    <p> Please type your name and click OK: </p>
    <input id="myInput" type="text" />
    <button style="margin-left: 10px;">
       OK
       <e:handler event="click">
```

```
                  <c:setText
                     select="concat('Hello: ',
                      id('myInput')/property::value,'!')"
                     destination="id('myBalloon')"
                     mode="replaceChildren" />
                  <c:setAttribute
                     with="id('myBalloon')"
                     name="open"
                     select="'true'" />
               </e:handler>
          </button>
          <b:balloon label="Backbase says:"
             id="myBalloon" mode="top-center"
             timeout="10s" width="250px" />
     </div>
```

In this example, using the Backbase Tag Library (BTL), XML Execution Language (XEL), and Command Functions libraries may look daunting to you. While in the later chapters of the book we will fill in the details, we want you to look at the code here, see that it is more compact than the JavaScript version and that it is pure XML instead of JavaScript encapsulated within XML tags. We will explain now what is going on from a higher level:

- In this example, the `<div>` tag contains the namespace declarations that we put at the `<html>` tag in the previous example. This is done not only to show you that you can put namespace declarations in any parent tag of the tag where the namespace is used, but also to prepare ourselves for modularization of the code. We could carve out the `<div>` tag with its contents and put it in a separate file. We could then put an XInclude instead. If you do this, the declaration on the `<html>` tag would be useless, while the declaration on the `<div>` tag would be just what you need, except that you would have to add the default namespace for XHTML again to make the file a self-contained proper XML.

- The `e:handler` tag does not have a `type` attribute here because using XML as content is the default.

- When the button is clicked, the value in the text node is concatenated from three string parts, where the middle part is an XPath expression that extracts the value from the input field.

- The destination of the newly created text node is the balloon.

- A `setAttribute` function from the Backbase Command Functions language is used to open the balloon.

- The `b:balloon` itself is the same as in the previous example.

We have now said "Hello!" using real Backbase BTL widgets and we peeked into XEL to see how we can code event handlers in a more structured way, choosing between JavaScript and XEL. You can use either, depending on your preferences.

The next example is a real AJAX example: we will communicate with a server asynchronously, and the updates are placed on the page doing a partial page reload, without refreshing the whole page.

Hello Server!

To many people, AJAX is almost synonymous with XMLHttpRequest, the API that allows client programs to communicate asynchronously with a server. This example page shows the "Hello World" example communicating via AJAX using a Backbase form. If you are using the Backbase AJAX framework, it is possible that you will never use an XMLHttpRequest object directly, because its use is made transparent to you. If you wish however, it is possible to use it.

Here, we will look at using an ordinary looking form, still the most common means to enter information to be sent to a server. Instead of refreshing the whole page, AJAX is used when you tell the framework that you want to put the response to the form submitted at a particular spot on your page, by using the bf:destination attribute. As a server scripting language, we use PHP in our example because we assume that the majority of developers will be able to understand it. In addition, we show what the response file that PHP generates looks like. You can see from its structure how you could code an AJAX response in other languages.

Below you can see a snapshot of what the result could be of executing the example:

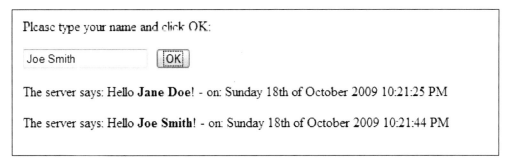

The page with the form

By now, you know the drill: create a file in the `helloWorld` folder, name it `helloServer.html`, and add a copy of the starter skeleton as content of this file.

Replace the part where it says `<!-- YOUR APPLICATION CODE GOES HERE -->` in the starter page skeleton, with the following code:

```
<div style="margin-left: 20px;">
    <p>Please type your name and click OK:</p>
    <form xmlns:bf="http://www.backbase.com/2007/forms"
        action="response.php"
        bf:destination="id('server-response-area')"
        bf:mode="appendChild" method="post">
        <input id="name" name="name" type="text" />
        <input type="submit" style="margin-left: 10px;"
            value="OK" />
    </form>
    <div id="server-response-area" style="background: #FFFFC8;"></div>
</div>
```

This form is not very interesting, except a few things that are as follows:

- Adding a `bf:destination` attribute to the form will cause the submitted data to be sent asynchronously. Instead of refreshing the complete page, the contents of the response will be put at the defined destination by the Client Runtime, at the `div` element with ID `server-response-area` in our example.

- We have also coded a `bf:mode` attribute with the value `appendChild`. This means that the response of the server will be put as the last child node of the `div` element. Every click of the **OK** button will add one more response line to the page, leaving intact what was there before. The `appendChild` value is the default. Therefore, we could have omitted it here.

We will be looking at the server side next.

The PHP response

From the action that is specified in the form, you can see that `response.php` will be invoked when the form is submitted. Therefore, you should create a file in the `helloWorld` folder and name it `response.php`. Add the following as content:

```php
<?php
  header('Content-type: application/xml');
  echo '<?xml version="1.0" encoding="UTF-8"?>';
?>
<div xmlns="http://www.w3.org/1999/xhtml">
   <?php
     $myname = $_POST['name'];
     echo " <p>";
     echo "The server says: Hello <strong>$myname</strong> ! - on: ";
     echo date('l jS \of F Y h:i:s A');
     echo " </p>\n";
   ?>
</div>
```

To see this "Hello Server" example in action, open a browser and type something like this in the address bar: `http://localhost/bookApps/helloWorld/helloServer.html`. Type something in the input field and click on **OK**. Change the input field and click on **OK** again. Repeat this a few times. You will see the list of responses grow, while the rest of the page is not touched. Some points to note are:

- This time you cannot execute the example from the file system by double clicking on the `helloServer.html` file, because the web server needs to be activated to interpret the PHP script.

- The server script that receives the request should be aware that it should not send a complete page in return, and that the response should be valid XHTML.

In order for the browser to recognize that it is XML that it receives, the response header must be set appropriately. Using PHP, you can do this as follows: `header('Content-type: application/xml');`. If your scripting language is JSP, you could code: `response.setHeader("Content-Type", "application/xml");`.

For those of you who are not so familiar with PHP, we show here an example of a response file that might have been generated by `response.php`, as an actual response file:

```xml
<?xml version="1.0" encoding="UTF-8"?>
<div xmlns="http://www.w3.org/1999/xhtml">
   <p>
      The server says: Hello <strong>John Doe</strong>! - on:
```

```
        Friday 30th of May 2008 12:50:43 PM
    </p>
</div>
```

The server response includes a timestamp of when the response is sent. We did this to show that the page really stays put and is only partially changed. By entering new information in the input field and clicking the **Submit** button, a new line will be appended in the yellow box where the server messages are shown.

XML and namespaces

If you know HTML, you also know XML, the Extensible Markup Language—just think of it as HTML where you can invent and specify your own tags.

To be more specific, XML is a general-purpose markup language, which means that you can describe and annotate the structure or formatting of text with it. HTML is a particular example of XML used to describe the structure and formatting of a web page.

Using XML, you can define a set of tags that together form a vocabulary for a specific subject. This is great if in all XML documents you would only need tags from one vocabulary, but probably you can imagine that this would be rather restrictive.

In this section, we give some background for the use of XML namespaces in the Backbase framework. As the W3C standard puts it, XML namespaces provide a simple method for qualifying element and attribute names used in Extensible Markup Language documents by associating them with namespaces identified by URI references.

Why do we need XML namespaces?

When XML was invented, there was no such thing as a namespace concept. The steadily increasing volume of XML data that was exchanged between different groups of people and different companies revealed a series of problems. One was that it was difficult to properly combine parts of different XML documents into new documents. Basically, these are the causes:

- An XML vocabularies collision problem. This means that two XML documents could have tags with the same name, while in each document this tag could have a different meaning or structure. For example, a `<language>` tag could have an attribute `version` if it is a programming language, or else an attribute `region`, to indicate where this particular form of natural language is spoken.

- An intended content recognition problem. This means that if I see a tag in a document that has tags from more than one vocabulary, I need to know to which vocabulary it belongs. For example, if you see a `<title>` tag, is this the title of a book, the title in an HTML document, or the title of a person, such as "Mrs." or "professor"? Similarly, is a `<border>` the border of a country or a border of an element on a web page?

In order to solve these issues, the mechanism of namespaces was introduced into XML. If you are familiar with a programming language like Java, the namespace concept is similar to the *package* concept in that language. It enabled authors to determine, on markup, vocabularies for their content and facilitated governance.

Declaring XML namespaces

You can recognize an XML namespace when you see an attribute that starts with `xmlns`. The part of the attribute that follows `xmlns:` is called a prefix. It is that part of the namespace declaration that actually sets up a link between a convenience token and a namespace. The namespace declaration scope is limited to the element where it was done and to the element's sub-tree. The names of these attributes are reserved: you cannot use an `xmlns` attribute or prefix for another purpose.

Let's consider a sample XML document that uses namespaces:

```
<?xml version="1.0"?>
<catalog
    xmlns="http://www.library.com/ns/catalog"
    xmlns:isbn="http://www.isbn.com/ns/isbn">
    <book isbn:id="1847196705" id="1">
        <title>Learning jQuery</title>
        <author>Karl Swedberg</author>
        <author>Jonathan Chaffer </author>
        <isbn:datePublished>February 2009</isbn:datePublished>
    </book>
    <book isbn:id="1847191444" id="2">
        <title>Joomla! Template Design</title>
        <author>Tessa Blakeley Silver</author>
        <isbn:datePublished>June 2007</isbn:datePublished>
    </book>
    <!-- More books -->
</catalog>
```

The catalog could serve as a description of books in a local library. The meaning and structure of the tags can be whatever the local library thinks is practical. In this document there is also the isbn namespace, which is used for tags that are relevant to the worldwide book register that the **International Standard Book Number (ISBN)** represents.

Use of namespaces with Backbase

The Backbase Client Runtime processes all the tags that are placed between script tags that have type="text/backbase+xml" as attribute. To the Backbase Client Runtime, the combination of the namespace and the tag name will determine what the engine will do to interpret the tag.

We call a set of tags that belong to a specific namespace a markup language. In the Backbase point of view, XHTML is just another markup language. It belongs to the http://www.w3.org/1999/xhtml namespace, which you must declare just like the specific Backbase namespaces.

We have already seen several namespaces in our examples. Below is a list of namespaces you can expect to be using with Backbase, together with their preferred prefixes:

```
xmlns = "http://www.w3.org/1999/xhtml"
xmlns:xi = "http://www.w3.org/2001/XInclude"
xmlns:xs = "http://www.w3.org/2001/XMLSchema"
xmlns:smil = "http://www.w3.org/2005/SMIL21/"
xmlns:b = "http://www.backbase.com/2006/btl"
xmlns:c = "http://www.backbase.com/2006/command"
xmlns:d = "http://www.backbase.com/2006/tdl"
xmlns:e = "http://www.backbase.com/2006/xel"
xmlns:bf = "http://www.backbase.com/2007/forms"
```

Although it is legal to use different prefixes bound to the same namespace URI in different documents as well as within the same document, it is often convenient to stick to using similar ones.

For each markup language in your application, you must add a namespace declaration. For example, if you are using BTL UI widgets, you will need to add a BTL namespace declaration to your document.

The engine does recognize namespace declarations placed outside its processing space. This means that the best place to declare namespaces for all languages processed by the Client Runtime is as high as possible in the DOM tree, for example the <html> tag.

Each XML document, even if it will be included into another document, must contain appropriate namespace declarations.

Here is an example of namespace declarations that you could use with some of the Backbase markup languages:

```
<script xmlns="http://www.w3.org/1999/xhtml"
    xmlns:b="http://www.backbase.com/2006/btl"
    xmlns:e="http://www.backbase.com/2006/xel"
    xmlns:xi="http://www.w3.org/2001/XInclude"
    type="application/backbase+xml">
<div>
    Given the correct widget prefixes,
    the Client Runtime can now
    process all XHTML, BTL, XEL, and XInclude elements.
    XHTML is the default namespace, so we don't have to give a
    prefix to the parent div tag.
</div>
</script>
```

Using namespaces in your application can be confusing at first and can be a source of problems for a Backbase beginner. A good piece of advice is to check your namespaces if you have an error that you do not understand. Soon, adding the right namespaces will become second nature.

A basic page layout

After having installed the Backbase framework and after having said "Hello World!" so many times, we would like to finish this chapter by doing real work.

Every web application page design starts with a basic page layout. This layout usually involves a part where menu items are shown, sometimes a row of tabs at the top of the page, sometimes a list of links as a column on the left, sometimes both.

In the olden days, we would partition a web page using HTML frames, where you could have a table-like layout. The advantage of using frames is that each frame contains its own document, allowing you to make your application more modular. This was a big disadvantage at the same time because the communication between multiple frames can become a problem and also you cannot easily print such a page.

As an alternative, you could use a pure HTML table layout. That is still the easiest way to design a page if the page is simple, but if you use a number of nested tables to layout your page, things can become tricky when you try to change something. Nowadays, most people say that tables should be used to display tables and that CSS should be used for layout. If you ever struggled with div elements floating in ways you could not imagine, you may still agree in principle, but hope for something better in practice.

The Backbase panelSet widget and related elements are designed to offer the best of both worlds—easy layout as with tables and modularity as with frames.

> The panelSet widget partitions the screen layout into rows and columns. When subdividing the panelSet, you use the panel element, or you can use another panelSet widget to further subdivide that row/column. You can specify a panelSet to have rows, columns, or both. By using the splitter="splitter" attribute/value pair, you can add a resizable border to your panelSet.

The Backbase framework has a set of example layouts that use panelSets available for you to use. You can find them in the demos folder of the Backbase package, or you can view them online at http://demo.backbase.com/layouts/.

If you would like to use one of these as a starting point for your own application, you will find you need to strip the application first. This is because they contain a lot of static information that is there to show what the page could look like. We made a very simple page layout that is inspired by these example layouts. However, we will start from the ground and work our way up so that we can expand the page to evolve to a real web application page later in the book. Below is a picture of this sample application:

We will put our application in a new folder. Create a subfolder of the `bookApps` folder named `myApp1`, or whatever name you like better. Create a file in the `app1` folder, name it `index.html`, and add a copy of the starter skeleton as content.

Add a CSS file reference to the head section in order to keep the styling we use:

```
<link rel="stylesheet" type="text/css" href="resources/app.css" />
```

The CSS file is not very interesting at this point. We suggest that you copy it from the downloaded source and put it into its own `resources` folder.

Replace `<!-- YOUR APPLICATION CODE GOES HERE -->` with the following content:

```
<div xmlns="http://www.w3.org/1999/xhtml"
    xmlns:b="http://www.backbase.com/2006/btl"
    xmlns:e="http://www.backbase.com/2006/xel">
    <div id="appHeader">
        <div class="appHeaderText">Backbase Basic Layout</div>
    </div>
    <b:panelSet columns="260px *" splitter="true">
        <b:panel>
            <xi:include href="menu.xml" />
        </b:panel>
        <b:panel class="btl-border-left">
            <xi:include href="content.xml" />
        </b:panel>
    </b:panelSet>
</div>
```

You see a simple `panelSet`, where its structure is clearly visible because the menu and the real content are included with the XInclude mechanism. This allows you to make a very modular setup of your application.

There are two files that are included by the XInclude mechanism: `menu.xml` and `content.xml`. For now, these files contain nothing interesting. Remember though that these files must have proper namespace declarations because their contents are loaded into Backbase space. Therefore, the `menu.xml` file looks like this:

```
<div xmlns="http://www.w3.org/1999/xhtml">
    <ul>
        <li>Menu item 1</li>
        <li>Menu item 2</li>
        <li>Menu item 3</li>
        <li>Menu item 4</li>
        <li>Menu item 5</li>
    </ul>
</div>
```

What is interesting is that when we expand this application in the following chapters, the index.html file will stay the same, while the development effort can concentrate on various modularized parts of the application.

Even if modularizing your application using XInclude from Backbase will be the only facility you'd use, this will be an important step in writing better applications. You could argue that you can achieve the same effect by using the include() function of PHP, or a similar function in another server scripting language. You should realize though, that this will make your client application dependent on the server language you are using.

Another disadvantage you may think of is that it requires extra communication with the server to use XInclude in this way. That is true, but if you have a performance problem with your application, probably something else is the cause. Kent Beck, the well-known inventor of Extreme Programming, says on this issue: "First make it right, then make it fast".

The code we have put in menu.xml and content.xml is just dummy text. Therefore, we are not repeating it here. In later chapters, we will start putting meaningful content into our basic application.

Your web directory structure could look as follows:

```
htdocs
  |-- backbase
  |             |-- 4_4_1
  |
  |-- bookApps
  |             |-- helloWorld
  |             |-- myApp1
  |                       |-- resources
  |                       |           |-- media
  |                       |           |-- app.css
  |                       |
  |                       |-- content.xml
  |                       |-- index.html
  |                       |-- menu.xml
```

In your whole application, there is only one file that contains references to your Backbase installation. That makes it a lot easier to set up a new application and to upgrade your Backbase installation for a new release.

To conclude this section, look back at what we have achieved. With very little code we have set up a structure for an application that we can easily extend or use as a skeleton for new applications.

Summary

What have we done so far?

- We have made sure that our development environment is right.

- We have downloaded and installed the Backbase framework.

- We have seen what we have to add to an HTML page to make it Backbase framework enabled.

- We have seen the famous "Hello World" in many variations: with only basic JavaScript, with a Backbase Tag Library widget and basic JavaScript, with a Backbase Tag Library widget and the Backbase XML Execution Language, and finally, using AJAX communication with a server script.

- We have started on a basic page layout for our web application using a `panelSet`.

- We learned something about XML and namespaces.

With only these few concepts and just a few Backbase widgets, you will be able to develop new web applications with improved results.

In the next chapter, we will expand our knowledge and take a look at the GUI widgets that are available in Backbase.

2
User Interface Development

The Backbase Tag Library (BTL) contains about fifty UI widgets—UI components that can be embedded in an HTML page—that help you to build a web page quickly. In this chapter, we will give an overview of BTL and a list of all elements available. We will briefly describe the structure of BTL, showing the base elements from which BTL widgets inherit, depending on their function.

 Widget, **element**, **control**, and **UI component** are terms that are almost synonymous and that can cause confusion. The Backbase documentation is sometimes vague about their meaning. We try to use widget for visible things on a page and element in a more generic way for things that can also be abstract or behavioral. We will avoid control, but the word is used sometimes in the Backbase documentation.

There are six BTL widgets intended to do the major work when laying out a web page. We will describe those in more detail, with examples. To make this work, we need some utility tasks, for which a special set of elements is available and we will describe those too.

With the layout widgets that we'll describe, we'll have enough knowledge to build a sample application specific for this chapter. This sample application, a BTL Exerciser, will show and execute all BTL examples that we'll show in this, and the following, chapters. The BTL Exerciser is built upon the basic layout that we showed at the end of the previous chapter.

Another topic will be styling of the web page and what you can do to make the Backbase widgets fit your style.

You are not expected to read this chapter as if it were a novel. Depending on your skill and interest, you can glance through the pages to see what widgets are available and find out how to code them, or you can read about the object-oriented structure of the widgets and their relationships.

Here is a complete list of subjects that we will discuss in this chapter:

- Squaring the circles: why an XML-based framework
- The Backbase Reference
- An overview of the Backbase markup languages
- XHTML within Backbase
- Overview of the Backbase Tag Library (BTL)
- The BTL abstract elements
- The BTL layout widgets
- The BTL utility elements
- Styling techniques
- A sample application that can show all BTL examples

As we cannot describe all the BTL widgets in this chapter, here is a table that lists where each category can be found:

Category	Chapter
Layout	2
Info & Notify	3
Actions & Menu	8
Grids & Trees	5
Forms	4
Multimedia	8
Windows & Dialogs	8
Utilities & Tools	2

Squaring the circles of web applications

There is an old saying that expresses the difficulty of trying to match things that inherently do not match: "Try to fit round pegs into square holes". In IT circles, the saying became popular to describe the difficulty of storing programming objects created, for example in Java, in a relational database table. If you think about it, this is exactly what many AJAX developers try to do: fit round JavaScript objects in square HTML tags.

The Backbase framework solves this problem by allowing you to write JavaScript code that is encapsulated as data within XML tags. This causes the pieces of JavaScript that you need in your application to become smaller and easier to write. The problem of unwanted global objects interfering in unexpected ways with other parts of your application, or with other frameworks that you may want to use, is solved in this way. We will discuss the background for these ideas in Chapter 7, which is about the Backbase Tag Definition Language.

Now, our task is to explain what the squares or the XML tags look like in the Backbase framework. We'll start with the tags that allow you to build a UI: XHTML and the built-in UI widgets, the Backbase Tag Library.

The Backbase Reference

The best source of information for all details concerning the Backbase framework is the API Reference. The content of the Reference is generated from the source code of the Backbase framework. This means that the API Reference is up-to-date, but also that its format may not be clear at first. We suggest that you take your time to become familiar with the API Reference, because the amount of detail it contains can be intimidating. There are two versions of the API Reference, one in the Windows Help format and one in HTML format.

From experience, we know that you will have the API Reference open on your desktop most of the time while developing, to look up widgets or functions you are using. Although, by having this book available, the need to search the Reference will be much less.

After opening the reference, click on the **Markup Languages** book, then on **BTL (b:)**, and next on **Elements**. You will see an alphabetical list of the widgets that are available in the BTL. Click on one and you will see its attributes, properties, methods, and events. You can click on almost anything to get more details, and to see inheritance, derived elements, attributes, and events.

Here is a typical API Reference page:

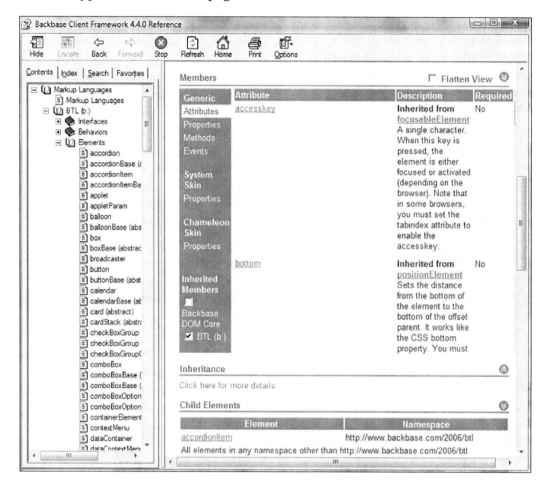

UI markup languages

As we have explained in Chapter 1, the Backbase framework implements a set of XML markup languages for the purpose of developing web applications. In this section, we will give an overview of those markup languages that are used to develop the visual part of your web application.

Believe it or not, after reading just the first chapter you will have a sound background to start developing Backbase web applications. So far, you have seen how to:

- Set up an application UI skeleton
- Specify the namespace definitions needed

- Put Backbase Tag Library widgets on the page
- Interact with a widget through an event handler

The key insight into understanding how to develop web applications with the Backbase framework is that you will develop XHTML documents as before, using familiar XHTML syntax and technology. In addition to what you could use before, you have a set of XML markup languages available that use their own XML namespaces. Not only can you use the languages that Backbase has developed, you can also develop your own markup language using the Tag Definition Language, as we will see in a later chapter.

For UI development, we need XHTML, forms, and BTL markup languages. Here is an overview of these:

Language	Standard	Description
Backbase Tag Library	No	The BTL (Backbase Tag Library) is a set of extensible UI widgets that shield you to a large extent from cross-browser problems and that you can use out of the box. These widgets use a declarative model familiar to anyone who knows standard HTML. Namespace: `xmlns:b = "http://www.backbase.com/2006/btl"`
Forms	No	The forms namespace contains a number of interfaces and base implementations for submission of forms and validation functionality that is shared between XHTML, BTL, and custom client controls. Namespace: `xmlns:bf = "http://www.backbase.com/2007/forms"`
XHTML	Yes	XHTML, as provided by Backbase, has methods, properties, and attributes that correspond almost exactly to XHTML 1.1 standards. For more information, refer to the W3C `http://www.w3.org/1999/xhtml`, the XHTML specification. Namespace: `xmlns = "http://www.w3.org/1999/xhtml"`

Language	Standard	Description
XInclude	Yes	XInclude is a mechanism to include other files, which facilitates the modularity of applications. For more information, refer to the W3C `http://www.w3.org/TR/XInclude`, the XInclude specification.
		Namespace:
		`xmlns:xi = "http://www.w3.org/2001/XInclude`

There are other markup languages as well, as you may have guessed from the list in Chapter 1. We will see details about these in later chapters.

Where is the source code?

The source code of the Backbase framework is available for you to view. In the package, you will find two versions of the code—a development version and an optimized version. The difference between the two is that the optimized version has all white space filtered out to minimize file size. For the same reason, the development version source code has no comments, but most of these comments can be found in the Reference.

If you open the package and then the `web` folder, you will see a structure as in the picture below (the release number may differ):

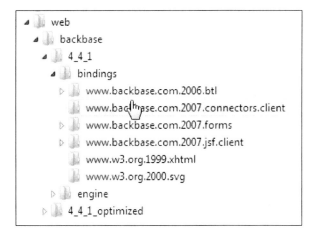

You may have guessed that the BTL definitions are in:

`web/backbase/4_4_1/bindings/www.backbase.com.2006.btl`

When you open this folder, you will see (we are showing only a part of the list):

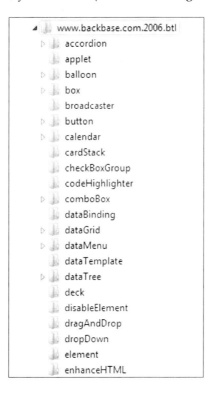

There is a folder for every element in BTL. Many folders have subfolders: `chameleon` and `system`, to accommodate the two skins that the Backbase framework provides for BTL, the chameleon, and the system skin.

Widgets' definitions are loaded in a lazy manner, which means only those definitions are loaded that are actually used.

XHTML

The overview in the previous section shows XHTML as one of the markup languages that you will need for UI development. Are we kicking in an open door here? Maybe, maybe not.

We hope you remember that all the Backbase code is contained within `script` tags with `type="application/backbase+xml"`; we called this a Backbase area. This means that a browser will not process any tags placed within this area directly. Instead, the Backbase Client Runtime will process them before being presented to the browser. This is the reason why XHTML is a markup language for the Client Runtime just like the other markup languages that it processes.

If you place a tag in a Backbase area that looks like an XHTML tag, in reality, it is a tag from the XHTML markup language implemented by Backbase. This offers some interesting possibilities: an XHTML language that complies fully with the W3C standards on all browsers, for example. There is some sugar on top of this, which adds a very important feature: AJAX support for form submission, form validation, and more.

The processing of the XHTML tags Backbase Client Runtime also has a drawback because it takes extra time. If you are not using any specific Backbase framework facility, this would just be a performance penalty. Therefore, if you have pieces of code where no Backbase markup language is involved, you should place it outside the Backbase area. You can have as many Backbase areas as you like.

As XHTML is just another markup language, you must declare its namespace while using it, which will almost always be the case. Therefore, the XHTML namespace is usually the default namespace that does not require a prefix.

We don't have to tell you what XHTML looks like because we assume that you already know it. We spend some time on it here anyway. The reason is that the Backbase Client Runtime is much less forgiving for sloppy code than most browsers are. If you see errors in your application, it is usually a good idea to check first for unclosed tags. In many cases, the Backbase debugger will give you a good indication of what is wrong.

XHTML 1.1 is in fact a refined version of HTML 4 with proper XML syntax enforced. We briefly hinted at what you should keep in mind when discussing the page skeleton. Here it is again, as a short checklist:

- Tags should be closed
- Element names as well as attribute names should be lowercase
- Attribute values should be enclosed in quotes, preferably double quotes by convention

An example of valid XHTML markup, where these things are used is:

```
<form action="action.php" method="post">
    Your email:
    <input name="email" type="text" />
```

```
<br />
<input id="flag" name="subscribe"
   type="checkbox" checked="checked" />
   <label for="flag"> Send me updates</label>
<input type="submit" value="Subscribe" />
</form>
```

Developing true client-side applications with pure XHTML is not an easy task, because the technology was designed to markup hypertext, not to develop Application User Interfaces. XHTML lacks sophisticated components for user input, interaction, and layout. The Backbase Tag Library is adding these building blocks. Let us take a closer look.

The Backbase Tag Library

The focus of this chapter is the Backbase Tag Library (BTL). BTL concerns itself with the visible aspect of a web application user interface. For its dynamic behavior, we need JavaScript, or the XML Execution Language and Command Functions tag libraries that we will cover in the next chapter.

When you are developing a user interface, you will find that you are solving the same problems over and over again:

- Create a layout
- Show a menu of options
- Have tabs to structure the space on a page
- Provide pop ups and tool tips
- Do form validation

These are just a few examples from a long list. The BTL is a set of UI widgets that can be used out of the box, which are extensible, and should appear the same in all browsers. By using these, you should be able to develop your website faster with a more robust result.

Backbase Tag Library widget overview

There are eight categories of BTL widgets for every aspect of layout and user interaction. If that is not enough, you can extend the BTL widgets to add new behavior or new looks. You can also develop your own widgets as we'll see in detail in the chapter about the Tag Definition Language.

The following schema shows an overview of the widgets that are available:

Layout	Info & Notify	Actions & Menu
• panelSet	• balloon	• button
• accordion	• infoBox	• contextMenu
• box	• toolTip	• menuBar
• deck	• loadingMessage	• toolBar
• navBox		• menuPopUp
• tabBox		• pager
Grids & Trees	**Forms**	**Multimedia**
• dataGrid	• calendar	• applet
• listGrid	• comboBox	• flash
• tree	• fileInput	
• treeGrid	• listBox	
	• slider	
	• spinner	
	• suggestBox	
Window & Dialogs	**Utilities & Tools**	
• window	• skinSettings	
• modal	• populator	
• taskBar	• label	
• windowArea	• codeHighlighter	
	• xhtml	

There is also a ninth category of BTL elements. They are special because they can appear as attributes on other tags to specify extra behaviors that can be applied to any UI element. An example of such a behavior is drag-and-drop. We will cover drag-and-drop in Chapter 6.

If you are using the Backbase Explorer that we encountered in the previous chapter to find examples for the BTL widgets (`http://demo.backbase.com/explorer/`), the schema shown above may be a handy reference to find widgets you are looking for.

We always use the b prefix when referring to BTL widgets, although you can use whatever (nonconflicting) prefix you want.

The BTL abstract elements

If you are interested mainly in learning what BTL widgets look like, then the subject of this section about abstract elements maybe a little too abstract. Feel free to skip it, but before you do, take a look at the picture of the inheritance relationships between abstract elements. The picture shows the attributes that are available on many BTL elements.

Most of these attributes will be familiar to you and remind you of a not so distant past when you were still coding HTML instead of XHTML. While coding XHTML instead of HTML, you should use class and style instead of more specific attributes like width or margin. However, while using BTL, you must partly unlearn this for the BTL elements because using class or style could upset the styling that is done for the BTL elements, to make them look as they do.

Abstract element inheritance structure

The BTL markup language was developed using the Backbase Tag Definition Language. This means that BTL widgets are objects that can inherit properties from other TDL objects. It also means that you are able to extend the BTL objects into customized objects suitable for your application.

The BTL objects that we are looking at in this chapter, the layout objects, inherit from more basic, abstract objects. It is useful to look at some of these abstract elements because their attributes can be used by inheritance on the layout objects. The BTL elements we will be looking at are element, containerElement, dimensionElement, postionElement, and visualElement. All layout BTL elements inherit from these.

Here is a diagram of the inheritance structure:

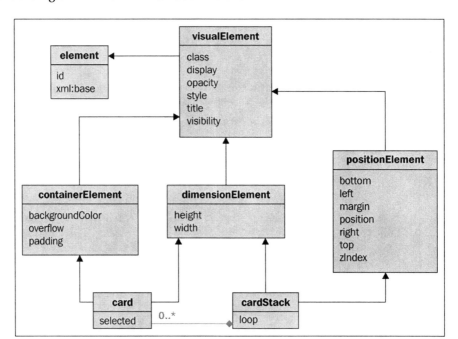

For those of you who are not so familiar with object-oriented models: the picture says that `element` is the object from which all others inherit. Therefore, for all BTL widgets, you can use the `id` and `xml:base` attributes, because these are defined on the `element` element.

The Backbase Tag Definition Language supports multiple inheritance. Therefore, a `cardStack` element can use the attributes of both `dimensionElement` and `positionElement`, and by looking further up in the tree, also of `visualElement` and `element`.

The relationship between `card` and `cardStack` says that a `cardStack` can contain zero or more `card` elements.

The picture does not describe the methods available. The only public methods that are interesting, belong to `cardStack`, which has the `next` and `previous` methods.

Now, let's look at some of the BTL elements in detail:

element

Base element from which all the elements in the BTL namespace are derived.

Attribute	Description
id	Unique ID of the element.
xml:base	Specifies a base URI other than the base URI of the document or external entity. The value of this attribute is interpreted as a URI reference.

Although `element` has no parent within the BTL namespace, it derives from the `element` JavaScript object in the DOM Core of the Backbase framework. The `element` JavaScript object implements the `node` interface, which means that all familiar DOM-related attributes and methods to append and remove children, and to navigate the DOM tree, are available. See the Backbase Reference for more details.

visualElement

An element from which all the visual elements in the BTL namespace are derived. This element takes care of some of the visual and interaction aspects.

[`visualElement` inherits from `element`.]

Attribute	Description
class	Used to set CSS classes to BTL elements. It is not recommended that this attribute be used, as it might break the styling of controls. More specific attributes are implemented to take care of certain styling properties. Font-related styling can be used safely.
display	Sets how the element is displayed. It works like the CSS `display` property. Because setting `display` can be tricky in some cases, the `true` and `false` values have been added. False does exactly the same as none, and true will reset the display property of the `viewNode`. The result is that the element is displayed according to the default rules or according to settings specified in the CSS classes.
opacity	Sets the opacity of the element, allowing you to see through it. It works like the CSS3 `opacity` property. It (decimal) ranges between 0.0 (not visible) to 1.0 (100% visible).

Attribute	Description
style	Used to set styles to BTL elements. It is not recommended that this attribute be used because it might break the styling of controls. More specific attributes are implemented to take care of certain styling properties. Font-related styling can be used safely.
title	Sets the title of the element.
visibility	Sets the visibility of the element. It works like the CSS visibility property. As opposed to setting the display, setting the visibility of the element does not change its dimensions. It will not disappear from the layout.

positionElement

This element implements attributes that can position the elements that inherit from it.

 positionElement inherits from visualElement.

Attribute	Description
bottom	Sets the distance from the bottom of the element to the bottom of the offset parent. It works like the CSS bottom property. You must add the proper CSS unit type.
left	Sets the distance from the left side of the element to the left side of the offset parent. It works like the CSS left property. You must add the proper unit type.
margin	Sets the margin around the element. It works like the CSS margin property. You must add the proper unit type.
position	Sets the position of the element. It works like the CSS position property.
right	Sets the distance from the right side of the element to the right side of the offset parent. It works like the CSS right property. You must add the proper CSS unit type (for example, px).
top	Sets the distance from the top of the element to the top of the offset parent. It works like the CSS top property. You must add the proper CSS unit type (for example, px).
zIndex	Sets the z-index of the element. It works like the CSS z-index property.

dimensionElement

This element implements attributes that set the dimensions of the elements that inherit from it.

 dimensionElement inherits from `visualElement`.

Attribute	Description
height	Sets the height of the widget. The widget height is relative to the height of its container.
width	Sets the width of the widget. The widget width is relative to the width of its container.

cardStack and card

There is a set of layout widgets that have a container—containment relationship. They use **cardStack** and **card** to inherit from. The widgets involved are:

- accordion and accordionItem
- deck and deckItem
- tabBox and tab

cardStack is the parent element for all widgets that represent a stack of cards. It allows users to navigate through items (cards). The content of the card on top will be visible.

cardStack has one attribute and a set of methods that can be called to navigate through the stack.

 cardStack inherits from `disableElement`, `dimensionElement`, and `positionElement`.

Attribute	Description
loop	When set to `true`, the `previous` or `next` methods will, when called, continue to select either the last or first item. If set to `false`, these methods will not continue to select an item when reaching the beginning or end of the list.

Method	Description
next	Selects the next item in the `cardStack` (that is not disabled). If the `loop` attribute is set to `false`, it will not select an item when the end of the list is reached. If set to `true`, it will continue with the first item in the list.
previous	Selects the previous item in the `cardStack` (that is not disabled). If the `loop` attribute is set to `false`, it will not select an item when the beginning of the list is reached. If set to `true`, it will continue with the last item in the list.

A `card` is an abstract element that provides the ability to enable and disable a widget. When the `selected` attribute is set to true, this card is the one that is shown when the `cardStack` is loaded into the page.

 `card` inherits from `disableElement`, `dimensionElement`, and `containerElement`.

Attribute	Description
selected	The selected state of the item (`true`/`false`).

This section does *not* sum up all the basic abstract elements implemented in BTL. For example, `disableElement` or `focusableElement` may interest you, for which you can find the details, as always, in the *Reference*.

There is another set of abstract elements that you will find mentioned in the Reference—the `base` element for each widget. Many widgets have a generic implementation that is common to both the system and the chameleon skin, and then specific implementations for each skin. The file structure for the `tabBox` widget, for example, is as follows:

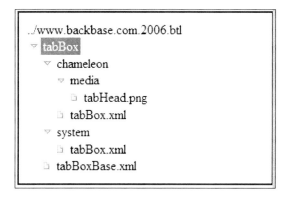

For both the chameleon and the system skin, there is a `tabBox` BTL object, which inherits from the `tabBoxBase` BTL object. In fact, it is the `tabBoxBase` object that inherits from all basic elements as described before. The `tabBox` itself conveniently inherits everything from its base object.

Just for fun, we created the previous picture from the following code snippet:

```
<b:tree xmlns="http://www.w3.org/1999/xhtml"
    xmlns:b="http://www.backbase.com/2006/btl">
    <b:treeBranch open="true">
        <b:label>../www.backbase.com.2006.btl/tabBox</b:label>
        <b:treeBranch label="chameleon">
            <b:treeBranch label="media" open="true">
                <b:treeLeaf label="tabHead.png" />
            </b:treeBranch>
            <b:treeLeaf label="tabBox.xml" />
        </b:treeBranch>
        <b:treeBranch label="system" open="true">
            <b:treeLeaf label="tabBox.xml" />
        </b:treeBranch>
        <b:treeLeaf label="tabBoxBase.xml" />
    </b:treeBranch>
</b:tree>
```

This code hardly needs explanation by now.

From now on, we will usually take the existence of the `base` element for granted and ignore it in our description of inheritance relationships.

Now, we have all the background we need to know how the layout widgets are constructed. With this in mind, you can use the information in the next section without needing to look into the Backbase API Reference because we will mention the specific attributes for each widget. By looking at the inheritance information that we showed earlier, you will know what inherited attributes you can use.

The layout widgets

BTL has a number of widgets that are intended to perform the most common layout tasks while developing an application user interface.

We will describe these widgets in this section and give you examples of their use. You can see the widgets in action by using the BTL Exerciser described at the end of this chapter.

We will look at the layout widgets in an alphabetical order. Therefore, the first one is accordion.

Accordion

An **accordion** efficiently groups together content, only showing the selected **accordionItem**.

 accordion and accordionItem inherit from cardStack and card. They do not have local attributes or methods.

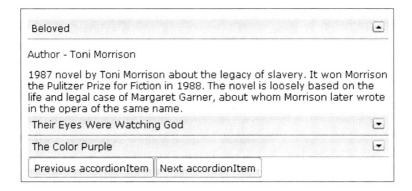

When a user clicks on one of the header panes in an `accordion`, the body pane of the `accordion` is revealed. All header elements are always visible. The sequence of panes is determined by the order of the child `accordionItem` elements. By setting the `selected` attribute to `true`, you can determine which `accordionItem` is selected when the widget is put on the page.

An `accordion` always has one and only one item open. If you open another item, the item that was open before will be automatically closed. The `navBox` is very similar to an `accordion` in appearance, but it can have as many items open as you like.

The `accordion` has `previous` and `next` methods (inherited from `cardStack`), to navigate between `accordionItems`. Note the `loop` attribute (inherited from `cardStack`) set on the `accordion`. When the `loop` attribute is set to a value of `true`, the `previous` and `next` methods will loop after reaching the first/last `accordionItem`.

The example that follows shows an `accordion`. The first snippet shows the `accordion` itself, the second snippet shows two buttons with `click` event handlers. These buttons can be used as an alternative way to navigate the `accordion`.

Note the use of the `b:label` element instead of the `label` attribute in the third `accordionItem`. This element allows for inserting more than just text into the label, for example, icons. Here's the code snippet that shows the `accordion`:

```
<b:accordion loop="true" width="250px">
    <b:accordionItem label="Beloved">
        <p>Author - Toni Morrison</p>
        <p> ... </p>
    </b:accordionItem>
    <b:accordionItem label="Their Eyes Were Watching God"
        selected="true">
        <p>Author - Zora Neale Hurston</p>
        <p> ... </p>
    </b:accordionItem>
    <b:accordionItem>
        <b:label>The Color Purple</b:label>
        <p>Author - Alice Walker</p>
        <p> ... </p>
    </b:accordionItem>
</b:accordion>
```

In the next snippet, each of the two buttons contains an XEL event handler (using the `handler` tag). When the button is clicked, the event is handled, and `previous` and `next` methods are called. These methods belong to the `accordion`. They allow navigation back and forward through the `accordion` items.

```
<b:button>
   Previous accordionItem
   <e:handler event="click">
      <e:call with="preceding::b:accordion[last()]"
         method="previous" />
   </e:handler>
</b:button>
<b:button>
   Next accordionItem
   <e:handler event="click">
   <e:call with="preceding::b:accordion[last()]"
      method="next" />
   </e:handler>
</b:button>
```

Look at the `e:call` statements in the event handlers for the buttons. The `with` attribute has the value `preceding::b:accordion[last()]` in both cases. This is an XPath expression that says "Find the set of elements in the DOM tree before this `button` element. Of these, select all accordions in the b namespace. Of these, find the last element".

> The support for XPath expressions is an important and powerful feature of the Backbase framework. Many attributes in the Backbase markup languages can have an XPath expression as their value. You can find details about XPath in the API Reference and the Application Development Guide. We will see more of it in the next chapter when we talk about XEL and commands.

Why is this complicated XPath expression preferable over the more simple XPath expression: `id('my-accordion')`? Well, in that case, I need to give the accordion an ID. Imagine that you have more than one accordion in your application UI, or more applications with `accordion` elements. You could then extend the `accordion` into a new widget that always has the `previous` and `next` buttons, and you would not have the problem of coping with `id` attributes in multiple `accordion` elements that cannot have the same value.

There is also a disadvantage. If you were not sure about the relative position of the buttons and the accordion, it would be difficult to use an XPath expression, while if you were using an ID, it would not matter.

A last remark before we look at the next widget. If you have many elements, such as a number of input fields in your `accordionItems`, then you may experience timing problems when the `accordion` is loaded. Look at the tips section later in this chapter for a solution to this problem.

Box

The **box** widget allows you to create a styled container for generic content. Use this to group components and define layout.

 box inherits from `containerElement`, `dimensionElement`, and `positionElement`. box does not have local attributes or methods.

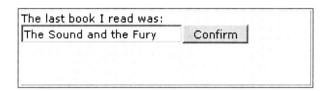

The box widget accepts text, images, and other BTL widgets.

The box is very similar to a `div` element. It has a default styling of a darker background. Here's the code snippet that shows the box widget:

```
<b:box width="300px" height="75px">
  The last book I read was:
   <div>
       <input type="text"
          size="25" value="The Sound and the Fury"
          name="lastBook"/>
       <button>Confirm</button>
   </div>
</b:box>
```

deck

The **deck** widget presents multiple panes, one at a time of which is visible, just like a deck of playing cards.

 deck and `deckItem` inherit from `cardStack` and `card` respectively. They do not have local attributes or methods.

Each pane in the `deck` is called a `deckItem` (it is really a `card`). The content of each `deckItem` element determines the content of the `deck`. The order of `deckItems` in the `deck` represents the sequence in which they will be displayed.

Booker Prize Winners:
2002 - Yann Martel
Previous Card   Next Card

While the `deck` has built-in `previous` and `next` methods (inherited from `cardStack`), you must create the buttons and handlers that trigger navigation between `card` elements in the `deck`. You will also be responsible for any other functionality that must occur while navigating between cards.

Here is a simple example of a `deck` with two buttons that navigate to the next and previous `deckItem` in the `deck`. One of the buttons is written in XEL, while the other is written in JavaScript.

The JavaScript version uses an XPath expression to find the deck. The JavaScript that you could use to find the element by ID is commented out.

```
<h1>Booker Prize Winners:</h1>
<b:deck id="mydeck" loop="true">
   <b:deckItem>2002 - Yann Martel</b:deckItem>
    <b:deckItem>2003 - DBC Pierre</b:deckItem>
   <b:deckItem>2004 - Alan Hollinghurst</b:deckItem>
   <b:deckItem>2005 - John Banville</b:deckItem>
   <b:deckItem selected="true">2006 - Kiran Desai</b:deckItem>
</b:deck>
<button>Previous Card
   <e:handler event="click">
      <e:call with="id('mydeck')" method="previous"/>
   </e:handler>
</button>
<button>Next Card
   <e:handler event="click" type="text/javascript">
      //var oDeck = bb.document.getElementById('mydeck');
      var oDeck = this.selectSingleNode('preceding::b:deck[1]');
      oDeck.next();
   </e:handler>
</button>
```

navBox

The **navBox** widget shows and hides levels of sub-navigation and further detail. Its appearance is the same as an `accordionItem`.

 navBox inherits from `containerElement`, `dimensionElement`, and `positionElement`.

navBox also inherits from `focusableElement`, `iconElement`, and `labelImplementor`.

Attribute	Description
open	If `true`, the widget will be open initially.
Method	**Description**
open	Opens the widget.
close	Closes the widget.

Each `navBox` has a header widget (defined by the value of the `label` attribute) and related content, which can be static or dynamic text, links, images, or other widgets. Clicking on the head widget expands or collapses the body widget with the related content as shown in the following screenshot:

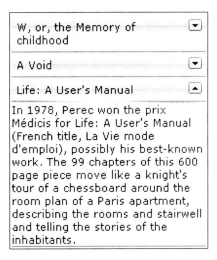

The `navBox` widget can expand multiple topics simultaneously. If you want to have only one topic visible at a time, you can use an `accordion` or a `tabBox`. Unlike the `accordion`, each `navBox` operates completely independent of the other, therefore, a set of `navBox` elements do not need a container like the `accordionItem` elements do.

Here is an example:

```
<b:navBox width="200px"
label="W, or, the Memory of childhood" open="false">
W ou le souvenir d'enfance, (W, or, the Memory of Childhood, 1975)
is a semi-autobiographical work, hard to classify. Two alternating
narratives make up the volume, one a fictional outline of a
totalitarian island country called "W", patterned partly on life in
a concentration camp, and the second, descriptions of childhood,
that merge towards the end when the common theme of the Holocaust is
explained.
</b:navBox>
<b:navBox width="200px" label="A Void" open="false">
Perec is also noted for his constrained writing: his 300 page novel A
Void (La disparition, 1969) is a lipogram, written without ever using
the letter "e". It has been translated into English by Gilbert Adair
under the title A Void (1994).
</b:navBox>
<b:navBox width="200px" label="Life: A User's Manual">
In 1978, Perec won the prix Médicis for Life: A User's Manual (French
title, La Vie mode d'emploi), possibly his best-known work. The
99 chapters of this 600 page piece move like a knight's tour of a
chessboard around the room plan of a Paris apartment, describing the
rooms and stairwell and telling the stories of the inhabitants.
</b:navBox>
```

panelSet

The **panelSet** widget partitions the screen layout into rows and columns.

`panelSet` inherits from `dimensionElement` and `positionElement`. See the table below for the attributes that are specific for `panelSet`.

`panel` inherits from `containerElement` and does not have local attributes or methods.

The panelSet has a number of specific attributes:

Attribute	Description
columns	Specifies the column dimensions, defining values, or a space-separated set of values in %, px, pc, pt, em, ex, in, cm, or mm. You can also use the wildcard asterisk "*" sign to fill the remaining space. You can use rows and columns attributes simultaneously to create a panel matrix.
fullScreen	Tells the panelSet to expand its area to the browser view port.
rows	Specifies the row dimensions, defining values, or a space-separated set of values in %, px, pc, pt, em, ex, in, cm, or mm. You can also use the wildcard asterisk "*" sign to fill the remaining space. You can use rows and columns attributes simultaneously to create a panel matrix.
splitter	The panelSet can be resized using a splitter when this attribute is set to true.
splitterSize	Size of the splitter between panels in the panelSet.

When subdividing a panelSet, you use the **panel** element, or you can use another panelSet widget to further subdivide that row/column. You can specify a panelSet to have rows, columns, or both. By using the splitter="true" attribute/value pair, you can add a resizable border to your panelSet.

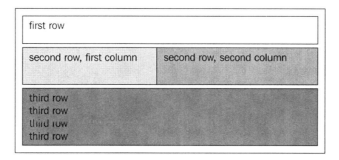

The orientation of the panelSet can be set using either the rows or columns attribute.

The number of rows or columns is defined by the number of space-separated unit values in the attribute. For instance, we create two columns by setting the columns attribute to "200px 600px". To create three columns, we should have set the attribute value to "200px 200px 600px". For five columns, you can use "50px 100px 100px 100px 50px". If not specified differently, the width of the panelSet widget will automatically adjust to the sum of the column widths.

Note that a panelSet with a width of 800px will have an empty space on the right for users with a screen resolution of 1024x768 or higher. This can be solved by using the "*" wildcard. This way, the row or column will fill up its container in the browser window. The asterisk wildcard can only be used once within the panelSet. For example, the five columns panelSet can also use "50px 100px * 100px 50px", where the third column will automatically adjust its width to ensure that the panelSet occupies the entire container area.

The panel and panelSet widgets behave like a div tag. By themselves, they do not have width or height. Therefore, you must add some styling to make a panelSet visible. A simple way to achieve visibility is to add the fullScreen="true" to the panelSet tag. Another option is to surround the panelSet with a div. For example:

```
<div style="width:600px; height:400px;">
```

Warning: Microsoft Internet Explorer performs slower if ancestor elements of a panelSet have the style attribute set to height: 100%. To resolve this, for the parent elements that have style="height: 100%", add the style attribute overflow: auto or overflow: hidden.

The panel tag represents the column or row as specified by the columns or rows attributes of panelSet. Therefore, it is important that there are as many panel tags nested in the panelSet as there are defined rows or columns. Child elements of the panel tag constitute the content of the panel.

It is also possible to use a nested panelSet tag instead of the panel tag. Be aware that there should eventually be as many panel tags as there are columns or rows defined in (nested) panelSets.

Here is a panelSet with panels example:

In the following example, there are three rows, where the second row is divided into two columns:

```
<div style="width:600px; height:200px;">
<b:panelSet rows="50px * 60px" splitter="true">
   <b:panel backgroundColor="#A9E9E2">first row</b:panel>
   <b:panelSet columns="30% *">
      <b:panel backgroundColor="#99FF99">
         second row, first column
      </b:panel>
      <b:panel backgroundColor="#FFCCFF">
         second row, second column
      </b:panel>
```

```
    </b:panelSet>
    <b:panel backgroundColor="#DF8E8E">
        third row
        <br />
        third row
        <br />
        third row
        <br />
        third row
    </b:panel>
</b:panelSet>
</div>
```

tabBox

A **tabBox** is a container for multiple items that can be selected through tabs.

tabBox and tab inherit from cardStack and card.

tabBox is focusable by inheriting from focusableElement.

tab can have a label by inheriting from labelImplementor.

tabBox and tab do not have local attributes or methods.

This is how a tabBox widget looks:

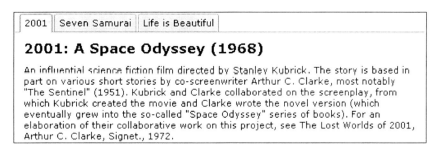

When a user clicks on one of the header panes in a tabBox widget, the body pane of the tabBox is revealed. All the header elements are always visible. The sequence of panes is determined by the order of the child tab elements. The value of the label attribute determines the text header of each tab.

The tabBox is functionally similar to an accordion. The difference between the two widgets is their visual presentation. While the tabBox has a horizontal orientation that looks like a Rolodex or tabbed address book, the accordion has a vertical orientation.

You can navigate between tabs by using the left and right arrow keys.

Here is a BTL `tabBox` example. Note how you can put other XHTML or BTL widgets inside a `tab`:

```
<b:tabBox>
    <b:tab label="Person">
        <div class="container">
            <table class="form-table">
                <tbody>
                    <tr>
                    <!-- omitted code: input form fields,
                         we just leave the birth date to show
                         the b:calendar -->
                    <tr>
                        <td class="form-left">
                            <label
                                for="input_person_birth_date">
                                Birth Date:</label>
                        </td>
                        <td class="form-right">
                            <b:calendar
                                name="person_birth_date"
                                id="input_person_birth_date"/>
                        </td>
                    </tr>
                    </tr>
                </tbody>
            </table>
        </div>
    </b:tab>
    <b:tab label="Address"/> <!-- this tab is empty -->
</b:tabBox>
```

`tabBox` is the last of the layout widgets. So far, we have concentrated on the visual and static aspects of a web application page. What happens and how to code it when a user interacts with your application, will be shown in detail in the next chapter. We conclude the description of widgets in this chapter by showing a few utility elements.

The BTL utility elements

There are a number of elements in the BTL library that only have a utilitarian purpose. Here is a short overview of these. In particular, you will see `populator` used in our BTL Exerciser sample application to lazily load tab panel contents.

codeHighlighter

This is an internal element that you can use to show code in a nice way. All examples in the API Reference are shown using the highlighter. For example, see the following section about the `label` widget for how the picture of the label example is followed by the highlighted source code. The highlighter can be used as follows:

```
<b:codeHighlighter>
    <!-- your valid piece of XML here -->
</b:codeHighlighter>
```

label

Many BTL widgets support a `label` attribute, where, for example, you can specify a simple text to be shown in a title bar. If you need more than simple text, you can use the `label` element, which allows markup and icon images within your label.

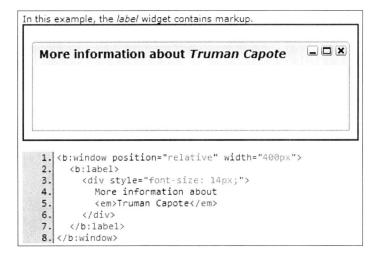

populator

populator is a utility widget that implements lazy loading, allowing content to be loaded upon request.

Attribute	Description
events	Default: "select".
	Space-separated list of events that will trigger loading.
type	Default: "once".
	Specifies the behavior of lazy loading.
	If set to once, it will load the content only once. This is useful when working with static content that will not change. Setting this attribute to always will make the lazy loader connect to the server every time one of the events occur to which the populator element is listening.
url	Specifies the URL that will be loaded.

Method	Description
populate	Loads the resource specified in the url attribute.

A custom loading message can be placed inside the populator element.

This element is often used in conjunction with a tabBox, to load contents of a tab panel on request.

The loaded contents will be appended after the populator element. Any previously loaded contents will be removed.

skinSettings

This element can be used to set a number of styling attributes of the chameleon skin. We will give more detail about these settings in the section about styling later in this chapter.

xhtml and xml

xhtml is a tag that can be used within a Backbase area to signal the Backbase runtime engine that the contents between the start and end tag do not need to be processed. This is useful to optimize performance if you have a block of plain XHTML code. The following code snippet shows the use of xhtml tag:

```
<p style="border:1px solid blue">
    This XHTML code is processed by the Backbase Engine.
</p>
```

```
<b:xhtml>
    <p style="border:1px solid green">
        This XHTML code is processed by the client browser.
    </p>
</b:xhtml>
```

xml is a tag that does the opposite. It can be used for escaping back into an area that is processed by the Backbase Client Runtime, when used within the BTL xhtml tag.

You can place xml elements within an xhtml element to force processing by the Client Runtime.

Several attributes that affect the style of the xml element are available. In the example, backgroundColor is used. To make the background color visible, style="display: block;" must be specified.

```
<b:xhtml>
    <p>This is outside the Backbase space</p>
    <b:xml backgroundColor="yellow" style="display: block;">
        <p>This is inside the Backbase space</p>
        <b:calendar mode="inline" />
    </b:xml>
    <p>This is outside the Backbase space</p>
</b:xhtml>
```

Styling techniques for GUI widgets

This section talks about CSS and about the two skins available in the Backbase framework—the chameleon skin and the system skin.

We assume that you have experience working with CSS (Cascading Style Sheets). You probably did style your web pages by coloring texts and by filling areas with background images, or by drawing borders. Another aspect of using CSS is to specify layout for HTML, which you probably are familiar with too.

In this section, we will cover both aspects, that is, using CSS in Backbase applications as well as other facilities that are available.

Using CSS

CSS helps you to separate visual aspects of the application from its content markup. Generally speaking, you can use CSS to style many properties of your application markup, such as colors, fonts, sizes, positioning, and so on. The following example shows how an ID selector was used to give the calendar component a width:

```
<style type="text/css">
    #myCalendar { width: 200px; }
</style>
<b:calendar id="myCalendar" />
```

 Keep in mind that Internet Explorer doesn't support multiple class selectors. So, creating a rule .myclass1 .myclass2 will be applied only to elements that have either myclass1 and/or myclass2 classes specified.

Styling BTL components can also be done with CSS. However, here you need to follow certain conventions. Let's take a look at an example:

```
<style type="text/css">
    .btl-calendar-input { color: red; }
</style>
<b:calendar value="10/03/2009" />
```

Here, we gave a red color to the text that displays the calendar value. The class selector we used was constructed by concatenating the following parts with a - character: btl, indicating the BTL component namespace, calendar for the name of the component, and input, indicating that this style is to be applied to the component's input field.

You can style other BTL components in a similar way.

Skinning

When a set of widgets share a common skin, a consistent look and feel is propagated throughout the web application.

The Backbase Client Framework provides two skins for all renderable BTL elements: a system skin, which has the same look and feel as the Windows XP classic skin, and a modern, configurable chameleon skin. This is how a slider widget looks in system skin:

Here's how the same `slider` widget looks in chameleon skin:

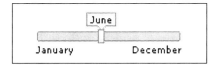

You can change the skin used by altering the `backbase/4_4_1/bindings/config.xml` file. In this file, alter the value of the `href` attribute in the `include` statement to reflect the `system` skin file (`config.xhtml_btl.system.xml`) or the `chameleon` skin file (`config.xhtml_btl.chameleon.xml`).

For example, to change the skin to a chameleon skin, you can use this code:

```
<include xmlns="http://www.w3.org/2001/XInclude"
  href="config.xhtml_btl.chameleon.xml" />
```

The Backbase Client Framework provides a few different options to alter the look and feel of Backbase widgets. The application developer can alter the chameleon skin simply by updating attribute values in the skin settings.

The BTL skinSettings widget

When using the chameleon skin, a tag called `skinSettings` is available. This tag has attributes that allow you to alter the background and text colors of the chameleon skin.

The `slider`, in this example, will be yellow; the button will have a purple border when pressed, and the `calendar` will show a variety of colors when dates are clicked:

```
<b:skinSettings activeText="cyan" highlightText="green"
activeBackground="yellow" activeBorder="purple" />
   <p>
   <b:slider id="mySlider"
      max="30" min="0" step="2" value="15" />
   </p>
   <p>
      <b:button> This is a button </b:button>
   </p>
```

```
<p>
    <b:calendar mode="inline" />
</p>
```

Default colors are represented by the default values of attributes of the `skinSettings.xml` widget. By changing these attributes, you alter the stylesheet settings.

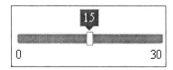

Refer to the API Reference for the default values of the `chameleon` skin.

Many features of the Backbase chameleon skin cannot be customized as easily as it may seem from this story. One reason is the use of background images and the other reason is that the intricate interplay of the various CSS settings can easily be upset if you change things.

If you don't want to use the `chameleon` skin, or you only want to alter a subset of the `chameleon` skin widgets, or want to create your own skin, you will have to extend widget(s) using TDL. Refer to the *Widget Development Guide* for more information.

Height problems

When putting GUI widgets on a page, it may happen that they look different than what you expected in the browser. Especially, the `panelSet` has a tendency to not appear at all, causing frustration to developers. Let's look at the cause and its solutions.

It can happen that the container element of the widget does not have a height set. In that case, the container will be sized according to the contents of the container. By default many BTL widgets do have a height of 100%, but if the height of the container is not set, this may be 100% of zero. The widget will collapse and will not be visible.

Solutions to these problems are as follows:

- Don't use `height: 100%` but use a fixed height.
- Set a height to the container. While using 100%, please understand that you're setting a size relative to the (offset) parent. You are actively setting a relative size. If you are not aware of the size of the (offset) parent, you may have to start with setting the height of the `html` element to 100%.

Part of the issue is the browser behavior. Take the following test case:

```
<!-- -->
<!DOCTYPE html PUBLIC "-//W3C//DTD XHTML 1.1//EN"
    "http://www.w3.org/TR/xhtml11/DTD/xhtml11.dtd">
<html xmlns="http://www.w3.org/1999/xhtml">
    <head>
        <style type="text/css">
            html { background-color: blue; }
            body { background-color: red; }
        </style>
    </head>
    <body> </body>
</html>
```

You will find that in Firefox, the color you see will be blue. In Internet Explorer, in quirks mode, it is red. In IE, in standards mode, it will be blue, but with a red bar (even if there is no content in the body). The conclusion is that the body does not have a height initially (the content would determine the height). A height of 100% of something that has no height will result in no height.

The next step is to give the body a height. If we want "full screen" behavior, we will use 100%. However, the screen will still only show a blue background. Setting a height to the html element quickly solves this.

There is much more to tell about skinning and ways to change the looks of BTL elements. When appropriate, we will add some more information about this subject in our examples.

A BTL Exerciser

In this section, we introduce an example application, a BTL Exerciser, which you can use to execute the BTL examples shown in this chapter and later chapters. This application uses functionality learned in this chapter and it gives a simple way to see what the examples that are described in this chapter look like when executed. Each of the examples is stored in a separate file. This makes it easy to look at the code or to add your own examples. The picture below shows the application showing the `tabBox` example:

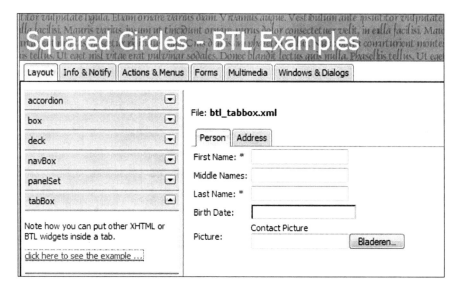

The BTL Exerciser application builds upon the *Basic Layout* application that we made in the previous chapter. If you want to follow along building this application, then make a copy of the `myApp1` folder in the same `examples` folder, and name it `btlSamples`, or some other name that you like better.

The application structure

The structure of the application is similar to what we had in the first chapter, while showing the basic application layout.

In the `btlSamples` folder, you will see the `index.html` file that contains the `include` statements for the Backbase framework libraries and also, there is the `app.xml` file, which contains the basic application layout.

We have some subfolders in the `examples` folder:

- `resources`: contains application-specific widgets, CSS files, and images.

- `panels`: contains the definitions for the tab panels, as we will see.

- The BTL examples are contained in two folders: `descriptions` and `examples`. Their name says it all. You will find files in these with names such as `btl_accordion.xml`, `btl_balloon.xml`, and so on.

See the picture below for an overview of this structure. The Backbase framework does not enforce a directory structure such as, for example, the Ruby on Rails framework does. However, we recommend setting a structure for yourself that allows you and your co-workers to find all application-related items quickly.

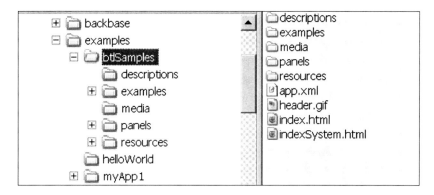

The starting point to find out how an application works is of course `index.html`. Therefore, we will look at its content now.

index.html

Make sure that the code for the Backbase area in `index.html` looks like this:

```
<script type="text/backbase+xml" style="height:100%">
   <xi:include
      href="../../backbase/4_4_1/bindings/config.xml" />
   <xi:include href="resources/bindings/squared.xml" />
   <xi:include href="app.xml" />
</script>
```

In addition to the `config.xml` file that is there to include the Backbase widgets and tag libraries, we also include `resources/bindings/squared.xml` and `app.xml`. The `squared.xml` file is there to include our own custom built widgets. As you will see shortly, we used a widget that we built for this application. We will explain how to build custom widgets and how this works in Chapter 7, which is about the Tag Definition Language. For now, just copy the `resources` folder from the sample code provided with this book.

app.xml

The `app.xml` file contains the main user interface layout for the application. We have chosen to make a more complex layout than in the "Basic Layout" application because we needed space for some fifty examples. We gave each category of BTL widgets its own tab, and on each tab panel there is a layout like the one in the "Basic Layout". The code looks as follows:

```
<div xmlns="http://www.w3.org/1999/xhtml"
xmlns:b="http://www.backbase.com/2006/btl" style="height: 100%;">
   <div id="appHeader">
   <div class="appHeaderText">
      Squared Circles - BTL Examples</div>
   </div>
   <b:tabBox height="100%">
      <b:tab class="mainTab" label="Layout">
         <b:populator
            events="DOMNodeInsertedIntoDocument select"
            url="panels/layout.xml" />
      </b:tab>
      <b:tab class="mainTab" label="Info & Notify">
         <b:populator url="panels/infoNotify.xml" />
      </b:tab>
      <b:tab class="mainTab" label="Actions & Menus">
         <b:populator url="panels/actionMenu.xml" />
      </b:tab>
      <b:tab class="mainTab" label="Forms">
         <b:populator url="panels/forms.xml" />
      </b:tab>
      <b:tab class="mainTab" label="Multimedia">
         <b:populator url="panels/multimedia.xml" />
      </b:tab>
      <b:tab class="mainTab" label="Windows & Dialogs">
         <b:populator url="panels/windowsDialogs.xml" />
      </b:tab>
   </b:tabBox>
</div>
```

For the `tabBox` used in our application, the tab panel contents are not coded directly, but they are loaded from another file with a `populator` element. The `populator` element differs from `XInclude` because the file is loaded in a lazy manner—only when you click on a tab to select it, are the contents loaded. In our case, the contents will be loaded once because we did not specify a `type` attribute and therefore, its default value is assumed to be `once`.

Note that for the first tab we also specified an `events` attribute, which shows a `DOMNodeInsertedIntoDocument` value, in addition to the `select` value, which is the default. This is because the `select` event is not fired when the `tabBox` is loaded for the tab that is the selected tab, by default the first one.

Tab panel content

Let's look at the content of one of the tab panels. The content of all of them is very similar. We chose the panel for the multimedia category of widgets. Here's the content of the tab panel:

```
<div xmlns="http://www.w3.org/1999/xhtml"
  xmlns:b="http://www.backbase.com/2006/btl" style="height: 100%;">
    <b:panelSet columns="200px *" splitter="true">
        <b:panel>
            <xi:include href="menus/multimediaMenu.xml" />
        </b:panel>
        <b:panel class="btl-border-left">
            <div class="examplePanel">
                <p> Flash and Applets. </p>
            </div>
        </b:panel>
    </b:panelSet>
</div>
```

Each tab panel contains its own `panelSet` to create its layout. Each `panelSet` uses a layout that is very similar to the basic layout that we described in Chapter 1.

We have chosen here to load the real content of the left part of the panel with an `XInclude`. This means that the code is loaded statically when the `tabBox` is loaded into the web application user interface. If the user interface of the application would have many tabs of which you expect only a few will be used, then you should use a `populator` element instead to load the contents more dynamically. You should also use it if the contents of each tab are very large or if the contents should be refreshed whenever the tab is selected.

You could argue that the use of XInclude here is modularization taken too far, which results in too many small files. This is a matter of choice. Try to experiment whatever size of files and modules works for you to make the code more clear to read and therefore, easier to maintain. Recognize though, that you indeed have a choice without resorting to server-side inclusion of code fragments, for example, by PHP or JSP processing.

The menu in each tab panel

In the example above, you saw a reference to the menu file to be included. What does it look like? Let us take as example the menus/infoNotifyMenu.xml file. It contains the code that shows a menu with a set of navBox widgets, one for each BTL widget in the category that the tab panel represents:

```
<div xmlns="http://www.w3.org/1999/xhtml"
    xmlns:b="http://www.backbase.com/2006/btl">
  <b:navBox label="balloon" open="false">
    <sq:navLink example="btl_balloon" />
  </b:navBox>
  <b:navBox label="infoBox" open="false">
    <sq:navLink example="btl_infoBox" />
  </b:navBox>
  <b:navBox label="toolTip" open="false">
    <sq:navLink example="btl_toolTip" />
  </b:navBox>
</div>
```

We have chosen a set of navBox elements over an accordion because we wanted all navBox elements to be closed, whereas for an accordion there will always be one accordionItem open.

The code looks simple enough, but what does <sq:navLink example="btl_infoBox" /> mean? Or the other navLink elements? Well, think about what we would like to see when you click on a navBox tab:

- The navBox should open and we would like some descriptive text to appear for each example that is available for the particular BTL widget that is in the title of the navBox.

- A standard text will be appended to each description: **click here to see the example...**

- When you click on the **click here** text, the example should be loaded and shown in the panel to the right of the menu area.

The following code snippet implements this for the case when we want to look at the `infoBox` test case:

```
<div>
    <b:populator events="DOMNodeInsertedIntoDocument"
        url="../../descriptions/btl_infoBox.xml" />
    <a href="javascript:">
        click here to see the example ...
        <e:handler event="click">
            <c:load url="../../examples/btl_infoBox.xml"
                destination="following::b:panel[1]"
                mode="replaceChildren" />
        </e:handler>
    </a>
</div>
```

Our `sq:navLink` is an encapsulation into a widget that we made ourselves for the code in the snippet above. Instead of having to copy the code above fifty times, each with slightly different content, we now only have to code one line for each of the widgets. We will explain more about it in Chapter 7, which describes the Tag Definition Language.

The code in the snippet does the following:

- Load the description for the `infoBox` example underneath the `navBox` header using a `populator` widget.
- Load the code for the example itself in the `panel` on the right. The `populator` does not allow us to specify a target for the contents of the file to be loaded, therefore, we are using the more powerful `c:load` command to accomplish this. We will explain the Backbase commands including `c:load` in the next chapter.

You have already seen some of the code for the examples and their descriptions. Therefore, we assume that you already know what the files to be loaded, which are in the `descriptions` and the `examples` folders, will look like.

We can conclude that we have built with very simple means a rather extensive and dynamic application that shows the power of Backbase Tag Library.

Summary

In this chapter, we took a closer look at the Backbase Tag Library and in particular the layout widgets.

The proper layout of an application user interface involves styling with CSS. We described how CSS can interact with the BTL widgets and how you can go about styling in your web application. We created a web application that can show all BTL examples, basically just using the BTL layout widgets.

In the next chapter, we will give more detail about the execution logic of a web application—commands and XEL.

3
Writing the Application Logic

In this section, we will learn the basic concepts of scripting with the Backbase framework. First, we will look into the Application Programming Model and see how simple and intuitive it is. Then, we will present an overview of technologies and APIs available, including specific Backbase event handling. After that we will get acquainted with XML Execution Language (XEL), a markup-based programming language that can be used instead of, or together with, JavaScript. At the end of this section, we will provide some notes about XPath because XPath expressions can be used as value for many XEL attributes. Then, we will be ready to dig into details of the built-in functions that the Backbase framework provides—the *Command Functions*.

At the end of the chapter, we will present the BTL widgets in the *Info and Notify BTL widgets* section, followed by a sample application that is very similar to the BTL Exerciser we saw in the previous chapter. This version, the Command Functions Exerciser, allows you to see the examples for the Command Functions, making use of some of the features explained in this chapter.

Here is a detailed list of the subjects that we will cover in this chapter:

- The Application Programming Model—what it is and what it consists of
- Overview of the Backbase APIs—the bb object, the W3C DOM, events, and utility functions
- Events—Event flow, the three ways of registering event handlers, event APIs, and custom events
- Backbase utility functions, bb object functions, and Command functions
- XML Execution Language—variables, conditional logic, functions, XEL, and JavaScript
- Some remarks about the use of XPath with the Backbase framework
- Command functions to manipulate the DOM or to manipulate elements

- Info and Notify BTL widgets
- A Backbase Command Exerciser

In the following table you can find where the various categories of command functions are discussed:

Category	Chapter
Manipulate the DOM	3
Manipulate Elements	3
CSS related	-
Asynchronous load	4
Behavior	6
Other	8

The application programming model

In the previous chapter, we have seen how to layout the User Interface with XML and how to style it. We also looked into XHTML and several BTL widgets. Some of those widgets had interaction capabilities, as you may remember. These interaction capabilities are part of their implementation; we did not have to write a single line of code to enable this behavior. You could also see that the widgets we used had no real communication with each other. We were concentrating on their visual aspects. It is clear that we need more if we want to develop an interesting application.

In a real application, the interaction with the UI components triggers actions. For example, parts of the UI can be hidden or shown, or data can be visualized dynamically. Simply, interactions enable user work flow.

In the previous chapter, we never talked about what the web application looked like internally in the browser after the application XHTML document is loaded. We will see something about this now. In more abstract terms, we will be talking about the *programming model* of a Backbase application, meaning that we will describe in a general way what the facilities are that a client web application will use.

When an XHTML document is loaded into a browser, the browser will parse the elements and put them into an application tree, generally referred to as the Document Object Model (DOM). The browser ignores everything that is placed between `<script type="application/backbase+xml">` and `</script>` tags, the Backbase areas we defined in Chapter 1. The content of such a Backbase area, which we will sometimes call a Backbase markup fragment and which should consist of proper XML, is parsed by the Backbase framework core engine in exactly the same way as the browser does with the XHTML elements. This means that the Backbase markup fragment is inserted into a Backbase application tree.

The Backbase application tree has a standard DOM programming API for accessing and modification of its content at runtime. If you know the HTML DOM API or the XML DOM API, then you also know the Backbase DOM API because they are the same. The execution of code in a web application usually starts with some user interaction. For example, the user enters text into an input box, or clicks on a node in a tree. Once the user interaction has taken place, an event is dispatched to the appropriate object in the application UI tree. It carries information about the event name and other details. If there is a listener (or handler) for the event, it is invoked and the handler script is executed.

To summarize this introduction: The programming model of a Backbase application involves a DOM that is similar to an XML or HTML DOM, with the corresponding API. To interact with a Backbase web application, we need event handlers that are registered to a specific DOM node. The content of the event handlers form the application logic of our application.

Overview of the Backbase APIs

The Backbase Framework delivers a comprehensive and well-balanced set of APIs for developing applications. Some of these APIs are JavaScript-based, others are XML-based. The XML-based APIs always have a JavaScript equivalent API. The opposite is not always true, as we will see when we talk in more detail about XEL. The overview we are giving in this section is mainly based in the JavaScript interface that the Backbase framework provides.

The APIs can be divided into two groups:

- The low level APIs that have the Document Object Model at the heart, enabling fundamental functions
- The high level APIs that wrap common implementation patterns into simple calls

For both the low level and the high level APIs, there exist JavaScript implementations that are collected together in the bb object.

The bb object

The bb JavaScript API gives you the ability to interact with the Client Runtime; it is the gateway to the Backbase APIs using JavaScript. You can use the API for calling methods, checking properties, string functions, XML manipulation, DOM methods, and utility functions. This object covers both the low level and the high level API.

Almost anything that you can do with the bb JavaScript API, you can also do with XEL and the declarative Command Declarative API. The Backbase framework provides a dual (JavaScript and XML) API so that developers can work with the Client Runtime according to their development preferences and skill sets.

The bb object is documented in the API Reference.

Low level APIs—the W3C DOM family

The Document Object Model is a family of platform- and language-neutral interfaces that allow programs to access and manipulate structured documents, for example, XML or HTML documents. The Backbase framework supports the following DOM modules:

- The **DOM Core** module enables base objects such as Text, Element, Document, and others. This module presents the document tree and it allows APIs to access and manipulate its structure and contents.

- The **DOM Events** module enables a uniform event system that introduces event flow through a document structure. It allows registration of event handlers and provides ways to access event contextual information. Event flow means that events are propagated through the DOM tree. We will explain more about this in the *Events* section later in this chapter.

- The **DOM XPath** module enables APIs to query the document tree nodes by using the XPath selection language. Although the DOM Core already has all primitive APIs required to navigate the tree, it is more efficient and powerful to use XPath because it significantly simplifies the use of the DOM.

- The **CSS Selectors API** module enables an alternative selection language instead of XPath, for use with structured documents: the CSS Selectors. This is the youngest technology in the family of DOM-related specifications yet it is one of the most widely adopted. We assume that you are familiar with it. There is no custom support for it in the Backbase framework.

The Document Object Model

As we noted earlier, Document Object Model is at the very heart of the Backbase framework and it is the primary or low level API to the application UI. Some developers consider the DOM to be complex, whereas others consider it to be too complex. In fact, the DOM is rather simple, nice, and compact, as we hope to explain.

There are three aspects that need to be taken care of—traversing and modifying the document tree, and handling events on its nodes.

Traversing the document tree

The first task we would need to complete when scripting almost anything against the DOM is usually locating elements to operate on. DOM has many means to do that, including pure traversal consisting of walking through parents of elements, siblings, and children.

Often, it is practical to give the widget an identifier by specifying an `id` attribute in the markup. Such an element can be found by calling `getElementById` document method.

It is not always possible to give an `id` to every element we are going to work with. Other APIs are available in this case, where the most powerful one is `bb.evaluate`. It allows you to use XPath expressions to find nodes.

Here are the APIs relevant for document traversal:

- `getElementById`
- `getElementsByTagName` and `getElementsByTagNameNS`
- `bb.evaluate` and `bb.evaluateSmart`
- `bb.selector.query` and `bb.selector.queryAll`
- `getAttribute` and `getAttributeNS`

Some methods in the list above cannot be called directly on the `bb` object. Instead, they can be called on the `bb.document` object. In the next example, we find a collection of all `b:calendar` elements in the application:

```
var aCalendars = bb.document.getElementsByTagName("b:calendar");
```

 In an XHTML application, you can find the root node of the DOM with the `document` property. Similarly, the root of a Backbase area is available as the `bb.document` property. The `bb.document` property shows only the root of a Backbase application fragment and not the HTML nodes that may be outside it.

Modifying the document tree

At application runtime, widgets may need to be adjusted to reflect the state of the application. For example, an action in the application could become unavailable and the corresponding `menuPopupItem` might need to be disabled, so that the user would not be able to activate it. This could be done by setting a `disabled` attribute on the `menuPopupItem` element.

It is also possible that we would need to dynamically create UI elements or even fragments consisting of multiple elements. For example, an application user might want to attach more files to a message and therefore, additional XHTML `input` elements might need to be added to the UI to allow this. The `createElementNS` method from the `document` object is used in this case. This method returns an instance of a widget from a certain namespace that is provided as argument. Once an instance of element is created, it can be added to the application DOM tree.

These are APIs relevant for document modification:

* `createElement` and `createElementNS`
* `appendChild`, `insertBefore`, `removeChild`, and `replaceChild`
* `setAttribute`, `setAttributeNS`, `removeAttribute`, and `removeAttributeNS`

The NS suffix for the API methods mean that this is a namespace aware version of the API.

The next example features the creation of a new `menuPopUpItem` widget and adding it to the application UI:

```
var oMenuPopup = bb.document.getElementById("my_menupopup");
var oMenuPopupItem =
  bb.document.createElementNS("http://www.backbase.com/2006/btl",
  "b:menuPopupItem");
oMenuPopupItem.setAttribute("label", "New menu item 1");
oMenuPopup.appendChild(oMenuPopupItem);
```

Dealing with events

When talking about the programming model, we said that dealing with events is the most important aspect of implementing the application logic. You can still use the low level `on...` attributes on the XHTML tags, such as for example:

```
<div onclick="alert('I am clicked')">Click me</div>
```

Probably, you will often *not* use this option of handling events because using an XEL event handler will allow you to use the specific Backbase events. Also, as we have already seen, XEL event handlers are much easier to write, even if you use JavaScript instead of XEL.

As handling events is an important topic, which cuts through the low level and high level API separation, we will discuss it now separately.

Events

Events refer to any kind of interaction with the application. An event can be dispatched as a result of user input, such as a button click. A change in the system, such as the loading of an external snippet, can also trigger the dispatching of an event. In your application, you will see an event only when you indicate this to the browser by registering an event handler.

DOM event flow and cancelable events

All events in the Backbase framework follow the DOM event flow. The three phases (capture, target, and bubble) of the DOM event flow determine how an event is dispatched through the application. During the **Capture Phase** of event propagation, the event follows a path from the root of the DOM tree down to the target node. The event can be handled at any ancestor of the target node. The **Target Phase** takes place when the event reaches the target node. In the **Bubbling Phase**, the event is dispatched back up from the target node (the node handled or that has an attached listener) to the root of the tree.

See the next chart for an example:

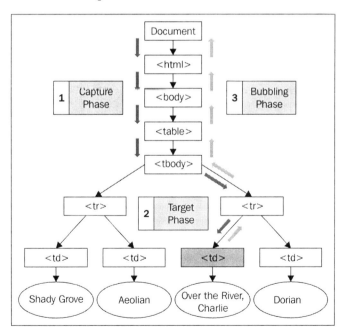

Implementations may have a default action associated with an event type. An example is the HTML `form` widget. When the user submits the form, usually by pressing on a submit button, the event `submit` is dispatched to the widget and the default action for this event type is generally to send a request to a web server with the parameters from the form.

A *cancelable* event is an event associated with a default action that is allowed to be canceled during the DOM event flow. At any phase during the event flow, the triggered event listeners have the option of canceling the default action or allowing the default action to proceed.

Registering event handlers

For a Backbase application, there are generally three ways of registering event handlers:

- Using markup with an XEL handler element
- Using markup with XEL handler attributes
- Using JavaScript and the DOM events API

Using markup with an XEL handler element

We have seen this type of event handler before in our "Hello Backbase!" examples. It is the most common way to specify and register an event handler. Here is an example:

```
<script xmlns="http://www.w3.org/1999/xhtml"
  xmlns:e="http://www.backbase.com/2006/xel"
  type="application/backbase+xml">
  <xi:include href="../../backbase/4_4_1/bindings/config.xml" />
  <input type="text" id="age">
    <e:handler event="change" type="text/javascript">
       alert(this.getAttribute('value'));
    </e:handler>
  </input>
</script>
```

Let's explain the code:

- The `handler` tag indicates that the parent of the tag (the `input` element in our example), will handle a particular event type.
- The `event` attribute specifies which event (in this case: "change") to handle.
- Code nested within the `handler` tag represents the functional code to be executed when the event is triggered.

- The `type` attribute specifies what execution language will be used. In this case, we are using JavaScript by setting the `type` attribute to `text/javascript`. You could set the `type` attribute to `application/xml` and write functionality using XML Execution Language.

Using markup with XEL handler attributes

Instead of the familiar `onchange="..."` or other `on...` event handling, you can write `e:onchange="..."` and use Backbase-specific functionality in the handler.

```
<script xmlns="http://www.w3.org/1999/xhtml"
  xmlns:e="http://www.backbase.com/2006/xel"
  type="application/backbase+xml">
  <xi:include href="../../backbase/4_4_1/bindings/config.xml" />
  <input type="text" id="age"
     e:onchange="alert(this.getAttribute('value'))" />
</script>
```

This is handy if the event handler is very short, such as one or two statements. Otherwise, it is preferable to use the XEL event handling.

Using JavaScript and the DOM events API

The third possibility is to add an event handler using the `addEventListener` method on the node where you want to register the event.

```
var oElement = bb.document.getElementById("age");
oElement.addEventListener("change", function(oEvent) {
   alert(this.getAttribute('value'))
}, false);
```

The examples above have just an `alert` as the content of the event handler. Of course, you will need to do more interesting things when handling events. The next step in understanding how a web application works, and in particular, a Backbase web application is to understand what the content of these event handlers can be and which APIs are available to you as a web application developer. We will see more of this in the high level Backbase APIs.

Besides the ability to trigger a script or to update the UI state, an event handler can also affect the event flow itself. It can stop event propagation or prevent the default action associated with this event type from executing.

The Backbase framework offers the possibility to dispatch events from the application logic into the UI tree, although this is not a common thing to do. Especially this should never happen for events implemented in the framework. Creating an event object with a certain interface is done by calling the `createEvent` function that is available on Backbase `document` object. Once the event object is initialized with `initEvent` or another method specific to a certain interface, it can be dispatched into the tree.

> The events in the Backbase DOM implementation support the three phases of propagation we described earlier—*capture*, *target*, and *bubble*. Within a Backbase area, this will happen always, even within a browser that might miss certain propagation phases completely outside this area (Hello Internet Explorer!).

APIs relevant for dealing with events

The low level APIs for event handling are:

- `stopPropagation` and `preventDefault`
- `createEvent`, `initEvent`, and `dispatchEvent`
- `addEventListener` and `removeEventListener`

In the sample below, we show how calling `stopPropagation` prevents executing an `alert` call from the element's parent.

```
<div e:onclick="alert('I shall not be called when my child is
  clicked')">
  <div e:onclick="event.stopPropagation()">
     Click (initiate) and stop event propagation.
  </div>
</div>
```

As we indicated earlier, the Backbase framework has more events available than most browsers offer. It also standardizes the events for you, which means that when using the Backbase framework, you will always have the same set of events available, regardless of whether the specific browser used supports it.

Event types

Event types refer to the kind of events that can occur in an application. They may have to do with mouse movement (`click`, `mouseover`), keyboard commands, system changes (`load`, `DOMNodeInsertedIntoDocument`), or other interactions with the application. They can be used as the value of the `event` attribute of an XEL `handler` tag, or as an `onEvent` HTML event attribute.

The Backbase framework supports the following event standard types:

- DOM level 3 event types (sub-set)
- Backbase framework (non-DOM) events
- BTL widget custom events

The Backbase Application Development Guide and the Reference give a complete list of the supporter DOM level 3 events. Here, we list only the specific Backbase events:

Event Type	Description	Bubbles	Cancelable
keypress	Dispatched when the user presses an alphanumeric key.	Yes	Yes
mousewheel	Dispatched when the mouse wheel button is rotated.	Yes	Yes
contextmenu	Dispatched when a context menu is triggered.	Yes	Yes
mouseenter	Fires when the user moves the mouse pointer into the object.	No	No
mouseleave	Fires when the user moves the mouse pointer outside the object boundary.	No	No

BTL widget custom events

Each widget contains its own API—a set of attributes, properties, methods, and event handlers for the user to hook into. Sometimes, a widget or a behavior that can be attached to a widget creates custom events. These events may add extra or changed functionality to existing events (overriding) or they may exist because a widget/behavior has a particular specific functionality that we want the application to react to. In Chapter 6 we will see a number of these events that can be triggered when adding drag-and-drop or resize behavior to a widget.

Custom event creation

Just as custom events were created in the BTL widgets, you can create and dispatch your own custom events in the body of an XEL handler.

It takes three steps to create and dispatch an event. First, you create the event object. Second, you initialize that event and set its properties (including the event name). Lastly, you dispatch that event (when the change event is handled on the input field) to an event target. Here is a somewhat artificial example:

```
<img id="shoppingCart" src="media/adg_shopBlueOrig.png">
    <e:handler event="shoppingCartInvoked" type="text/javascript">
        alert('I am the shoppingCartInvoked handler!');
    </e:handler>
</img>
<input type="text">
    <e:handler event="change" type="text/javascript">
        var oShoppingCartImage =
          bb.document.getElementById('shoppingCart');
        var oEvent = bb.document.createEvent('Events');
        oEvent.initEvent('shoppingCartInvoked', false, false);
        oShoppingCartImage.dispatchEvent(oEvent);
    </e:handler>
</input>
```

In the example, we create the `shoppingCartInvoked` event by using the `initEvent` function in the event handler for the input field. The event is then dispatched to the specified target, the image of a shopping cart, which handles the event by showing an alert.

`createEvent()` and `dispatchEvent()` are methods of the DOM `document` object, while `initEvent()` is a method of the DOM `event` object. Refer to the API Reference for details.

We will stop our discussion of lower level APIs here and turn our attention to the utility functions that are available and then to the XEL language.

Backbase utility functions

Although using the low level API is enough to code any UI-related task in your application, it is not always efficient to do so as you will often end up writing similar code constructs. The Backbase utilities wrap common routines into tasks that can be called in a more simple and intuitive manner.

We introduced the `bb` core object already. It contains basic functions and properties necessary to build applications. These functions include the ability to call other methods and functions, property getting and setting, application construction and destruction processes, and model-view-controller manipulation. These methods on the `bb` object are used like any JavaScript method. See the API Reference for a complete list.

The bb object utility functions

The following list describes the type of objects available with the `bb` object:

Objects	Description
array	Utility functions for array objects.
browser	Provides information about the client browser.
command	JavaScript API for the Command Functions methods.
console	JavaScript API for the `bb.console` methods. These methods are only available when the debugger is loaded.
cookie	On this object, you can find API functions to set and get cookies.
exec	On this object, you can find functions related to execution flow.
history	Utility functions for handling history and bookmarking.
html	Utility functions that handle HTML-related functions in a browser-independent way.
smil	Utility functions for SMIL animation.
string	Utility functions for handling string objects.
time	Utility functions for time calculation.
ui	User Interface related functions.
uri	Utility functions for resolving a URI
xml	Utility functions for XML objects.

Backbase Commands

In the list above that specifies the types of `bb` object functions you saw the `bb.command` functions mentioned. These command functions have a declarative equivalent, the Command Functions markup language.

We have already encountered several commands in the first and second chapter because almost every event handler will contain one. For example, there were several `alert` commands, a `setText` to set the balloon text, and a `load` function to dynamically load parts of the code.

When using commands declaratively in an application, the command namespace must be declared in a parent tag of the element.

- The command namespace URI is: `http://www.backbase.com/2006/command`.
- The command conventional prefix is `c:`.

We categorized the command functions for you as follows:

Manipulate the DOM	Manipulate Elements	CSS related
• getAttribute	• blur, focus	• addClass
• setAttribute	• fireEvent	• setClass
• removeAttribute	• position	• removeClass
• copy	• scrollTo	• replaceClass
• create	• show, hide, showHide	• setStyle
• destroy	• sort	
• move	• tile	
• setText	• transform	
Asynchronous load	**Behavior**	**Other**
• load	• addBehavior	• alert
	• setBehavior	• bookmark
	• removeBehavior	• trace

 In a later section of this chapter, we will look at the commands that manipulate the DOM or specific elements. The other commands will be covered in a later chapter.

The Backbase XML Execution Language (XEL)

The Backbase Client Framework offers XEL, an XML markup language, which can be used in many circumstances as an alternative to JavaScript. This section will introduce you to the main XEL elements.

Before we turn our attention to XEL itself, let us try to clarify when you should use JavaScript and when you should use XEL. Remember that we showed two versions of the "Hello Backbase" balloon example in Chapter 1. In both cases, they used an XEL event handler tag to describe what should happen in case the user clicks on the **OK** button. In the first example, the content of the element was coded in JavaScript and in the second example we used XEL. This suggests that you can use XEL or JavaScript interchangeably. Just use whatever you like better for a specific situation.

By specifying either `text/javascript` or `application/xml` (which is usually the default), you can indicate the choice you made. When making a choice, keep this in mind:

- XEL code is usually shorter and it may be easier to see what is going on for UI designers. Therefore, using XEL should be preferred in event handlers.
- The actions you code within an event handler are often command functions. Of each command function, there are JavaScript versions, but also declarative versions that you can use with XEL.
- XEL is not a complete programming language. Therefore, there may be circumstances where it is not possible or feasible to use XEL.
- XEL has a learning curve. Therefore, if you are an experienced JavaScript developer, you may be tempted to *not* use it, apart from the XEL `handler` tag.
- Sometimes it is preferable to use JavaScript because of the slightly better performance you may be able to achieve.

XEL is a programming language. Therefore, we will describe *variables*, *operations*, *control logic*, and *functions*.

XEL features
XEL can be used to perform the following tasks:

- Adding an event handler to an element
- Implementing presentation logic
- Extending a widget instance
- Creating and destructing elements
- Allowing one widget to communicate with another widget
- Loading data asynchronously

A namespace declaration is needed while using XEL tags. We use the `e:` prefix in our examples: `xmlns:e="http://www.backbase.com/2006/xel"`.

We already described the most important element of XEL, the event handler. To understand how to implement presentation logic with XEL, it is best to assume that it is a real programming language. We will see later that it is missing some features in this respect, but that has hardly an effect on its usability.

The first things to look at are variables.

Variables in XEL

Variables, attributes, and properties. What is the difference?

- Attributes can be set by giving them a value when placing a widget on a page. Their initial value is visible on the UI. Their value can only be of a string type. The scope of an attribute is within its widget.

- Properties are the attributes of widgets or objects. They can only be set and retrieved programmatically. The type of a property can be any type that is allowed in JavaScript. The scope of a property is local to the object it belongs to.

- Variables are part of XEL as a programming language. Their value can be anything, including node sets, and their scope can be local or global.

Declaring variables

In XEL, variables can be declared using the `variable` element.

In this example, we define a variable name as `myVar` and we define its value as `myInitialValue`, which is an XPath string:

```
<e:variable name="myVar" select="'myInitialValue'" />
```

While declaring a variable, the value of the `name` attribute represents the variable name. You will use this value while accessing the variable somewhere else in your application. XEL variables can have strings, elements, or entire node sets as value.

There are a number of ways to assign a value to the variable. For example, you can use an XPath expression in the `select` attribute.

In the next example, we assign all the `div` elements in the document to the variable `myVar`:

```
<e:variable name="myVar" select="[//div]" />
```

Alternatively, you can use the `e:data` tag as a child of the `variable` tag to assign its content to the variable, as in the next example:

```
<e:variable name="myVar">
   <e:data type="text/plain">
      My initial value
   </e:data>
</e:variable>
```

You can use the `e:data` tag combined with an `xi:include` tag to load an entire file into a variable on startup of the page.

```
<e:variable name="external_data">
   <e:data type="text/xml">
      <xi:include href="data/movies_20.xml" />
   </e:data>
</e:variable>
```

Instead of `xi:include`, you can use `c:load` to load an entire file into a variable. This is the preferred way for setting the value of a local variable as it may appear in an event handler because the file will only be loaded when the variable is parsed and not when the document is parsed, as would happen with `xi:include`.

```
<e:handler event="click">
   <e:variable name="external_data">
      <c:load url="data/movies_20.xml" />
   </e:variable>
</e:handler>
```

Variable scope

Variable scope indicates where you can access a declared variable. XEL variables can take local or global scope depending on the position of the `variable` declaration. If you declare a variable within an XEL function body, then the variable will have a local scope. Therefore, it will only be accessible within that function. If the variable is declared elsewhere in a document, the variable will have a global scope and it can be accessed anywhere in that document.

Retrieving variable values

The value of a variable is available either in an XPath or a JavaScript expression.

In XPath expressions, variables are recognized using the $ sign. Here is an example of getting the value of a variable named `myVar`. In the example, a button is defined that shows an alert when clicked. The alert displays the value of the variable `myVar`, which is defined in the previous statement as `myValue`.

```
<e:variable xmlns:c="http://www.backbase.com/2006/command"
  name="myVar" select="'myValue'" />
<b:button xmlns:c="http://www.backbase.com/2006/command">
    Click
    <e:handler event="click" type="application/xml">
       <c:alert select="$myVar" />
    </e:handler>
</b:button>
```

XEL variables are also accessible as JavaScript variables in the body of a `handler` or `function`:

```
<b:button xmlns:c="http://www.backbase.com/2006/command">
    Click
    <e:handler event="click" type="application/xml">
       <e:variable name="myVar" select="'myValue'" />
       <e:script type="text/javascript">
          alert(vars['myVar']);
       </e:script>
    </e:handler>
</b:button>
```

Notice that we moved the declaration of the `myVar` variable inside the `e:handler` function, because the JavaScript `vars[]` array is only available within the scope of a function.

Setting properties and variables

You can use the `e:set` element to set object properties as well as XEL variables. You use the attribute `property` and `select` to determine what you would like to set. Here is an example. An accordion is shown and an XEL `set` element sets the `selectedIndex` property.

```
<b:accordion id="myAccordion">
    <e:handler event="DOMNodeInsertedIntoDocument">
       <e:set property="selectedIndex" select="'1'" />
    </e:handler>
    <b:accordionItem label="Beloved">
       <p>Author - Toni Morrison</p>
```

```
    </b:accordionItem>
    <b:accordionItem label="Their Eyes Were Watching God"
      selected="true">
       <p>Author - Zora Neale Hurston</p>
    </b:accordionItem>
    <b:accordionItem label="The Color Purple">
        <p>Author - Alice Walker</p>
    </b:accordionItem>
  </b:accordion>
```

Getting and setting attributes

In XEL, you get and set attributes in a slightly different way than you get and set properties or variables. This is because we tap into the existing DOM standard, which already has `setAttribute` and `getAttribute` methods. In this example, we will click on one button to shrink its `width` attribute:

```
<b:button id="button" width="600px">
   Click me to shrink the width of the button...
   <e:handler event="click" type="application/xml">
      <e:call method="setAttribute" name="'width'"
        value="'100px'" />
   </e:handler>
</b:button>
```

Notice that both the `name` and `value` attributes accept XPath expressions, which is why we place the attribute value inside single quotes.

Conditional execution in XEL

XEL has a number of operators that you can use to perform conditional processing.

Conditional logic

In XEL, conditional logic can be expressed through the `if` element or `choose`/`when`/`otherwise` elements. The `if` element allows you to make a single test.

The `if` and `when` elements use the `test` attribute to determine logical conditions. The value of the `test` attribute can be an XPath or a JavaScript expression.

Warning: The XEL language has no `else` construct. If you need conditional logic of this kind, you can use the `choose`/`when`/`otherwise` elements.

Use the `test` attribute while evaluating a single test. As there are no parentheses around the test, it is interpreted as XPath. Note that the JavaScript and XPath test syntax have subtle differences, (`1==1`) as opposed to `1=1`. The XPath test may also be written as: `1 eq 1`. Click on the text, and an alert message should appear.

```
<div>
    <e:handler event="click">
        <e:if test="(1=1)">
            <e:script type="text/javascript">
            alert('This XPath test is true');
            </e:script>
        </e:if>
    </e:handler>
    testMe
</div>
```

The `choose`/`when`/`otherwise` elements allow you to create a logic structure with more than one condition. The `choose` element is a container for one or many `when` tags. Each `when` element constitutes one condition. The `otherwise` element provides functionality if all the conditions in the `when` elements return false. The following example shows a function that will toggle the width property of a button based on the value of a variable named `sWidth`.

Use `e:choose` while evaluating multiple conditional statements. It is very similar to a case construct in most programming languages.

```
<e:function name="toggleWidth">
    <e:argument name="sWidth" required="true" />
    <e:body>
        <e:choose>
            <e:when test="$sWidth='600px'">
                <e:call with="id('button1')"
                  method="setAttribute"
                  name="'width'" value="'60px'" />
            </e:when>
            <e:otherwise>
                <e:call with="id('button1')"
                  method="setAttribute"
                  name="'width'" value="'600px'" />
            </e:otherwise>
        </e:choose>
    </e:body>
</e:function>
<b:button id="button1" width="200px">
    <e:handler event="click">
```

```
        <e:call function="toggleWidth">
            <e:with-argument name="sWidth" select="@width" />
        </e:call>
    </e:handler>
    Click me!
</b:button>
```

Iterators

In XEL, iterators and looping structures can be created with the for-each element. The for-each element allows you to iterate over a node set:

The handler in the clickable div loops through the children of the div with id="parent". At each node, text is inserted, where the destination is the current div in the for-each loop. The loop breaks when the div with id="d" is reached.

```
<div id="parent">
    <div id="a">a</div>
    <div id="b">b</div>
    <div id="c">c</div>
    <div id="d">d</div>
    <div id="e">e</div>
</div>
<div> Click to see the for-each loop
    <e:handler event="click">
        <e:for-each select="[id('parent')/div]">
            <c:setText destination="."
              select="' -- inserted text node -- '" />
            <e:if test="@id='d'">
                <e:script type="text/javascript">
                    alert('Breaking the loop with the ' +
                        'XEL break element -- ');
                </e:script>
                <e:break />
            </e:if>
        </e:for-each>
    </e:handler>
</div>
```

The value of the select attribute determines the node set. The XPath expression [id('parent')/div] selects all the div child elements of the element with an id of parent. In each element, a text node will be inserted in the child widget a.

The `break` element allows you to break from an iterator. In this case, when the `for-each` statement executes the element with an `id` of `d`, it will execute a JavaScript alert and then stop execution. As a result, the command to create a new text node will not operate on the `div` elements with an `id` of `e`.

Functions in XEL

Just as in JavaScript, XEL allows you to define functions. After an XEL function is defined, it can be called using either JavaScript or XEL in exactly the same way as you would call a JavaScript function.

[Defining functions in XEL is generally a very bad idea. Don't do it!]

Of course, you need JavaScript functions and XEL offers you an easy way to define them. However, if you develop a web application of any size and if you use other people's work, like third-party frameworks, you must be very careful to not end up with spaghetti and naming clashes. All good JavaScript frameworks use the namespace to avoid interference problems and, of course, the Backbase framework does this too, by using the `bb` object to contain all Backbase specific functions.

If you confine your code within event handlers or within methods of widget definition objects that you define with the Tag Definition Language, you are able to conquer complexity by dividing your code into pieces with local scope only, or by forcing the circles of JavaScript into the squares of Backbase widgets. However, defining XEL functions provides you with the ability to create code with a global scope and this allows you to create spaghetti again.

You can read in the Backbase Application Development Guide how to define functions if you really think you need one. We must confess though, that the examples that follow contain a few function definitions, intended to make it easier to clarify an XEL element. Our apologies!

Because you may need to call a function someone else wrote, for example a function of the `bb` object, we show how to call a function with XEL.

Calling a function or method

To call an XEL function, use the `e:call` element within an `e:handler` or `e:function` body:

```
<!-- first we define a function ;-) -->
<e:function name="alertBox">
   <e:body type="text/javascript">
   alert('This alertBox function creates a JavaScript alert box.');
   </e:body>
</e:function>
<b:button>
   Click Me!
   <e:handler event="click" type="application/xml">
      <e:call function="alertBox" />
   </e:handler>
</b:button>
```

The `call` element allows you to call an XEL function or an API method. To call an XEL function, you add the `function` attribute—the value is the name of the function. For a method, you replace the `function` attribute with the `method` attribute:

```
<b:button>
   Click Me!
   <e:handler event="click" type="application/xml">
      <e:call method="setAttribute"
         name="'width'" value="'300px'" />
   </e:handler>
</b:button>
```

Passing a function argument

To pass an argument value to an XEL function, you can use the `with-argument` tag as a child of the `call` element:

```
<b:button>
   Click me for XEL function passing text into alert...(1)
   <e:handler event="click">
      <e:call function="flexibleAlertBox">
         <e:with-argument name="myAlertText"
            select="'Argument Value'" />
      </e:call>
   </e:handler>
</b:button>
<e:function name="flexibleAlertBox">
   <e:argument name="myAlertText" required="true" />
   <e:body type="text/javascript">
```

```
        alert(myAlertText);
      </e:body>
   </e:function>
```

The value of the `name` attribute must match the value of the `name` attribute specified in the function `argument`. The argument value is specified in the `select` attribute. The value can be an XPath or a JavaScript expression, and can return a string value, an integer, or object.

You can also pass an argument value to an XEL function as an attribute/value pair of the `call` element. The attribute name corresponds to the argument named as specified in the function, and the value is the argument value. In this example, we will have two buttons (with two `handlers`) that call the same function. The handlers will pass different argument values and therefore, the function itself will react differently. In this way, we will be able to pass different values to the same `alertBox` function:

```
<b:button>
   Alert: Roses are Red
   <e:handler event="click">
      <e:call function="flexibleAlertBox"
         myAlertText="'Roses are red'">
         <e:with-argument name="myAlertText"
            select="'Roses are red'" />
      </e:call>
   </e:handler>
 </b:button>
<b:button>
   Alert: Violets are Blue
   <e:handler event="click">
      <e:call function="flexibleAlertBox"
         myAlertText="'Violets are blue'" />
   </e:handler>
</b:button>
<e:function name="flexibleAlertBox">
   <e:argument name="myAlertText" required="true" />
   <e:body type="text/javascript">
      alert(myAlertText);
   </e:body>
</e:function>
```

The first handler will show the `with-argument` element as a child of the `call` element, while the second handler will pass the argument value as an attribute/value. Both pass a value to the function. When the user clicks on each button, they will see a different alert value.

With the `call` element, you can call JavaScript functions. However, JavaScript functions do not have named arguments; they simply pass them in a predefined order. As a result, while using XEL to call a JavaScript function that requires an argument, you need to have syntax to name each argument. To accomplish this, the attribute name of the first argument is `argument1`, the second argument is named `argument2`, and so forth. Here's an example of calling the JavaScript `alert` function:

```
<div>
    Click me!
    <e:handler event="click">
        <e:call function="alert"
            argument1="'Alert function!'" />
    </e:handler>
</div>
```

One advantage of using the `with-argument` element (rather than an attribue/value pair) is that you can call another function or method to get the argument value. In this example, we call the `doAlerting` function. In the `getAlertValue` function, we introduce the `return` element, which returns a value:

```
<b:button>
    <e:handler event="click">
        <e:call function="doAlerting">
            <e:with-argument name="alertValue">
                <e:call function="getAlertValue" />
            </e:with-argument>
        </e:call>
    </e:handler>
    Click me!
</b:button>
<e:function name="getAlertValue">
    <e:body>
        <e:return select="'257'" />
    </e:body>
</e:function>
<e:function name="doAlerting">
    <e:argument name="alertValue" required="true" />
    <e:body type="text/javascript">
        alert(alertValue);
    </e:body>
</e:function>
```

The returned value can be determined from the children of the `return` tag (for example, a literal value or an XEL variable) or from the value of a `select` attribute on the `return` element.

Passing context

When a `handler` has executable code in its body, the context is by default the parent widget of the `handler`, and the functional code inside the handler operates on that parent widget. This context is passed to any functions or methods called in the handler, so that the function is operating on the parent widget of the `handler`. For example, if a handler is the child of a button, the executable code inside the handler will operate on the button.

However, if the parent widget is not the correct widget to operate on, then you will need to specify the correct element(s). In XEL, the `with` attribute is responsible for specifying context. By targeting a widget or a widget set using XPath, we can reset the context. In the following example, when we click on one button, we set the `disabled` property of a second button. Because the default context is the first button (the button we click), we need to specify the second button as our proper context.

Similar to passing arguments, context can also be passed as an attribute/value pair.

```
<b:button id="button1">
   Click me to disable the other button ....
   <e:handler event="click" type="application/xml">
      <e:set with="id('button2')"
        property="disabled" select="true()" />
   </e:handler>
</b:button>
<b:button id="button2">
   By clicking the other button, this one will be disabled...
</b:button>
```

 As a best practice, we like to specify `with` as the first attribute. That way, we immediately know on what element(s) the functional code will operate.

Using JavaScript in XEL

One of the powerful features of XEL is that you can still use JavaScript within the body of an XEL execution block. You can even evaluate JavaScript in the value of `select` attributes and other attributes. This gives you not only flexibility, as you can choose the best way to create your execution logic, but the power of both languages.

Most of the time when you use JavaScript, it will be in the body of an XEL function, handler, or `script` element. To specify that you will write the handler of a function or body in JavaScript, you give the `type` attribute a value of `text/javascript`:

```
<e:function name="myFunction">
   <e:body type="text/javascript">
      alert('The body of this function is written in JavaScript!');
   </e:body>
</e:function>
```

Even if you specify that you will write the handler or body function in XML, you can still mix up XEL and JavaScript by nesting your JavaScript code in a `script` tag:

Use when you need to embed some JavaScript code in an XEL handler or function body that is set to a type of XML.

```
<div>
   <e:handler event="click">
      <e:set variable="myVar" select="'my variable'" />
      <e:script type="text/javascript">
         alert('This line is written in JavaScript inside the XEL
            script tag!');
      </e:script>
   </e:handler>
   Click mc!
</div>
```

This concludes our description of XEL. The next section contains some notes about XPath that are useful when you are writing XEL code.

XPath

XML Path Language (XPath) is a W3C language for targeting parts of an XML document. When working declaratively, XPath gives you a powerful mechanism to select and operate on the DOM nodes of your application. It also gives you the ability to perform logic and basic programming functions.

In the Backbase framework, you will generally use XPath when working with XEL or with declarative `command` attribute values.

 For example, the frequently used `select` attribute is set to accept an XPath expression to target an element.

Here is a code fragment that targets all `div` elements in the application: `select="//div"`.

XEL and command attributes are set by default to be in "string mode", where the accepted value is a string, or in "XPath mode", where the accepted value is an XPath expression. In the API Reference, the attribute type will state the default mode.

The Backbase framework supports XPath version 1.0 (and some 2.0 functions). When you can use an XPath expression as an attribute value, you can use any supported XPath command.

We will not spend more time and paper on the explanation of XPath in this book, except for some notes on how attribute values are evaluated. You can find a short reference in the Backbase Application Development Guide and in the API Reference. We hope that you will see the power of using XPath by looking at the examples we provide.

The Backbase implementation follows the standard. Therefore, we refer you to the W3C for the complete XPath specification.

Evaluating attribute values

Different languages evaluate attribute values in different ways. For example, in XHTML, attribute values are always evaluated as strings. In contrast, while some XEL and command attributes are also evaluated as strings, especially attributes such as `name` and other attributes (notably attributes that point to an element, like `select`) accept both XPath and JavaScript as valid values. With XPath and JavaScript syntax at your disposal, you can create complex XPath expressions that point to a node or node set or JavaScript functions as attribute values.

String mode

When the attribute is evaluated by default as a string, you can force it to evaluate as XPath by using curly brackets {} inside the double quotes (""). Otherwise, the value within the double quotes will be processed as the string.

XPath mode

Here is a quick syntax guide for attribute evaluation when the attribute should be evaluated as XPath:

Syntax	Explanation	Attribute value
`'blue'` or `"blue"`	Considered a string, without further evaluation.	`blue`
`//div`	Evaluated as an expression, where the first item of the resulting sequence is used.	First `div` widget only
`[//div]`	Evaluated as an expression, where all the items of the resulting sequence are used.	All `div` elements in document
`{/div/my:elem}`	Evaluated as an expression, where the first element of the result sequence is cast to a string type.	String value of `my:elem` element
`javascript: alert('Alert Box');, javascript:6+3;`	The values after the colon are evaluated as a expression. No return statement is expected.	`Alert Box` (in the alert), 9

As we saw in the description of the Backbase programming model, the functions that we need to actually perform some work after having determined the logic flow with XEL are the Command Functions. The next two sections describe some of these commands.

Commands to manipulate the DOM or elements

In this section, we provide details about commands that manipulate single elements or the sets of elements in the DOM. The other commands will be covered in a later chapter.

If you look at the descriptions for the commands, you will see that many attribute names are shared. We describe some of these here, so that we do not have to repeat them for every command.

Very common attributes are `select` and `with`:

Attribute	Type	Description
`select`	String (XPath)	Input value to the command.
`with`	String (XPath)	The targeted element.

Another set of commands is intended to manipulate the DOM. These commands share the `destination` and `mode` attributes:

Attribute	Type	Description
destination	String (XPath)	Destination of the reated/copied/moved/replaced element.
		The value is a valid XPath or JavaScript expression that refers to an element
mode	String (XPath)	Specifies how the node will be placed in the DOM tree. If you do not specify this attribute, `appendChild` will be assumed.
		The possible values are:
		`replace`: Replace the selected destination node.
		`replaceChildren`: Replace its children.
		`firstChild`: Place as the first child.
		`insertBefore`: Insert before the selected node.
		`insertAfter`: Insert after the selected node.
		`appendChild`: Append to the selected destination node. This is the default.
		`lastChild`: Append to the selected destination node.

Manipulating elements

This is a set of commands that do something to a single element.

focus and blur

With the `focus` and `blur` commands, you can dynamically set or remove focus from any element. Both these commands have the `with` attribute:

- `focus`: Sets focus on an element.
- `blur`: Blurs (removes focus from) the current focused element.

In the following example, we use the buttons to blur or focus `button 1`:

```
<b:button>
    Click to set focus on button 1
    <e:handler event="click">
        <c:focus with="id('button1')" />
    </e:handler>
</b:button>
<b:button>
    Click to blur button 1
    <e:handler event="click">
        <c:blur with="id('button1')" />
    </e:handler>
</b:button>
<b:button id="button1">
    button 1
</b:button>
```

fireEvent

It fires an event on the targeted element.

The `fireEvent` command supports the `with` attribute and also the following specific attributes:

Attribute	Type	Description
bubbles	Boolean	Determines whether the event should bubble.
cancelable	Boolean	Determines whether the event could be canceled.
event	String	The type of event that should be dispatched.

position

Changes the position of an element on the screen and sets the position of the `viewNode`. The target element is repositioned relative to the destination element. This destination element is specified by the `destination` attribute. The relative position type is determined by the `mode` attribute.

The `position` command supports the `destination` and `mode` attributes, and also the following specific attributes:

Attribute	Type	Description
x	String	X-coordinate of the element position. Expressed as XPath.
y	String	Y-coordinate of the element position. Expressed as XPath.

Here is an example:

```
<b:button>
   Click to reposition the destination widget.
   <e:handler event="click">
      <c:position with="id('movedElement')"
         destination="id('destinationElement')"
         mode="after-start" x="200px" y="100px" />
   </e:handler>
</b:button>
<div style="position:absolute;" id="movedElement">
   Element to be moved
</div>
<div id="destinationElement">
   Destination element
</div>
```

scrollTo

It scrolls an element into view in the browser.

The `scrollTo` command supports the `with` attribute.

setText

Creates an XML text node and places it in the DOM tree. Useful to dynamically add text nodes based on user interaction.

Use the destination and mode attributes to specify where and how the element is placed in the DOM tree.

The `setText` command supports the `destination`, `mode`, and `select` attributes.

In the next example, the value of a text node is set based on a change event in the input field. The change event occurs when you press *Enter* or click your mouse outside the input field.

```
<div id="myDiv" style="border: solid 1px red;" />
<p>
    A change to the input field will add a text node containing
    the value of the input field to the preceding div
    as first child.
</p>
<input type="text">
    <e:handler event="change">
        <c:setText select="property::value"
            destination="id('myDiv')" mode="firstChild" />
    </e:handler>
</input>
```

show, hide, and showHide

These commands allow showing or hiding elements dynamically.

The show command shows an element. When the show command is issued, it will first check if a show method is defined on the controller. If this is the case, the method is called. Otherwise, it will set the display style property to its default value (or to block if it is still not displayed). The element to be shown is determined by context.

The hide command hides an element. When the hide command is issued, it will first check if a hide method is defined on the controller. If this is the case, the method is called. Otherwise, it will set the display style property to none. The element to be hidden is determined by context.

Using showHide, the specified element will either be displayed or hidden, based on the current state. When the showHide command is issued, it will first check if a showHide method is defined on the controller. If this is the case, the method is called. Otherwise, it will change the display style property. If the element is visible, the display style property will be set to none. If the element is invisible, the element will be displayed.

The show, hide, and showHide commands support the with attribute.

The three buttons in the next example cause a widget to be shown or hidden:

```
<div id="showHideDiv" style="display:none;">
    This widget is toggled by c:showHide.
</div>
<b:button>
```

```
            Show preceding div element
            <e:handler event="click">
                <c:show with="id('showHideDiv')" />
            </e:handler>
    </b:button>
    <b:button>
            Hide preceding div element
            <e:handler event="click">
                <c:hide with="id('showHideDiv')" />
            </e:handler>
    </b:button>
    <b:button>
            Show/Hide preceding div element
            <e:handler event="click">
                <c:showHide with="id('showHideDiv')" />
            </e:handler>
    </b:button>
```

sort

This is a generic sorting command. It will generally be used on XHTML tables or a group of similar elements, though they do not have to be the same. When sorting a table, the sort target is a th or td element. When sorting a group of elements, the sort target is the parent element.

The sort command supports the with attribute and the following specific attributes:

Attribute	Type	Description
by	String	Specifies the sort value. This is a string that is resolved to a function that gathers the value to sort. By default, the result is "return this.textContent".
algorithm	String	Specifies how to sort. Possible values are string and smart.
		If the value is smart, then a smart algorithm is applied to the values of sort. This is the default value.
		If the value is string, then a string sort algorithm is used.
order	String	Specifies the sort direction.
		If the value is ascending, then the values sorted in ascending order. This is the default value.
		If the value is descending, the values are sorted in descending order.

Here is one example. The source code provided with the book contains two more examples. By default, sorting works on the `textContent` of an element. You can use `sortValue` if you want to use some other value like the sort attribute in the `td` elements of the table.

```
<table id="sorttable">
   <thead>
      <tr>
         <th id="col1">col1</th>
         <th id="col2">col2</th>
      </tr>
   </thead>
   <tbody>
      <tr>
         <td sort="b">a</td>
         <td>4</td>
      </tr>
      <tr>
         <td sort="a">b</td>
         <td>3</td>
      </tr>
      <tr>
         <td sort="c">c</td>
         <td>2</td>
      </tr>
      <tr>
         <td sort="d">d</td>
         <td>1</td>
      </tr>
   </tbody>
</table>
<b:button>
   Sort JS
   <e:handler event="click"
      type="application/javascript">
         bb.command.sort(bb.document.getElementById('col1'),
            false,
            'return this.getAttribute("sort")');
   </e:handler>
</b:button>
<b:button>
   Sort XEL
   <e:handler event="click">
      <c:sort with="id('col1')"
```

```
            order="ascending"
            by="return this.getAttribute('sort')" />
        </e:handler>
    </b:button>
```

tile

It tiles the content of the targeted element. Items must be absolutely positioned and have a fixed width and height.

Attribute	Type	Description
animate	String	Animates the tiling or places the tiles at their final position at once.
		true: Items will be animated when tiled. Default.
		false: Items will be tiled at once.
orientation	String	The orientation in which the tiled items will be rendered.
		rows: Tiled items will be rendered in rows. Default.
		columns: Tiled items will be rendered in columns.
rowmargin	String	The margin between rows. The value should be specified in a similar way as you would specify a width or height attribute; for example, in pixels (px).
columnmargin	String	The margin between columns. The value should be specified in a similar way as you would specify a width or height attribute; for example, in pixels (px).
maximum	Integer	The maximum row width or column height. Whether it is the row width or column height depends on whether the orientation is set to rows or columns. The value should be specified in a similar way as you would specify a width or height attribute; for example, in pixels (px).

Here is an example:

```
<div style="height: 500px;">
    <b:button>
        Tile the child elements of the "parent" div.
        <e:handler event="click">
            <c:tile with="id('parent')"
                orientation="rows" max="300px"
                rowmargin="50px" columnmargin="50px" />
        </e:handler>
    </b:button>
    <div id="parent"
        style="width: 800px; height: 400px; border: 1px solid
        black; position:absolute; top:200px;">
```

```
<img style="position:absolute;width:200px;"
    src="http://www.google.nl/intl/nl_nl/images/logo.gif" />
<img style="position:absolute;width:200px;"
    src="http://www.google.nl/intl/nl_nl/images/logo.gif" />
<img style="position:absolute;width:200px;"
    src="http://www.google.nl/intl/nl_nl/images/logo.gif" />
<img style="position:absolute;width:200px;"
    src="http://www.google.nl/intl/nl_nl/images/logo.gif" />
<img style="position:absolute;width:200px;"
    src="http://www.google.nl/intl/nl_nl/images/logo.gif" />
    </div>
</div>
```

transform

It transforms XML with an XSL stylesheet. Parameters that can be used with `transform` are described next. It uses the browser's XSLT 1.0 implementation.

The `transform` command supports the `destination`, `mode`, and `select` attributes, and the following specific attribute:

Attribute	Type	Description
stylesheet	String (Xpath)	The location of the XSL stylesheet (Valid URL) or data stored in a variable.

Here is an example of using the `transform` command. The transformation itself follows the rules of XSLT. If you are interested, you can see this example (and all others) in action using the Command Exerciser provided with the book.

```
<b:button>
    Click to transform...
    <e:handler event="click">
        <e:variable name="source">
            <c:load url="data/transform.xml" />
        </e:variable>
        <e:variable name="stylesheet">
            <c:load url="data/stylesheet.xsl" />
        </e:variable>
        <c:transform select="$source"
            stylesheet="$stylesheet"
            destination="id('myDiv')" mode="lastChild" />
    </e:handler>
</b:button>
<div id="myDiv">
    Load contents of transformation below this line...
    <hr />
</div>
```

param

It adds a parameter to be added to the transform action.

The `param` command supports the `name` and `select` attributes.

 This element can only be used as a child of the `transform` command.

This example shows a parameter to be added to the transform action.

```
<c:transform select="$datasource"
   stylesheet="$stylesheet"
   destination="id('output2')" mode="replaceChildren">
   <c:param name="stringvalue" select="' Nice book '" />
   <c:param name="nodevalue" select="$datasource//content" />
</c:transform>
```

Manipulating the DOM

In this section, we are looking at a set of commands that help you to create, copy, or move elements. These commands are: `copy`, `copy-of`, `create`, and `destroy`. These commands use the `destination` attribute to specify where the element should be placed in the DOM tree and the `mode` attribute to specify how the element should be put at its destination.

copy

Copies an element and recreates it in the destination location.

Use the `destination` and `mode` attributes to specify where and how the element is placed in the DOM tree.

The element to be copied is determined by the context. Therefore, you should use the `with` attribute if the context is not the current node.

The next example copies an existing widget and places it in the view tree.

```
<div style="width: 200px; border: 1px solid red;">
   Element to be copied
</div>
<div id="container"
   style="width: 400px; border: 1px solid black;">
    Copy container
</div>
```

```
<div>
   Click to copy first widget as last child of second element
   <e:handler event="click">
      <c:copy with="preceding-sibling::*[2]"
         destination="id('container')" mode="appendChild" />
   </e:handler>
</div>
```

create

Creates and renders a fragment based on a provided XML fragment. The provided XML fragment is the model fragment. Controllers will be created and the view nodes are rendered using the templates. After creation, the fragment is placed inside the DOM tree or returned (if no destination is specified).

Use the destination and mode attributes to specify where and how the fragment is placed in the DOM tree. If the destination attribute is omitted, then the created fragment will be returned.

An XML fragment can be provided by the select attribute or inline as a child of the create command.

The destination and mode attributes are described earlier in this section. The select attribute determines what will be created.

You can use the create command to create a widget and append it at the proper location:

```
<div id="myElm"
  style="border: 1px solid black; width: 300px;">
   Created elements will be the last children of this widget.
</div>
<div>
   <p>Click to create new elements</p>
   <e:handler event="click">
      <c:create destination="id('myElm')" mode="appendChild">
         <div>
            <div>New widget 1</div>
            <div>New widget 2</div>
            <div>New widget 3</div>
         </div>
      </c:create>
   </e:handler>
</div>
```

attribute

It sets an attribute and an attribute value on the created parent element. This element can only be used as a child of the `create` command.

The `attribute` command supports the following attributes — `select` and `name`.

And in addition, it supports the following attribute:

Attribute	Type	Description
namespace	String	The namespace of the attribute (optional).

Use the `value-of` attribute in the next example, to create a text value and the `attribute` to create a new attribute with a corresponding value. The value displayed is the total number of nodes on the pages, which increments by one each time you click the **Click here** text. Because the new element is created as `firstChild`, it will appear as the first node in the `div`, before all other text nodes.

```
<div id="myElm4"
  style="border: 1px solid black; width: 300px;">
    Elements will be created as first child of the div with id:
    myElm4.
</div>
<div>
    <p>
        Click to create new elements with attributes
        <code>value-of</code> and <code>attribute</code>.
    </p>
    <e:handler event="click">
        <c:create destination="id('myElm4')" mode="firstChild">
            <div>
                <c:value-of select="count(//*)" />
                <c:attribute name="style"
                  select="'background:#0f0'" />
            </div>
        </c:create>
    </e:handler>
</div>
```

copy-of

It creates a copy of the selected XPath expression. This element can only be used as a child of the `create` command.

The `copy-of` command supports the `select` attribute.

Use the `copy-of` attribute to create a copy of an existing widget within the template of your `create` command. The `copy-of` widget must have a parent element that is created.

```
<e:variable name="data" type="application/xml">
    <e:data type="text/xml">
        <div style="width: 100px; background: #cccccc;">
            <div>Element to be copied </div>
        </div>
    </e:data>
</e:variable>
<div id="myElm2"
    style="border: 1px solid black; width: 300px;">
    Created elements will be the last children of this widget.
</div>
<div>
    <p>Click to create new elements with copy-of</p>
    <e:handler event="click">
        <c:create destination="id('myElm2')">
            <div>
                <c:copy-of select="$data/div" />
            </div>
        </c:create>
    </e:handler>
</div>
```

value-of

It creates a text node of the selected XPath expression. This element can only be used as a child of the `create` command.

The `value-of` command supports the `select` attribute.

We saw an example for the `value-of` command with the example for the `attribute` command.

destroy

It destroys the element. Use the `with` attribute to determine the element to be destroyed. The value is a valid XPath or JavaScript expression that refers to an element.

When an element is removed from the DOM, it is not automatically destroyed. An explicit call to `destroy` is necessary to delete it from the memory.

The code in the following example destroys the first preceding div found and removes it from the memory. When there is no more div to be found, you will see an error message:

```
<div>
   We will destroy this widget and remove it from memory 1.
</div>
<div>
   We will destroy this widget and remove it from memory 2.
</div>
<div>
   We will destroy this widget and remove it from memory 3.
</div>
<div>
   We will destroy this widget and remove it from memory 4.
</div>
<div style="border: solid 1px red;">
   Click to destroy widget.
   <e:handler event="click">
      <c:destroy with="preceding::div[1]" />
   </e:handler>
</div>
```

move

It moves the element to a new target location.

Use the destination and mode attributes to specify where and how the element is placed in the DOM tree. The with attribute determines which element is to be moved.

This example moves an existing widget to another location:

```
<b:button>
   Click to move "to be moved" widget into "container" element
   <e:handler event="click">
      <c:move with="id('tobemoved')"
         destination="id('container')" mode="firstChild" />
   </e:handler>
</b:button>
<div id="container"
  style="border:1px solid black; width: 400px;">
   <div id="a" style="border:1px solid green; width: 200px;">
      1st child widget in container
   </div>
```

```
   <div id="b" style="border:1px solid blue; width: 200px;">
      2nd child widget in container
   </div>
   <div id="c" style="border:1px solid red; width: 200px;">
      3rd child widget in container
   </div>
</div>
<div id="tobemoved"
  style="border:1px solid red; width: 200px;">
   widget to be moved
</div>
```

The DOM manipulation commands also include the `getAttribute`, `setAttribute`, and `removeAttribute` commands. We do not describe these explicitly here. You will find examples in other places.

This concludes the description of two categories of commands that we wanted to describe in detail in this chapter. You will find more commands in later chapters.

Info and Notify BTL widgets

In this section, we expand our knowledge of the Backbase Tag Library with a new set of BTL widgets. These widgets help build the dynamic interaction with a user.

 The Info and Notify BTL widgets inherit from `containerElement` and `dimensionElement`. See Chapter 2 for a description of these elements and the attributes they support.

balloon

The `balloon` widget displays an image similar to that of a dialogue box in a comic book. We have seen the `balloon` already in the "Hello World" examples. You can find a slightly different example in the supplied source code.

In addition to the elements already noted, `balloon` also inherits from `labelImplementor`, which means that you can use a `label` attribute, or a nested `label` element.

The `balloon` widget supports the following specific attributes:

Attribute	Type	Description
mode	String	Location of the balloon, relative to the container element. Its values can be: top-right (default), top-center, top-left, bottom-right, bottom-center, bottom-left.
open	Boolean	The element is opened/expanded by default.
timeout	String	The time before the balloon disappears, based on a formatted time string (for example, "1:23:45.687" or "5h").

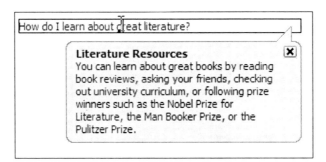

infoBox

The `infoBox` widget represents a box with content that appears below a widget. You must click on the enclosing element for the `infoBox` to appear. The contents of the `infoBox` can be text, images, or other widgets.

Attribute	Type	Description
for	XPath	XPath expression indicating the element(s) that open the `infoBox` on click and DOMActive events.
open	Boolean	The element is opened/expanded by default.

What do Joseph Conrad, Samuel Beckett, Jack Kerouac, and Vladimir Nabokov have in common?

None of them wrote in their native language. Conrad was Polish, Beckett wrote (after the mid-40's) in French, Russian was Nabokov's first language, and Kerouac was Quebecois.

Clicking outside the `infoBox` closes it. You can open an `infoBox` by calling the `open` method with a given context or by setting the `open` attribute to `true`.

Click on the text widget and receive advanced content information in the following example:

```
<p id="bookOutline"
   style="border:1px solid black; padding:3px; width:350px;">
   What do Joseph Conrad, Samuel Beckett, Jack Kerouac, and Vladimir
   Nabokov have in common?
</p>
<b:infoBox for="id('bookOutline')" width="200px">
   <p>
      None of them wrote in their native language. Conrad was Polish,
      Beckett wrote (after the mid-40's) in French, Russian was
      Nabokov's first language, and Kerouac was Quebecois.
   </p>
</b:infoBox>
```

loadingMessage

The `loadingMessage` widget displays a notification to the user while the application is loading. The message can be displayed using the `show` method, and removed using the `hide` method.

This example shows a `loadingMessage` that is displayed when a button is clicked:

```
<b:button>
   Load a file
   <e:handler event="click" type="text/javascript">
      var oLoadingMessage =
        bb.document.getElementById('sampleLoadingMessage');
      oLoadingMessage.show();
      setTimeout(
        function()
        {if(oLoadingMessage.viewNode)
           oLoadingMessage.hide()},
        3000);
   </e:handler>
</b:button>
<b:loadingMessage id="sampleLoadingMessage">
   <p>No file is being loaded.</p>
   <p>This is only an example.</p>
</b:loadingMessage>
```

It is not so easy to use the `loadingMessage` when the Backbase framework is starting up because of the well-known chicken-and-egg problem—you need the framework to be active before you can use the loading message. Therefore, most applications such as the Backbase explorer, use a custom loading message.

Personally, we dislike loading messages. If they are there to hide a performance problem, it's better to solve the problem. Otherwise, they just delay the appearance of your page.

toolTip

The `toolTip` widget allows you to provide a small piece of informative content when a user hovers over a widget. It takes the form of a small box with text that appears close to the element the user is moving his/her mouse over. You can create a `toolTip` by nesting the `toolTip` widget inside the related widget. The `toolTip` is displayed relative to the pointer and the enclosing widget.

`toolTip` has no local attributes.

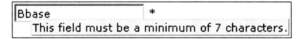

Here is an example:

```
<p>
    <input type="text" name="companyName" value="Bbase"/> *
    <b:toolTip>
        This field must be a minimum of 7 characters.
    </b:toolTip>
</p>
```

A Backbase Command Exerciser

In Chapter 2, we introduced an example application that allowed you to view all BTL examples and see them work. With so many new examples about the Backbase Commands, it would be nice to have a similar application to show these.

We could have copied the BTL Exerciser and just changed the names in the menu items and so on. We have chosen to make some changes to the UI though, to be able to use some of the new widgets and commands for this chapter. As before, each of the examples is stored in a separate file, which makes it easy to look at the code, or to add your own examples.

The result is a Backbase Command Functions Exerciser. The following screenshot shows it for the `create` command example:

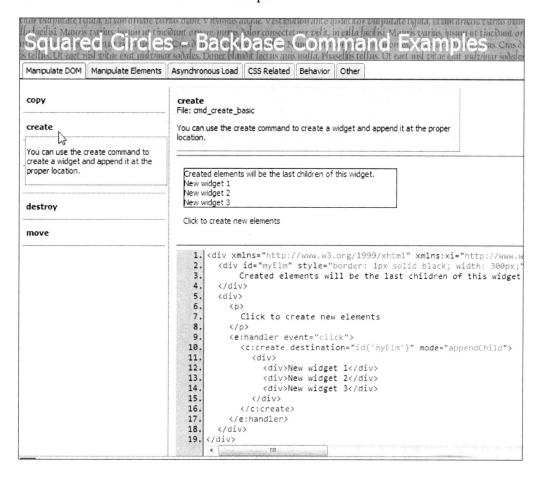

The Command Functions Exerciser application has a similar `tabBox` and `panelSet` layout as the BTL Exerciser. Where it differs is the content of the menu panels—there are no `navBox` widgets anymore. Instead, there is just the name of the command and if you move your mouse over it, you will see a yellow `toolTip` with the description.

When you click on the name of a command, the content is shown in the panel to the right of the menu. The actual content is extended in this version by showing the description of the example above the live code, so you do not have to remember it from the `toolTip`. Below the live code, the source code is shown using the BTL `codeHighlighter` widget.

The fastest way to build this application is to copy the contents of `btlSamples` to `cmdSamples`, and then remove all examples and descriptions. Rename the panel and menu files to reflect the Command Functions categories.

Probably, you can figure out for yourself how to code `app.xml` and the panels. What is new are the menu files. We made a new widget, `sq:menuItemLink`, which does everything from showing the `toolTip` to creating the widgets that are shown in content panel.

It is still too early to explain how to build the `menuItemLink` widget. Therefore, we added plain code for one of the menu items, the `copy` command, which is equivalent to what the widget would have executed. Here is the code for `manipulatedomMenu.xml`:

```
<div xmlns="http://www.w3.org/1999/xhtml"
  xmlns:b="http://www.backbase.com/2006/btl"
  xmlns:c="http://www.backbase.com/2006/command"
  xmlns:e="http://www.backbase.com/2006/xel"
  xmlns:sq="http://www.squaringthecircles.com/squared">
  <!-- the code below is a replacement for:
     <sq:menuItemLink label="copy" example="cmd_copy" />
  -->
<div
  style="padding-left: 5px; border-bottom: solid 1px gray;">
  <b:toolTip width="200px" backgroundColor="yellow">
      <xi:include href="../../descriptions/cmd_copy.xml" />
  </b:toolTip>
  <p><strong>copy</strong></p>
    <e:handler event="click">
      <c:create
        destination="following::b:panel[1]"
        mode="replaceChildren">
       <div style="padding-left: 10px;">
          <b:box width="400px">
            <p><strong>copy</strong>
              <br />
              File: cmd_copy
            </p>
            <xi:include
              href="../../descriptions/cmd_copy.xml" />
          </b:box>
          <hr />
          <xi:include
            href="../../examples/cmd_copy.xml" />
          <hr />
          <b:codeHighlighter>
```

```
                    <xi:include
                      href="../../examples/cmd_copy.xml" />
                  </b:codeHighlighter>
                </div>
              </c:create>
            </e:handler>
          </div>
          <sq:menuItemLink
            label="create" example="cmd_create_basic" />
          <sq:menuItemLink
            label="create copy-of" example="cmd_create_copyof" />
          <sq:menuItemLink
            label="create attribute"
            example="cmd_create_valueof_attribute" />
          <sq:menuItemLink label="destroy" example="cmd_destroy" />
          <sq:menuItemLink label="move" example="cmd_move" />
        </div>
```

As you can see, the menu item is now really a `div` containing simple text, extended with a `toolTip` and a `click` event handler.

The event handler contains a `create` command, that creates a BTL box widget containing the name of the command, the file name where the example can be found, and the description included from the description filename. Below the box there are a set of horizontal lines, the live code, and the highlighted source code.

As we argued already several times, it is no fun to copy this code some thirty times for each command. Of course it would not have been very difficult to generate this code from a server script, but we hope you agree that it is a much cleaner solution to have a widget that shows the behavior we want at the client side of the web application.

There is one nasty line of code that we have to explain. We added the following line to `index.html`, just after the line that includes `config.xml`:

```
<xi:include href="../../backbase/4_4_1/bindings/www.backbase.com.2006.
btl/toolTip/chameleon/toolTip.xml" />
```

We need to do this because the lazy loading of widget definitions is not completely foolproof. Because we are creating the `toolTip` dynamically within a `create` command, the loader seems to miss it and therefore, we are loading it explicitly. There are a few circumstances where this is needed. Another reason why you may want to load widget definitions explicitly is to optimize performance, by being able to spend time loading at a moment when it is least noticed by your user.

On purpose, we did not spend effort to make the application better-looking than it is. A real web designer could beautify this application easily. What we wanted to show, however, is the bare bones of what you need to make a flexible and functional application that can easily be adapted if you change your mind on styling or layout.

Summary

The first part of this chapter was rather theoretical. As a naive user of the Backbase framework, you do not need to know all we described there. We hope that by explaining some fundamentals of web application development with the Backbase framework it will be easier to understand the structure of it. This understanding will then make it easier to develop good web applications.

In this chapter, we provided more detail about the execution logic of a web application. We looked at the Backbase programming model and the various APIs it provides. In particular, we looked at XEL and Command Functions.

Further, just a list of points to remember:

- The namespace for the BTL is defined as:
  `xmlns:b="http://www.backbase.com/2006/btl"`.

- Event handlers are part of XEL, the XML Execution Language. Event handlers can be attached to any element within Backbase space. They are coded as child tag to that element with: `e:handler`.

- The `type` of an event handler can be either `text/javascript`, or `application/xml`. The default is `application/xml`.

- In an event handler with type `application/xml`, you will use XEL to code the logic and Command Functions to code the functions to be performed. Each have their own namespaces:
  `xmlns:e = "http://www.backbase.com/2006/xel"` and
  `xmlns:c = "http://www.backbase.com/2006/command"`.

We added a few new BTL widgets to our repertoire, the Info and Notify widgets. We modified our sample application to show the Command Functions examples.

In the next chapter, we will look at forms and asynchronous communication.

4
Client-server Communication and Forms

In the previous chapter, we have looked more closely at how to write the application logic at the client-side of your web application, where JavaScript, XHTML, and the Backbase framework live.

Of course, that is only half of the story. In this chapter and the next, we are looking at communication with the other half of your web application — the part that resides on the server and is developed using a server-side scripting language, such as PHP, JSP, ASP, Ruby, and more.

This is a core chapter of the book. As you might expect from an AJAX Framework, the Backbase client can make asynchronous requests to a server and the server can respond with data or with dynamic parts of the page. We will look at communication using the `XMLHttpRequest` object API, which for many is synonymous to using AJAX. After we have covered the basics, we will discuss what the Backbase framework adds to it and how you can make use of this in an application.

We discuss forms in detail because submitting a form is the major way to send user input to a server. Being able to do this asynchronously has many implications for the total architecture of your web application. Some of these aspects are discussed by looking at the sample application.

To be able to communicate between client and server is useful, but if we are going to develop a real application, we need more. Therefore, we will step to the server-side and show you how AJAX communication can influence the architecture of a web application. Against popular belief, we think that the server-side of the application can become much easier than before, provided that you use data-driven widgets as much as you can and use a strict Model-View-Controller (MVC) approach as the overall architecture of your application. We will look at data-driven or data-bound widgets in the next chapter and at the MVC pattern in this one.

In our examples, we are going to use PHP as the server-side scripting language. We apologize here to our readers interested in Java. We know how to develop an application in Java (Ghica has been involved with Java development for about ten years). However, developing in PHP is much faster and the resulting code is more concise. Because the syntax of both Java and PHP are derived from the C language syntax, the PHP code should be easily understandable to Java developers.

We acknowledge that using Java, with JSP or JSF, is more appropriate for developing core applications in corporate environments, where also a large percentage of the Backbase framework users are located. However, for fast changing and dynamic applications, the use of PHP, Ruby, or similar languages seems to be on the rise everywhere, including within large corporations.

Remember also that the Backbase framework is server agnostic. This means that the client web application that you develop with the Backbase framework is unaware of what server language your application is using. You may see some signs of what the server language is, by looking at the URLs involved in calling server actions. However, you could even hide these by using some clever Apache web server mod-rewriting. We will not do this because it may make it more difficult to deploy our sample code in your own environment. Because the client application knows nothing about the server except the agreed protocol for communication, you can easily replace the server application with a similar one written in another language, as long as it adheres to the same API.

The sample application that we start developing in this chapter involves a *travel blog* site, where, if you are traveling, you can write blog entries about your travel experience for a specific trip. You can upload photos and show where you are on a Google map. Family or friends can follow your trip by visiting the site. In this chapter, we develop enough of this application to do something interesting with forms. In the next chapter, we will look at the display of public information for the travel site by using data grids. Google maps and photo upload will be added in a later chapter.

Here is a list of subjects that we will cover in this chapter:

- Overview of AJAX
- Asynchronous communication within the Backbase framework: the `XMLHttpRequest` object, the `JSONRequest` object, and the `load` command
- Working with forms:
  - Forms profiles
  - Form elements: `form`, `input`, and `fileInput`
  - Abstract BTL form elements

- ° BTL form widgets: `calendar`, `checkBoxGroup`, `comboBox`, and more
- ° Validating input fields

- AJAX and architecture, Model-View-Controller, and implementing MVC on the server
- The C3D travel blog sample application

 The code for the BTL and command function examples can be found in the *btlSample* and *cmdSample* exercisers that are part of the sample code for this book.

AJAX

In a book that has AJAX in its title, we cannot omit a section where we briefly introduce what AJAX stands for, although we assume that you are already familiar with it.

Asynchronous JavaScript and XML (AJAX) is a term that describes a collection of web development techniques and technologies for creating interactive web applications:

- Extensible HyperText Markup Language (XHTML) and Cascading Style Sheet (CSS) for presenting information.
- The Document Object Model (DOM), which is the browser's internal representation of a web page, manipulated through JavaScript to display information dynamically and to interact with the information.
- Extensible Markup Language (XML) and Extensible Stylesheet Language Transformations (XSLT) for data interchange between browser and server, and for data manipulation.
- The `XMLHttpRequest` object to exchange XML data asynchronously with the web server, using the HTTP protocol. This means that the client does not have to wait for the data exchange to complete before further user interaction with the application is possible. As a result, JavaScript processing can take place simultaneously with client-application interaction. Moreover, a completely new page request is not required in order for new data to be shown. Since only the necessary data is returned from the server, the user interface appears more reactive to user input.
- JavaScript to bind everything together. JavaScript is used to interact dynamically with the presented information. JavaScript functions can be used to change styling or content, as well as to manipulate the DOM tree.

From a technical perspective, the use of the XMLHttpRequest object allows applications to retrieve data from the server asynchronously. For example, the result of a long database query, while the user continues to interact with the application as presented in the browser page. Once the data transfer is complete, the JavaScript in the client updates only those parts of a web page that need updating by manipulating the DOM without refreshing the complete page (as required by conventional web applications), and without forcing the user to wait until communication with the server is complete.

From a conceptual perspective, AJAX technology allows you to build **Single Page Interface** (**SPI**) applications. These applications have only one complete XHTML document, in which the (dynamic) content of files or data sources will be loaded. End user interactions result in asynchronous data requests to the server instead of page requests. This results in partial updates of the user interface, thereby offering end users fast response, smooth transitions between states, and continuous and stable workflows.

The look and feel of an SPI AJAX application can be similar to a desktop application, where all interaction results in partial updates within one window instead of the traditional Multi-page Interface (MPI), where the browser page is reloaded after every button press or form submit.

For general information on AJAX, there are many books available today. One of our favorites is still the first one out—*"AJAX in Action"*, by *Dave Crane, Eric Pascarello, and Darren James*. The original article by Jesse James Garret is also still very readable. (See: http://www.adaptivepath.com/ideas/essays/archives/000385.php)

Asynchronous communication

The first letter "A" in the word AJAX stands for Asynchronous. You may wonder, however, what is asynchronous to what, and how is this possible?

When a page is loaded in the web browser, it starts its client-side life. In that period of time, many interesting things happen in modern web pages or web applications. For example, some animations could start running, some content could be updated, and so on.

True asynchronous processes in the browser do not exist, in any case, not when this book was written. This means that any of execution JavaScript code initiated, for example, by a user input event would have to be processed entirely before another event could happen. The same is true for JavaScript timeouts and intervals—they are not executed in parallel, but rather sequentially.

I/O operations can happen asynchronously though. Once initialized from synchronous JavaScript code, the request can start traveling to a remote server and back. As soon as the server replies with a portion of the data and this data has arrived at the client's web browser, the callback function of the requester object will be called. Then, the program, now populated with data, can continue its flow.

There are several APIs available in the Backbase AJAX Framework that you can use either with JavaScript or with XML to communicate with the server. In the following sections, we will have hands-on experience with each of them.

The XMLHttpRequest object

The XMLHttpRequest JavaScript object is known today to be at the heart of any modern AJAX application. But before this happened, it came quite a long way. XMLHttpRequest was first released with Internet Explorer 5 in the year 1999. Back in these days, this was a feature not used widely. Also, it was not known as XMLHttpRequest, but as XMLHTTP. Several years later, the Mozilla browser pioneered the reproduction of the XMLHTTP functionality with a new name of XMLHttpRequest. Other browsers followed in Mozilla's steps and JavaScript now had a powerful API for data communication.

The W3C standards specification for the XMLHttpRequest object can be found here: http://www.w3.org/TR/XMLHttpRequest/.

The Backbase AJAX Framework has a reimplementation of XMLHttpRequest object. Why is that? Web browsers, although trying to agree on implementation details and even working in a joint effort on XMLHttpRequest specification, still have multiple inconsistencies and sometimes even bugs in their implementation. Also, Internet Explorer, prior to version 7, had a different API call for instantiating the XMLHttpRequest object.

To solve these bugs and to bring consistency to the XMLHttpRequest object APIs, Backbase provides a wrapped version of the object that has extra features, for example, it enables script authors with sniffing facilities to serve browser-appropriate content to site visitors.

Take a close look at the example below. It is very simple. The script is expected to retrieve an XML document from the root folder of the web page:

```
var oRequest = new XMLHttpRequest;
oRequest.open("GET", "script.py", true);
oRequest.onreadystatechange = function() {
    if (this.readyState == 4) {
        alert(this.responseXML);
    }
```

```
}
oRequest.send(null);
```

If you have experience with using XMLHttpRequest in your projects, you will immediately see several potential problems. The first problem is using the this scope in the readystatechange event handler and also, in the old Internet Explorer browsers you could not write var o = new XMLHttpRequest; because the object XMLHttpRequest did not exist.

These and many other issues are resolved within the Backbase framework. Therefore, you do not need to think about them. You can just write code, as in the example given, in the way you expect it to work and it indeed works.

The JSONRequest object

JavaScript Object Notation (JSON) is a lightweight data-interchange format. It is rather popular with web developers as an alternative to using XML with the XMLHttpRequest object because it is perceived as being easier to use.

The JSONRequest JavaScript object is a non-standard API object used in many JavaScript frameworks and libraries. Unlike the XMLHttpRequest object, this API object cannot be instantiated and all its methods are static. You can find more information about its Backbase implementation in the Backbase framework's *API Reference*.

In the following example, we will post a JSON object to the server script:

```
var oData = {"firstName": "Sam","lastName": "Brown"};
JSONRequest.post("myscript.cgi", oData, function() {
    alert('done!');
});
```

The load command

In the previous chapter, we gave an overview of the command functions that are available with the Backbase framework. We then showed details of the commands that you can use to manipulate the DOM tree or its elements. Here, we show the load command, which is in a category of its own. You saw the load command already in various examples.

The load command does a bit more than the XMLHttpRequest object that we saw in the previous section because it also does something with the response it receives from the server. Here are the functions of load command:

- The load command uses the XMLHttpRequest object to load XML from the server. It then uses that XML (like the `create` command) as the code fragment.

- Use the `destination` and `mode` attributes to specify where and how the element is placed in the DOM tree. If the `destination` attribute is omitted, the loaded data will be returned.

- If the destination is outside a Backbase area, then the command also allows loading *invalid* XML, in which case the browser will be responsible for rendering the XML.

- If no content-type header is provided and the data is of type `String`, then the content-type header will be set to `application/x-www-form-urlencoded` for a post request.

- If no content-type header is provided and the data is of type XML node or XML document, then the content-type header will be set to `application/xml` for a request.

- The `load` and `error` events are fired on destination (if specified).

Here is a list of attributes that you can use with the `load` command — `async`, `data`, `destination`, `error`, `method`, `mode`, `select`, `success`, `type`, and `url`. We have encountered many of these before. Therefore, we restrict our description to the attributes that are specific to the `load` command or that we did not see before.

Attribute	Type	Description
url	String	The URL of the remote data to be loaded. The value is a valid URL string value expressed as an XPath expression.
method	String	Determines the request method. Can be any string value, but in general it is limited to GET (default) or POST.
error	JavaScript function	JavaScript string that will be executed when an error occurs during the load process.
success	JavaScript function	JavaScript string that will be executed when the load process is completed successfully.

Attribute	Type	Description
type	String	Determines the type of response that the `load` command should return.
		Warning: This may only work correctly when the `destination` attribute is omitted.
		• `application/xml`, default: `true`, `application/xml` Mime-type
		• `text/xml`, `text/xml` Mime-type
		• `application/javascript`, `application/javascript` Mime-type
		• `text/javascript`, `text/javascript` Mime-type
		• `text/plain`, `text/plain` Mime-type
async	Boolean	Determines whether the request should be done asynchronously.
		• `true` (default): Request is done asynchronously.
		• `false`: Request is done synchronously.
select	XPath	Data to be sent to the server along with the response URL. When the `method` attribute is set to `GET` and the data is of type string, the string will be interpreted as query string data, comparable to the name/value pairs at the end of a URL. If `method` is set to `POST`, it is equivalent to a form submit. When the data is of type `Node`, it will be serialized to a string and properly escaped to make it suitable for HTTP transport.
		Warning: When data is of type string, it must be properly escaped by you to make it suitable for HTTP transport.

In this example, the `c:load` function is used to load an external file:

```
<b:button>
    Click to load an external XML file
    <e:handler event="click">
        <c:load url="data/loadfiledata.xml"
            destination="id('receiver_element')" />
```

```
    </e:handler>
  </b:button>
<div id="receiver_element" style="border:1px solid green;">
    The contents of the external file will be loaded into this
    element.
</div>
```

header

It adds a header to the load action.

This element can only be used as a child of the `load` command.

Attribute	Type	Description
name	String	The header name. For example: `Content-type`.
select	String (XPath)	The header value. For example: `application/xml`.

The JavaScript load command

In the previous chapter, we introduced the `bb` object, which offers a set of utility functions. One of the types of functions available with the `bb` object is the command functions. In fact, for every command function that is available declaratively in the `xmlns:c="http://www.backbase.com/2006/command"` namespace, there is an equivalent function available with the `bb` object. Therefore, there is also a `bb.command.load` function.

The parameters you can use to invoke the `bb.command.load` function are similar to the ones available for the declarative `load` command, with the addition of headers, process, and contextNode. You should specify them in this order: `url`, `method`, `data`, `headers`, `destination`, `success`, `error`, `process`, `async`, and `contextNode`.

In the following example, the content of an external file is loaded into a `div` using the JavaScript `bb.command.load` function. A function is defined to show an alert when the load is successful. Similarly, you can define a function that handles errors.

```
<b:button>
  Click to load external XML file
  <e:handler event="click" type="text/javascript">
    var sUrl = "data/loadfiledata.xml";
    var oDest =
      bb.document.getElementById('receiver_element');
    var sMode = 'firstChild';
    var sMethod = "GET";
    var fnSuccess = function(){alert('success');};
```

```
        bb.command.load(sUrl, sMethod, '', null, oDest,
            sMode, fnSuccess);
    </e:handler>
</b:button>
<div id="receiver_element" style="border:1px solid green;">
    The contents of the external file will be loaded into
    this widget.
</div>
```

Working with forms

The Backbase framework provides extended functionality to submit and validate forms. As we said in the introduction to this chapter, a form is one of the most used means to send input to a server. The standard implementation of the `form` element and the elements that it can contain do not allow for asynchronous submission of data and for receiving the data on the same page.

In the first chapter, we already presented a simple example: *Hello Server!*, which showed how you can submit a form asynchronously and receive the results in an area in the page itself. We made use of specific attributes on the `form` tag that are provided with the Backbase framework: `bf:destination` and `bf:mode`. These two attributes determine what will be done with the result that the server sends back — where it will be placed on the page and how.

As you can see from the `bf` prefix used, these attributes are part of the `forms` namespace, which we briefly introduced in Chapter 2.

The form submission itself happens exactly as before, by clicking a **submit** button or by calling the JavaScript `submit()` function.

What does the forms support provided by the Backbase framework include?

- A complete implementation of the XHTML forms module to enable all standard form's tags, without browser quirks
- A set of BTL widgets, designed to be used in a form
- Synchronous or asynchronous form submission
- Validation, together with a messaging and feedback system

We will first look at some general aspects of Backbase form handling, next we will describe the BTL widgets that belong to the *forms* category and the last subject in this section is form validation.

The forms profiles

The *forms profile* extends BTL and XHTML with additional functionality — the AJAX submission functionality and the validation functionality that the Backbase framework offers for forms.

The forms profile files are automatically loaded when attributes in the `forms` namespace are used, for example, a `bf:destination` attribute on an HTML `form` element will trigger the loading of the forms profile. The profiles can also be loaded on demand with the following two lines at the start of your application:

```
<d:uses namespace="http://www.w3.org/1999/xhtml" src=
"backbase/4_3_1/bindings/www.w3.org.1999.xhtml/formsProfile.xml" />
<d:uses namespace="http://www.backbase.com/2006/btl" src=
"backbase/4_3_1/bindings/www.backbase.com.2006.btl/formsProfile.xml"
/>
```

> When you let the forms profile files load automatically, they are not applied retroactively to elements before the element that triggered the loading. For example, if you have an `input` element with a `bf:required` attribute inside a `form` without a `bf:destination` attribute (implying a Multi-page Interface submit), the form's code will only be loaded when it reaches the `bf:required` attribute, and the `form` element would not get the forms profiles' extensions.

The reason for the existence of the forms profiles is that the overhead of loading them can be avoided when not used.

Form elements

In the `forms` namespace, there are a number of elements available that are extended by the Backbase framework with regard to the XHTML standard. The two most obvious ones are `form` itself and `input`. For both of those there is a base abstract object to inherit from and an interface to implement. We are not going to bother you by explaining how this exactly works, what is interesting though is the extra attributes that are supported on these elements.

In addition to these two elements, we would like to discuss the Backbase framework specific `fileInput`, which provides a way to upload a file with an AJAX form.

Other Backbase framework-specific elements are `message` and `messages`, which we will introduce when we are discussing form validation.

The extended form element

The `form` element has the same functionality as the standard XHTML form. In addition, it supports the following attributes:

Attribute	Description
`bf:destination`	Destination of the response when the form is submitted. The value must be a valid XPath expression. If this attribute is omitted, the whole page will be refreshed with the contents of the response.
`bf:messagesRef`	A reference to a messages element. Inherited from `messengerBase`, an element we will not discuss here.
`bf:mode`	Specifies how the submission result is placed in the DOM tree. We have shown the valid modes before. `appendChild` is the default in this case. Look in chapter 3 for allowed values.

`bf:destination` and `bf:mode` are related to Asynchronous JavaScript and XML form submission, which we discussed earlier, while `bf:messagesRef` is related to form validation, which we will discuss shortly.

The extended input element

Similar to the `form` element, the `input` element will function according to the XHTML standard. Now, with these new attributes:

Attribute	Description
`bf:dataType`	Contains the XML Schema data type name with which to validate the value. Refer to the W3 specification for simple types at `http://www.w3.org/TR/2004/REC-xmlschema-2-20041028/datatypes.html`.
`bf:messagesRef`	A reference to a messages element. Inherited from `messengerBase` (not discussed here).
`bf:required`	If a field is required (`true`), a non-empty value for the input is required. When the field is not required (`false`), an empty value is accepted. If the attribute is absent or has the value default, no requirement checks are done.

fileInput

The `fileInput` widget is a replacement for the `input` element with `type="file"`.

It offers an input text field and a button. When the button is clicked, a dialog box showing the filenames in the file system. When the user selects a file, the path and filename is listed in the input field. Use this widget when your application requires file uploads in a Single Page Interface (SPI) environment. This widget only works for SPI submits. A regular HTML file input widget only works for Multi-page Interface (MPI) submits.

When the form containing this widget is submitted or the `submit()` method is called, the file upload will issue a separate request containing the selected file. You can use `fileInputParameter` child elements to specify parameters that have to be submitted along with the file. For example, this can be used to link two submission requests together through a unique ID.

Use the `fileInput` when uploading a file to your application. The `fileInputParameter` simply adds parameters that the server can read. These are passed to the server on upload. You can use this field, together with a hidden input field, to match the file upload with the form submit.

The following example actually works if you have the required PHP scripts available. These are included in btlSample exerciser that can be found in the code package for the book.

```
<form method="post" action="uploadForm.php"
   bf:destination="id('myFormDiv')">
   <input type="hidden" value="12345" name="uploadFormId" />
   <bf:fileInput action="fileUpload.php" name="myFile">
      <e:handler event="load" type="application/javascript">
         document.getElementById('myFileDiv').innerHTML =
            bb.getProperty(this,
               'responseHTML').documentElement.innerHTML;
      </e:handler>
      <bf:fileInputParameter name="uploadId" value="12345" />
   </bf:fileInput>
   <button type="submit">
      Upload the file!
   </button>
</form>
<div id="myFileDiv" style="border:solid 1px red;" />
<div id="myFormDiv" style="border:solid 1px blue;" />
```

We will use `fileInput` in a later chapter to upload photos to a web server, for our sample application, the travel blog site. You will see that it can be rather tricky to synchronize the file upload and form submit.

The abstract BTL form elements

In our overview of the BTL widgets, there is a *forms* category that contains a number of widgets intended to be used in forms. These are: `calendar`, `checkBoxGroup`, `comboBox`, `listBox`, `slider`, `spinner`, and `suggestBox`.

Just as we have seen in Chapter 2 for the layout BTL elements, there exist some abstract elements to implement generic behavior for form elements. We have no intention to present a boring long list of abstract elements here, however, knowing something about the abstract behavior that some of the form elements inherit can be helpful in using them.

The BTL elements we will be looking at are `focusableElement`, `dropDown`, `formList`, `formField`, and `rangeFormField`.

focusableElement

We have mentioned `focusableElement` before, but a longer description seems appropriate here because it determines the accessibility features of a widget, which is important in a form.

If managing focus is properly supported, it allows the user to navigate through an entire application using the keyboard. Supporting focus means supporting the following features:

- `accesskey`: By pressing an *Alt* + [key] combination, the widget that has that `accesskey` set will gain focus
- `focus`, `blur` methods: The methods to force focus/blur on a widget
- `focus`, `blur` events: The events that are dispatched when the widget receives focus or when focus is lost to the widget
- `tabindex`: Determines placement in the order in which widgets are focused by using *Tab* to cycle through focusable widgets

The `focus` feature is related to the `disabled` property, which means that when a widget is disabled, it should not receive focus.

Elements that support focus extend `focusableElement`. To avoid problems with disabling a `focusableElement`, it should be the last element in the list of extended elements.

Here is a description of the attributes:

Attribute	Type	Description
accesskey	Character	When this key is pressed, the element is either focused or activated (depending on the browser). Note that in some browsers, you must set the `tabindex` attribute to enable the `accesskey`.
tabindex	Integer	Manages the order in which controls can be accessed with the *Tab* key. A value of -1 removes a control from the tab sequence, and 0 is the default value for focusable controls. Values higher than 0 place a control earlier in the tab order, with 1 having the highest priority.

As mentioned above, the methods implemented by `focusableElement` are `focus` and `blur`.

 All widgets in the forms category inherit from `focusableElement`.

dropDown

This is the base element for drop-down widgets. `calendar`, `comboBox`, and `suggestBox` inherit from it. `dropDown` implements the list functionality that displays the items in the drop-down widget.

formField, formList, and rangeFormField

`formField` is the element that implements basic functionality for `formList` and `rangeFormField` that both inherit from it. `formField` has no local attributes.

`formList` implements functionality for form widgets that can contain a list of options. `checkBoxGroup`, `comboBox`, `listBox`, `slider`, and `suggestBox` inherit from it. `formList` has no local attributes.

`rangeFormField` provides `min` and `max` attributes for derived elements to create a value range.

Attribute	Type	Description
max	Integer	Sets the upper limit of the value.
min	Integer	Sets the lower limit of the value.

`calendar`, `slider`, and `spinner` inherit from it.

After this groundwork, we are ready to look at the form widgets themselves.

The BTL form widgets

In this section, we describe the *forms* category of the BTL widgets.

calendar

The `calendar` presents a visual representation of a month in Gregorian calendar format. Click the arrows to navigate to the desired month and year, and select a date in the presented month by clicking the appropriate number. The date is then populated in an input field, which is read-only. The `format` option will cause the date to be shown as, for example, `21-September-07`.

`calendar` inherits from `focusableElement`, `dimensionElement`, `positionElement`, and `rangeFormField`. It supports the following local attributes:

Attribute	Description
disabledDates	List of dates (in yyyy/MM/dd format) and weekday names (according to language attribute) to disable in the calendar. Supported delimiters are comma, semicolon, and space.
format	A pattern for formatting the value of the attribute. Values represent possible patterns for day, month, and year options. For example, M/d/yy is 12/7/58, d-MMM is 7-Dec, d-MMMM-yy is 7-December-58, MMMM is December, and MMMM yy is December 58. The default value (for the default language, English) is MM/dd/yyyy. Note that when specifying a date pattern with a full or abbreviated day (ddd or dddd), the numeric value (d or dd) should also be included (for example, dddd dd or dddd MMMM d, yyyy). For a full list of acceptable values, see the *Backbase API Reference*.
language	Display language. Languages are represented by two letter language codes.
max	The last date (in yyyy/MM/dd format) of the calendar. Dates after this date will be disabled in the calendar.
min	The start date (in yyyy/MM/dd format) of the calendar. Previous dates will be disabled in the calendar.
mode	Specifies whether the calendar will be shown completely inline or partially inline with a pop up.
readonly	When set to true, the user is not allowed to change the value.
value	The (initial) value of the control.

Here is a picture of what a calendar looks like:

The calendar can be displayed in line or as a pop-up menu.

There are a few languages for which the calendar is supported—English, German, and Dutch. Other languages can be added easily, look in the API Reference for an example.

This example shows a calendar that is visible by default (mode="inline"). It also specifies: language="nl", which means that the selected date is displayed in Dutch.

```
<b:calendar mode="inline" language="nl" format="d-MMMM-yy" />
```

checkBoxGroup

The checkBoxGroup is a form element that contains checkBoxGroupOptions. It works in a similar way to an XHTML select. Multiple options can be selected at the same time. XHTML can be used to influence the way the options are structured. For example, a table can be used to display the options in several rows. The checkBoxGroup should not contain other form elements.

Multi-page Interface (MPI) submits are not supported.

checkBoxGroup inherits from disableElement, containerElement, dimensionElement, positionElement, and formList, and it does not have any specific attributes.

In the next example, navBox elements are used to organize the options into appropriate subgroups. In order for a server script to know what the entered values are, a name attribute has to be supplied on the checkBoxGroup tag. If a value attribute has been supplied on a checkBoxGroupOption, then that value will be submitted instead of the text content; see the value for the **Trivial Pursuit** game after submission. (You will need a server script to see it. It is provided with the code.)

```
<style type="text/css">
    .option { display: block; }
</style>
<strong>Hobbies and Interests</strong>
<form action="cb_response.php"
    bf:destination="id('server-response-area')"
    bf:mode="appendChild" method="post">
    <b:checkBoxGroup name="hobbies[]" style="margin-top:20px">
        <b:navBox label="Sports" class="btl-bevel-left-right"
          padding="5px 10px" width="200px" open="true">
          <b:checkBoxGroupOption class="option">
              Football
          </b:checkBoxGroupOption>
          <b:checkBoxGroupOption class="option">
              Baseball
          </b:checkBoxGroupOption>
          <b:checkBoxGroupOption class="option">
              Swimming
          </b:checkBoxGroupOption>
        </b:navBox>
        <b:navBox label="Music" class="btl-bevel-left-right"
          padding="5px 10px" width="200px" open="false">
          <b:checkBoxGroupOption class="option">
              Pop
          </b:checkBoxGroupOption>
          <b:checkBoxGroupOption class="option">
              Easy Listening
          </b:checkBoxGroupOption>
          <b:checkBoxGroupOption class="option">
              Classical
          </b:checkBoxGroupOption>
           <b:checkBoxGroupOption class="option">
              Jazz
          </b:checkBoxGroupOption>
          <b:checkBoxGroupOption class="option">
              New Age
          </b:checkBoxGroupOption>
        </b:navBox>
        <b:navBox label="PC/Console Games"
          class="btl-bevel-left-right"
          padding="5px 10px" width="200px" open="false">
          <b:checkBoxGroupOption class="option">
              First Person Shooter
          </b:checkBoxGroupOption>
          <b:checkBoxGroupOption class="option">
```

```
            Adventure
        </b:checkBoxGroupOption>
        <b:checkBoxGroupOption class="option">
            Platform
        </b:checkBoxGroupOption>
        <b:checkBoxGroupOption class="option">
            Simulation
        </b:checkBoxGroupOption>
    </b:navBox>
    <b:navBox label="Traditional Games"
        class="btl-bevel-left-right"
        padding="5px 10px" width="200px" open="false">
        <b:checkBoxGroupOption class="option">
            Bridge
        </b:checkBoxGroupOption>
        <b:checkBoxGroupOption class="option">
            Chess
        </b:checkBoxGroupOption>
        <b:checkBoxGroupOption class="option">
            Draughts
        </b:checkBoxGroupOption>
        <b:checkBoxGroupOption class="option">
            Scrabble
        </b:checkBoxGroupOption>
        <b:checkBoxGroupOption value="trivp"
            selected="true" class="option">
            Trivial Pursuit
        </b:checkBoxGroupOption>
    </b:navBox>
</b:checkBoxGroup>
<br/>
<input type="submit"
    style="margin-left: 10px;" value="OK" />
</form>
<div id="server-response-area" />
```

And here is what it looks like:

comboBox

The comboBox shows an input field and a drop-down value list. When the user selects an item in the value list, the input field is populated with that value. By default, the user can type a value directly into the input field; you can disable this functionality by setting the value of the readonly attribute to true. The value list can be hard-coded or bound to a data set, and the input value can be validated.

comboBox inherits from focusableElement, dimensionElement, positionElement, formList, and dropDown. It has the following specific attributes:

Attribute	Description
filter	Specifies whether options will be filtered when a user enters a value in the element.
readonly	Specifies whether a user can enter a value in the element.

Here's what a comboBox looks like:

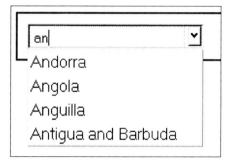

The comboBox implements filtering functionality. If the filter attribute is set to true when the user types a letter into the input field, then only the values in the list that begin with that letter are displayed. Typing second and third letters further reduces the possible list of values.

In the example, the readonly attribute is set to false. Therefore, custom values can be typed in the comboBox. The filter attribute is set to true, which means that after each character typed, only the remaining possible options will be shown.

```
<b:comboBox id="countryList" readonly="false" filter="true">
    <b:comboBoxOption>Afghanistan</b:comboBoxOption>
    <b:comboBoxOption>Albania</b:comboBoxOption>
    <b:comboBoxOption>Algeria</b:comboBoxOption>
    <b:comboBoxOption>American Samoa</b:comboBoxOption>
    <b:comboBoxOption>Andorra</b:comboBoxOption>
    <b:comboBoxOption>Angola</b:comboBoxOption>
    <b:comboBoxOption>Anguilla</b:comboBoxOption>
    <b:comboBoxOption>Antigua and Barbuda</b:comboBoxOption>
    <b:comboBoxOption>Argentina</b:comboBoxOption>
    <b:comboBoxOption>Armenia</b:comboBoxOption>
    <b:comboBoxOption>Aruba</b:comboBoxOption>
    <b:comboBoxOption>Ascension Island</b:comboBoxOption>
</b:comboBox>
```

listBox

The `listBox` widget displays a value list in a box. The list can be created inline or bound to a data source. By setting the `multiple` attribute to `true`, the user can select one item or many items (using *Ctrl* + click or *Shift* + click) from the value list. The `size` attribute determines the number of visible rows in the box.

`listBox` inherits from `focusableElement`, `dimensionElement`, `positionElement`, and `formList`, and it supports these specific attributes:

Attribute	Description
multiple	If set to a value of true, the `listBox` will allow the selection of multiple values.
size	The number of items displayed in the `listBox` (clipped items will create a vertical scroll bar).

Here is what a `listBox` looks like:

The `listBox` is populated with child `listBoxOption` widgets. Setting the `selected` attribute on the `listBoxOption` widget to `true` selects the `listBoxOption` by default.

This example shows a `listBox` with `listBoxOptions` that make up the list items.

```
<h1>Contemporary Dutch Fiction</h1>
<b:listBox size="5" multiple="true" name="myListBox">
    <b:listBoxOption>The Discovery of Heaven</b:listBoxOption>
    <b:listBoxOption selected="true">The Assault</b:listBoxOption>
    <b:listBoxOption>A Heart of Stone</b:listBoxOption>
    <b:listBoxOption>All Souls Day</b:listBoxOption>
    <b:listBoxOption>The Third Voice</b:listBoxOption>
</b:listBox>
```

slider

The `slider` widget allows the user to move a *grippy*, or a rectangular cursor, along a linear path that represents a text or numerical range. The location of the grippy along the slider range corresponds to a particular value. Each grippy is a holder of this value and position. These values can either be strings or numbers. The `orientation` attribute of the slider allows you to orient the slider either horizontally or vertically.

`slider` inherits from `focusableElement`, `dimensionElement`, `positionElement`, `rangeFormField`, and `formList`. It supports the following local attributes:

Attribute	Description
fill	If this attribute is `true`, the `slider` will have an area that is highlighted with specific color. For a `slider` with one grippy, it will be the area from the beginning of the scale to where the grippy is positioned. For a `slider` with two grippies, it will be the area between the grippies. In other cases, nothing is highlighted.
max	The highest number in a numerical range. The `slider` cannot represent a number higher than the value of this attribute.
min	The lowest number in a numerical range. The `slider` cannot represent a number lower than the value of this attribute.
orientation	Determines whether the positioning of the `slider` is horizontal or vertical.
showLabels	Boolean value to indicate if a label should be displayed.
showToolTip	Indicates if a `toolTip` should be displayed.
snap	Boolean value to indicate if the `slider` should snap to the closest value.
step	The value by which the `slider` *jumps*. With a step of 3, a min of 1, and a max of 10, the possible values would be 1, 4, 7, and 10.
value	The attribute that sets the initial (default) value.

This is what a `slider` looks like:

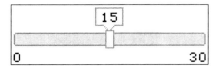

The grippy is defined using the `sliderGrippy` element. If there is no child `sliderGrippy` defined, one instance will be created automatically. You can define any number of `sliderGrippy` elements for this `slider`, each having its own value. Therefore, each following grippy cannot have a value that is smaller than the value of the previous grippy.

Each `sliderGrippy` represents this separate value and position holder. For backward compatibility, the `slider` widget also contains a `value` attribute, a `value` property, and a `defaultValue` property, which redirect to the same properties and attributes of the initially defined grippy.

A user can work with only one grippy at a time. This grippy should be active at the time that the user works with it. The user selects the active grippy by clicking on it. The active grippy receives all the mouse movements and keyboard controls. Programmatically, the active grippy is represented by the `activeGrippy` property. Setting this property changes the active grippy at runtime.

A `slider` is typically used on a form. When a user needs to enter a numerical value, especially if there is a wide range of values, a `slider` is easier to use than a `spinner` or a standard input field. Because the `slider` widget has attributes for `min`, `max`, and `step` (the increment/decrement amount between values), a `slider` becomes even more useful when the numerical value has a set range or must be incremented by a value larger than one. Using two grippies, you can define the control for intuitive entering of a range of values.

A more complicated scenario would involve a relationship between the `slider` and a `data` widget. For example, the value on the `slider` could determine the maximum price for items that you want to buy on a vacation. When the `slider` value is changed, the data in a `data` widget is filtered, so that only items less than the maximum price are displayed.

The `sliderOption` widget handles text values for the `slider`. Use the `sliderOption` widgets as children of the `slider` when you want to predefine a non-standard item list for the `slider`.

Here is an example of a BTL `slider` with horizontal and vertical orientation:

```
<b:slider id="myHorizontalSlider"
    max="30" min="0" step="2" value="15" />
<b:slider id="myVerticalSlider"
    max="0" min="-30" value="-15" orientation="vertical" />
```

This is an example of a BTL `slider` with non-numerical `sliderOptions`:

```
<b:slider value="Wednesday">
    <b:sliderOption>Sunday</b:sliderOption>
```

```
    <b:sliderOption>Monday</b:sliderOption>
    <b:sliderOption>Tuesday</b:sliderOption>
    <b:sliderOption>Wednesday</b:sliderOption>
    <b:sliderOption>Thursday</b:sliderOption>
    <b:sliderOption>Friday</b:sliderOption>
    <b:sliderOption>Saturday</b:sliderOption>
</b:slider>
```

spinner

The `spinner` allows you to increment or decrement a numerical value by entering a value in an input field, clicking up and down arrows with the mouse, or using the up and down arrow keys.

`spinner` inherits from `focusableElement`, `dimensionElement`, `positionElement`, and `rangeFormField`. It has these local attributes:

Attribute	Description
decimals	Sets the number of decimals to be used for the precision of the `spinner` value.
step	Sets and reports the size of the changes made when the arrows are clicked or the up and down keys are pressed.
stringAfter	The text to be added after the value when it is displayed.
stringBefore	The text to be added before the value when it is displayed.
value	Value of the `spinner`.

This is what a `spinner` widget looks like:

You can set the minimal numeric value of the `spinner` using the `min` attribute. The maximum numeric value is set using the `max` attribute (inherited from `rangeFormField`).

This spinner example uses `max` and `min` attributes to create bounding values:

```
<b:spinner id="myspinner" min="50" max="100" step="5" value="75"
    stringAfter="%" />
```

suggestBox

Much like the XHTML `select` element or `comboBox` widget, the `suggestBox` is a form widget of which the submitted value is selected from a list of options. It can be used to limit the size of the list for large datasets. Where the `comboBox` shows all the options in the list, the `suggestBox` only shows the options that are suggested. This means that the user does not have to go through a large list of options in order to select one. Note that the number of suggestions that are displayed can be limited using the `suggestMaximum` attribute. Setting this attribute may result in usability and performance improvements when the `dataSource` contains a very large number of suggestions.

`suggestBox` inherits from `focusableElement`, `dimensionElement`, `positionElement`, `dataObserver`, `formList`, and `dropDown`, and it also has some specific attributes:

Attribute	Description
select	Specifies a query for the data that has to be shown in the `suggestBox`. Currently, this can only be an XPath query of which the context is a row in the `dataSource`.
suggestDelay	Specifies the delay in milliseconds before suggestions are actually made. This reduces the amount of unnecessary suggestions when a user is still typing a value.
suggestMaximum	Specifies the maximum number of suggested options that are visible.
suggestStartLength	Specifies the minimum input string length for which suggestions will be displayed.

The following screenshot shows a `suggestBox`:

Unlike the `comboBox` or `listBox`, the `suggestBox` does not need the options to be listed as child elements of the `suggestBox`. Instead, it can retrieve the options from a `dataSource`.

Currently, the suggestBox only supports using a local XML dataSource. In the next chapter, you will see much more about data sources and we will show how you can extend the suggestBox to use a remote data source after we have discussed TDL.

The suggestBox in this example allows you to find a specific country from a list of countries easily by typing the first few letters of the country name. You could keep the names of the countries in an XML file and read it into a variable. Here, we provided the first few lines of this file as local data. To find the value of a suggestBox, consider that its behavior is very similar to an input field. The dataContainer is used to specify inline data. This inline data can be included using xi:include.

```
<b:dataSource e:behavior="b:localData" name="mySource"
  dataType="application/xml">
  <b:dataContainer>
    <countries xmlns="">
      <country><name>Afghanistan</name></country>
      <country><name>Albania</name></country>
      <country><name>Algeria</name></country>
      <country><name>American Samoa</name></country>
      <country><name>Andorra</name></country>
      <country><name>Angola</name></country>
      <country><name>Anguilla</name></country>
      <country><name>Antigua and Barbuda</name></country>
    </countries>
  </b:dataContainer>
</b:dataSource>
<b:suggestBox name="country" dataSource="mySource" select="*[1]" />
```

Validating input fields

Anyone who fills in a form now and then has been confronted with the frustration of making mistakes. Sometimes, you must deal with a server that sends unfriendly error messages, and then wipes out the input that has already been entered.

You can enhance the user experience considerably by checking the values in the form fields for validity before the form is sent to the server. The user should also see a meaningful error message when values are entered incorrectly or when a value that is required was not provided.

The Backbase framework offers several built-in facilities to validate user input. There are also many ways to extend this validation.

Required fields

We start with a very simple validation. An error message is displayed when you try to submit the form while the name field is not filled in.

Here is the code for a form with Backbase form widgets:

```
<div xmlns:xi=http://www.w3.org/2001/XInclude
   xmlns:c="http://www.backbase.com/2006/command" id="center">
   <fieldset title="Check Out" id="checkOut">
      <legend>Check Out</legend>
      <div class="row">
         <div class="lspan">
            <label for="name">Name:</label>
         </div>
         <input class="inputText"
            type="text" name="name" id="name"
            bf:required="true"
            bf:messagesRef="id('required_field')" />
         <span> * </span>
         <bf:messages id="required_field">
            <bf:message event="invalid"
              class="errorMessage" facet="required">
               <div>This field is required.</div>
            </bf:message>
         </bf:messages>
      </div>
      <div class="row rowOdd">
         <div class="lspan">
         </div>
         <button type="submit">
            Order the T-shirt
         </button>
      </div>
   </fieldset>
   <p>
      Fields marked with * are required.
   </p>
</div>
```

Two attributes (bf:required="true" and bf:messagesRef="id('required_field')") are added to the input field. We have seen these attributes in our description of the extended input field for forms. You should also notice the messages container.

The `required_field` identifier refers to a `messages` container, which displays or hides the message depending on the validity of the field when the user tries to submit the form. The `messages` container can have more than one message if you want; for example, one for each kind of error that you would like to catch.

When the `invalid` event occurs, the message content is made visible. In our example, red text appears to inform the user that the field is required. You can try this by pressing the **Order the T-shirt** button without entering a value in the name field.

When you fill in some values in the form and press the **Order the T-shirt** button, a simple static text is displayed. This is what it would look like:

Data type validation

Making sure that a field is filled in is of course useful, but often you want more. You would want to make sure whether the field value is a valid email address, home address, or phone number, or a date, and so on. To help with this problem, the Backbase framework supports the XML schema data types specification, and provides the `bf:dataType` attribute for applying type validation rules to input tags.

This code shows a form with a select box, where the options should be a valid language abbreviation. The `name` field is required, `age` has a custom type, and the `zipcode` has a Backbase-specific type.

```
<select name="language" id="language
   bf:dataType="xs:language">
  <option value="" />
  <option value="nl">Dutch</option>
  <option value="en-GB">English (British)</option>
  <option value="en-US">English (US)</option>
  <option value="ja">Japanese</option>
</select>
<input name="name" id="name" bf:required="true" />
<input name="age" id="age"
```

```
      bf:dataType="example:minimum-age-12" />
 <input name="postcode" id="zipcode"
      bf:dataType="b:zipcode-nl" />
```

By default, the XML schema data types provide a number of built-in data types. There are various possibilities to extend the types with custom values and checking rules. You can find details for this in the Backbase documentation.

The XML schema specification itself provides the most common validation rules. For example, the value of the bf:dataType attribute in the select element of the earlier example, xs:language, is a standard simple type.

Additionally, Backbase delivers a few extra simple types such as email and creditcard. These are extra validation rules that are not part of the XML schema specification.

The age input field in the example also specifies a data type: minimum-age-12. This simple type definition ensures that the field only allows an integer value greater than 12.

```
<xs:schema xmlns:xi="http://www.w3/org/2001/XInclude"
    xmlns:xs="http://www.w3.org/2001/XMLSchema"
    targetNamespace="http://example.org/ns/my-datatypes">
    <xs:simpleType name="minimum-age-12">
       <xs:restriction base="xs:nonNegativeInteger">
             <xs:minInclusive value="12" />
       </xs:restriction>
    </xs:simpleType>
</xs:schema>
```

This custom simple type is a composite of two XML schema rules. The restriction xs:nonNegativeInteger refers to a built-in simple type that states that the value must be an integer greater than or equal to zero. We then further restrict that simple type by adding the minInclusive constraint, ensuring that the value must be an integer greater than or equal to twelve.

We only showed some simple validation types here. If you need more, all facilities are there to define them. The main purpose of this section was to give you an impression of what is possible. We will add more complex validation to our sample application in later chapters.

For inspiration and to see what is possible, you could take a look at the **Rich Forms Demo** that can be found on the **Demos** page: http://bdn.backbase.com/client/demos. We do not recommend taking this demo as a starting point for your own development because it is very specific to the example it implements.

AJAX and architecture

By now, you know how to communicate with the server and how to load data or code asynchronously. What effect does this have on the architecture of your application? We are going to shift our attention from the details of asynchronous communication to a more abstract level where we are talking about overall web application architecture. After that, we'll make some remarks on how this can be implemented on the server. The actual examples of both client and server code will be given in the next section, where we discuss the travel blog site sample application.

In February 2005, when the term AJAX became known to the world via Jesse James Garret's article *AJAX: A New Approach to Web Applications*, (see for a reference the *AJAX* section, covered earlier in this chapter), web developers suddenly realized that it was possible to create web applications with the same interactive look-and-feel as desktop applications.

It was not new technology because all aspects of AJAX already existed, but the understanding of how these technologies could be integrated caused a steep increase in attention for new ways to do web application development.

In practice, the development of web applications has not become easier since AJAX came on the scene as we already explained at the start of Chapter 1. Nowadays, the effective web developer needs to have expert knowledge about (X)HTML, XML, AJAX, JavaScript, CSS, the Document Object Model (DOM), and a server-side language like JSP, PHP, ASP, or Ruby, to name a few. He needs to know about browser quirks, server application architecture, database access, and the business domain that the application covers.

It is no wonder that few web applications' frontends do nothing more than show some glitzy JavaScript stuff and that the UI code of many applications has become the spaghetti that we know so well from the eighties, the days before object oriented programming was invented.

By now, there are hundreds of JavaScript UI and AJAX libraries available, some better known than others. It is not enough to have these libraries to make our development easier. In fact, although we can make web applications that are more powerful and more user friendly, in general, they have also become more complex.

The natural course of events for a new technology is that after making things more complex, eventually, the community will understand how the technology works. The new technology will be merged with older, similar ones, and simpler paradigms will arise. We think the same is true for the AJAX technology now.

We have seen that the Backbase framework can act as a unifying technology for the client-side of web applications, which is a great step forward in managing the complexity of such applications. This does not help us if we cannot find means to also manage the complexity of the server application and the web application as a whole. Let's look at it.

AJAX is about communication between a web server application and a web client. As you will understand now, each of the two is an application in its own right. Both together compose the web application as the user will experience it. The question arises: what should be in the client application and what should be in the server application?

Older wisdom helps us out here. IT architects have known for a long time that you should split your application in layers. The appropriate way to do that is by using the MVC pattern, which we will describe in the next section.

Model-View-Controller

The Model-View-Control design pattern, or MVC for short, is maybe the first design pattern documented as such—a **design pattern** is a general solution to a common problem. The MVC pattern was originally written down by Trygve Reenskaug in 1978. This is roughly what he said:

- A *model* is a representation in an application of knowledge in a particular problem domain
- A *view* is the presentation of the model to a user
- A *controller* defines the interaction between a user and the application

This definition is just as valid today as it was in 1978 and every good application has a strategy for separating models from views and a discussion where the controller should be placed.

Our web application really consists of three parts as we argued in the previous section. For each part, you can apply the MVC separation separately. In fact, you can use the MVC pattern for each component within your application and you have to strike a balance between too much structure that cuts your application in pieces that are too small and the complexity of spaghetti without structure.

Looking at our web application from a helicopter perspective, it is clear that the *model* should be on the server and that the client acts as a *view*. We place the controller also on the server. Why? Because the server is more secure and does not allow (at least in principle) the user to assume any role he/she would like (being a super administrator, for example), with the risk of destroying precious data.

Let us delay the question of how you can use the MVC pattern for the client application until later. First, we will look at the server-side because the structure of your server application determines to a large extent the complexity of your total application.

Implementing MVC on the server

A while ago, we started looking for a PHP framework that could help with setting up an architecture for our web applications. We evaluated a few and we tried a few, but finally, none fit our requirement. Then, we came across some remarks by Rasmus Lerdorf, the original creator of PHP (`http://toys.lerdorf.com/ archives/38-The-no-framework-PHP-MVC-framework.html`):

> *So you want to build the next fancy Web 2.0 site? You'll need some gear. Most likely in the form of a big complex MVC framework with plenty of layers that abstracts away your database, your HTML, your JavaScript and in the end your application itself. If it is a really good framework, it will provide a dozen things you'll never need.*

Rasmus continues arguing that it is better to develop your own framework that exactly fits your needs. This framework should be so simple that six months from now you will understand it at a glance. We will develop such a framework. You will see what it looks like in the next section when we introduce our travel blog site.

Of course, you are wondering now why we did not use the same argument and develop our own client framework instead of using the Backbase framework. Well, the truth is, Sergey did this indeed, but he was also a core developer of the Backbase framework. For average web developers, it is not possible to develop a framework that would abstract most quirks from all modern browsers and that can implement the dynamic widgets that we need these days. As we argued in our introduction about architecture in the previous section, the Backbase framework acts as a unifying technology, which is needed to keep complexity at bay, just like object-oriented technology gave a handle to manage complexity in the late nineteen-eighties.

In addition, the Backbase framework is more than a framework. It includes the Tag Definition Language, which constitutes an essential part of the value of what is offered by Backbase. We will discuss TDL in detail in a later chapter. Also, think of it this way: Rasmus had to create PHP first, before he could create his *no-framework PHP MVC framework*. Developing your own language is not interesting to most developers and why should you if there are good languages to choose from?

The server controller

A basic principle for a controller on the server is that it should act as the single, exclusive entry point of all communication with the server. This has an important advantage—only a single script is needed to handle *session management*, *user authorization*, and *input filtering*. This makes handling security much easier. By the way, input filtering can be done automatically for PHP since release 5.2.

In our no-framework framework, all other PHP scripts only contain classes and therefore, cannot be executed directly by typing their URL in the address bar of the browser. This is also an important security feature because authorization for a script is not in the script itself, which could be wrongly handled or forgotten by the developer.

The server model

We try to design our application in such a way that most server scripts can be just simple providers of data to the client. They will need access to a database to do this. We have a simple database framework available for you too. You need a framework in this case not to protect you from writing SQL, but to protect you from inadvertent SQL injection problems. The framework also offers you a choice of interfaces for MySQL and SQLite.

Having only scripts that do simple requests for data and return that data as XML will be a major simplification of your server application. Contrast this with the Multi-page Interface approach where you had to weave data with HTML to build a complete page, for every user request. In this chapter, we only look at requests that result from submitting a form or from a `load` command. In the next chapter, the data-bound widgets will be responsible for the requests for data.

The server view

Everything that is visible from the client is sent to it from the server. Using AJAX technology and the Backbase framework, it is possible to separate out those parts of an application that contain static text and those parts that contain dynamically generated content. Static parts do not need to be generated. By using data bound widgets and by sending only XML with data and not (X)HTML to the client, we can avoid writing complicated server scripts that need to generate (X)HTML.

However, we did find that it is not possible to avoid code generation totally, sometimes because of performance reasons, and sometimes because of restrictions that we did not know how to solve yet.

We round this topic off with a cute quote from Martin Fowler. If you don't know him, then check out his books. He is a very well-known author and authority on everything related to object-oriented application analysis, design, and implementation, with examples mostly in Java.

Scriptlets

On page 351 of his book, *Patterns of Enterprise Application Architecture,* Martin Fowler defines a **scriptlet** as:

> *A piece of arbitrary programming logic in a server page, such as ASP, JSP or PHP.*

On page 337, he writes:

> *I think that scriptlet code has the same relationship to well-designed software that professional wrestling has to sport.*

He then argues that we should separate out the programming logic from the presentation logic in much the same way as web application programmers have learned to use templates or template languages to separate model from view. This is still valid, although the need for templates that are used to generate HTML should be much less than before.

The C3D travel blog site

After the rather abstract and high level description of what our server code should look like, we are ready to step down and get our hands dirty with some real code. But, not immediately! First, we introduce our web application and describe a set of requirements for it.

At the time of writing this chapter, one of the authors (Ghica) was in China, accompanying her husband on a university exchange. To keep family and friends informed of their whereabouts and adventures, they registered for a Dutch travel blog site.

The site serves its purpose, but the user interface is annoying, to say the least. This gave us the idea that maybe this user interface could be improved and that it actually would provide an example where we could show many of the features of the Backbase framework, as you will see.

Why *C3D*? Well, this book is about JavaScript *circles* and how to square them into Backbase widgets. On the other hand, traveling is about the *globe*, which is really a 3D circle.

We have no intention to compete with this Dutch site or with its international cousin, www.travelblog.com. Rather, our site will be a private site for a limited amount of registered users and their friends.

You can use the source code provided as such and upload it to your own site, or you can use the examples and the mini framework provided, to develop something entirely different, for example, a web shop.

Here is a quick preview of the first prototype of the site for this chapter, at the time when you enter a new trip:

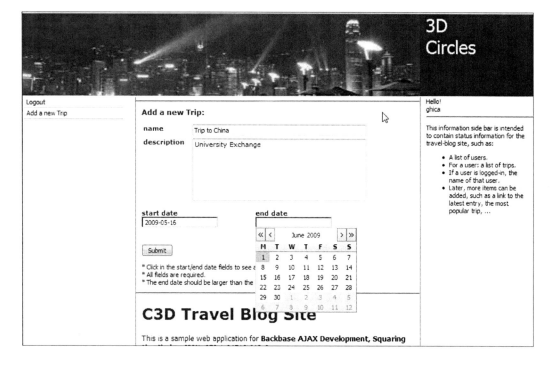

The first thing that has to be done while developing an application is to write down a list of requirements.

Requirements for the C3D site

Some of you may remember the times when the requirements for an application were documents of two hundred or more pages, which were then cast in concrete. This was a good starting point for the failure of your project because it was usually impossible to match the requirements and if you could, it would turn out to be not what your customer wanted by the time you finished. Therefore, we restrict our requirements to a short informal list:

- The C3D site is a site where a restricted set of users can blog about their travel experience and upload photos to show next to a blog entry
- It will be possible to place small Google maps next to a blog entry to indicate where on earth the traveler is when writing a blog entry
- Everyone can view the trips made by the registered users and be informed of selected updates to the site

This chapter addresses the design of the web application and the first point in the list. The next chapter will show how the blog entries can be displayed using a data grid and in Chapter 11 we will add the Google map facility.

Design

There are many ways of designing a web application. The most accepted ways are either to start with *use cases*, or with frontend *user interface* design:

- Because this is an experimental example, we let our informal list of requirements be the use cases
- The user interface design is just the thirteen-in-a-dozen page layout that you saw for our example applications in Chapters 2 and 3

It is important to note here that if we change our mind about the visual aspect of the user interface, we can usually rearrange it without having to change any of the interface logic.

Our favorite next step is to create a data model.

Data model

Creating a data model is a quick way of starting the design of a small application. For a large application, starting with an object model is more usual. However, in our opinion, the best object models closely resemble good data models, and this is true for applications of any size.

You create the data model by listing all the things that are important for your application and that you want to keep track of in a database. After some shuffling, we came up with the following model:

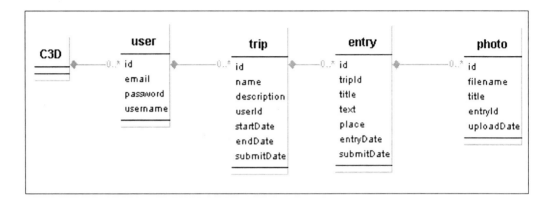

This is an extremely simple model that says:

- The C3D site has a number of *users*. Note that we do not need to create a table that represents the site because it has no attributes.

- Each user can make a number of *trips*. Each trip can have a number of blog *entries* associated with it. Each entry can have zero or more *photos* associated with it.

- Note that we store when a trip was added or when a blog entry was made. However, a user can still choose the dates to which a trip or entry applies. This allows you to make entries at a later date than the date you are describing in your blog.

- We will store photos outside the database. It is not difficult to do, but it may take up a lot of space.

The straightforward SQL that you can create from this model is included in the code provided with the book.

Page layout

Finally, we are going to show some real implementation. Unfortunately, we are going to violate some of the principles we were arguing about earlier, as we need to address something more important: *usability*.

We started out with a starter page containing a layout very similar to what we have been doing before, using a panelSet. When our first prototype was ready, we uploaded it to a server that sits somewhere in Europe and quickly found out that we had a problem looking at it via our good, but rather slow, Internet connection in China.

An essential part of a good user experience for a site is that the first page should appear quickly. After that, a user may be willing to wait a few seconds. Using a panelSet has the effect of putting a blanket on top of your application, through which all interactions go. Moreover, lots of Backbase functionality needs to be loaded just for this panelSet.

We solved our problem by replacing the panelSet with an ordinary table. With the advent of better CSS support in most browsers, people tend to frown upon the use of tables, and surely we could have found a way to get the same layout with just CSS and a few div tags. However, a well-placed table can save you a lot of frustration and in this case there are no hidden, generated, and nested tables that can upset our layout.

We also changed the file type from .html to .php. We could now replace the XInclude statements by PHP include statements. The difference is, of course, that the code is included at the server, and not by an extra request after the page is loaded. The BTL bindings in the config.xml must always be included using XInclude.

The body part of index.php now looks like this:

```
<body>
    <script type="text/backbase+xml" height="200px">
        <xi:include
          href="../../backbase/4_3_1/bindings/config.xml" />
    </script>
    <table style="width:100%; height: 100%" border="0"
        cellpadding="0" cellspacing="0">
        <tbody>
            <tr>
                <td colspan="2" style="overflow:
                  hidden;height:140px;">
                    <img src="resources/media/hongkong.jpg"
                      width="100%" height="140px" border="0" />
```

```
    </td>
    <td style="width:200px; height:140px;
      margin-bottom: 20px;" valign="top"
      align="right">
      <div class="appHeaderText"
        style="background-color: #2e1f34;
        height:140px;padding-left:10px;">
          3D<br />Circles
      </div>
    </td>
  </tr>
  <tr>
    <td style="width:200px;height:100%;
      overflow: hidden;" valign="top">
      <script type="application/backbase+xml">
        <div id="menu-area"
          style="width:180px;height:100%;
          overflow: hidden;">
           <?php $req=initialmenu;
             include "initcntrl.php"; ?>
        </div>
      </script>
</td>
    <td class="btl-border-left" valign="top">
      <script type="application/backbase+xml">
        <div id="trip-area"></div>
      </script>
       <div id="app-content">
       <?php include "content.xml"; ?>
       </div>
    </td>
     <td class="btl-border-left"
       style="width:200px;" valign="top">
       <script type="application/backbase+xml">
         <div id="login-info"
           style="padding-left: 10px;
           font-color: navy;">
            <?php $req=userinfo;
              include "initcntrl.php"; ?>
         </div>
       </script>
        <div id="app-info">
        <?php include "info.xml" ?>
        </div>
     </td>
```

```
        </tr>
      </tbody>
    </table>
  </body>
```

Your startup page will look like this:

Remember that this is a prototype still. There is some code in this version that we are not so proud of. We will improve some of it in later chapters.

Good use of IDs

You may have guessed that we are not strong advocates of the use of IDs in your XHTML. If you are dynamically loading code, then IDs are not guaranteed to be present when you think they are. There is also the danger of loading a code fragment twice and consequently, errors with duplicate IDs will result.

There are also circumstances where the use of an ID is OK. When you design a web application page, there will be static parts of the application, such as the area at the top where the header is placed, an area at the side where the menu items are and an area in the middle where the dynamic content of a page is loaded. Usually, you define `div` elements where the contents of these areas will be loaded and because these elements will stay on the page during the whole execution process of your web application, it is a good idea to give these `div` elements an ID. With CSS you can determine where these `div` elements are placed on the page, and the IDs make it easier to target dynamic content to be loaded.

To make it easier to understand the code in the next sections, we give here a diagram of the IDs we are using:

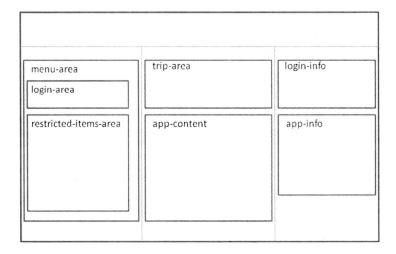

Server application structure

The structure of our C3D application is similar to the one we used before. There is a root directory, called c3da (we will have also a c3db version, and so on), and there are several subfolders, each with a specific purpose. Here is a picture of it:

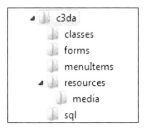

c3da is a subfolder of myApps. Another subfolder you will see is the fw folder. *FW* stands for framework, but it typically is a no-framework framework because it only contains a small set of database classes, a class loader typical for PHP5, and a few other things. As before, the Backbase code is one-level up.

We promised that we would structure our server code according to the MVC pattern. Therefore, we should look at each of those parts. Let's start with the controller.

The C3D controller

Basically, there is only one server script that can be called from the client: `cntrl.php`.

`cntrl.php` can accept a number of parameters, as either GET or POST requests. The main one is the `req` parameter, which tells the `cntrl.php` script what it should do. The code of this script is as follows (for brevity, we do not show all actions):

```php
<?php
if (!isset($_SESSION)) {
    session_start();
}
header('Content-type: application/xml');
echo '<?xml version="1.0" encoding="UTF-8"?>';
require "../fw/setPaths.php";
require 'config.inc.php';
ob_start();
switch ($_REQUEST['req']) {
    case "login":
        $login = new login();
        $login->check($_POST['username'], $_POST['password']);
        break;
    case "logout":
        $login = new login();
        unset($_SESSION['c3d']['username']);
        $login->setLoginMenu();
        break;
// more case statements here
    default:
        echo "*** invalid request ***";
}
$out1 = ob_get_contents();
ob_end_clean();
echo createResponseElement($out1);
?>
```

Do you think that this controller is too simple? Maybe not! For example, remember that input filtering to prevent cross-site scripting is done transparently by PHP, SQL injection is handled by our database access classes, and this controller is the only way you can communicate with the application. Its sole task is to make sure that only those tasks are called for which the user of the site is authorized.

As for any PHP script that is part of an application, we should make sure first that there is a session present that can keep information about our site user, such as whether the user is logged on, which trip he/she is looking at, and so on.

You see two files included from our small `fw` framework, these contain the class loader we were talking about and the database access classes. There is also a function defined in `setPaths.php` with the name `createResponseElement()`. This function embeds the code that is sent back by the model classes in a `div` with all necessary namespace declarations.

The `config.inc.php` file contains database information, such as database user and password. If you are using our sample code in your own environment, you should adapt these values to fit your setup.

For those of you not familiar with PHP: the `ob_start()`, `ob_get_contents()`, and `ob_end_clean()` functions allow to save output that otherwise would be echoed immediately, into a string. This string can then be used to create the response with the `createResponseElement()` function.

You may have noticed in the `index.php` script the invocation of `initcntrl.php` script. This is not really a controller, but a script that offers a shortcut solution to the problem of inserting dynamic code into the initial page.

It can happen that the user clicks on **Refresh** in his browser. This will result in a new invocation of the `index.php` script. Because it is not nice to destroy the session this user already had available, the initial page must be able to show the proper menu items in this case. To avoid unnecessary round-trips to the server, which as we found out in China gives the site a slow appearance, a custom script, `initcntrl.php`, was written for this case. We will refactor this code in Chapter 11 in such a way that `initcntrl.php` is not needed anymore.

The C3D model

The model classes are the classes that are called from the controller script `cntrl.php`. Right now, there are only three classes—a class that handles login and logout, a class that handles inserts into a database table (for the moment only *trips*), and a class that does some work to set up the initial menu.

The C3D view

The view is not stored in classes but in XML files and some of it is still hidden in PHP model classes. They should go to PHP templates for which we have an extremely simple facility in our `fw` framework. We will refactor this in a later version of the C3D application.

`index.php` clearly belongs to the view too.

Login and logout

A user must be logged in to add a new trip, to add blog entries, or to upload photos. To do so, he or she will click on the `login` menu item. A form will appear in which the user can type a username and a password.

A request is sent to the server, which is handled by the controller script. When the password is OK, the `logout` menu item will replace the login form and all menu items that only a logged-in user can see will be added. For now, this is only the `add trip` menu item.

When the user logs out, the `login` menu item should reappear and anything that was viewable only by logged-in users should be removed.

Before login, the following code is placed in the menu area:

```
<div xmlns="http://www.w3.org/1999/xhtml"
   xmlns:b="http://www.backbase.com/2006/btl"
   xmlns:c="http://   www.backbase.com/2006/command"
   xmlns:e="http://www.backbase.com/2006/xel"
   class="app_menu_item">
   <a href="javascript:">Login</a>
   <e:handler event="click">
      <c:load url="../forms/UserLogin.xml"
         destination="id('login-area')"
         mode="replaceChildren" />
   </e:handler>
   <!-- make sure that areas where there is info about
      logged-in users are empty -->
   <e:handler event="DOMNodeInsertedIntoDocument">
      <c:create destination="id('login-info')"
         mode="replaceChildren">
         <div />
      </c:create>
      <c:create destination="id('restricted-items-area')"
        mode="replaceChildren">
         <div />
       </c:create>
       <c:create destination="id('trip-area')"
         mode="replaceChildren">
         <div />
       </c:create>
   </e:handler>
</div>
```

This code says that at a `click` event the form should be loaded. As the code for the form is very straightforward, we do not show it here.

Because we do not know whether the placement of the `login` menu item on the page is the result of logging out, we make sure that all restricted areas are replaced with empty `div` elements.

The `logout` menu item looks as follows:

```
<div xmlns="http://www.w3.org/1999/xhtml"
    xmlns:b="http://www.backbase.com/2006/btl"
    xmlns:c="http://www.backbase.com/2006/command"
    xmlns:e="http://www.backbase.com/2006/xel"
    xmlns:xi="http://www.w3.org/2001/XInclude" class="app_menu_item">
    <a href="javascript:">Logout</a>
    <e:handler event="click">
        <c:load url="../cntrl.php?req=logout"
            destination="id('login-area')"
            mode="replaceChildren" />
    </e:handler>
    <e:handler event="DOMNodeInsertedIntoDocument">
        <c:create destination="id('login-info')"
            mode="replaceChildren">
            <div>
                Hello!
                <xi:include href="../cntrl.php?req=getuser" />
                <hr />
            </div>
        </c:create>
    </e:handler>
</div>
```

When the `logout` item is clicked, a request is sent to the controller. The controller will just reset the user information in the session.

The placement of the `logout` menu item on the page must be the result of a successful login. Therefore, when the menu item is inserted into the DOM, a `create` command will place a greeting in the `login-info` area.

Add a trip

The last thing we would like to discuss for this version of the C3D web application is the addition of a new trip by a user.

You have seen that the `add trip` menu item will appear when a user has successfully logged in. When you click this item, a form will appear in the middle section of the page. You have already seen what it looks like in an earlier section. Here is the code:

```
<div xmlns="http://www.w3.org/1999/xhtml"
  xmlns:b="http://www.backbase.com/2006/btl"
  xmlns:bf="http://www.backbase.com/2007/forms"
  xmlns:d="http://www.backbase.com/2006/tdl">
  <d:uses namespace="http://www.w3.org/1999/xhtml"
    src="../../../backbase/4_3_1/bindings/www.w3.org.1999.xhtml/
    formsProfile.xml" />
  <d:uses namespace="http://www.backbase.com/2006/btl"
    src="../../../backbase/4_3_1/bindings/www.backbase.com.2006.btl/
    formsProfile.xml" />
  <hr />
  <h2 style="margin: 10px;">Add a new Trip:</h2>
  <form bf:destination="id('trip-area')"
      bf:mode="replaceChildren" action="../cntrl.php"
      method="post">
    <input type="hidden" name="req" value="insert" />
    <input type="hidden" name="dbtable" value="c3d_trip" />
    <table>
      <tbody>
        <tr>
          <td valign="top">
            <label for="name">name</label>
          </td>
          <td>
            <input type="text" name="name"
              style="width:300px;"
              bf:required="true"
              bf:messagesRef="../../td/bf:messages[1]" />
          </td>
          <td valign="top">
            <bf:messages>
              <bf:message
                event="invalid"
                class="errorMessage"
                facet="required">
                <span>A name for your trip is required</span>
              </bf:message>
            </bf:messages>
          </td>
        </tr>
        <tr>
          <td valign="top">
            <label for="description">description</label>
          </td>
          <td>
```

```
                <textarea name="description"
                    bf:required="true"
                    bf:messagesRef="../../td/bf:messages[1]" />
            </td>
             <td valign="top">
               <bf:messages>
                   <bf:message
                     event="invalid"
                     class="errorMessage"
                     facet="required">
                      <span style="margin-top: 0px;">
                          A description for your trip is
                          Required
                      </span>
                   </bf:message>
               </bf:messages>
            </td>
        </tr>
    </tbody>
</table>
 <div style="height: 50px; clear:left; margin-top:10px;">
    <div style="float:left; width:200px;">
        <label for="startDate">start date</label>
        <br />
         <b:calendar name="startDate" format="yyyy-MM-dd"
           bf:required="true"
           bf:messagesRef="../../div/bf:messages[1]" />
     </div>
    <div style="float:left;">
        <label for="endDate">end date</label>
        <br />
        <b:calendar name="endDate" format="yyyy-MM-dd"
           bf:required="true"
           bf:messagesRef="../../div/bf:messages[2]" />
    </div>
    <div style="float:left;">
        <bf:messages>
            <bf:message event="invalid"
              class="errorMessage"
              facet="required">
              <div style="padding-left: 10px;">
                  Start date is required</div>
           </bf:message>
        </bf:messages>
        <bf:messages>
```

```
        <bf:message event="invalid"
          class="errorMessage"
          facet="required">
           <div style="padding-left: 10px;">
               End date is required</div>
        </bf:message>
       </bf:messages>
     </div>
   </div>
   <div style="clear:left; margin-top: 10px;">
     <input type="submit" value="Submit" />
   </div>
 </form>
 <div style="padding-left: 10px;">
   <p>
     * Click in the start/end date fields to see a calendar.
     <br />
     * All fields are required.<br />
     * The end date should be larger than the start date.
   </p>
 </div>
 <hr />
</div>
```

Here are some points to note:

- We apologize for using a table in this form. After struggling an hour or more with floating `div` elements jumping all over the page, we felt this is something that we should not repeat and gave up.

- The forms profile is loaded at the beginning. This is done because we want to make sure it is there.

- There are two hidden fields in the form that specify the request to the controller, an `insert` request and the database table this applies to. This is just a convenient way to pass these request parameters to the server. Whether a user is allowed to do the insert (a hacker could have changed the form) is checked again by the controller. Therefore, it is not a security risk to use a hidden field here.

- There are two simple fields to enter the name and a description for the trip.

- There are two `calendar` fields to specify the start and end date for the trip. We specified a format for the calendar: `format="yyyy-MM-dd"`. This format makes the resulting value acceptable as input for MySQL.

- All fields have the `bf:required="true"` attribute, which means that they are all required to be filled in. We tried to associate individual error messages to each field and to display them next to the field where the error occurs.

- There is one thing missing from this form: the check that the end date should be larger than the start date. To properly do this the Backbase way, we need to write some TDL. Therefore, we defer this to the Chapter 7, *Creating UI Components*, where TDL is discussed.

We take a short look back at what we discussed about our C3D sample application:

- We motivated the choice of this application and we gave an overview of its requirements.

- We showed its overall design according to the MVC pattern.

- A data model and several examples of the code were given.

- We certainly did not show all code. Specifically, we left out the PHP model classes and mini framework classes because we consider it outside the scope of this book to tell you how to access a database. Of course, the code is available for you to look at.

Even considering its limited functional scope, there are still certain things missing, both in the client application as in the server application, such as checking start and end date when adding a trip and validating the input fields again.

In the following chapters, we will expand the scope of the application by implementing the display of trip information, adding blog entries, and adding photos.

Summary

This was a long chapter where the subjects ranged from low level details about asynchronous communication between client and server to high level web application architecture. To develop solid web applications, at least a conceptual knowledge of these subjects is required.

We showed you the details of forms support in the Backbase framework and listed the BTL widgets available in this category.

We started to apply the knowledge acquired in these first four chapters to design and to develop a sample application for a travel blog site, the C3D application. This application will be expanded in future chapters.

In the next chapter, we will look at *data-bound* widgets.

5
Data-bound Widgets

Every web application contains data. In the beginning of the Web era, data, structure, and formatting were sent in one package from the server to the browser, as you all know. Then, CSS came along to separate formatting from data and structure. To separate structure and data, more is needed: still most web applications prepare the whole web page on the server and fill tables, select boxes, or other widgets that contain dynamic data, by weaving structure and data together.

Data binding makes the next step possible—the separation of structure and content.

Data binding is an interaction between a `dataSource` and a `dataObserver`. A `dataSource` only knows about data and how to retrieve it from a server. A `dataObserver` knows how to access the data presented by the `dataSource` and it maps the data retrieved onto elements that can be displayed in a browser.

If the data content is not put within HTML elements, it must be made available separately to the client web application. It is probably clear to you that usually AJAX communication is used for this. The "X" in AJAX suggests that the format the data is sent in should be XML. For practical purposes, that is mostly true in our book, but in reality, it is also rather popular to send data using the JavaScript Object Notation (JSON) format.

JSON is more lightweight than XML and easier to assemble. If you are sending lots of data, then this can be a performance advantage. But JSON is also less secure because there is a possibility to put data into a JSON stream that can be interpreted as malicious JavaScript.

Smart data-bound web applications do not need to send lots of data. You will never send more than what fits on a page and XML data is just as easy to assemble if you use a server framework and some sound design principles, as we will see later in this chapter. Therefore, we assume that all data will be XML, with some exceptions that should be transparent to the user of the Backbase framework.

In this chapter, we will look at data grids and other widgets that are data bound. We will discuss in detail what data binding is and why this is important for Rich Internet Application websites.

The Backbase framework offers the possibility to develop data-bound widgets. These are not sent in a rendered form from the server to the client, but are rendered in the client using content that is received as data from the server. Similarly, these widgets have the possibility to let their data content be updated by the user and these updates be sent back to the server transparently.

The interest for these so called data-bound widgets as a means to enable true Rich Internet Application applications is increasing steadily. We stumbled upon a survey a while ago that lists the features that people find most important in a framework. It lists that *data widgets* and *grids* are the top two features (`http://www.athenz.com/app/decision/statistics/ajax`) valued by the respondents to the survey. You will see that the Backbase framework does fulfill these requirements beautifully.

A central element to be used with the data binding facilities is the BTL `dataSource` element. This is the element that communicates with the server to receive data and provide this data in a uniform format to the data-bound widgets on the client. All data-bound widgets depend on `dataSource` to receive or update the data they are bound with.

Paired with a `dataSource` is a `dataObserver`. All data-bound objects inherit from `dataObserver`, which provides the interface definitions that these objects should adhere to.

There are several widgets in BTL that have built-in data-binding facilities, such as `dataGrid` or `dataMenu`. In addition, if the widget of your choice does not implement data binding, you can easily add the facilities you need.

The format of this chapter will be slightly different from that of the earlier chapters. We will concentrate on fundamentals of data binding and on examples for one particular widget: the BTL `dataGrid`. Even restricting ourselves to these topics will make this the longest chapter in the book. However, with this information, you will be well equipped to find out all you need for the other data-bound widgets available.

Finally, with our new knowledge, we will rework and expand our C3D sample application and make it into a usable prototype.

Here is a list of subjects that we will cover in this chapter:

- Why data binding is important and the server-side of it.
- Data-binding fundamentals, the `dataSource` element. Local and remote data sources.

- Making an HTML element data bound: `dataUL`.
- The data-bound BTL widgets.
- `DataGrid` and its eleven features—common header menu, header context menu, data paging, column drag-and-drop, column freezing, one-click editing, editing and focusing together, instant editing, collapsible info block, form editing, and live scrolling.
- Showing trips and trip entries for the C3D travel blog.

Why is data binding important?

To answer this question, we take a look at a simple example and we will contrast a non data-bound and a data-bound solution to display a set of data.

The inspiration for this example is associated with our experience in developing the *C3D travel blog* sample application. While being away in China, we were entering our travel experiences in the travel blog. We split up our long trip into parts, to get a better overview and to have more than one trip to show you, with realistic content. Therefore, we now have a list of trips, although still from only one user.

Assume that we would like to show an overview of the trips on our C3D website. We could display a simple HTML table, and it would look like this:

name	description	startDate	endDate
Amsterdam - Hong Kong	From Amsterdam to Hong Kong and one day in the city.	2009-05-16	2009-05-18
Changsha and Zhangjiajie	Conference TAMC 2009 in Changsha and post-conference tour to Zhangjiajie.	2009-05-18	2009-06-24
Guangzhou, Sun Yat-Sen University	Stay at the Sun Yat-Sen University, where Peter teaches game theory.	2009 05 24	2009-06-24
Guilin	A three day tour to the famous scenery of Guilin and surroundings.	2009-06-13	2009-06-15
Hong Kong and return to Amsterdam	A few days in Hong Kong and travel back home.	2009-06-24	2009-06-26

Even if you use fancy MVC techniques to develop your server-side application and templates to produce the view output, the final HTML source that is sent to the client browser has the data content mixed with the HTML table structure tags, as in the following code snippet:

```
<table border="1">
   <tr>
      <th width="150px">name</th>
      <th width="350px">description</th>
```

```
         <th width="100px" valign="top">startDate</th>
         <th width="100px" valign="top">endDate</th>
      </tr>
      <tr>
         <td>Amsterdam - Hong Kong</td>
         <td>From Amsterdam to Hong Kong and one day in the city
         </td>
         <td>2009-05-16</td>
         <td>2009-05-18</td>
      </tr>
      <!-- More rows here ... -->
      <tr>
         <td>Hong Kong and return to Amsterdam</td>
         <td>A few days in Hong Kong and travel back home.</td>
         <td>2009-06-24</td>
         <td>2009-06-26</td>
      </tr>
   </table>
```

This means that despite all your troubles to keep your server application clean, the client-side application has no MVC separation anymore for the table structure and its contents. If the amount of data is small and the data itself is static, that is no problem because you would never touch the client-side code. The situation changes when you are developing a Rich Internet Application. Consider these possibilities:

- The data is dynamically retrieved from a database and can change easily

- The amount of data is very large and cannot be displayed on one page

- The way the data is displayed needs to be flexible, allowing sorting of cell values in a column, reordering or hiding columns, or formatting cells

- Inline editing of the table is a requirement for your application

If you try to implement these features in your server application, you will find that the HTML your application produces will become very messy sooner or later. In addition, for every new table you are using you must more or less reinvent the wheel.

The solution to this problem is to use *data binding*. This means that the client web application provides the structure for the data and the data itself is retrieved dynamically from the server using AJAX requests.

What would the code look like when using a `dataGrid` from the Backbase framework? Here is a snippet from our C3D sample application:

```
<b:dataGrid width="100%"
   e:behavior="b:dataGridSortOneColumn"
   sortDirection="descending" sortField="startDate">
   <b:dataGridCol dataField="name"
      dataClass="t-area" width="150px">
      name
   </b:dataGridCol>
   <b:dataGridCol dataField="description"
   dataClass="t-area" width="250px">
      description
   </b:dataGridCol>
   <b:dataGridCol dataField="startDate" width="90px">
      start date
   </b:dataGridCol>
   <b:dataGridCol dataField="endDate" width="90px">
      end date
   </b:dataGridCol>
   <b:dataSource e:behavior="b:remoteData"
      url="../cntrl.php?req=tripdata"
      dataType="application/xml"
      requestType="application/xml" />
</b:dataGrid>
```

As you can see, in the client web application, there is no data content visible to the developer. He/she has only to deal with designing an appropriate structure to display the data. The data itself is retrieved by a special element named `dataSource`. Do not worry about the details yet, just notice that the table rows are sorted according to the start date column in descending order.

This is what the table from the previous picture looks like using a `dataGrid`:

name	description	start date ⌄	end date
Hongkong and return to Amsterdam	A few days in Hongkong and travel back home.	2009-06-24	2009-06-26
Guilin	A three day tour to the famous scenery of Guilin and surroundings.	2009-06-13	2009-06-15
Guangzhou, Sun Yat-Sen University	Stay at the Sun Yat-Sen University, where Peter teaches game theory.	2009-05-24	2009-06-24
Changsha and Zhangjiajie	Conference TAMC 2009 in Changsha and post-conference tour to Zhangjiajie.	2009-05-18	2009-06-24
Amsterdam - Hongkong	From Amsterdam to Hongkong and one day in the city.	2009-05-16	2009-05-18

Of course, you will not be fooled by the better looks of this grid: with appropriate CSS, you can make the original table look just as good. You may appreciate though, that out of the box this `dataGrid` has additional behavior that you can easily invoke. For example, the `e:behavior="b:dataGridSortOneColumn"` specification allows you to click on any column header and sort the rows in the table according to the values of the cells in that column.

If you keep the data locally on the client, the Backbase framework will handle the sorting and other functional behaviors that you may have specified. When using a remote data source, such as in the example in this section, your server script must be able to send the data according to the request received, such as ordering by values in a specific column.

This brings us to the point of the data binding itself. The `dataSource` widget acts as the spider in a web here. Its `url` attribute tells which server script will be invoked via an Ajax request when new data is needed. The server is asked to return an XML document by using `dataType="application/xml"`. The `dataSource` receives this XML document (alternatively it could be a JSON document) and supplies the data to its associated data-bound widgets (there could be more than one). The widget (in our example, a `dataGrid`) is responsible for rendering the data in the right way.

By looking at a part of the content of the XML document that could be sent back in this example, it may become clear how the mapping from database data to `dataGrid` content, the data binding, is established:

```
<records totalRecords="5" date="2009-06-16">
    <record>
        <id>1</id>
        <name>Amsterdam - Hongkong</name>
        <description>
```

```
    From Amsterdam to Hongkong and one day in the city.
    </description>
    <user>ghica</user>
    <startDate>2009-05-16</startDate>
    <endDate>2009-05-18</endDate>
  </record>
  <record>
    <id>2</id>
    <name>Changsha and Zhangjiajie</name>
    <description>
      Conference TAMC 2009 in Changsha and post-conference tour to
      Zhangjiajie.
    </description>
    <user>ghica</user>
    <startDate>2009-05-18</startDate>
    <endDate>2009-06-24</endDate>
  </record>
 <!-- More records -->
</records>
```

The `dataField` values in the `dataGridCol` elements correspond with the tag names in the XML document. To see the mapping to the data in the database, recall the structure of the `c3d_trip` table:

```
CREATE TABLE c3d_trip (
    id int(11) NOT NULL auto_increment,
    name VARCHAR(30),
    description TEXT,
    userId int(11),
    startDate DATE,
    endDate DATE,
    submitDate DATE,
    PRIMARY KEY (id)
) TYPE=MyISAM;
```

You will see that the XML tag names correspond to the column names in the table. In this way, we have a one-to-one mapping of columns in the `dataGrid` to columns in the table. However, this is mainly for convenience.

Actually, the Backbase framework provides much more complicated ways to do this mapping if you need it. Also, on the server-side, you may have complex queries to work with, where you will have to pull some tricks to get the column names right. However, if you use common sense naming conventions and design principles, then you probably never will have to deal with a situation more complex than the one described here.

The server-side of data binding

Our story so far, assumes that automagically the right data will appear in the right format at the client's doorstep after the client application made an AJAX request to the server. Of course, this is not a realistic assumption.

The Backbase framework claims to be **server agnostic,** meaning it does not know anything about what type of server it is dealing with. Therefore, it gives little attention in its documentation to application development on the server-side. This is understandable because there are many different programming languages that can be used and opinions about the right server-side architecture may vary.

In this book, we advocate a specific overall architecture according to the MVC design pattern for the web application, as we explained in the previous chapter. This is not enough for the data binding to work. The Backbase framework's data-bound widgets make specific assumptions about the structure of the data that is sent and it will make our development a lot easier if we develop some server-side functionality to help with this.

You already know that we have a database framework that is used with the C3D sample web application. It may be small and simple, but it does exactly what we need—connects to a database, executes a query, returns the results, and prevents SQL injection.

For this iteration of the development of our C3D application, we have added a class to this framework that takes a query, sends it off to the database classes, and converts the returned result to XML. It is called `bb_remoteDataSource`. When we show the new functionality added to the sample C3D application, we will show you some of its code.

Knowing now that we have this `bb_remoteDataSource` class available, what should we do to reply to a request to provide the XML as shown above? What you see next is the essential piece of code, taken from a class named `showTrips` in the `c3db` version of the application:

```
public function readTrips() {
   $sQuery=
      'SELECT t.id as id, name, description,
         u.username as user, startDate,
         endDate FROM c3d_trip t, c3d_user u
      WHERE t.userId = u.id';
   $sCountQuery =
      'SELECT COUNT(*) as iCount FROM c3d_trip';
   $datasource = new bb_remoteDataSource();
   return $datasource->asXml($sQuery, null, $sCountQuery);
}
```

Let's discuss this short piece of PHP:

- The query asks for all trip rows to be returned and it includes the username by joining the `c3d_trip` table with the `c3d_user` table.

- In our `dataGrid`, we are not using the username at the moment because so far there is only one user. If we need it later, we just add a column to the `dataGrid` and it will be shown.

- There is a second query that returns the number of rows in the result query. This second query can be useful if the first query is complex and the number of rows returned can also be found with a simpler query. The `pager` element needs to know this value because it must be able to display the number of pages in the result. In our example, the root element of the XML document has the attribute `totalRecords="5"` . This is the total number of rows in the table that can be used by the `pager`.

- We instantiate a new object of the class `bb_remoteDataSource`. Next, we ask to return XML, as converted from the query result. Because there is no parameter substitution in this example, the second argument in the call the `asXML` method is null.

- The `bb_remoteDataSource` class returns XML as a result of calling its `asXML` method. We have shown what this XML could look like in the previous section of this chapter. The tag names used here are `record` and `records`. These names are ignored by the `dataSource` because of the way we have set this up, just the tag names within a `record` tag matter. By making these tag names the same as the column names of the result of the SQL query, we can write a server script that generically handles the requests from our `dataSource`.

- Maybe you noticed the little downward pointing triangle in the header of the `startDate` column and saw that the dates were sorted as the last date first. You may have wondered why there is no ORDER BY in our query. This is because the `dataGrid` asks for the sorting by: `sortDirection="descending"` and `sortField="startDate"`. The server script (in our case `cntrl.php`) receives a request for ordering the rows and the `bb_remoteDataSource` class picks up the request parameters, modifies the SQL query, and returns the desired result.

- If you are interested in knowing what the request to the server really looks like, then an easy way to see it, is to execute the example in a Firefox browser, open *Firebug* and look at the request parameters. Of course, you must have the Firebug plugin installed.

This was a long explanation for a few lines of code. We hope to have convinced you of two things: a simple server framework to handle requests for data from a remote data source is very useful, and data binding makes your application more transparent and easier to develop.

We did not discuss all aspects of writing server-side scripts with respect to data binding. For example, the simple grid we were showing here does not allow for updates to be made. Our C3D sample application does not have the possibility for updating yet. This topic will be covered in the section *The eleven features of dataGrid*. For server-side code, you could look at the PHP code provided with these examples.

Historical note: On the Backbase developer website (`http://bdn.backbase.com`), you may find traces of older products, such as a JSF edition of the framework and a Java Data Services module. These products were discontinued in favor of their new flagship product, the *Rich Portal*, built upon the Backbase Client Framework.

Data-binding fundamentals

In fact, by looking at the design of the data-binding facilities, we have encountered another example of the *Observer pattern*. The first example was the MVC pattern that we used to partition our total web application into client and server layers.

The original description of the Observer pattern can be found in the famous **Gang of Four** (GOF) book (*Design Patterns: Elements of Reusable Object-Oriented Software, by Erich Gamma* and others), which we can sincerely recommend to read. Although it is already almost fifteen years old, its diagrams are in a pre-UML dialect, and its C++ code examples may not look so familiar, the content is still very valid. For your convenience, if you do not own the book, we found an online version of the Observer pattern, copied from the book, here: `http://www.research.ibm.com/designpatterns/example.htm`.

The purpose of the *Observer pattern* as stated by the Gang of Four is:

> *Define a one-to-many dependency between objects so that when one object changes state, all its dependents are notified and updated automatically.*

The overview picture shown in the following figure is based on the actual implementation of the data-binding features in the Backbase framework. Therefore, the class names differ from those in the book.

In the case of the Backbase framework and as applied to data binding, the object that can change state is the `dataSource`. The dependent objects that will be notified of such state changes all inherit from `dataObserver`. The concrete objects that inherit from `dataObserver` in the Backbase framework are for example `listGrid`, `dataGrid`, and `suggestBox`. The next diagram shows the inheritance structure:

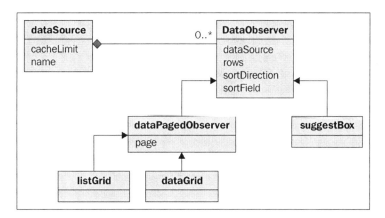

- A dataSource can have references to zero, one, or more dataObserver elements

- One of those observers can send a message to the dataSource to change the state of the dataSource

- When that happens, the dataSource will notify all its known dataObserver elements, which then can update their displayed data

Although a dataSource can have as many dataObserver elements attached to it as you like, in practice, there will mostly be only one.

How does a dataSource set its state? Behind the scenes it needs to obtain data from somewhere. Here, another design pattern comes into play, the *proxy* pattern. The intent of this pattern is described as:

> *Provide a surrogate or placeholder for another object to control access to it.*

This means that the dataSource allows its dataObserver elements access to the data via a defined API, independent of how the data is actually stored or made available.

The *other object* that the proxy pattern refers to, provides the real implementation hiding behind the API of the dataSource. It is attached to the dataSource in form of a so-called behavior. For now, we just say that a behavior is a generic functionality that can be attached to an element. We will see more behaviors in the next chapter, for example, to handle resizing of elements or drag-and-drop. The three behaviors that can be associated with a dataSource are indicating whether the dataSource will handle *local*, *remote*, or *static* data. You can specify these on the dataSource as follows:

- e:behavior = "b:localData", or

- e:behavior = "b:remoteData", or

- e:behavior = "b:staticData"

Let's look at the elements involved in data binding in more detail.

dataSource

The object that takes the role of being able to change state is the dataSource object. It also acts as a proxy to provide data when attaching behaviors. By itself, the dataSource inherits directly from element and has these attributes:

Attribute	Description
cacheLimit	The maximum number of records, usually rows in a grid that are kept in a cache by the dataSource. A high number can increase performance if large amounts of data need to be kept, at the cost of memory usage.
name	Optional name of the dataSource. The value of this attribute will be used to match with the value of the dataSource attribute of a dataObserver that wants to use this dataSource.

The methods that are available for dataSource are mostly intended to be able to attach and detach observers. The only method that you may want to use directly is the refresh method, which tells all attached observers to refresh their data.

The most important aspect of providing the data to a dataSource object is whether this data will be available *statically, locally,* or *remotely.* We will now look at the various ways to provide the data.

Local data sources

What is the effect of specifying e:behavior = "b:localData" as attribute on a dataSource element? First of all, it means that all the data is available in the client application. Even though the observer widget may not see all data simultaneously, no request to the server is needed when the observer widget requests new data.

For example, think of a data grid that can display 10 rows, while 100 rows are available on the client. A pager will handle the pagination of the data that is displayed.

The easiest way to make data available in the client locally is by using a dataContainer—an element that can contain inline data. Here is an example:

```
<b:dataSource e:behavior="b:localData"
    dataType="application/xml">
    <b:dataContainer>
        <xi:include href="tripdata.xml" />
    </b:dataContainer>
</b:dataSource>
```

tripdata.xml contains the actual data. It is indeed local data because the XInclude causes it to be included when the dataSource element is loaded.

The data content itself in tripdata.xml is the same as in the snippet we have shown before containing the XML trip data.

`dataType="application/xml"` tells the `dataSource` that its data is in XML format, as opposed to JSON. You may wonder why the `dataType` attribute was not shown in the list of attributes of `dataSource`, while it appears as such in the previous example. The effect of attaching the `localData` behavior to it is that it can now use the attributes that are defined for the `localData` behavior, which are as follows:

Attribute	Description
`asynchronous`	Immediately returns on a request without waiting for the results.
`dataSelect`	XPath expression to select records on which to operate. The default value points to the `dataContainer` child node inside the control.
`dataType`	Determines the language in which the data is stored, its value is either `application/xml` or `application/json`.

There are also interesting methods available for the `localData` behavior:

Method	Description
`pushData`	Sends the data to a server.
`sendRequest`	Sends request data to the server.

Refer to the Backbase API Reference for details of the arguments for these methods.

Remote data sources

If the data to be displayed is too large to be contained on the client, or highly dynamic, you can choose to load only portions of the data in the client and request data from the server only when needed.

We have already seen an example of a remote `dataSource` in the section *The server-side of data binding*. The code for this `dataSource` looked like this:

```
<b:dataSource e:behavior="b:remoteData"
    url="../cntrl.php?req=tripdata"
    dataType="application/xml"
    requestType="application/xml"/>
```

The `remoteData` behavior, our proxy object, has the same attributes as the `localData` behavior, with a few extra. They are as follows:

Attribute	Description
method	HTTP method used to open the connection (GET or POST).
requestType	Determines the data type in which the request is sent to a server. (application/xml or application/json).
url	Points to the URL where the data is stored. Usually, a server script that returns the data as result.
useTimestamp	Determines if a timestamp is used in the URL to prevent caching of requests.

A `dataSource` with `remoteData` behavior communicates with a server, by definition. The information it sends to the server is sent in a specific format, in order for the server to be able to decode the request and send an appropriate response.

The following table gives an overview of the set of parameters that are sent:

Parameter	Values	Default	Description
request	-	-	An XML or JSON string containing the request parameters and associated data.
action	read, sort, create, update, delete	-	The action that is to be performed on the data set.
rangeStart	-	-	The range start index for which data should be sent.
rangeEnd	-	-	The range end index for which data should be sent (inclusive).
sortDirection	ascending, descending	-	The direction in which the data should be sorted.
sortField	-	* [1]	The field (column) to be sorted.
dataType	application/ xml, text/json	application/xml	The format in which the data should be returned.
requestType	application/ xml, text/json	text/json	The format used for the parameter value.

You have already seen how these parameters arrive at the server in case the request is sent as JSON data. Later, we will see examples of how a server script can deal with these requests.

Static data sources

There is a third way of referring to data from a data source—the `staticData` behavior. It differs from the previous two by not allowing any operations on the data, such as sorting or editing. Similar to the `localData` behavior, the `staticData` behavior can be used with the `dataSelect` and `dataType` attributes. This behavior can be useful if you have a small amount of static data that needs to be displayed quickly and does not need to be updated.

dataObserver

The other fundamental object besides `dataSource` that participates in the data binding pattern is the `dataObserver` object. The `dataSource` object is a concrete object where the additional functionality is added by way of behaviors, as we have discussed in the previous sections. The `dataObserver` on the other hand, is an abstract object that the concrete widgets such as `dataGrid` and `suggestBox` inherit from.

In fact, any widget that is bound to data should inherit from `dataObserver`. `dataObserver` contains several attributes, properties, and methods that are used for data binding; the attributes are:

Attribute	Description
dataSource	The name of the `dataSource` element to which a connection is made. The value of this attribute must match the value of the `name` attribute of a `dataSource` element.
rows	The number of visible rows.
sortDirection	Indicates whether the initial sort direction is ascending or descending. With remote data sources, this attribute is passed as a parameter in data requests.
sortField	The field used for sorting. With remote data sources, this attribute is passed as a parameter in data requests.

The dataUpdate method

Of the methods available for `dataObserver`, we only describe the `dataUpdate` method. This method is automatically called by the data binding mechanism. This method must be reimplemented by all widgets that inherit from `dataObserver` because they will all need to determine how to display the data that is made available by the `dataSource`. In the next section, we will show an example of a `dataUpdate` method, as implemented for a custom, data-bound bulleted list.

The `dataUpdate` method has two arguments:

- `action`—a string, the value of which depends on what is supported by the particular `dataSource` behavior. Possible actions can be `create`, `read`, `update`, or `delete`.

- `records`—contains an array of identifiers of records that have been updated. For example, when the action is `read`, the array contains the identifiers of all the records that should be visible.

The `btl.dataSource.getValue` function is used to retrieve a value in a record. The first argument of this function is the reference to the `dataSource` that is observed. The second argument is the unique identifier of a record, which is usually one item in the `records` array. The third argument is the query string to query the data in the record.

Make an HTML element data bound

Before we dive into the description of the complex `dataGrid` widget, we would like to illustrate the data binding concept in depth by creating our own widget, a data-bound bulleted list. We need to use some Tag Definition Language to achieve this, which is not covered yet. Fear not, we will explain what we are doing and if needed, you can peek into Chapter 7.

Our goal is to show a bulleted list of the names in the `c3d_trip` table.

Creating the data source

To feed our data source with data, we need to extract it from the database. For the purpose of this example, we have done this in advance and have stored the result in an XML file, which allows us to use the trip information as local data. We showed the contents of this file earlier in this chapter.

We already talked about how to create a `dataSource` for this example. We show it again here:

```
<b:dataSource e:behavior="b:localData"
   dataType="application/xml" id="tripdata">
   <b:dataContainer>
      <xi:include href="tripdata.xml" />
   </b:dataContainer>
</b:dataSource>
```

Look back at the section about *Local data sources* for an explanation of the attributes and contained elements of this dataSource.

We gave the dataSource widget an id attribute with value tripdata. In most cases, you can avoid giving the dataSource an ID, for example, by placing the dataSource element as a child element of its observer (a dataGrid or other data-bound widget).

Define the new widget

To create a new widget definition, we must give it a *name* and a *namespace*. As name, we use dataUL and mimicking the conventions that Backbase uses for its namespaces, we have chosen http://www.squaringthecircles.com/squared, for which we use the sq prefix. The outline for our widget definition using Tag Definition Language then becomes:

```
<d:tdl xmlns="http://www.w3.org/1999/xhtml">
    <d:namespace
       name="http://www.squaringthecircles.com/squared">
       <d:element name="dataUL" extends="b:dataObserver">
          <d:template type="application/xhtml+xml">
             <!-- template code here -->
          </d:template>
          <d:method name="dataUpdate">
             <!-- the method here ... -->
          </d:method>
       </d:element>
    </d:namespace>
</d:tdl>
```

It requires no rocket science to see that we defined a new element with the required name and namespace. Just three points:

- The dataUL extends dataObserver. Therefore, dataUL inherits all the properties and methods from dataObserver. This also means that the new element should have a dataUpdate method because the one defined on dataObserver is abstract.

- The template tag defines the visible XHTML.

- The method tag has a name attribute with the value dataUpdate. This means that we are defining a dataUpdate method here. We will look at its implementation now.

The dataUpdate method

As said, the dataObserver object is abstract, and elements extending it must implement the dataUpdate method. The following listing shows the implementation for our dataUL widget:

```
<d:method name="dataUpdate">
    <d:argument name="action" />
    <d:argument name="records" />
    <d:body type="text/javascript">
        if(action == 'read'){
            var oSource = this.getProperty('dataSource');
            for(var i = 0; records.length > i; i++){
                var oLi = bb.document.createElement('li');
                var sTripName = btl.dataSource.getValue(oSource,
                    records[i], 'name');
                oLi.appendChild(
                    bb.document.createTextNode(sTripName));
                this.appendChild(oLi);
            }
        }
    </d:body>
</d:method>
```

Here are some points to note:

- When the method dataUpdate is called by the dataSource, two arguments will be provided—action and records. We described this in the previous section.

- The code in the body of the dataUpdate method shows that only a read action is acted upon.

- If it is a read action, the second argument, which contains the data records available, is iterated through. For every record, a new bullet item is created and the value of the name tag in the record is retrieved using the dataSource associated with the dataUL element. This value is used to create a text node for the bullet item.

We are now done with defining the widget.

Show the data-bound bulleted list

To use our new widget, we must make sure that our widget definition is included on the page and that we provide a namespace declaration. We can then create a bulleted list from our trip data simply as follows:

```
<sq:dataUL dataSource="tripdata" />
```

The `dataSource` with the `id="tripdata"` will serve the contents of `tripdata.xml` to the `dataUL` widget.

The result of the opening the page will be:

This completes the example showing a custom data-bound widget. We saw here that we can make any element data bound, including simple HTML elements as done in this example, by displaying a bulleted list that receives its content from a `dataSource`.

The data-bound widgets

There are a number of widgets available in the Backbase framework that can use a `dataSource` to provide the data content for the widget. These are as follows:

- `dataGrid`
- `listGrid`
- `dataMenu`
- `dataTree`
- `suggestBox`
- `treeGrid`

We already described the suggestBox in the previous chapter. The details for the remaining data-bound widgets could fill the rest of this book. Therefore, we made a choice and here we will only discuss the dataGrid and the fieldEditor that is handy when allowing editing of a grid. At the time of writing this book, the dataGrid is still a *Release Candidate*, as opposed to the listGrid, which has very similar functionality and is fully deployed. Our reason for choosing the dataGrid instead of the listGrid is that the dataGrid is better performing, more powerful, and more flexible. The dataGrid was developed as a replacement for the listGrid.

dataGrid

The dataGrid is a powerful mechanism for displaying tabular data. The dataGrid supports sorting, value formatting, and editing. Furthermore, there are some styling possibilities and it is possible to show smaller parts of data through a paging mechanism, rather than showing all data at once. It fetches the data from a dataSource that is specified with the dataSource attribute. The widget provides high performance and can work with thousands of cells.

The dataGrid is similar to a listGrid in functionality. However, the listGrid offers more formatting functionality out of the box, while the dataGrid will perform up to three times better for large amounts of data.

For the dataGrid widget, there are several built-in behaviors available:

- For sorting: dataGridSortOneColumn
- To edit a dataGrid, you need to add the dataGridEditCell behavior to the dataGrid
- For column freezing: dataGridFreezingUI

The most interesting elements that the dataGrid inherits from are: focusableElement, dimensionElement, and dataPagedObserver.

The dataGrid element has a set of specific attributes that you can use on top of the ones from the inherited elements . These attributes are described as follows:

Attribute	Description
defaultColumnWidth	Default column width.
frozenColumns	Number of initially frozen columns.
liveScrolling	Indicates whether live scrolling is enabled for the dataGrid.
maxPages	Maximum number of pages.
readonly	Indicates whether the dataGrid can be edited or not.
sortable	Determines whether the columns in the dataGrid can be sorted or not.

In addition to these attributes, there are also the attributes that are available when specifying a behavior such as `e:remoteData`, for which you saw the attributes earlier in this chapter.

The contents and format of a `dataGrid` can be specified with a number of child elements, first of all, the `dataGridCol` that specifies the columns. A `dataSource` can also be specified as child of a `dataGrid`, which is practical if the `dataSource` is only used in conjunction with the `dataGrid` of which it is a child, because in this case, you do not need an ID for the `dataSource`, opening possibilities to use the grid in a custom widget.

You have seen a simple example of using the `dataGrid` at the beginning of this chapter and a set of complicated examples are given in the section *The eleven features of dataGrid*. Before we start with these examples, we provide a description of `fieldEditor`, a widget that you can use to customize the editing facilities of a `dataGrid`.

Grid editing and fieldEditor

In many cases, it will be sufficient to specify the `dataGridEditCell` behavior when editing of the grid should be possible, because the default editing capabilities of the grid column elements will be sufficient. If you need custom editing facilities, you can use a `fieldEditor`.

A `fieldEditor` is used to define the content of a `dataGrid` cell when it is edited. For example, you can add a `select` element in the editor with predefined options, which will be displayed when the specific cell is edited. A `fieldEditor` can also be used for other data-bound elements such as `listGrid` and `treeGrid`.

Let's look at an example:

```
<b:dataGrid width="100%"
   e:behavior="b:dataGridSortOneColumn
      b:dataGridEditCell"
   sortDirection="descending"
    sortField="startDate" rows="10">
   <b:dataGridCol dataField="name"
      dataClass="t-area" width="150px">name</b:dataGridCol>
   <b:dataGridCol dataField="description"
      dataClass="t-area" width="250px">description
      <b:fieldEditor>
         <b:xhtml>
            <textarea />
         </b:xhtml>
      </b:fieldEditor>
```

```
    </b:dataGridCol>
    <b:dataGridCol dataField="startDate" dataType="date"
       width="90px">start date
    </b:dataGridCol>
    <b:dataGridCol dataField="endDate" dataType="date"
       width="70px">end date</b:dataGridCol>
    <b:dataSource e:behavior="b:remoteData"
        url="../c3db/cntrl.php?req=tripdata"
        dataType="application/xml"
        requestType="application/json" >
        <b:dataSchema identifier="id"/>
    </b:dataSource>
  </b:dataGrid>
```

The example should look familiar to you because it uses the same `dataGrid` that we used in the beginning of this chapter. There are some differences now that allow us to edit the grid:

- You can see that the grid has `dataGridEditCell` specified as behavior. This makes all cells editable. You can restrict columns from being editable by specifying that they are `readonly`.

- We added `dataType="date"` to the `startDate` and `endDate` columns. This will have the effect that a `calendar` widget will appear when clicking on a cell in these columns. We do not need a `fieldEditor` to make this happen.

- The trip description can be rather long, but the default editor for a string type column is an input field. Therefore, we specified a `textArea` here to have a larger area that can be used to enter text. We have put `b:xhrml` tags around the `textArea` to tell the Backbase runtime engine that it does not need to touch this element.

- The `dataSource` will send an update request to the server with the changes made to the grid. The server needs to know which records are involved, in order to be able to do a proper update of the database tables. For this purpose, we need to send an ID. We can achieve this by adding a `dataSchema` to the grid, and giving it the attribute `identifier="id"`, where id is the name of our identifier column. A `dataSchema` allows for intricate mappings between the XML received from the server and the columns in the grid, but as we said earlier, avoid this if possible.

The full source code, including the server-side PHP code, can be found with the source code for this book, as is the case for the code for the eleven features discussed in the next sections.

The eleven features of dataGrid

The dataGrid is a complex widget that offers a variety of features. Some are easy to make use of, because their functionality is pre-built and they can easily be added by attaching a behavior with e:behavior attribute. Others require additional coding, but thanks to the dataGrid, the architecture of this coding is still simple.

In this section, we present eleven examples of using the dataGrid. The source code for the examples can, as always, be found in the source code package for the book; they are placed in the folder dataGrid11.

The examples show various display, interaction, and editing facilities. They make use of a rather large table that contains fake personal data. The table is stored in an SQLite database and there is a PHP script to access the data. This PHP script is rather different from the server framework classes we are using for the C3D sample application because it is a custom built piece of code, made for just this table and for SQLite access. It contains many tips and tricks that are worth looking at. However, here we will concentrate on the client-side of the examples.

The dataSource used is the same in all eleven examples:

```
<b:dataSource name="mySource" dataType="application/json"
  e:behavior="b:remoteData"
  url="../data/dataSqlite3Contacts.php?dataType=json">
  <b:dataSchema identifier="id">
    <b:dataField name="First" select="firstName" />
    <b:dataField name="Last" select="lastName" />
    <b:dataField name="Gender" select="gender" />
    <b:dataField name="Email" select="email" />
    <b:dataField name="Country" select="country"
        format="style[color:darkblue]" />
    <b:dataField name="Origin" select="origin" />
    <b:dataField name="Status" select="status" />
    <b:dataField name="Birthdate" select="birthdate" />
    <b:dataField name="Rating" select="rating" />
    <b:dataField name="liedetector" select="liedetector" />
    <b:dataField name="Name" select="name" />
    <b:dataField name="Age" select="age" />
  </b:dataSchema>
  <e:handler event="error" type="application/javascript">
    alert('data source error:\n' + event.message)
  </e:handler>
</b:dataSource>
```

We will not show complete listings for all examples because that would take too much space and it would not help with understanding of the described features. We will indicate for each example what the filename is and where you can find the particular code for that example.

Now, let's look at the eleven features of dataGrid:

Common header menu

The source code for this example can be found in xml/menu.xml.

We will start our walk through the features of dataGrid with a very simple example: enabling common context menu for column headers. In many applications, the header menu that is activated when you click your right mouse button is the same for all columns. Such a menu can then offer often used functionality. In this example, you can hide or show columns.

The grid definition is as follows:

```
<b:dataGrid rows="20" height="400px"
    e:behavior="b:dataGridSortOneColumn">
    <!-- The dataSource goes here -->
    <b:dataGridColGroup class="test-69F-bold">
        <img src="../media/11.png" />
        <b>Names</b>
        <b:dataGridCol dataField="First" width="150px"
            dataType="html">
            <img src="../media/26.png" />
            <b>First name</b>
        </b:dataGridCol>
          <b:dataGridCol dataField="Last" label="Last name" />
    </b:dataGridColGroup>
    <b:dataGridCol dataField="Gender" label="Gender" />
    <b:dataGridCol dataField="Email" label="Email"
        display="false" />
    <b:dataGridCol dataField="Country" label="Country" />
    <b:dataGridCol dataField="Rating" label="Rating" />
    <!-- The menu pop-up goes here -->
    <!-- The contextmenu event handler goes here -->
</b:dataGrid>
```

Here is a picture of the grid in action:

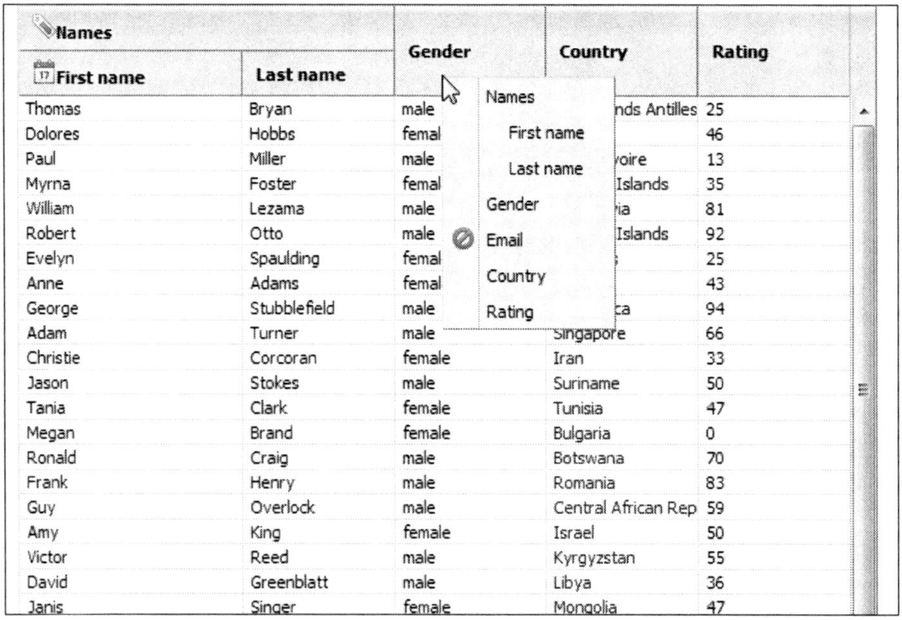

By using a `dataGridColGroup` element to contain `dataGridCol` elements, you can, as the name suggests, group columns together. See the previous screenshot for what this will look like.

Next, we show the code for the context menu:

```
<b:menuPopUp id="gridContextMenu">
   <b:menuPopUpItem label="Names" />
   <b:menuPopUpItem>
      <b:label style="padding-left:15px">
         First name</b:label>
   </b:menuPopUpItem>
   <b:menuPopUpItem>
      <b:label style="padding-left:15px">
      Last name</b:label>
   </b:menuPopUpItem>
   <b:menuPopUpItem label="Gender" />
   <b:menuPopUpItem label="Email" />
   <b:menuPopUpItem label="Country" />
   <b:menuPopUpItem label="Rating" />
<!-- A  click in the menu hides or shows corresponding
      column or columns group -->
```

```
<e:handler event="DOMActivate"
    type="application/javascript">
    var oMenuItem = event.target;
    if (oMenuItem){
        if ( oMenuItem.hidden) {
            oMenuItem.column.show();
        }
        else {
            oMenuItem.column.hide();
        }
    }
</e:handler>
</b:menuPopUp>
```

The menu has an event handler that causes a column to be hidden or shown as a toggle when its name is clicked.

In order to achieve the required behavior when interacting with the grid, we will listen to the contextmenu menu event on dataGrid element. Once it occurs, we will check the origin of the event and if it is the dataGrid header, we will walk through the collection of dataGrid columns and apply column states to the menu items.

```
<!-- show the menu -->
<e:handler event="contextmenu" type="application/javascript"> <![CDATA[
    var oCell =
        bb.selector.queryAncestor( event.viewTarget,
        "td.btl-grid-header");//show the menu only in the header
    if ( oCell) {
        var oMenu =
         bb.document.getElementById('gridContextMenu');
        if (oMenu) {
            //draw columns state
            var oGrid = oMenu.getProperty('parentNode');
            var aCols = oGrid.getProperty('columns');
            var aItems =
                oMenu.getElementsByTagName('b:menuPopUpItem');
            var iHiddenCount = 0, iLastVisible = -1;
            for( var i = 0; aCols.length > i; i++ ){
                var ind = i + 1;
                aItems[ind].column = aCols[i];
                if (aItems[ind].hidden =
                    aCols[i].getProperty('hidden')) {
                    bb.html.addClass(
                    aItems[ind].viewNode, 'contextMenu-hidden');
                    iHiddenCount++;
```

```
                }
                else {
                    bb.html.removeClass( aItems[ind].viewNode,
                        'contextMenu-hidden');
                    iLastVisible = ind;
                }
                aItems[ind].setAttribute('disabled', 'false');
            }
            var oGroup =
                oGrid.getElementsByTagName
                    ('b:dataGridColGroup')[0];
            aItems[0].column = oGroup;
            if (aItems[0].hidden =
                oGroup.getProperty('hidden'))
                bb.html.addClass( aItems[0].viewNode,
                    'contextMenu-hidden');
            else
                bb.html.removeClass( aItems[0].viewNode,
                    'contextMenu-hidden');
            //disable some items to prevent hiding last column
            var iGroupVisibleColumns =
                (aItems[1].hidden ? 0 : 1) +
                (aItems[2].hidden ? 0 : 1);
            if (iHiddenCount >= 6 - iGroupVisibleColumns)
                //all hidden except group's columns
                aItems[0].setAttribute('disabled', 'true');
            else
                aItems[0].setAttribute('disabled', 'false');
            if (iLastVisible >= 0 && iHiddenCount >= 5)
                //one column is visible
                aItems[iLastVisible].setAttribute('disabled',
                    'true');
            oMenu.open(oCell, 'at-pointer');
            event.preventDefault(); //prevent browser menu
        }
    }
]]></e:handler>
```

Header context menu

The source code for this example can be found in `xml/menu2.xml`.

This is a variation of the previous example. It will also enable the column header context menu, but in a little bit different way.

The `dataGrid` used is the same as in the previous example. Therefore, we are not showing it here. The `menuPopUp` is different from the previous one. It does not act on all columns but on a specific column and row. This allows you to perform actions such as sending an e-mail to the address in the selected row. You are also able to delete rows, which then will be permanently deleted. In a later example, there is an option to restore the table from a backup copy.

Here is the code for the `menuPopUp`:

```
<b:menuPopUp id="gridContextMenu">
   <b:menuPopUpItem align="left" label="Hide column">
      <e:handler event="click" type="application/javascript">
         this.getProperty('parentNode').context.column.hide();
      </e:handler>
   </b:menuPopUpItem>
   <b:menuPopUpItem label="Sort column">
      <e:handler event="click" type="application/javascript">
         var oContext =
            this.getProperty('parentNode').context;
         oContext.grid.sortColumn( oContext.column);
      </e:handler>
   </b:menuPopUpItem>
   <b:menuPopUpItem label="Send message to ..."
      disabled="true">
      <e:handler event="click" type="application/javascript">
         alert('Message sent');
      </e:handler>
   </b:menuPopUpItem>
   <b:menuPopUpSeparator />
   <b:menuPopUpItem label="Delete ..." disabled="true">
      <e:handler event="click" type="application/javascript">
         var oContext =
            this.getProperty('parentNode').context;
         oContext.grid.deleteRecords( [oContext.recordId]);
      </e:handler>
   </b:menuPopUpItem>
</b:menuPopUp>
```

In the next picture, you see what the menu looks like when activated over a header. When you activate it over a row, you will see the other options too.

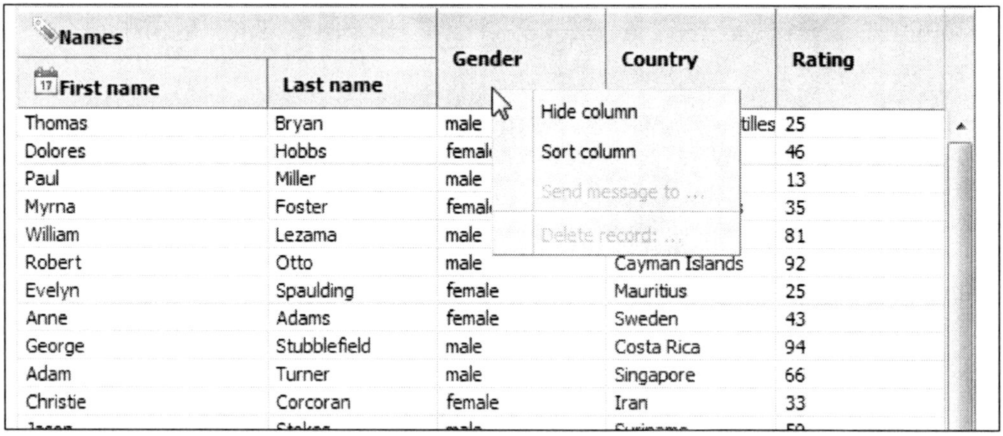

The following code is from the `contextmenu` event handler on the `dataGrid`:

```
<!-- show the menu -->
<e:handler event="contextmenu" type="application/javascript">
    var cell = bb.selector.queryAncestor(
        event.viewTarget, "td");
    var oCol = this.getColumn( cell);
    if ( oCol) {
        var oMenu =
            bb.document.getElementById('gridContextMenu');
        if (oMenu) {
            if (oCol) {
                var aCols = this.getProperty('columns');
                var iVisibleCount = 0;
                for( var i = 0; aCols.length > i; i++ )
                    if (!aCols[i].getProperty('hidden'))
                        iVisibleCount++;
                //initialize menu items
                var bGroup = bb.instanceOf(oCol, btl.namespaceURI,
                    "gridColGroup");
                var bVisible = !oCol.getProperty('hidden');
                var aItems =
                    oMenu.getElementsByTagName('b:menuPopUpItem');
                //Hide
                aItems[0].setAttribute('display',
                    bVisible ? '' : 'none');
                aItems[0].setAttribute('disabled',
                    iVisibleCount > 1 ? 'false' : 'true');
```

```
//Sort
aItems[1].setAttribute('disabled',
    bGroup ? 'true' : 'false');
var recordId = this.getRecordId( cell);
var oDataSource = this.getProperty('dataSource');
var bNoRecord = recordId === null || recordId == '';
var sName = bNoRecord ? '...' :
    btl.dataSource.getValue( oDataSource, recordId,
    'Name', false);
//send message
aItems[2].setAttribute('label',
    'Send message to ' + sName);
aItems[2].setAttribute('disabled', bNoRecord);
//delete row
aItems[3].setAttribute('label',
    'Delete record: ' + sName);
aItems[3].setAttribute('disabled', bNoRecord);
oMenu.context =
    {'grid' : this,
        'column' : oCol, 'recordId' : recordId};
oMenu.open(event.viewTarget, 'at-pointer');
event.preventDefault();
            }
        }
    }
</e:handler>
```

Data paging

The source code for this example can be found in `xml/paging.xml`.

Paging is a powerful mechanism that is often useful when a large dataset needs to be displayed in `dataGrid`. Instead of loading and rendering huge amounts of data at once, we can retrieve smaller page-size datasets, thus reducing traffic and load on both, the server as well as the client.

The most important widget here is the `pager`. You can place it, for example, next to the `dataGrid`. In order to provide you with a granular control over its functional behavior, there are several more widgets that you can put into `pager` as children—`pagerButton`, `pagerSeparator`, and `pagerJumper`. Take a look at the next code snippet and you will quickly find out how to make use of the features:

```
<b:dataGrid id="testGrid" rows="50"
  height="600px" width="auto">
    <!-- The columns are placed here -->
</b:dataGrid>
```

```
<b:pagerBar width="auto">
   <b:pager for="id('testGrid')" width="250px">
      <b:pagerButton type="First" />
      <b:pagerButton type="Previous" />
      <b:pagerSeparator />
      <b:pagerJumper />
      <b:pagerSeparator />
      <b:pagerButton type="Next" />
      <b:pagerButton type="Last" />
   </b:pager>
</b:pagerBar>
```

The next picture shows what the `pager` looks like when used with the `dataGrid`:

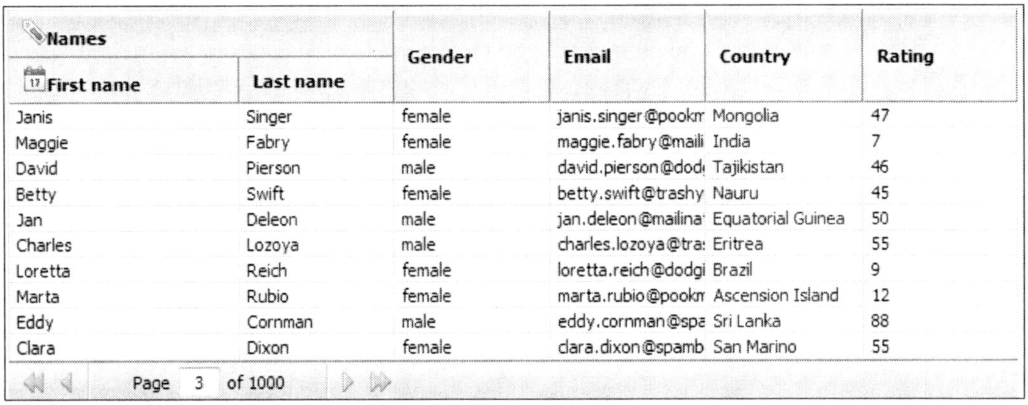

Names		Gender	Email	Country	Rating
First name	Last name				
Janis	Singer	female	janis.singer@pookm	Mongolia	47
Maggie	Fabry	female	maggie.fabry@maili	India	7
David	Pierson	male	david.pierson@dod	Tajikistan	46
Betty	Swift	female	betty.swift@trashy	Nauru	45
Jan	Deleon	male	jan.deleon@mailina	Equatorial Guinea	50
Charles	Lozoya	male	charles.lozoya@tra	Eritrea	55
Loretta	Reich	female	loretta.reich@dodgi	Brazil	9
Marta	Rubio	female	marta.rubio@pookn	Ascension Island	12
Eddy	Cornman	male	eddy.cornman@spa	Sri Lanka	88
Clara	Dixon	female	clara.dixon@spamb	San Marino	55

Page 3 of 1000

Column drag-and-drop

The source code for this example can be found in `xml/columnDnD.xml`.

In some applications, it can be useful to allow end user to move columns around within the `dataGrid` widget. If a user is more interested in viewing column A and column B, he will probably want to move these columns in front. This can improve the user's experience and in the end his/her efficiency working with dataset.

Adding a reorderable columns feature to a `dataGrid` is as simple as adding the `b:gridColumnDnD` behavior to its list of behaviors:

```
<b:dataGrid rows="50" height="600px"
   e:behavior="b:gridColumnDnD">
   <!-- The columns are placed here -->
</b:dataGrid>
```

In the following screenshot, we have tried to catch the act of dragging the **Gender** column behind the **Email** column:

Names					
First name	Last name	Gender	Email	Country Gender	Rating
Thomas	Bryan	male	thomas.bryan@mail	Netherlands Antilles	25
Dolores	Hobbs	female	dolores.hobbs@poc	Mali	46
Paul	Miller	male	paul.miller@spambo	Cote d'Ivoire	13
Myrna	Foster	female	myrna.foster@span	Falkland Islands	35
William	Lezama	male	william.lezama@mail	Yugoslavia	81
Robert	Otto	male	robert.otto@pookm	Cayman Islands	92
Evelyn	Spaulding	female	evelyn.spaulding@s	Mauritius	25
Anne	Adams	female	anne.adams@trash	Sweden	43
George	Stubblefield	male	george.stubblefield	Costa Rica	94
Adam	Turner	male	adam.turner@spam	Singapore	66
Christie	Corcoran	female	christie.corcoran@s	Iran	33

It will certainly be more convincing if you try this for yourself.

Column freezing

The source code for this example can be found in `xml/columnFreeze.xml`.

Another useful feature of the `dataGrid` widget is *column freezing*. When a dataset has more columns than what can be viewed at a time within the `dataGrid` viewport, it may be useful to freeze several first columns so that when scrolling the rest of columns horizontally, the frozen ones' position would be persisted at the start.

In order to achieve the described behavior, we only need to add `b:gridFreezingUI` behavior to the `dataGrid` and that's it! The initial amount of frozen columns can be specified in the `frozenColumns` attribute. At runtime, this value can be updated when a change is caused by the user interaction or the script.

In the code snippet below, you see that the number of frozen columns is 2. For brevity, we left out the code for the columns. To make the column freezing more interesting, there are more columns in the `dataGrid` than in the previous examples.

```
<b:dataGrid rows="10" height="auto" width="600px"
    e:behavior="b:dataGridFreezingUI" id="testGrid"
    frozenColumns="2">
    <!-- the columns go here -->
</b:dataGrid>
```

The next picture shows the effect of the column freezing when you move the scrollbar to the right.

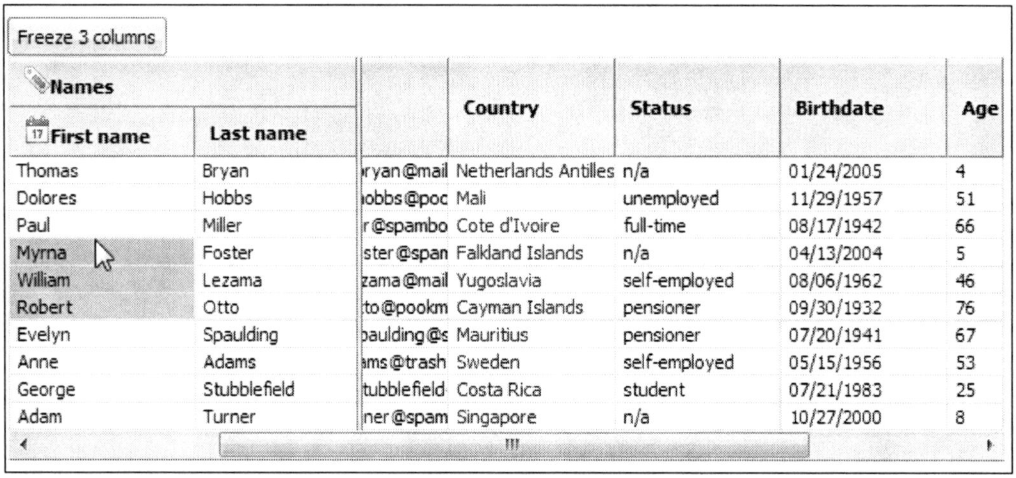

Names		Country	Status	Birthdate	Age
First name	Last name				
Thomas	Bryan	ryan@mail Netherlands Antilles	n/a	01/24/2005	4
Dolores	Hobbs	obbs@poc Mali	unemployed	11/29/1957	51
Paul	Miller	r@spambo Cote d'Ivoire	full-time	08/17/1942	66
Myrna	Foster	ster@span Falkland Islands	n/a	04/13/2004	5
William	Lezama	zama@mail Yugoslavia	self-employed	08/06/1962	46
Robert	Otto	to@pookm Cayman Islands	pensioner	09/30/1932	76
Evelyn	Spaulding	aulding@s Mauritius	pensioner	07/20/1941	67
Anne	Adams	ms@trash Sweden	self-employed	05/15/1956	53
George	Stubblefield	tubblefield Costa Rica	student	07/21/1983	25
Adam	Turner	ner@spam Singapore	n/a	10/27/2000	8

At the top of the picture, there is a button. When clicked, the number of frozen columns will be changed to 3, using the following code:

```
<b:button width="7em">
   Freeze 3 columns
   <e:handler event="click" type="application/xml">
      <c:setAttribute with="id('testGrid')"
         name="frozenColumns" select="3" />
   </e:handler>
</b:button>
```

If you try the example and move your mouse over the rows in the grid, you will see that the cells in the column under the mouse are animated with various shades of a blue color. This is an example of simple tricks that you can do with the grid. We are using a functionality here that we haven't discussed yet. Therefore, the code may pose problems to you right now. We will cover animation and view handling in the following chapter.

```
<e:handler event="mouseenter" match="td.btl-grid-data"
   type="application/javascript">
   //track the mouse
   var oAnimationInfo = {
      attributeName: "background-color",
      attributeType:"CSS", dur: "500ms",
      from:"#7CF", to: "#FFF"
   }
```

```
    var cell = event.currentView;
    bb.smil.animateColor(cell, oAnimationInfo);
</e:handler>
```

One-click editing

The source code for this example can be found in `xml/editor.xml`.

In the previous sections, we have learned about features that mainly concerned `dataGrid`'s general appearance and behavior. Here, we will start looking into more practical aspects—enabling data editing within the `dataGrid` widget.

- Click on a cell to start editing.

- Pressing the *Esc* key leaves editing mode without saving.

- Clicking on another cell saves the current cell if its contents are changed and editing the new cell is started.

- Leave editing mode: Press the *Esc* key without saving, or the *Enter* key with saving the current changes. Use the arrow keys *PageUp*, *PageDown*, *Home*, *End*, *Home + Home*, and *End + End* to move edit focus.

- Press *Enter* key or *F2* key to start editing or you may just start typing (not too fast, this is still an experimental feature).

The magic is made possible with the `fieldEditor` element, child of `dataGridCol`, and with the `b:dataGridEditCell` behavior attached. Place a user input widget into that element and you are done. The `dataGrid` widget will do the rest of the work.

First, we show the `dataGrid` itself with columns having a default editor:

```
<b:dataGrid dataSource="mySource" rows="50"
    width="600px" height="600px"
    e:behavior="b:dataGridEditCell">
    <b:dataGridColGroup>
        <img src="../media/11.png" />
        <b>Names</b> <!-- default editor: input -->
        <b:dataGridCol dataField="First">
            First name</b:dataGridCol>
            <!-- default editor: input -->
        <b:dataGridCol dataField="Last" label="Last name" />
    </b:dataGridColGroup>
  <!-- columns with special editors go here -->
</b:dataGrid>
```

The remaining columns have specific editing capabilities, either because we attached a specific editor or because their data type is something else as string. Here is a picture of one of the custom editors in action:

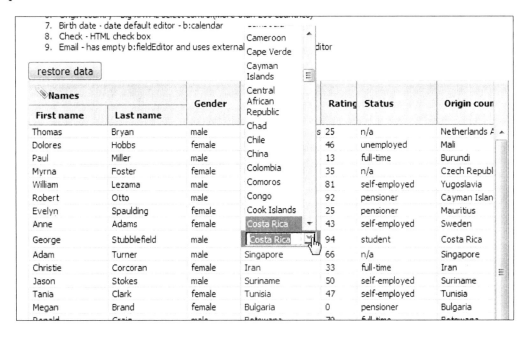

In the next editor, the cells in the Gender column show two radio buttons when edited. Here is the code:

```
<!-- editor: radio buttons inside b:xhtml -->
<b:dataGridCol dataField="Gender" width="6em"
    title="Radio buttons inside b:xhtml">
    Gender
    <b:fieldEditor>
        <b:xhtml>
            <input name="gender" type="radio"
                value="male" id="male" />
            <label for="male">Male</label>
            <br />
            <input name="gender" type="radio"
                value="female" id="female" />
            <label for="female">Female</label>
        </b:xhtml>
    </b:fieldEditor>
</b:dataGridCol>
```

The Country column cells show a large comboBox when edited:

```
<!-- editor: big b:comboBox -->
<b:dataGridCol dataField="Country" label="Country">
    <b:fieldEditor>
        <xi:include href="bigCombo.xml" />
    </b:fieldEditor>
</b:dataGridCol>
```

For the Rating column, a spinner will be shown by default because the data type is number:

```
<!-- default editor: spinner -->
<b:dataGridCol dataField="Rating" label="Rating"
    width="4em" dataType="number"
    title="default editor - spinner" />
```

The Status column has an XHTML select box:

```
<!-- editor: XHTML control -->
<b:dataGridCol dataField="Status" title="XHTML control">
    Status
    <b:fieldEditor>
        <select style="width:100%">
            <option>full-time</option>
            <option>n/a</option>
            <option>part-time</option>
            <option>pensioner</option>
            <option>self-employed</option>
            <option>student</option>
            <option>unemployed</option>
        </select>
    </b:fieldEditor>
</b:dataGridCol>
```

The Origin column has a big select box:

```
<!-- editor: a large XHTML select control -->
<b:dataGridCol dataField="Origin" width="150px"
    title="Large XHTML select control">
    Origin country
    <b:fieldEditor>
        <xi:include href="bigSelect.xml" />
    </b:fieldEditor>
</b:dataGridCol>
```

The `Birth Date` column has a `calendar` as editor by default because it has a *date* data type:

```
<!-- default editor: calendar -->
<b:dataGridCol dataField="Birthdate" dataType="date"
   title="default editor - calendar">
   <img src="../media/26.png" />
   Birth date
</b:dataGridCol>
```

The `Age` column cannot be edited:

```
<b:dataGridCol dataField="Age" label="Age"
   dataClass="readonly"
   readonly="true" width="3em"
   title="Read only field. Try to change a birtdate field." />
```

The `Check` column has a `checkbox` input:

```
<!-- editor: checkbox -->
<b:dataGridCol dataField="liedetector"
   width="50px" title="checkbox">
   Check
   <b:fieldEditor>
      <input type="checkbox" value="pass" />
      Pass
   </b:fieldEditor>
</b:dataGridCol>
```

Here is an example of an external editor with which you can edit the e-mail address. Firstly, we'll have a look at the screenshot of an external editor:

Now, let's look at the code:

```
<!-- editor: external editor -->
<b:dataGridCol dataField="Email" label="Email"
   title="external editor and edit events">
   <b:fieldEditor>
      <e:handler event="editStart"
```

```
        type="application/javascript">
    var arr = this.getProperty('value').split('@');
    var eName = document.getElementById('name');
    eName.value = arr[0];
    var eSite = document.getElementById('site');
    eSite.value = arr[1];
    bb.html.position(eName.parentNode, this.viewNode);
    //show the editor form
    eName.parentNode.style.display = 'block';
    eName.focus();
</e:handler>
<e:handler event="editFinish"
        type="application/javascript">
    var eName = document.getElementById('name');
    this.setProperty('value', eName.value + '@' +
        document.getElementById('site').value);
    eName.parentNode.style.display = 'none';
</e:handler>
    </b:fieldEditor>
</b:dataGridCol>
```

The external editor needs some sneaky invisible buttons, which are made visible when the editor is invoked:

```
<b:xhtml>
    <div style="display:none;
        background-color:#F96;position:absolute;
        top:200px;left:200px;width:300px;padding:20px;">
        <input id="name" style="width:120px;" />
            @
        <input id="site" style="width:120px;" />
        <p>
            <button onclick=
                "bb.document.getElementsByTagNameNS(
                btl.namespaceURI, 'dataGrid')[0].
                editFinish(true)">
            Save
            </button>
            <button onclick=
                "bb.document.getElementsByTagNameNS(
                    btl.namespaceURI, 'dataGrid')[0].
                        editFinish(false)">
            Cancel
            </button>
        </p>
    </div>
</b:xhtml>
```

On the picture, you can also see the **restore data** button we promised earlier. It allows you to mess up the table and start over again with a fresh copy.

```
<button onclick=
   "btl.dataSource.actionRequest(
      bb.document.getElementsByTagName('b:dataGrid')[0],
         'restore')">
   restore data
</button>
```

Here is the event handler of the dataGrid that does the refresh when a response from a restore is received:

```
<!-- update the whole grid with restored data -->
<e:handler event="actionResponse"
   type="application/javascript">
   if (event.action == 'restore')
      this.refresh();
</e:handler>
```

Editing and focusing together

The source code for this example can be found in xml/editor2.xml.

The editing experience would be greatly improved if it was possible to work with data using keyboard only. Jumping between cells with the *Tab* key without the need to touch the mouse can easily be enabled with the b:gridRowFocusAndSelect behavior. Having two behaviors, the new one and the one used in the previous example, will turn our grid into a full-blown spreadsheet:

- Editing
- Focusing and selecting

The code for this example and the previous example is the same, except for the added behavior. Therefore, we only show the dataGrid element:

```
<b:dataGrid dataSource="mySource" rows="50"
   width="600px" height="600px"
   e:behavior="b:dataGridRowFocusAndSelect
   b:dataGridEditCell">
   <!--   columns, event handlers, editors etc. go here -->
</b:dataGrid>
```

	Rating	Status	Origin country	Birth date	Check	Email
Antilles	25	n/a	Netherlands Antilles	01/24/2005	pass	thomas.bryan@mail
	46	unemployed	Mali	11/29/1957	pass	dolores.hobbs@poc
	13	full-time	Burundi	08/17/1942	pass	paul.miller@spambo
ds	35	n/a	Czech Republic	04/13/2004	pass	myrna.foster@span
	81	self-employed	Yugoslavia	08/06/1962		william.lezama@mail
ds	92	pensioner	Cayman Islands	09/30/1932		robert.otto@pookm
	25	pensioner	Mauritius	07/20/1941	pass	evelyn.spaulding@s
	43	self-employed	Sweden	05/15/1956	pass	anne.adams@trash
	94	student	Costa Rica	07/21/1983	pass	
	66	n/a	Singapore	10/27/2000	pass	
	33	full-time	Iran	06/09/1979	pass	
	50	self-employed	Suriname	11/06/1947		
	47	self-employed	Tunisia	10/01/1919		
	0	pensioner	Bulgaria	09/20/1934	pass	
	70	full-time	Botswana	06/20/1964		
	83	n/a	Romania	06/21/1999		frank.henry@pookm
n Rep	59	self-employed	Central African Republic	08/20/1987	pass	guy.overlock@dodg
	50	student	Israel	06/25/1987	pass	amy.king@pookmail
	55	pensioner	Kyrgyzstan	08/23/1937	pass	victor.reed@dodgit

george.stubblefield @ dodgit.com

[Save] [Cancel]

Instant editing

The source code for this example can be found in `xml/instantEdit.xml`.

In this example, a contrast is made between two `dataGrid` elements, one with the usual editing capabilities and another one (actually the first one shown) with inline editing elements where all the changes are sent to a server immediately. We are only showing a picture:

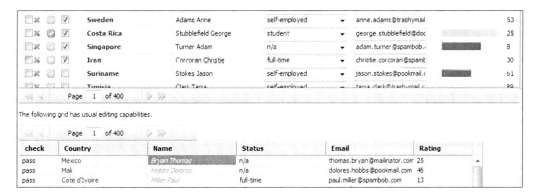

Collapsible info block

The source code for this example can be found in `xml/infoBlock.xml`.

When you try this example, you will notice the tiny **+** signs in the first column. When you click on one, it gets replaced by a **-** sign and underneath, in an orange block, the details for that row are shown.

In this example, actually in the previous example also but we did not tell you then, an architectural feature of the Backbase framework surfaces, which we tried to hide from you before. This is the existence of two layers in the Backbase areas, a *controller* layer and a *view* layer. We will talk more about this in Chapter 7, which is about the Tag Definition Language. For now, you should know that the view layer, as seen by the browser, contains an ordinary HTML table representing the `dataGrid`, while the controller layer contains the column structure and the functionality that you have seen in action in the previous examples.

What happens in this example is that when you click on the **+** sign, an extra row in the HTML table is made visible that was created when the `dataGrid` was created. We show only relevant parts of the code, first the `dataGrid`:

```
<b:dataGrid dataSource="mySource" id="testGrid" rows="25"
  width="auto" height="auto">
  <!--    the column contains +/- to toggle the info section -->
  <b:dataGridCol render="none" resizable="false"
     dataClass="render-image-toggle" width="16px" />
  <b:dataGridCol dataField="Name"
     label="Name" width="150px" />
  <b:dataGridCol dataField="Email" label="Email"
     width="250px" />
</b:dataGrid>
```

Next, we show the event handler that acts like a field creator:

```
<e:handler event="pageRefreshed" type="application/javascript">
   //render column #1 with +/-
   var grid = this;
   var oDataSource = this.getProperty('dataSource');
   var eTemplate =
      document.getElementById('template').firstChild;
   //use selector API to get just created cells
   var arr =
     bb.selector.queryAll( grid.viewNode, 'td.render-image-toggle');
   for(var i=0; arr.length > i; i++) {
      //now render their content—create controls
      var cell = arr[i];
      var row = cell.parentNode;
```

```
var eToggle = document.createElement('div');
bb.html.addClass( eToggle, 'image-toggle');
//move viewNode to the required place
cell.appendChild(eToggle);
var recordId = this.getRecordId(cell);
//add information block
var eRow = document.createElement('tr');
row.parentNode.insertBefore( eRow, row.nextSibling);
//hide it
eRow.style.display = 'none';
var eCell = eRow.appendChild(
   document.createElement('td'));
eCell.setAttribute('colSpan', '3');
var eInfo = eCell.appendChild(
   eTemplate.cloneNode(true));
var eInfoTable = eInfo.firstChild;
eInfoTable.rows[0].cells[1].
   appendChild( document.createTextNode(
      btl.dataSource.getValue(
         oDataSource, recordId, 'First')));
eInfoTable.rows[1].cells[1].
   appendChild( document.createTextNode(
      btl.dataSource.getValue(
         oDataSource, recordId, 'Last')));
eInfoTable.rows[2].cells[1].innerHTML =
   btl.dataSource.getValue(
      oDataSource, recordId, 'Rating', 'rating');
eInfoTable.rows[3].cells[1].innerHTML =
   btl.dataSource.getValue(
      oDataSource, recordId, 'Country');
eInfoTable.rows[4].cells[1].
   appendChild( document.createTextNode(
      btl.dataSource.getValue(
         oDataSource, recordId, 'Age')));
eInfoTable.rows[5].cells[1].
   appendChild( document.createTextNode(
      btl.dataSource.getValue( oDataSource,
         recordId, 'Birthdate')));
bb.html.addEventListener(
   eToggle, 'click', function(event){
      var div = event.target || event.srcElement;
      if( bb.html.hasClass(div, 'image-toggle-open')) {
         bb.html.removeClass(div, 'image-toggle-open');
         //hide info block
```

```
                    div.parentNode.parentNode.
                       nextSibling.style.display = 'none';
                 }
                 else {
                    bb.html.addClass(div, 'image-toggle-open');
                    //show info block
                    div.parentNode.parentNode.
                       nextSibling.style.display = '';
                 }
                 //redraw grid for IE
                 grid.getProperty('gate').doLayout();
              }, false);
           //drop the class name on rendered cells to avoid
           //re-rendering on update and on paging
           bb.html.removeClass(cell, 'render-image-toggle');
        }
     </e:handler>
```

And finally, here is the XHTML code that acts as a template for the detail values:

```
<b:xhtml style="display:none;" id="template">
   <div style="margin:5px;background-color:#F96;">
      <table>
         <tr>
            <td>First Name:</td>
            <td />
         </tr>
         <tr>
            <td>Last Name:</td>
            <td />
         </tr>
         <tr>
            <td>Rating:</td>
            <td />
         </tr>
         <tr>
            <td>Country:</td>
            <td />
         </tr>
          <tr>
            <td>Age:</td>
            <td />
         </tr>
         <tr>
            <td>Birth date:</td>
```

```
            <td />
        </tr>
    </table>
  </div>
</b:xhtml>
```

We conclude this part of the example with a picture of the info block that appears when the **+** sign is clicked:

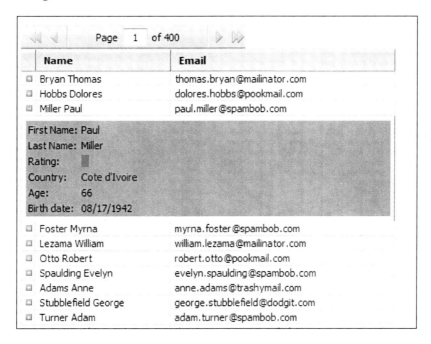

Form editing

The source code for this example can be found in `xml/formEdit.xml`.

This example is a rather extended mini-application. We included it here because it might be useful to you. We will not show the code in the book, but give a description that should be enough to get you started when you look at the source code:

- The grid can be edited by the form on the right-hand side of it
- The grid does not have any editing behavior
- Any changes are sent to a `dataSource` directly
- The form displays the values of the selected row in the grid
- You can edit the values in the form

- In case **Create** is pressed, a new row will be added to the grid
- In case **Save** is pressed, the selected row will be updated

The picture below should make the intention of the example clear:

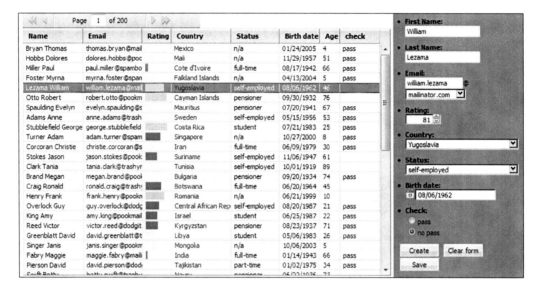

Live scrolling

The source code for this example can be found in `xml/livescrolling.xml`.

The last feature we want to highlight in the series is the live scrolling. When `dataGrid` widget is first initialized, it will normally get only the first page rendered. Later on, when the user starts scrolling through the virtual dataset, the widget will retrieve and render a page if it is not yet available, thus implementing lazy initialization behavior.

Adding live scrolling to a `dataGrid` element is done by specifying two important attributes: `livescrolling` and `maxPages`. The first turns on the live scrolling behavior and the second instructs the `dataGrid` what the maximum amount of pages is that can be rendered at any time.

```
<b:dataGrid
    e:behavior="b:dataGridSortOneColumn
        b:dataGridEditCell b:gridColumnDnD"
    rows="40" height="600px"
    livescrolling="true" maxPages="10">
    <!-- the dataGrid columns go here -->
</b:dataGrid>
```

Here is a picture of the live scrolling behavior. It shows that, if you are scrolling too fast, a big page number will be shown. As soon as the data is available, the number will disappear and be replaced by the `dataGrid` contents:

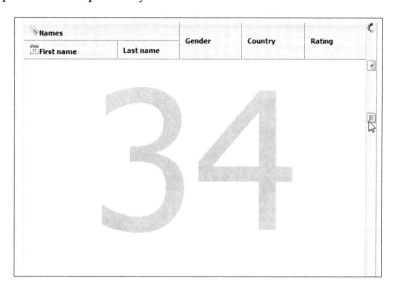

This was the last of the eleven features of the `dataGrid` element. We hope to have given you a taste of what is possible with this powerful widget.

Continue the development of the C3D application

In the previous chapter, we introduced the C3D application. Back then, you could only see a page skeleton, you could log in and log out, and you could add a trip.

In this chapter, we will add two major functional items:

- Add a trip entry. Each trip can contain several entries that describe the details of a specific part of the trip.
- Show a list of trips, a list of entries for a trip, and entry details.

After we have added these features, the first prototype of the site is usable and can accept real data as you can see on the example site that we made available for you: `http://www.squaringthecircles.com/bookApps/c3db/`.

Of course, some highly desirable features are still missing: *photo uploads*, *editing of trip descriptions and trip entries*, and *e-mail notification*, to name a few. Some of these we will add in later chapters.

Adding a trip entry

The first feature we will add is the ability to enter details for a trip. The entry form we need to make looks very much like the form we used for entering new trips as you can see in the next screenshot:

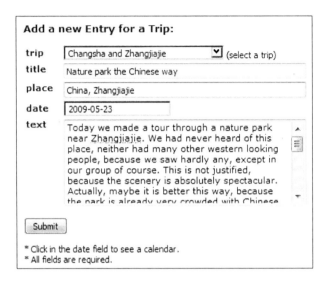

There is one obvious difference: the trip entry has to be related to a trip, and therefore, we would like to add a data-bound `comboBox`, which allows you to choose from the available trips. Because new trips could be entered at any time, it is necessary to build the options in the `comboBox` dynamically. First, we considered using a `suggestBox`, which is already provided by the Backbase framework and which is data bound. We decided *not* to use it because the user needs to type some letters before suitable choices can be made and this is hard if you have no idea what the trip names are. Therefore, we had to develop our own widget.

In this case, we already have a pretty good idea how to do this, as we have the experience of developing the `dataUL` widget. To summarize, we need to define a widget that extends from `comboBox` because we need the `comboBox` behavior, and from `dataObserver` because we want to make the widget data bound. The new widget should implement its own `dataUpdate` method.

Here is first the code, and after the code, we will explain the details:

```
<d:namespace
    xmlns:sq="http://www.squaringthecircles.com/squared"
    name="http://www.squaringthecircles.com/squared">
    <d:element name="dataComboBox"
        extends="b:comboBox b:dataObserver">
```

```
<d:attribute name="dataSource" />
<d:attribute name="valueSelect" />
<d:attribute name="optionSelect" />
<d:method name="dataUpdate">
    <d:argument name="action" />
    <d:argument name="records" />
    <d:argument name="actionObj" />
    <d:body type="text/javascript">
        this.callSuper('dataUpdate', [action, records,
            actionObj]);
        if (!(action == 'read' || action == 'sort'))
            return;
        var oSource = this.getProperty('dataSource');
        var sValueQuery =
            this.getAttribute('valueSelect');
        var sQuery = this.getAttribute('optionSelect');
        var aResults = [];
        for (var i = 0, iMax = records.length; i < iMax; i++)
        {
            var sLabel =
                btl.dataSource.getValue(oSource,
                    records[i], sQuery);
            var sValue =
                btl.dataSource.getValue(oSource,
                    records[i], sValueQuery);
            var oOption = {};
            oOption.value = sValue;
            oOption.label = sLabel;
            aResults[aResults.length] = oOption;
        }
        for (var j = 0, jMax = aResults.length; jMax > j, j++)
        {
            var oOption =
                bb.document.createElementNS(
                    btl.namespaceURI, 'comboBoxOption');
            var oText =
                bb.document.createTextNode(aResults[j].label);
            var sValue = aResults[j].value;
            if (sValue) {
                oOption.setAttribute('value', sValue);
            }
            oOption.appendChild(oText);
            this.appendChild(oOption);
        }
//}
```

```
        </d:body>
      </d:method>
    </d:element>
  </d:namespace>
```

Our data-bound combobox has been named `dataComboBox`; it is placed in the `http://www.squaringthecircles.com/squared` and has three additional attributes defined:

- `dataSource`: Obviously, we need to be able to identify the `dataSource` used for the `dataComboBox`.

- `valueSelect`: This should identify the ID to be used to send to the server, in order for the server to use as identification for the option selected. We need this attribute because just sending an index back would not be sufficient to identify the option selected.

- `optionSelect`: This is what the user will see in the drop-down list of the `dataComboBox`.

It is not obvious what the content of the method should be. But, we have an example at hand—the `dataUpdate` method of `suggestBox`! We can just *borrow* it from the definition that we find in: `backbase/4_4_1/bindings/www.backbase.com.2006.btl/suggestBox/suggestBoxBase.xml`.

The `dataUpdate` method for `dataComboBox` is slightly simpler than the one for `suggestBox` because we do not have to bother about a maximum number of options to attach. And, of course, we need to create a `comboBoxOption` instead of a `suggestBoxOption` to be appended to the drop-down list.

To be able to use this new widget, we place it into its own file, named `dataComboBox.xml`. And, we place this file in the `../bookApps/c3db/resources/bindings/www.squaringthecircles.com` folder. Here, we are using a convention similar to what the Backbase framework has for storing TDL definitions of widgets.

At the startup of the application, we should make sure that all the resources we need are loaded, including the definition of our `dataComboBox`. We achieve this by putting the names of all custom widgets (we have only one right now) in a special file. Here, it is called `../bookApps/c3db/resources/bindings/squared.xml`:

```
<d:tdl xmlns="http://www.w3.org/1999/xhtml"
  xmlns:d="http://www.backbase.com/2006/tdl">
    <d:namespace
       name="http://www.squaringthecircles.com/squared"
       xml:base="www.squaringthecircles.com/">
       <d:uses element="dataComboBox" src="dataComboBox.xml" />
    </d:namespace>
</d:tdl>
```

In our `index.php` script, we include `squared.xml` using XInclude.

The next thing to look at is the placement of the `dataComboBox` in the trip entry form. Here is the code. We only show the row in the table that contains the `dataComboBox` widget:

```
<tr>
   <td>
      <label for="tripId">trip</label>
   </td>
   <td>
      <sq:dataComboBox name="tripId" width="200px"
         valueSelect="*[1]"
         optionSelect="*[2]" bf:required="true"
         bf:messagesRef="../../td/bf:messages[1]">
         <b:dataSource e:behavior="b:remoteData"
            url="../cntrl.php?req=tripdataforuser"
            dataType="application/xml"
            requestType="application/xml" />
      </sq:dataComboBox>
       (select a trip)
   </td>
    <td valign="top">
       <bf:messages>
          <bf:message event="invalid"
             class="errorMessage" facet="required">
             <span>You must select a trip</span>
          </bf:message>
       </bf:messages>
    </td>
</tr>
```

As always, you can find the complete code for the form in the provided source code package for the book.

Note the XPath expressions used as value for the `valueSelect` and `optionSelect` attributes. These will find the values of the `id` tag (the first tag in each record) and `name` tag (the second tag in each record) in the XML data.

Also, for the `dataComboBox`, you can use form validation. Here, if you do not make a choice, which means a blank option, the error message will be displayed when you try to submit the form.

We are not finished with our dataComboBox yet. There are still three points to consider — the url on the data source, the data that is sent to the server when the form is submitted, and the menu item we must add to enable the display of the form.

The query result that is requested from the server is named tripdataforuser. The controller will invoke the readTripsForUser() function in the showTrips() class. We have seen a very similar function earlier in this chapter. However, it was not restricted to one user. Now, it looks like this:

```
public function readTripsForUser() {
    $sQuery=
        'SELECT id, name, description, startDate,
            endDate FROM c3d_trip
          WHERE userId = :userId ORDER BY startDate DESC';
    $sCountQuery =
        'SELECT COUNT(*) as iCount
            FROM c3d_trip WHERE userId = :userId';
    $aParameters = array();
    $aParameters['userId'] = $_SESSION['c3d']['user-id'];
    $datasource = new bb_remoteDataSource();
    return $datasource->
        asXml($sQuery, $aParameters, $sCountQuery);
}
```

We limit the trips returned to the trips that belong to the user who is logged in because it is undesirable that a user could make entries for a trip of another user. At the moment of writing this chapter, there is only one user who has entered trips, so the result will be the same for now. You can see that the user-id is entered as a parameter into the query. This helps prevent SQL injection because the parameters are all checked and will never be part of the SQL string directly.

What will the server script, which receives the submitted form, see? We ask Firebug for help again, and we see this:

```
POST http://snippetviewer/bookApps/c3db/cntrl.php  200 OK 41ms
   Headers  Post  Antwoord
   dbtable  c3d_entry
 entryDate  2009-06-24
     place  China, Guilin
       req  insert
      text  We made a tour on the Li river. This must be the most famous excursion in one of the most famous touristic
            spots in China.
     title  Splendid Scenery
    tripId  5
```

We see a tripId parameter that has as value the trip ID with which we want to associate this trip entry. As you can see, the server script does not need to be aware of the special widget we were using to obtain this value.

A last thing we need to do is add a menu item that allows a logged-in user to display the trip entry form. This is done in the same way as the **Add a new Trip** menu item was added. Because we did not show this in the previous chapter, we show it here now.

After a successful login, the `login` class delegates to the `menuItems` class to set up the `restricted-menu-area`. Remember that what is returned by the server is inserted into the `menu-area` area because the login menu specified this as destination. What is returned is only a `div` element, which is empty, except for a set of handlers. The one for the **Add a new Trip Entry** menu item looks like this:

```
<e:handler event="DOMNodeInsertedIntoDocument">
   <c:load destination="id('restricted-menu-area')"
      url="menuItems/addTripEntryItem.xml"
      mode="lastChild" />
</e:handler>
```

What happens is that the event is fired when the `div` node is inserted into the document. This will cause the `c:load` command to execute, which puts whatever it finds at `menuItems/addTripEntryItem.xml` into the `restricted-menu-area`. This happens to be:

```
<a href="javascript:">
   Add a new Trip Entry
</a>
<e:handler event="click">
   <c:load url="../forms/EntryInsert.xml"
      destination="id('trip-area')"
      mode="replaceChildren" />
</e:handler>
```

This is indeed our menu item, which when clicked, will cause the add trip entry menu to be loaded in the center area on the screen with id `trip-area`. This multi-step process looks complicated at first. However, it is necessary to load the code in this way because the reply to a request can only go to *one* destination, while often, we want to put items in more than one area, or the destination is dependent on the result of a server action, such as, if the login fails, the form should stay and an error message should appear, instead of the appearance of the restricted menu items.

Show trips and trip entries

So far, we have entered quite a lot of data into the C3D application, but it seems to have fallen into a black hole. So, now is the time to show the world what we have written.

We thought it would be nice if we could show the information in a tree-like structure. When you ask for the trip data to be shown, you will initially see just a `dataGrid` with trip names and descriptions.

But, if you click on the + sign that can be found in front of every row, you will see the entries that have been made for that particular trip. The text for the entries will be shortened and by clicking on **more...**, the full text of the entry is shown.

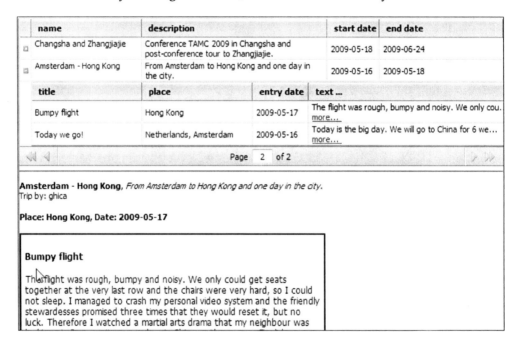

The widget we developed builds on the example of the `dataGrid` that showed a *collapsible info block*. In that example, the collapsible block contained a non-Backbase area. Here, we extend this by allowing the info block to contain Backbase widgets (in our case, another `dataGrid`).

Why are we not using a `treeGrid` instead of building such a complicated widget? For two reasons: the first one is that for a `treeGrid` the inner structure of the rows must be the same as the outer structure. This is not the case in our example. The second reason is that, when using a `treeGrid`, we must build rather complicated XML to tie the inner structure to the outer one. In our implementation, we can use the generic remote data source class we built in PHP.

We used this widget before in a scorecard application where statistical data from a large school with 20,000 students was presented about absence/presence, classroom occupancy, and so on. You could look at an overview for the whole school and then drill down via a sub-school and class or group to an individual student. This was very helpful to the school to obtain the necessary funds from the government.

This is again an exercise in using TDL while the introduction to this language is still a chapter away. Therefore, we will not further explain the code here. You have seen most of the building blocks already though, therefore, with some effort, you should be able to go through the code on your own.

Let's just see some of the code for using the `plusDataGrid` and `plusDatGridCol`:

```
<sq:plusDataGrid class="innerGrid" width="100%"
    e:behavior="b:dataGridSortOneColumn"
    overflow="visible" sortDirection="descending"
    sortField="startDate" rows="3">
    <sq:plusDataGridCol render="none"
        field1="id"
        include="cntrl.php?req=tripentrygrid"
        resizable="false" />
    <b:dataGridCol dataField="id" display="none">
        id
    </b:dataGridCol>
    <b:dataGridCol dataField="name"
        dataClass="t-area" width="150px">
        name
    </b:dataGridCol>
    <b:dataGridCol dataField="description"
        dataClass="t-area" width="250px">
        description
    </b:dataGridCol>
    <b:dataGridCol dataField="startDate" width="90px">
        start date
    </b:dataGridCol>
    <b:dataGridCol dataField="endDate" width="70px">
        end date
    </b:dataGridCol>
```

```
    <b:dataSource e:behavior="b:remoteData"
       url="../cntrl.php?req=tripdata"
       dataType="application/xml"
       requestType="application/xml" />
  </sq:plusDataGrid>
  <!-- the pager bar goes here -->
```

This looks like a normal grid with a peculiar first column, a `plusDataGridCol`, and there is a `dataSource` that is responsible for retrieving a list of all trips. The `plusDataGridCol` indicates that it will include whatever is returned from `cntrl.php?req=tripentrygrid`, which happens to be a `dataGrid` with trip entries. The value of the `field1` is the trip ID, which is used to find the entries for the selected trip.

Even if you cannot understand the code that we have introduced here for defining the new widgets, you would probably be able to use them in your application anyway. This is a strong point for using the Tag Definition Language: a specialist in developing widgets will develop the `plusDataGrid` and a specialist in UI development will develop the page in which the `plusDataGridCol` is used.

We also made it very clear that the work done in another project for a totally different purpose can very conveniently be reused. Here, our scorecard widget, which was developed for a school, turned into a trip entry browsing widget for the C3D sample application.

Summary

In this chapter, we have discussed data binding, data-bound widgets in the Backbase framework, and how you can make your own.

The most powerful data-bound widget in the Backbase framework is the `dataGrid`. With eleven examples, we explored many details of using this grid.

The work on our C3D travel blog sample application continued with the definition of a trip entry form, and a grid that could seamlessly display both trips and entries belonging to a trip.

In the next chapter, we will describe drag-and-drop and animation with SMIL.

6

More Dynamic Behavior

The word *more* in the title of this chapter suggests that we will cover a subject that we have described before. Indeed, we are continuing with what we started in Chapter 3: the three dynamic aspects of application development—*traversing the document tree*, *modifying the document tree*, and *dealing with events*.

Let's have a level check. What we have covered so far:

- **Traversing the document tree**: We indicated how you can find elements by *ID* or by *tag name*, using the bb object. There is also XPath that you can conveniently use to give a value to those attributes in XEL, which are used to set a node value in the DOM—for example, the often-used select attribute.

- **Modifying the document tree**: We discussed how you can use the APIs according to well-known web standards, as implemented by the bb object. On a higher level, you can use the XML Execution Language (XEL) and the applicable command functions. We described both in Chapter 3. XSLT transformations can be considered as a way to implement modifications of the DOM tree. We showed an example of how you can do this using the Backbase framework in Chapter 3.

- **Dealing with events**: In almost every example, we made use of an event handler to describe the interaction with the user that should take place. You might be familiar now with how to write these in either JavaScript or XEL. We also covered some finer points, such as how to create your own events.

Elements in the DOM tree can move or change shape in ways other than described above, by drag-and-drop, by animation, and so on. The Backbase framework has implemented support for some of these.

In the Backbase framework, there is a possibility to extend the dynamic behavior of any element in a generic way, conveniently called *behaviors*. We saw some specific behavior for the `dataGrid` that could be added to it, such as *sorting* or *cell editing*. Here, our main topic will be the generic *drag-and-drop* behavior. We will also describe the *resize* behavior that you can attach to an element.

We will look at several *command functions* that you can use to handle behaviors, either in combination with XEL or with JavaScript. In particular, you can use these commands for adding or removing behavior to or from an element. You will find these commands after the section on behaviors.

Using *animation* is a popular way to make a website more dynamic. The Backbase framework has a partial implementation of the **Synchronized Multimedia Integration Language** (**SMIL**) standard that is worth exploring, which we will do in this chapter.

The last subject in this chapter is about the **broadcaster/observer** functionality as it is implemented in the Backbase framework. You will remember that we have seen the observer pattern described in the previous chapter as the fundamental pattern behind *data binding*. There is also a more generic implementation in the Backbase framework, known as the broadcaster/observer support.

Here is a list of subjects we will cover in this chapter:

- Behaviors: a definition
- Drag-and-drop and resize behaviors
- Commands affecting behaviors
- The broadcaster/observer pattern
- UI animation with SMIL
- An SMIL example for the C3D travel blog

Behaviors

A **behavior** is a dynamic functionality that can be added to a UI widget. Backbase widgets are object-oriented objects. This means they have a state, which is kept in *properties* and a dynamic behavioral functionality, which is coded in *methods*. A behavior is actually an object that a widget can inherit from. If you add the behavior to an UI widget, by coding for example: `e:behavior="b:drag"`, the widget will now inherit all attributes, properties, and methods that are defined for the behavior (the capability to be dragged in this example).

We have already seen a large number of behaviors in the previous chapter. Remember that if you specify `e:behavior="b:remoteData"` on a `dataSource` element, the `dataSource` will be able to communicate with a server and you will have extra attributes that you can use with the `dataSource`, such as a `url` attribute to specify the destination of a request for data. Similarly, you could make a `dataGrid` sortable, by specifying `e:behavior="b:dataGridSortOneColumn"` on the `dataGrid` tag as attribute.

Frequently used examples of behaviors in the Backbase framework are drag-and-drop and resize. These two behaviors are the main focus of this chapter.

- **drag-and-drop**: This is an action that can be applied to a UI widget. By clicking with a mouse on that widget and keeping the mouse button down, you can move the mouse and drag the UI widget with it. When you release the mouse, the widget is dropped at the new location.

- **resize**: It is another action that can be applied to most UI widgets. It involves dragging a corner or a border of a widget with a mouse to a new location. When the mouse button is released, the size of the widget will be adapted in such a way that the dragged corner or border will now be at the new location.

Drag-and-drop and resize are applied on a particular widget using the `behavior` attribute and the name of the behavior as the attribute value. This will allow a number of additional attributes, events, and methods to be applied to the widget, namely those that are provided with the behavior. We will see in the next sections what these attributes, events, and methods are.

Developers new to Backbase are often confused by the namespace prefixes that must be used. In the `dataGrid` examples, you have seen that the name of the attribute `behavior` must be prefixed with `e:`. This is because `behavior` belongs to the XEL namespace. The value of the attribute is the name of the behavior, such as `localData`, `dataGridCellEdit`, or `resize`. As we have explained above, these behaviors are objects. The predefined Backbase behavior objects are all defined in the BTL namespace and must therefore be prefixed with `b:`.

In the next chapter, we will see that you can also define your own behaviors. The names of these must then be prefixed with the prefix you defined for your custom namespace. Another confusion is that attributes belonging to the behavior that you specified for a widget must *not* be prefixed, such as the `url` attribute of `b:remoteData`. This is because the behavior is like a superclass to the object to which the behavior is applied, as we explained in the previous paragraph. Therefore, the `dataGrid` where the behavior `b:remoteData` is used just inherits the `url` and other attributes.

Drag-and-drop

We already defined what drag-and-drop is in the previous section. Briefly, it is a way to move a UI widget using your mouse.

The *drag-and-drop* support in the Backbase framework consists of three behaviors. Therefore, behaviors that are defined in the BTL namespace are:

- `dragBase`: It fires the basic events associated with drag-and-drop
- `drag`: It inherits from `dragBase` and offers a set of attributes that you can use to customize the dragging behavior of the widget it is attached to
- `dragTarget`, which implements receiving draggable elements

As usual, in this book, we will show details of *attributes* and in this case, because we are talking about the drag-and-drop behavior, we will explain *events* first and then a series of examples.

dragBase

`dragBase` implements a set of events that form generic drag-and-drop behavior. Each event has a list of properties available when it is fired. Using these properties, you can investigate who initiated the drag and where, what is dragged, where the dragged element is located, and so on.

Event	Description	Properties
drag	Fires continuously during a drag operation.	pageX, pageY, viewTarget, dragInitiator, dragSource, dragTarget, and dragViewTarget.
dragDrop	Fires when the mouse button is released during a drag-and-drop operation.	dragInitiator and dragSource.
dragEnd	Fires when the user releases the mouse at the close of a drag operation.	dragInitiator and dragSource.
dragEnter	Fires when the user drags the object to a valid drop target.	viewTarget, dragInitiator, dragSource, dragTarget, and dragViewTarget.

Event	Description	Properties
dragLeave	Fires when the user moves the mouse out of a valid drop target during a drag operation.	viewTarget, dragInitiator, dragSource, dragTarget, and dragViewTarget.
dragOver	Fires continuously while the user drags the object over a valid drop target.	viewTarget, dragInitiator, dragSource, dragTarget, and dragViewTarget.
dragStart	Fires when the user starts to drag an object.	startX, startY, viewTarget, and dragManager.

Disregard the attributes with *view* in their name for now. We will talk about *models*, *views*, and *controllers* in the next chapter as they apply to the layers of the Backbase framework. You can probably guess the meaning of most other properties. Otherwise, the API Reference has descriptions.

The dragManager is a special object that you can use to customize dragging and dropping. We will show an example of its use later in this chapter.

drag

drag inherits from dragBase and implements a draggable element. The element receives dragStart, drag, and dragEnd events.

Attribute	Description	Value
dragBehavior	Defines whether the dragged item will be moved when dropped. drop indicates that the element will be moved in the tree. move indicates that the element will be absolutely positioned at the new location.	drop and move.
dragConstraint	Defines an element that serves as a boundary for the dragged element.	The value is a valid XPath expression. If the expression selects more than one node, only the first node is used.
dragGroup	Defines a list of tag words, delimited by a blank. A drag target checks this list to determine if it will accept the element.	List of strings.
dragItem	Defines a tag word. A drag target checks it to determine whether it will accept the element.	String
dragMode	Defines what the element looks like while it is being dragged.	outline, real, and symbol.

Attribute	Description	Value
dragSymbol	Defines the dragSymbol when using dragMode="symbol". The result of the XPath can be either a node to which a clone is moved or a string that will be converted to an HTML element.	XPath
dropMode	Defines what should be done when the element is dropped on a drop-zone.	move and none.
useDragClass	By default, the element can be dragged from any point, but this can be changed using drag classes. The class values can be: • btl-dragItem: behavior defined by dragBehavior • btl-dragMove: overrides dragBehavior to move value • btl-dragDrop: overrides dragBehavior to drop value	true and false.

Note that if useDragClass is set to true, the user selection of content within the source element is not prevented. To prevent the user selection of content within the element to which a drag class is applied, use the bb.html.disableUserSelect method.

dragTarget

It implements receiving draggable elements. The element receives dragEnter, dragOver, dragLeave, and dragDrop events. When the source element is moved to a new element in the tree, the default behavior is to append as last child to the receiving element.

This behavior is activated by specifying the b:dragReceive attribute on the receiver.

Having looked at the behavior objects that are available to support drag-and-drop operations, we can now look at some examples.

 All the source code for the *behavior* examples can be found in the bookApps/behaviors folder. For each example, there is a .html and a .xml file with the same filename. The actual source code is in the .xml part. The .html part is there to start things and to provide a short description.

Basic dragging and dropping with widgets

In this section, we look at the attributes you can specify to make a widget draggable and what you can do to make a widget into an element that can receive draggable widgets.

In the following example, you see a widget that can be dragged to a receiver:

```
<div class="dnd-container" style="left:50px;">
    Draggable<br />Item
    <div class="drag-tile" e:behavior="b:drag" />
</div>
<div class="dnd-container" style="left:200px"
  b:dragReceive="*">
    Drag
    <br />
    Receiver
</div>
```

Before we explain the code, let's see a picture:

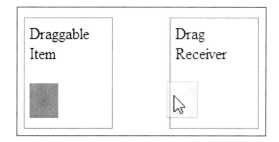

From looking at the picture, you can guess that we left out the CSS styling, which was used to make the draggable `div` into a blue square and to style the containers used. Apart from this, the code shown is all you need to enable *drag-and-drop* behavior:

- `e:behavior="b:drag"` is specified as an attribute on the draggable widget.

- `b:dragReceive="*"` is specified on the receiver. The * means that there are no constraints on the draggable widget that can be dropped.

Drag constraints

We can give a draggable widget extra properties that can help to constrain where the widget can be dropped, and which parts of the widget can be used as a handle to drag it.

dragItem

The next example is similar to the previous one. It shows four draggable items, now with the `dragItem` attribute specified. There are two receivers, one saying `b:dragReceive="odd"` and the other `b:dragReceive="even"`. Here's the code:

```
<div class="dragReceive-container"
  style="left:50px; height:auto" b:dragReceive="*">
  Integers
  <div class="dragReceive-tile" e:behavior="b:drag"
    dragItem="odd">
    1
  </div>
  <div class="dragReceive-tile" e:behavior="b:drag"
    dragItem="even">
    2
  </div>
  <div class="dragReceive-tile" e:behavior="b:drag"
    dragItem="odd">
    3
  </div>
  <div class="dragReceive-tile" e:behavior="b:drag"
    dragItem="even">
    4
  </div>
</div>
<div class="dragReceive-container" style="left:200px"
  b:dragReceive="odd">
  Odd
</div>
<div class="dragReceive-container" style="left:350px"
  b:dragReceive="even">
  Even
</div>
```

Here is a picture:

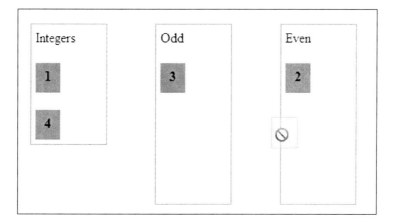

In this example, the `dragItem` attribute specifies the type of element that can be dragged. The receivers must specify the same value in their `b:dragReceive` attribute to be able to receive the dragged element. Therefore, blue squares can be dropped in either the **Odd** or the **Even** container. You can drag all of them back to their original container.

dragGroup

Another attribute that may be practical to use is the `dragGroup` attribute. First, let's look at the code:

```
<div e:behavior="b:drag" dragMode="real" dragGroup="cat"
  class="dnd-container" style="left: 50px;">
    <img src="media/igor.jpg" />
    <div dragItem="cat" class="cat-tail">
     Drag here...
    </div>
</div>
<div b:dragReceive="cat" class="dnd-receiver"
  style="left: 350px;">
    <div>
        Igor!!
    </div>
</div>
```

Now, the picture:

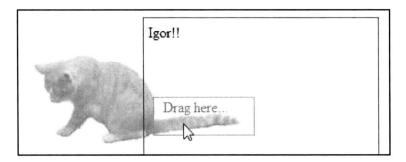

As you can see, the cat can be dragged only by its tail (the real Igor would bite you if you tried!). This is achieved by specifying a `dragGroup` attribute on the `div` that contains the image and an overlay `div` with a `dragItem` attribute for the part that can be clicked upon and be dragged.

Because we used `dragMode="real"`, you see the real cat being dragged, instead of only an outline.

useDragClass

This is another way to achieve the same effect: Igor can only be dragged by his tail. This effect is achieved by using a `useDragClass` attribute with the value `true`. The overlay `div` should now contain a `class` attribute that in our example contains the value `btl-dragItem`, which means that the value for the `dragBehavior` is used. We did not specify this attribute; its default value is `drop`. The code for the `div` containing the image and its overlay now becomes:

```
<div e:behavior="b:drag" dragMode="real"
  dragItem="cat" useDragClass="true"
  class="dnd-container" style="left: 50px;">
  <img src="media/igor.jpg" />
  <div dragItem="cat" class="cat-tail btl-dragItem">
    Drag here
  </div>
</div>
```

 dragMode="real" should be used carefully. Only in simple cases and when the dragged elements are kept within simple elements, will this mode work properly. In complex pages, you should create your own symbol that can be dragged appropriately.

dragConstraint

A constraint of a different type, indicating where an item can be dragged, is the `dragConstraint` attribute. It defines the boundaries for a draggable widget. The value for the attribute must be a valid XPath expression.

We illustrate this by coding an on-off switch, remotely modeled after the switches found in an iPhone to change the settings:

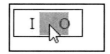

The switch is a simple table with one row and two columns. The table has a background image with the *on* and *off* symbols. When you slide the switch, it won't be appealing if you could move the switch all over the page. Therefore, the sliding is constrained within the only row of the table. Here's the code:

```
<table style="background-image: url(media/onoff.jpg);">
    <tbody>
        <tr>
          <td class="switch" b:dragReceive="switch1">
            <div class="red" e:behavior="b:drag"
                dragConstraint="../.."
                dragItem="switch1" dragMode="real">
            </div>
            <e:handler event="dragEnd"
              type="application/javascript" phase="capture">
                alert('hi! you switched me off');
            </e:handler>
          </td>
          <td class="switch" b:dragReceive="switch1">
            <e:handler event="dragEnd"
                type="application/javascript" phase="capture">
                alert('hi! you switched me on');
            </e:handler>
          </td>
        </tr>
    </tbody>
</table>
```

The code has `dragConstraint="../.."` specified for the `div` that represents the switch. This constraint means that the switch can be dragged within the element that is two parents up, therefore the `tr` element.

You will notice that `phase="capture"` is specified. This is done because the `dragEnd` event does not bubble. This example will need version 4.4.0 or greater of the Backbase framework to work properly.

We inserted two alerts to tell you what happens. This is done to show that it can indeed be used to control settings in a configuration or other on-off information.

Reverting a dragged element

In many drag-and-drop scenarios, the dragged element should not be moved or dropped to a new location, but only a copy or parts of the dragged element should be placed at the target location. Imagine a shopping cart to which you can drag products from a catalog. It would be really strange if the product would disappear from the catalog after it was dragged to the shopping cart!

In the well-known *prototype/scriptaculous* framework, this is easy to do: just specify `revert="true"` on the dragged element and it will happen. For the Backbase framework, however, it is surprisingly difficult to find out how to do it, although the implementation is fairly easy. Here, we reveal the secret for the first time!

We present a schematic scenario of a book shop. You will see images of books that can be dragged to a shopping cart area and if you change your mind, you can drag the book from the shopping cart to the waste basket. This is a very simple implementation, which only intents to show reverting of a dragged element. Therefore, there are no products, but only images in the catalog and there are no order lines in the shopping cart with quantity or price information.

We will implement the reverting as follows:

- We specify `dropMode="none"` on the dragged element. This means that when the element is dropped, it will always stay at the starting location.
- When dropped, we will clone the element and append the clone copy at the target location.

Because of some problems with the cloning of behaviors in the Backbase framework, we need to specify a new element using TDL. Actually, that gives us the opportunity to show an alternative way of specifying dragging capabilities: just inherit from `b:drag`!

The next picture should give you an impression of what happens when a picture is dragged to the shopping basket. You see a full basket, but all four books are still there in the books container.

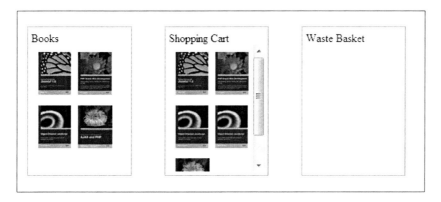

```
<d:namespace xmlns:sq="http://www.squaringthecircles.com/squared"
  name="http://www.squaringthecircles.com/squared">
  <d:element name="bookTile" extends="b:drag img">
     <d:attribute name="dropMode" default="none" />
     <d:attribute name="class" default="bookTile" />
     <d:attribute name="dragItem" default="book" />
  </d:element>
</d:namespace>
```

The element `bookTile` in the previous code is about the simplest element you can imagine; it is an image that you can drag and it has some extra attributes.

Now, we can put some books in a catalog on our web page:

```
<div class="dragReceive-container" style="left:50px;">
   Books
   <br />
   <sq:bookTile src="media/184719530X.png" />
   <sq:bookTile src="media/1847193633.png" />
   <sq:bookTile src="media/1847194141.png" />
   <sq:bookTile src="media/1904811825.png" />
</div>
```

Next, we can code the shopping cart:

```
<div class="dragReceive-container" style="left:250px;">
   Shopping Cart
   <div style="width:100%; height:90%; overflow: auto;"
     b:dragReceive="book">
   </div>
   <e:handler event="dragDrop"
     type="application/javascript" phase="capture">
     var oElement = event.dragSource;
```

```
        if (oElement.getAttribute("dropMode") == "none") {
           oElement = oElement.cloneNode();
           oElement.setAttribute("dropMode", "move");
           oElement.setAttribute("dragItem", "cart");
           event.target.appendChild(oElement);
        }
     </e:handler>
  </div>
```

The cloning takes place in the `dragDrop` event handler. We also change the `dropMode` and `dragItem` attributes, which enables the element to be dragged to the waste basket in the hopefully unlikely case that the shopper changes his mind.

Finally, here is the wastebasket:

```
<div class="dragReceive-container" style="left:450px"
  b:dragReceive="cart">
  Waste Basket
  <br />
  <e:handler event="dragEnd"
     type="application/javascript" phase="capture">
     var oElement = event.dragSource;
     bb.command.destroy(oElement);
  </e:handler>
</div>
```

Please note that this example requires version 4.4.0 or greater of the Backbase framework to run because of the `phase="capture"` attribute in the event handler. There is another way to implement reverting that also works in earlier versions. The idea is to drop the element normally and to recreate the element at the drag-initiating location when the dragged element is dropped, something like this:

```
<div class="book-tile">
  <img src="resources/media/mybook123.png"
    e:behavior="b:drag" />
  <e:handler event="DOMNodeRemoved">
     <c:create destination="." mode="appendChild">
        <img src="resources/media/mybook123.png"
          e:behavior="b:drag" />
     </c:create>
  </e:handler>
</div>
```

The disadvantage of this approach is that it may cause a flicker on the page and it may take extra time to recreate the element.

Advanced dragging and dropping with widgets

In this section, we look into how you can customize a drag-and-drop operation to match the requirements of the widget. For this, we use the `dragBase` behavior to hook into the events.

Drag-and-drop columns inside a table

For this example, we first define a table which has the `dragBase` behavior defined. By doing this, we receive the `dragStart` event when the user initiates a drag-and-drop operation. In this example, we simply show an alert when a `dragStart` is initiated, indicating the node name of the element that was dragged.

In the handler of the `dragStart` event, we can implement a specific behavior to do the dragging and dropping. If we do not define anything, it will not start the drag-and-drop operation.

```
<style type="text/css">
    .mySymbol {
        border: 1px solid black;
        background: red;
        position: absolute;
    }
    .mySymbol.btl-drag-target { background: lightgreen; }
</style>
<table border="1" e:behavior="b:dragBase">
    <thead>
        <tr style="-moz-user-select: none;">
            <th>Column 1</th>
            <th>Column 2</th>
            <th>Column 3</th>
            <th>Column 4</th>
        </tr>
    </thead>
    <tbody>
        <tr>
            <td>Content 1</td>
            <td>Content 2</td>
            <td>Content 3</td>
            <td>Content 4</td>
        </tr>
    </tbody>
    <!-- The handlers go here ... -->
</table>
```

We need to add some logic for the `dragStart` and `dragEnd` events:

- `dragStart`: Checking if we are on the head of the table when the drag starts
- `dragStart`: Creating the symbol we are going to drag
- `dragStart`: Starting the drag-and-drop operation using `btl.drag.dragManager.doDrag()`
- `dragEnd`: Destroying/removing the symbol we have created in the `dragStart`

We need to add the logic that detects if our mouse is on top of an element where the column can be dropped. We do this by iterating over the table head cells and checking if the current mouse position is at the target location of the table head. This is made visible because the `dragManager` adds the `btl-drag-target` class to the symbol, changing it from red to green.

- When this is the case, we call the `btl.drag.dragManager.acceptDragDrop()` to accept the drag-and-drop
- If this is not the case anymore, we call the same `btl.drag.dragManager.acceptDragDrop()` but then without any arguments to reset it

We also implement the `dragDrop` event handler that does the logic when the column is dropped on another column. This event will only fire when the target is accepted, in general, when `btl.drag.dragManager.acceptDragDrop()` is called with a valid element as argument.

The following snippet defines the custom code for the `dragStart`, `drag`, `dragDrop`, and `dragEnd` events to accommodate custom (symbolic) drag-and-drop for table column reordering.

```
<e:handler event="dragStart" type="application/javascript">
    // Check for head
    if (event.viewTarget.nodeName == 'TH') {
        //Create the symbol
        var oSymbol = document.createElement('div');
        oSymbol.className = 'mySymbol';
        oSymbol.innerHTML = event.viewTarget.textContent ||
            event.viewTarget.innerText;
        document.body.appendChild(oSymbol);
        this.symbol = oSymbol;
        //Start the drag operation
        btl.drag.dragManager.doDrag(this, event.viewTarget,
            event.startX, event.startY, oSymbol,
            20, 20, 0.8, false,
            event.viewTarget.parentNode.childNodes);
    }
</e:handler>
```

```
<e:handler event="drag" type="application/javascript">
    <![CDATA[
    //Find the column currently under the mouse
    var oTHs = this.viewNode.getElementsByTagName('th'),
        i = 0, oTH;
    var iFoundIndex = null;
    while(oTH = oTHs[i++]) {
        var oCoord = bb.html.getBoxObject(oTH);
        if (event.pageX &gt; oCoord.left &amp;&amp; event.pageX
            &lt; oCoord.left + oCoord.width) {
            if(oCoord.width / 2 &gt; event.pageX - oCoord.left) {
                iFoundIndex = oTH.cellIndex;
            }
            else
                iFoundIndex = oTH.cellIndex + 1;
        }
    }
    if (iFoundIndex !== null &amp;&amp; iFoundIndex !=
        event.dragSource.cellIndex &amp;&amp;
            event.dragSource != oTHs[iFoundIndex == 0 ? 0 :
                iFoundIndex - 1 ]) {
        //Accept the drag-and-drop
        this.iFoundIndex = iFoundIndex;
        btl.drag.dragManager.acceptDragDrop(this);
    }
    else {
        //Deny the drag-and-drop
        btl.drag.dragManager.acceptDragDrop();
    }
    ]]>
</e:handler>
<e:handler event="dragDrop" type="application/javascript">
    //Move all cells from that column to the new column
    var iCurrentIndex - event.dragSource.cellIndex;
    var iNewIndex = this.iFoundIndex;
    var aTRs = this.viewNode.rows, i = 0;
    while(oTR = aTRs[i++]){
        oTR.insertBefore(oTR.cells[iCurrentIndex],
            oTR.cells[iNewIndex]);
    }
</e:handler>
<e:handler event="dragEnd" type="application/javascript">
    document.body.removeChild(this.symbol);
    this.symbol = null;
</e:handler>
```

The next picture shows **Column 4** being dragged:

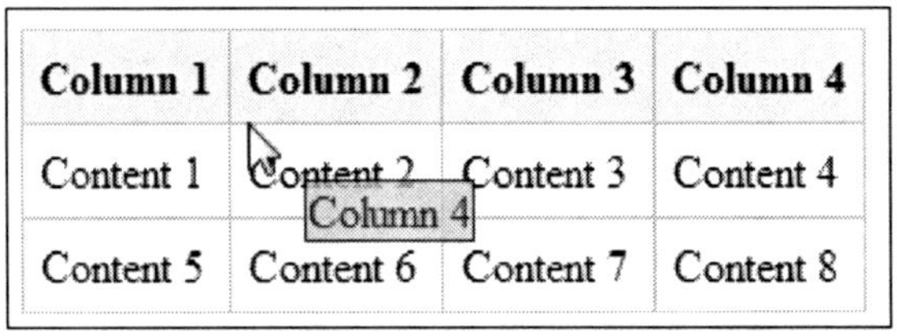

Column 1	Column 2	Column 3	Column 4
Content 1	Content 2	Content 3	Content 4
	Column 4		
Content 5	Content 6	Content 7	Content 8

The example code for the book contains the complete example.

Resize

The resize behavior allows you to click on the border or a corner of a widget and drag its border so that the widget becomes smaller or larger. When the user clicks on the border of a resizable widget, the icon changes into a double arrow.

Attributes of the resize behavior allow control over the resizable edges of an element, minimum and maximum resize capabilities, and the visualization of the widget in the process of resizing:

Attribute	Description
maximized	Defines if the element size is maximized.
minimized	Defines if the element size is minimized.
resizeConstraint	Defines an element that serves as the boundary for the resized element. The value must be a valid XPath expression. If the expression selects more than one node, only the first node is used.
resizeEdges	Defines a list of space-separated values representing the edges of the element that can start a resize action. By default, the element can be resized by all edges.
resizeGripSize	Defines the size in pixels of the region around an element edge where resizing can be started.
resizeMaxHeight	Defines the maximum height of the resized element. Use px as a valid CSS length value.
resizeMaxWidth	Defines the maximum width of the resized element. Use px as a valid CSS length value.

Attribute	Description
resizeMinHeight	Defines the minimum height of the resized element. Use px as a valid CSS length value.
resizeMinWidth	Defines the minimum width of the resized element. Use px as a valid CSS length value.
resizeType	Defines the visual representation of resizing. Its value can be outline, line, or real.

Using the resize behavior

As with other behaviors, you apply the resize behavior by adding the e:behavior attribute to a particular markup element.

The basic syntax for the resize behavior applied to a box widget is shown in this example. An absolute position for the resizable box is specified to give it enough space in all directions.

```
<b:box e:behavior="b:resize" width="100px" height="100px"
  position="absolute" left="50px" top="100px" />
```

The above example allows the user to resize the widget in any direction. Pressing the *Esc* key returns the last resized element to its original size. The picture below shows a basic resize operation:

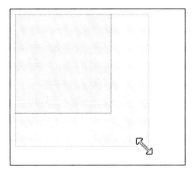

resizeEdges

Sometimes, you may want to restrict which borders the user can resize. If a widget must retain a fixed relation to another element, or is positioned at one side of the application, you may want to disable the ability to resize that border.

The resizeEdges attribute allows you to specify which edges of the widget can be used to resize it. In the example, only the top and right edges can be dragged for resizing. Absolute positioning is used to provide sufficient room.

```
<b:box e:behavior="b:resize"
  width="100px" height="50px"
  position="absolute" left="50px" top="100px"
  resizeEdges="top right" />
```

The `resizeEdges` attribute accepts four possible space-separated values: `left`, `right`, `top`, and `bottom`.

resizeMin and resizeMax

The `resizeMinHeight` and `resizeMinWidth` attributes allow you to specify a minimum size for the element's new size. The following example lets you increase the width and height as much as you want, but limits the minimum width and height to 100 pixels:

```
<b:box e:behavior="b:resize" width="30px" height="30px"
  resizeMinHeight="100px" resizeMinWidth="100px" />
```

Similar to the `resizeMinHeight` and `resizeMinWidth` attributes, you can use `resizeMaxHeight` and `resizeMaxWidth` attributes to constrain the size of a resizable widget.

resizeType

The `resizeType` attribute defines what the new border looks like when the widget is in the process of being resized. By default, the `resizeType` is set to `outline`. This shows a straight line that represents the new boundary of the element on the three edges that are being altered. The `line` value only shows a line on the edge that is currently being moved. There is also a `real` value that re-renders the box as it is being moved.

resizeConstraint

As with the drag-and-drop behavior, you can set additional limits (besides size itself) on the resize action. The `resizeConstraint` attribute allows you to use an XPath expression to define a boundary for a resized widget.

In this example, we set the `resizeConstraint` attribute specifying that the widget can be resized no larger than its parent:

```
<div style="width: 200px; height: 200px; border: 1px solid black;">
  This is the parent div widget.
  <div style="width: 100px; height: 100px; border: 1px solid red;"
    e:behavior="b:resize" resizeConstraint="..">
    This div cannot be resized larger than the parent widget.
  </div>
</div>
```

The following picture shows what happens when you try to resize the constrained element from the example outside its container.

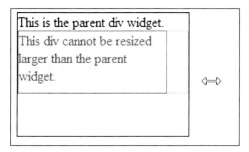

Advanced uses of resize scenarios could involve storing the new position of a widget so that the widget is already resized the next time the user views the application or allowing the user to reset the widget to a previously resized position.

Resize custom events

The resize behavior has three custom events that you can hook into. These events cover each phase while resizing a widget. They will come in handy when your needs exceed the out of the box functionality of the resize behavior and attributes. Most often, you won't necessarily want to override the default behavior of the events, but you might want to hook into the events in order to add additional functionality.

The resize custom events are:

Event	Description
resize	Fires when the size of the object is about to change. The event can be cancelled.
resizeEnd	Fires when the resizing ends (mouseup). Sets the new dimensions of the object and completes the resize process. The event can be cancelled.
resizeStart	Fires when the user begins to change the dimensions of the object. The event bubbles and can be cancelled.

Additionally, there are *properties* these event objects can have available:

- resizeEdges: Space-separated list of current moving edges and their types.
- originalLeft: Original left border position of the resized widget.
- originalTop: Original top border position of the resized widget.
- originalWidth: Original width of the resized widget.

- `originalHeight`: Original height of the resized widget.
- `newLeft`: New left border position of the resized widget. Can be modified by the event handler.
- `newTop`: New top border position of the resized widget. Can be modified by the event handler.
- `newWidth`: New width of the resized widget. Can be modified by the event handler.
- `newHeight`: New height of the resized widget. Can be modified by the event handler.
- `realWidth`: Real, box sizing independent width of the resized widget.
- `realHeight`: Real, box sizing independent height of the resized widget.

The following example uses the `resizeEnd` event to start an action (here, just a simple alert) to show the idea:

```
<b:box e:behavior="b:resize" width="100px" height="100px"
  position="absolute" left="50px" top="100px">
  Resize me!
  <e:handler event="resizeEnd" type="text/javascript">
    alert('The new right edge is at: ' + (event.newLeft +
    event.newWidth) + 'px');
  </e:handler>
</b:box>
```

In the source code provided with this book, you can find two more examples about resizing widgets. We show a part of the code for each here:

Custom Grippies

This example can be found in: `bookApps/behaviors/resize_custom_grippy.html`. In this example, an image can be resized by dragging one of the custom-defined grippies:

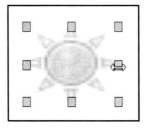

The example uses some ugly code, such as an XEL function, which we had advised not to use. For brevity of the example, we left it in:

```
<e:function name="doResize">
    <e:argument name="edge"/>
    <e:argument name="elm"/>
    <e:argument name="event"/>
    <e:body type="application/javascript">
        btl.resize.startResize(elm.controller, elm,
            edge, event.clientX + bb.viewport.scrollLeft,
            event.clientY + bb.viewport.scrollLeft, elm);
    </e:body>
</e:function>
```

The doResize function is called when the mouse is held down on one of the blue square grippies, as you can see from the following code:

```
<div e:behavior="b:resizeBase" style="position:absolute;
    left:200px; top:200px; width:100px; height:100px;">
    <div class="grippy" style="top:45%; left:0px;
        cursor: w-resize;"
        onmousedown="doResize(btl.resize.WEST,
        this.parentNode, event || window.event);"/>
    <div class="grippy" style="top:0px;left:0px;
        cursor: nw-resize;"
        onmousedown="doResize(btl.resize.NORTHWEST,
        this.parentNode, event || window.event);"/>
    <div class="grippy" style="top:0px;left:45%;
        cursor: n-resize;"
        onmousedown="doResize(btl.resize.NORTH,
        this.parentNode, event || window.event);"/>
    <!-- more grippies here -->
    <img src="media/weather-clear.png" width="100%" height="100%"/>
</div>
```

In the doResize XEL function, the btl.resize.startResize function is used to do the actual resizing. This function has a large number of arguments that you can find described in the Backbase API Reference.

You need quite a bit of code to make these custom grippies. In the way it is coded here, you would need to do the same for every image or any other element that needs these custom grippies. Therefore, this example is a good prospect for the building of a custom behavior. This (developing a custom behaviour) would make it easy to attach these custom grippies to any widget. We will see in the next chapter how custom behaviors can be developed.

Resizing table columns

This example can be found in: bookApps/behaviors/resize_custom_table.html.
This example has a simple table-like structure, the one we used for dragging columns
to a new position. Here, some fairly involved event handlers are defined to allow a
column to be resized.

Column 1	Column 2	Column 3	Column 4
Content 1	Content 2	Content 3	Content 4
Content 1	Content 2	Content 3	Content 4

This is how the resize takes place using event handlers:

- The mousemove event is used to find out whether the mouse is on top of a
  header element and near an edge. In that case, a resize cursor is shown.

- The mousedown event will start the resize if appropriate and show
  a resize line.

- The resizeEnd event will hide the line and finish.

We will not show all of the code for this example, but to give you a flavor of what
is involved, here is the mousedown event handler:

```
<e:handler event="mousedown" type="application/javascript">
<![CDATA[
   //Only when we are near an edge
   if( this._.resizeEdge && event.viewTarget.nodeName ==
      'TH' ) {
      //Select the correct cell for resizing and store
      // it on the object internal (for resizeEnd event)
      this._.resizeElm = this._.resizeEdge &
         btl.resize.RIGHT ?
            event.viewTarget : event.viewTarget.
               parentNode.parentNode.rows[0].
               cells[event.viewTarget.cellIndex - 1];
      //We use a line as symbol
      var oSymbol = document.getElementById('resizeLine');
      //Start the resize
      btl.resize.startResize(this, this._.resizeElm,
         btl.resize.RIGHT,
         event.clientX + bb.viewport.scrollLeft,
         event.clientY + bb.viewport.scrollTop,
            oSymbol, 20, 20);
      //Set the symbol height to the table height
```

```
        oSymbol.style.height = this.viewNode.offsetHeight+'px';
    }
]]>
</e:handler>
```

You will probably understand what is going on, but maybe you also notice that the code contains undocumented functionality, such as `this._.resizeEdge`. Unfortunately, there seems to be no easy alternative to achieve the same effect. We can just say that much more is possible using the Backbase framework than meets the eye and that there is room for improvement of both the framework and the documentation!

By now, you probably know more about resizing elements than you ever wanted to know. Therefore, we're going to stop discussing this subject. We will round up this section about *behaviors* with a description of the commands you can use to manage them.

Commands for the behaviors

In Chapter 3, we introduced the Backbase Command Functions and in their overview, you could find a set of commands to manipulate *behaviors*. These are three commands that are intended to add, remove, or set a behavior.

The behavioral commands, by now, have all the very familiar `select` and `with` attributes.

addBehavior

It adds the specified behavior to the targeted element.

Clicking of the button causes the `resize` behavior to be added. This can be achieved by using the following code:

```
<b:button>
   Click to add resize behavior to newly resizable widget.
   <e:handler event="click">
      <c:addBehavior with="id('resizable_element')"
         select="'b:resize'" />
   </e:handler>
</b:button>
<div id="resizable_element" style="border:1px solid green;
  width:100px; height:100px;">
   Can only be resized after the button is clicked.
</div>
```

removeBehavior

It removes the specified behavior from the targeted element.

Clicking of the button causes the `resize` behavior to be removed. Here's the code for removeBehavior:

```
<b:button>
   Click to remove resize behavior from currently
   resizable widget.
   <e:handler event="click">
      <c:removeBehavior with="id('resizable_element')"
         select="'b:resize'" />
    </e:handler>
</b:button>
<div id="resizable_element" e:behavior="b:resize"
  style="border:1px solid green; width:100px; height:100px;">
   Will not be resizable after the button is clicked.
</div>
```

setBehavior

It sets the specified behavior on the targeted element.

Clicking of the button causes the `resize` behavior to be set. This behavior will *replace* other behaviors as shown in the next code snippet:

```
<b:button>
   Click to set resize behavior on widget.
   <e:handler event="click">
      <c:setBehavior with="id('resizable_element')"
         select="'b:resize'" />
   </e:handler>
</b:button>
<div id="resizable_element" e:behavior="b:drag"
  style="border:1px solid green; width:100px; height:100px;">
   Can only be resized after the button is clicked.
   Will not be draggable after button is clicked.
</div>
```

Broadcaster/observer

In the previous chapter, about data binding, we introduced the *observer pattern*. Data binding is a rather specific use of the observer pattern, where changes to the data made by one observer are notified to other observers so that they are able to update their views. Here, we are looking at a more generic implementation of this pattern.

Observer is a design pattern associated with broadcasting changes in state of a single object (commonly referred to as the broadcaster) to one or more observers. In a web application, the state of an object can be defined by the values of its attributes. Indeed, for a Backbase application, the pattern determines how changes to any of the attributes of a broadcasting element are propagated to observing elements.

Any element can be used as a broadcaster in a Backbase application or it can be a special BTL element named `broadcaster`.

For an element to be an observer, it should have its XEL `observes` global attribute set to a valid `id` of the broadcaster. Because the `observes` attribute is defined in the XEL namespace, you must then have a proper prefix, usually `e:` declared.

The following listing demonstrates how a change to the setting of the broadcaster `style` attribute will be propagated automatically to the `style` attribute of two observing elements:

```
<b:broadcaster id="colorChanger" style="color: turquoise" />
<div e:observes="colorChanger">Observer 1</div>
<div e:observes="colorChanger">Observer 2</div>
<b:button label="Observer"
  e:onclick="bb.document.getElementById('colorChanger')
  .setAttribute('style', 'color: yellow');">
   Set the broadcaster style attribute
</b:button>
```

Whenever an attribute of the broadcaster is changed, a `broadcast` event is dispatched to the elements that observe the broadcaster. By default, this event causes the attributes of the observers to be synchronized with those of the broadcaster.

Each time a page is loaded that contains a broadcaster, its attribute values, if specified, are propagated to all observers. This is why in the previous and next examples, the `style` of the observer elements is set to "`color: turquoise`" immediately after the load.

Setting the broadcaster attributes causes the `broadcast` event to be fired on observers. The following example will alert about `style` attribute modification:

```
<b:broadcaster id="colorChanger" style="color: turquoise" />
<div e:observes="colorChanger">
   Observer
   <e:handler event="broadcast" type="application/javascript">
   alert('div style about to be changed');
   </e:handler>
</div>
<b:button label="Observer"
   e:onclick="bb.document.getElementById('colorChanger')
   .setAttribute('style', 'color: yellow');">
    Set the broadcaster style attribute
</b:button>
```

In certain cases, it may be necessary to influence the observer/broadcaster default behavior (which is to synchronize the attributes of the observers with those of the broadcaster). To override the default behavior, it is necessary to intercept the `broadcast` event, perform a custom action, and prevent the default action that synchronizes the attributes.

The following example demonstrates how to override the default synchronization action, making use of information about attribute changes that is carried over by the `event` object:

- `attrURI`: stores the namespace Uniform Resource Identifier (URI) of the changed attribute.

- `attrName`: stores the name of the changed attribute.

- `attrValue`: stores the setting that the default event applies to the attribute. Here's the code:

```
<b:broadcaster id="colorChanger" style="color: turquoise" />
<div e:observes="colorChanger">
   Observer
   <e:handler event="broadcast" type="application/javascript">
      <![CDATA[
      if (!event.attrURI && event.attrName == 'style' &&
         event.attrValue == 'color: yellow') {
         bb.document.getElementById('colorChanger')
            .setAttribute('style', 'color: red');
         event.preventDefault();
      }
      ]]>
```

```
        </e:handler>
    </div>
    <b:button label="Observer"
        e:onclick="bb.document.getElementById('colorChanger')
        .setAttribute('style', 'color: yellow');">
        Set the broadcaster style attribute
    </b:button>
```

When is the observer pattern useful? Imagine we have an application with a menu bar, context menus, a tool bar, and a shortcut. It could be the case that several items in these bars/menus are intended to invoke the same functionality, for example, creating a new entry in a list.

If we had defined a broadcaster with an ID "brd_new" and set the menus to listen to that broadcaster, we could easily enable or disable the calls to the functionality by managing a `disabled` attribute in a single location: on the broadcaster. The same broadcaster could also be used to share the textual representation of such a command, by, for example, means of a shared `label` attribute.

Here is a similar example, where the picture says it all: by deselecting the **Enable** checkbox, all elements below it are disabled:

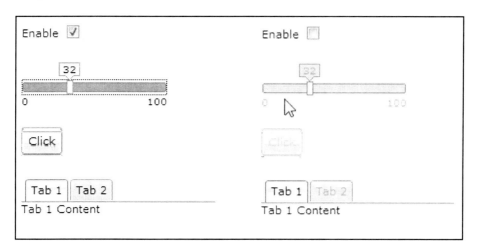

But you'd probably like to see the code too. So, here's the code:

```
<script type="text/javascript">
function setState(event) {
    event.target.setAttribute('disabled',
        event.attrValue=='true'?'false':'true');
    event.preventDefault();
}
```

```
    </script>
    <label>Enable
        <input id="checkbox" type="checkbox" checked="checked">
            <e:handler event="change" type="text/javascript">
                var oBroadcaster =
                    bb.document.getElementById('broadcaster');
                oBroadcaster.setAttribute('disabled',
                    this.getProperty('checked')?'false':'true');
            </e:handler>
        </input>
    </label>
    <b:broadcaster id="broadcaster" disabled="false" />
    <b:slider e:observes="broadcaster" margin="20px 0 20px 0" e:broadcast=
    "setState(event)" />
    <b:button e:observes="broadcaster"
        margin="0 0 20px 0" e:broadcast="setState(event)"
            e:onclick="alert('Click!')">
        Click
    </b:button>
    <b:tabBox height="200px" width="200px">
        <b:tab label="Tab 1">Tab 1 Content</b:tab>
        <b:tab label="Tab 2" e:observes="broadcaster"
            e:broadcast="setState(event)">
            Tab 2 Content</b:tab>
    </b:tabBox>
```

This example can be found in the Backbase Explorer, where you can try it for yourself.

Animating the UI

To spice up the look of your website, it can be functional to include some animation into your UI.

SMIL animation

Support for SMIL is built-in the Backbase core framework.

Synchronized Multimedia Integration Language (SMIL, pronounced "smile") version 2.1 is an XML-based language that allows interactive multimedia presentations. Using SMIL, you can describe the temporal behavior of a presentation, associate links with media objects, and describe the presentation layout. You can apply SMIL elements to widgets (such as XHTML or BTL elements) to add rich animation functionality.

You can find more information and the complete SMIL specification at: `http://www.w3.org/TR/SMIL2/`.

Support for SMIL is built into the core, and while you do need to include the correct namespace declaration, you do not need to include any extra files. Here's the correct SMIL namespace declaration: `http://www.w3.org/2005/SMIL21/`.

The Client Runtime supports the following SMIL 2.1 modules:

- `BasicAnimation`
- `BasicInlineTiming`

SMIL elements can be used inside contexts that can contain XEL execution tags, for example, within an XEL `handler` or `function` tag, and any TDL function body.

The following example changes the CSS `border-color` and `border-width` style attribute values of an XHTML `span` widget over a five second period.

```
<span style="border-color:#dddddd; border-style: solid;
  border-width:1px;">
  Click me to see the border color and width
  change over the next ten seconds...
  <e:handler event="click" type="application/xml">
     <smil:animate attributeName="border-color"
       dur="5s" values="#660000;#006600"
       fill="freeze" />
     <smil:animate attributeName="border-width"
       dur="10s" from="5px" to="10px" fill="freeze" />
  </e:handler>
</span>
```

In this example, you will actually see three states. At first, the `span` style is specified by the initial border color and width style properties. Secondly, there's the style when the widget is clicked (the beginning of the animation), and lastly, you see the style values at the end of the animation.

The `animate` widget is perhaps the most basic SMIL widget. The value of the `attributeName` attribute determines the style to be animated, while the `dur` attribute specifies how long it will take (the duration) from the beginning to the end of the animation.

Style attributes of the same element may have different animation durations. The border-color, for example, will change over a five-second period, but it will take ten seconds for the border-width attribute to increase from five to ten pixels. Most of the time, you will use the from and to attributes to specify the beginning and ending, and sometimes, you will use the values attribute that can also specify a number of intermediate values.

In the following example, the size of an image increases when the mouse is over that image. The animation for the mouseenter event is performed using the JavaScript API for SMIL, whereas the animation for the mouseleave event is performed using the XHTML API for SMIL.

```
<img src="media/weather-clear.png"
  alt="weather-clear" class="tile">
  <e:handler event="mouseenter" type="text/javascript">
      var oAnimationInfo = {
          attributeName: "height",
          attributeType:"CSS",
          dur: "1s",
          to: "250px", fill: "freeze"
      }
      // animate the height
      bb.smil.animate(this, oAnimationInfo);
      // animate the width
      oAnimationInfo.attributeName="width";
      bb.smil.animate(this, oAnimationInfo);
  </e:handler>
  <e:handler event="mouseleave" type="application/xml">
      <smil:animate attributeName="height" attributeType="CSS"
          dur="1s" to="50px" fill="freeze" />
      <smil:animate attributeName="width" attributeType="CSS"
          dur="1s" to="50px" fill="freeze" />
  </e:handler>
</img>
```

In the next and last animation example, we define a *behavior* to perform the animation on every row of a table. Although we will show how to define behaviors only in the next chapter, we assume that you will understand the code, knowing how drag-and-drop or resize works.

The following example gradually changes the CSS background-color of a table row. When the mouse enters the table row, which is detected by the handler tag defined in the behavior, the CSS background-color will transform from white (#FFFFFF) to purple (#7d8fce) in 250ms (dur="250ms"). On mouse leave, it will return to white in one second.

```
<d:namespace xmlns:sq="http://www.squaringthecircles.com/squared"
   name="http://www.squaringthecircles.com/squared">
   <d:behavior name="fx-color">
      <d:handler event="mouseenter" type="application/xml">
         <smil:animate attributeName="background-color"
            dur="250ms" to="#7d8fce" fill="freeze" />
      </d:handler>
      <d:handler event="mouseleave" type="application/xml">
         <smil:animate attributeName="background-color"
            dur="1s" to="#fff" fill="freeze" />
      </d:handler>
   </d:behavior>
</d:namespace>
<table xmlns:sq="http://www.squaringthecircles.com/squared"
   cellspacing="0" cellpadding="0" border="0"
   class="expenseTable">
   <thead>
      <tr>
         <th style="width: 60px;">Date</th>
         <th style="width: 150px;">Expense</th>
         <th style="width: 50px;">Amount</th>
         <th style="width: 200px;">Comment</th>
      </tr>
   </thead>
   <tbody>
      <tr e:behavior="sq:fx-color">
         <td>10-04-08</td>
         <td>Flight</td>
         <td>$1354.33</td>
         <td>Roundtrip from Amsterdam to New York.</td>
      </tr>
       <!-- more rows ... -->
      <tr e:behavior="sq:fx-color">
         <td>13-04-08</td>
         <td>Taxi</td>
          <td>$45.80</td>
         <td>Ride to JFK Airport.</td>
      </tr>
   </tbody>
</table>
```

Here is a screenshot:

Date	Expense	Amount	Comment
10-04-08	Flight	$1354.33	Roundtrip from Amsterdam to New York.
10-04-08	Taxi	$47.20	Ride to Marriott on Fifth Avenue.
11-04-08	Dinner	$278.67	Meal with clients at Kobe Club.
13-04-08	Hotel	$920.54	3 nights at Marriott on Fifth Avenue.
13-04-08	Taxi	$45.80	Ride to JFK Airport.

Adding animation to the C3D example application

So far, we have not been able to show photos, taken during a trip, in the C3D sample application. One major reason for this is that we haven't yet explained how you can upload photos to the server. In Chapter 4, there was an example using the `fileInput` widget. The use of that widget is not as straightforward as it seems in this example. This is because JavaScript cannot access the local filesystem and therefore, the file is uploaded in an `iframe` asynchronously from the rest of the form. Therefore, we faced some challenges in handling the uploaded photo on the server.

To describe how we solved this problem is outside the scope of this chapter. In Chapter 11 we show how synchronization can work for the C3D application.

Assuming that we have a set of photos uploaded and available now, we would like to use animation to be able to scroll smoothly through these photos in thumbnail form and maybe show an enlargement in a modal window if a user clicks on a photo.

For the smooth scrolling of the thumbnails, we borrowed an SMIL example from the Backbase Explorer. For our C3D application, it looks like this (the example code is placed in the `bookApps/animation` folder):

Although this is a very nice code for the purpose of the example in the Backbase Explorer, for our C3D travel blog, we need to do more work to integrate it into the application and to make it into a useful and reusable UI component. This is what we are going to discuss in the next chapter, when we will look at the Tag Definition Language in detail. We will then show the adapted code that is suitable for use in the C3D sample application.

Summary

This was a not-so-long chapter with a seemingly diverse number of subjects. However, they all were related to *dynamic behavior* of a web application and as such this chapter was a continuation of the topics presented in Chapter 3.

To summarize, we talked about:

- **Behaviors**: generic functionality that you can attach to any Backbase element
- The **drag-and-drop** behavior and the many options that you have to influence the dragging of elements and the things you can do when the element is dropped
- The **resize** behavior with its options
- **Command functions** to add, remove, or set behaviors dynamically
- The **broadcaster/observer** elements and functions
- Animation with **Synchronized Multimedia Integration Language** (SMIL)

In the next chapter, our subject will be the *Tag Definition Language*, finally!

7
Creating UI Components

There have already been a few key chapters in this book. For example, what would a book about an AJAX framework be without a chapter about client/server communication? Or, without a chapter about data-bound widgets, the elegant way to divide data content, and view structure in a widget made possible by AJAX?

Here is another key chapter. Its title could have been: *Squaring the Circles of Web Applications*, which also could have been the subtitle of this book. It is about building your own UI component with the Tag Definition Language (TDL), where the UI component is encapsulated as an XML tag in a custom namespace to allow it to be placed on a web page as a first class citizen, just like any XHTML or BTL element.

Even the most complete library of UI widgets will never cover all the requirements of a particular application. The standard way of extending what you need is adding some JavaScript here and there, often resulting in a spaghetti bowl of JavaScript functions that is hard to untangle, maintain, and extend. If you are using a JavaScript library or framework, it takes maybe a bit longer before your code becomes spaghetti; however, because you basically add JavaScript code to existing XHTML tags, the friction stays between two entangled syntaxes: the XML declarative syntax and the JavaScript procedural syntax.

It doesn't need to be that way! The Tag Definition Language allows you to build new declarative elements according to the XML syntax, where the JavaScript is encapsulated in local, small pieces of code that are used for event handling and object methods. This chapter is going to explain how.

Here is a list of subjects that we will cover in this chapter:

- Component models and technologies
- Introduction to the Tag Definition Language
- Simple widgets: templates, attributes, and resources
- Widget event handling

- Widgets as objects: classes, properties, methods, constructors, and destructors
- Composite widgets
- Inheritance, interfaces, and extending BTL
- Behaviors
- The limits of creating UI components

Component models and technologies

The Tag Definition Language of Backbase is *not* the only existing language that offers the facility to build custom UI components as XML elements. The notion of XML tag libraries may be more familiar to Java developers using JavaServer Pages or the like, but also on the client-side there are several products that allow you to define new XML tags and use these as UI components. We list some of these here briefly:

- HTML Components (HTCs) is a Microsoft technology available for the Internet Explorer providing a mechanism to implement components in script as Dynamic HTML (DHTML) behaviors.
- XBL (XML Binding Language) is an XML-based markup language used to declare the behavior and look of XUL widget (a UI widget in a Mozilla browser).
- The new, XBL 2.0 version of the specification is adopted by the W3C standards body as a recommendation. No industrial-strength implementation exists yet.
- The Backbase TDL: one of its unique features is that it works with all modern browsers and that it does not require a plugin.

Introduction to the Tag Definition Language (TDL)

The Backbase framework provides a binding language called Tag Definition Language (TDL). The TDL is XML-compliant and has its foundations in object-oriented programming languages. It provides a set of elements and attributes required for the definition of new widgets or tags. The TDL serves as a means to bind classes to document-level markup elements. The Backbase implementation of XHTML and all the BTL widgets are constructed with the TDL.

Widgets

At the start of Chapter 2, we defined a *widget* as a visible "thing" on a page. Throughout the book, we have tried to avoid confusion by using the term widget in this way and using *element* for more general "things", not necessarily visible. *Control* is synonymous to widget, but we try not to use it. A *tag* is nothing but the name of a widget, as you already know from XML.

In a more technical sense, we are going to use the term *widget* for any JavaScript object that you can define using TDL. In the Backbase framework, all BTL "things" are defined with TDL, therefore, `accordion`, `calendar`, `button`, `spinner`, and `tabBox` elements are all Backbase widgets. What this means we will see later in this chapter.

Sometimes, we will call a widget that is an element defined in TDL a *UI component*.

The advantages of using TDL

We have already said several times that the major advantage of using the Backbase framework is the possibility of using TDL—the possibility to define your own widgets or to easily change existing ones.

Because TDL is an object-oriented language, it allows you to do all the things that you can do with objects: define widgets as classes, extend existing widgets, add new behavior or presentation to a widget, and compose multiple widgets into one larger widget.

Object-orientation

We argued several times now that TDL is great because it is an object-oriented (OO) language. Maybe you cannot follow this reasoning, either because you are not so familiar with OO, or because you do not think that OO is a good idea at all, or because you do not know how OO is implemented in TDL. Let us address all three points.

Object-oriented concepts

OO is a rather elusive concept that is implemented differently in each modern programming language. The most pure OO language that we know of is Smalltalk, where everything is an object, but this language is hardly mainstream today. Other languages that may be more familiar to you are Java, C++, and C#, where there are objects and classes, or PHP, which has similar facilities but where OO is implemented as a kind of afterthought and where it is too easy to write applications without one single object. There is also Ruby, increasing in popularity, which we do not know enough about. And of course, there is JavaScript, which is object-based and therefore, does not support classes.

In each case, there are commonalities: objects are blocks of code that provide abstraction, encapsulation, and polymorphism.

Abstraction means that you are looking at your code from a higher level. Simply said: if you are implementing an object that describes a *car*, then call it `car` and not `obj123`. In the late eighties of the previous century, this was not as obvious as it is now. Using these concepts made it possible to cross the bridge between business analysts and software developers, and resulted in software that was closer to what users expected and that was easier to maintain.

Encapsulation, or information hiding, means that all data and behavior (routines, functions, or methods that access this data) are put in one place and that a clear API is defined, describing how the state can be accessed and the behavior be manipulated. This means that the implementation of an object could change without changing the API and therefore, without impacting the rest of the application. This adds further to the abstraction of the objects.

For example, if you want to put a calendar on your page, then you would like to write `<b:calendar/>` because that fits within the XML way of coding on a page containing HTML, instead of a set of `div` tags, with custom and vague CSS class names, and where you have to hunt the implementation inside CSS files and JavaScript libraries throughout your application. TDL allows you to do the simple thing—put an XML tag on your page (`<b:calandar />` in our example).

Polymorphism, or literally "many forms", has to do with the inheritance or extension capabilities of most OO languages. It allows you to define a more abstract concept, say *vehicle* and then extend it into *car* and *truck*, which are both vehicles. All vehicles drive on roads, but depending on the law, trucks may have a maximum speed that is different from a car. Still, you can code a sentence such as: "give me the maximum speed of this vehicle", and you would get a different answer depending on whether the object was a car or a truck.

Inheritance also relates to *method overriding*. In our maximum speed example, the vehicle class would have a `getMaximumSpeed` method, and both the car as well as the truck would have a method with the same name, each returning a different value. Maybe there is also a `three-wheel-car` class that would extend the `car` class, but allow a lower maximum speed. It could have its own `getMaximumSpeed` method that would override the method with the same name in the superclass.

In some languages, such as Java, you can also use interfaces to implement polymorphic behavior. For example, there could be a `print` interface that could apply to very diverse objects that have no inheritance relationship to each other (except `Object`, the granddad of all objects in Java).

OO and TDL

How is OO implemented in the TDL language?

- TDL supports *objects* and *classes*. To stay with our vehicle example, a class could be `car`. Whereas, an object or instance of this class could be my `Peugeot` model `406` with color `green`. Or, in case of our calendar, the class `calendar` is coded as a TDL element definition. We will see how to make these in the rest of this chapter. The object is the `<b:calendar format="d-MMMM-yy" />` on our page, where we have chosen a specific format. You define a class in TDL using the `element` tag.

- TDL supports *inheritance*. A car inherits all the properties and behavior of a vehicle, such as the capability to drive on a road, having wheels, and a maximum speed. A `calendar` inherits from `dimensionElement`, `positionElement`, and a few others, as we have seen in Chapter 4. Inheritance can be indicated on a TDL element by using the `extends` attribute.

- TDL supports *multiple inheritance*. This means that a TDL element can inherit from more than one TDL element. This is different from multilevel inheritance. Multiple inheritance has one specific danger: if your class has two superclasses both containing a method of the same name (for example: `print`), then which method will be chosen to be executed? Within TDL, this will be the first method found.

- TDL has *interfaces*. An interface specifies a set of methods that will be implemented for a class. An interface is coded using the `interface` tag. You can declare that a class will adhere to an interface by coding the `implements` attribute on the `element` tag.

- TDL clearly supports *encapsulation* because it allows you to put data (properties) and behavior (methods) together in an object. TDL does not support *private* or *protected* properties and methods, like Java. Private data and behavior allows the developer to protect an object from unauthorized or accidental wrong access. We think this is a minor problem, considering that Smalltalk does not support this either.

OO and web applications

The third question we were asking was whether the use of object-orientation is a good idea for web applications. You will be using OO if you want to manage and control the complexity of an application.

In the olden days, when each piece of behavior was allowed to access any piece of data, the complexity of an application would grow exponentially with its size. In an OO application, the access to data by pieces of behavior is very restricted and also abstracted through encapsulation. Therefore, a well-designed OO application will grow only linearly with size.

While web applications are evolving from simple HTML pages to complex and complete business applications, it is necessary to keep the complexity of these applications within manageable bounds. OO allows you to do that.

Model-View-Controller

In Chapter 4, we talked about the Model-View-Controller (MVC) architecture of the C3D travel blog application as a whole. In a modern web application, it is not enough to layer your application by putting just the *view* on the client and the *controller* with the *model* on the server. Disregarding for now how you can structure the application on the server further, let us turn our attention to the client.

We already said that the client part of a web application can be considered as an application in itself; therefore, you could structure the client web application using an MVC approach again. In fact, a Backbase application is more like a set of interacting UI components, where each component follows an MVC design pattern. Discussing MVC in this chapter refers to developing UI components and not to developing client applications. You can get a feeling for the MVC structure of each UI component by taking a look at the debugger. When you open the debugger, you will see a **Model** and a **View** tab that shows model and view information for each component. We will talk more about the debugger in the next chapter, but for now, you should know that you can open the debugger by pressing the *Esc* key. We show here some examples of useful information that you can find.

In case you had an accordion on your page, you will find a `b:accordion` tag with child `b:accordionItem` tags on the **Model** tab page. You can double-click on the tab and a list of interesting attributes, methods, handlers, and more will appear on the right-hand side. If you click on the **View** tab, you will see a number of nested `div` tags that have suggestive class names like `btl-accordion` and `btl-accordionItem`. The view part is what the browser sees and renders in your browser window. The model and controller parts are the parts you see as a developer.

Generally speaking, a widget has an abstract (non-visual) part that provides functionality and logic. We call that the widget *controller* and it is implemented as a JavaScript object. The widget will also have a *view* part that adds the visual presentation of the widget. This is actually not yet what you see on the browser window, it is the DOM tree as built by the **Client Runtime** from your TDL definitions or from other predefined elements. This DOM tree is interpreted by the browser to build the visual browser window.

The *model* part of your widget is the XHTML that the developer codes on a page, such as `<yourNamespace:yourWidget ... />` or `<b:accordion>...</b:accordion>`.

If we refer to *the* controller, we mean the controller layer, representing all controllers and their interaction together. If we refer to *a* controller, we mean a specific controller object for a specific widget.

You may also see the terms **modelNode, viewNode**, and **viewGate**:

- The `modelNode` API is browser dependent. Generally, there should be no reason to access this. Do not confuse this with the model part of your UI component.

- The `viewNode` is accessed if you need to change or control the appearance of your widget. It is the root node of the visual structure that represents your widget.

- Manipulating the view node directly should only be done if you are sure that this is browser independent. Otherwise, you can use the `bb.html` object that has many utility functions to allow browser-independent access to view nodes.

- The `viewGate` is the node where new presentation child-nodes will be appended by the framework (if required).

You can reach these nodes from a controller by coding `this.modelNode`, `this.viewNode` or `this.viewGate`. We will see examples later in this chapter.

Widget creation with TDL

With TDL you can extend BTL widgets, create your own custom widgets to be used by application developers, or even create your own custom XML languages that can be visualized by the client browser.

Overview of the TDL elements

Before we start explaining each TDL element by showing examples, let us briefly present an overview of the available tags. First, here is a list of the tags we already saw because they allow you to define classes of TDL elements:

Tags	Description
element	Declares an element within a namespace. It must be child of a namespace tag. This tag defines a class in TDL. The element is instantiated as an object when the XML tag is placed on the page.
property	Declares a property of an element. Properties are similar to attributes, but are intended to keep the internal state of a widget. As opposed to properties, which can only have a string data type, properties can be of any data type allowed for JavaScript. Child elements of property can be getter and setter. With getter, you can customize the value that is returned when the value of a property is requested. With setter, you can define a piece of code to be executed when a property value is set.
method	Defines a method on an element. Child elements of method can be argument and body.

These three tags are the basic building blocks of the OO constructs in the TDL language.

The next list of TDL elements can determine the appearance of a widget that you define using TDL:

Elements	Description
resource	Adds a resource to the namespace, document, or element (for example, a CSS stylesheet or JavaScript).
template	Templates define the content of a widget definition. You can use a content element once within the template to insert view contents for a specific instance of an element into the template. It also provides the insertion point for child elements of the widget.
content	Used within a template element to specify where the children of the element will be inserted into the visual representation template.

Elements	Description
attribute	Declares an attribute of an element. Attributes can be used to define the appearance of a specific instance of a widget. Although attributes can be get and set, they should not be confused with properties, as explained later in this chapter. The changer and mapper elements can be used to customize the setting of an attribute.

A very important TDL element is the handler element. With this element, you can apply event handlers to your own widgets in a predefined way, similar to the handler element of the XEL language that we already saw so many times.

Here are the tags that keep TDL definitions together and that put these definitions into a namespace.

Tags	Description
tdl	The tdl tag can be used as the root tag for a widget definition. namespace is the only child element a tdl element can have. You only need to use this tag if you have no other root element for your XML document.
namespace	The TDL-specific child elements that you will see are: element, interface, and resource. Any element is allowed as a child to namespace.

Finally, there is the document element that never seems to be used. It is intended to extend bb.document. We will ignore it.

Simple widgets

Simple widgets are the ones that are static. Maybe they have a CSS class applied or maybe there are attributes that help to change the appearance of the widget.

Building a TDL widget definition

In this section, we'll discuss how to get a TDL definition off the ground. The basic skeleton for a new widget built in TDL has three elements: the tdl root tag, a namespace identifier, and a widget declaration using the element tag.

The following example shows the required code necessary to create a widget skeleton. For each TDL definition, you will need a namespace tag that will contain one or more element tags.

```
<?xml version="1.0"?>
<d:tdl xmlns:d="http://www.backbase.com/2006/tdl">
```

```
<d:namespace
   name="http://www.squaringthecircles.com/squared">
   <d:element name="yourWidget">
   <!--
      children of the d:element tag consist of widget attributes,
      properties, methods, etc.
   -->
   </d:element>
   <d:element name="yourWidgetToo">
    <!--
      you can have more than one element within a namespace
    -->
   </d:element>
   </d:namespace>
</d:tdl>
```

You can place TDL on your application page or in a separate file. We will describe later in this chapter how to do this. For a production environment of your application, it is recommended to put TDL widget definitions in external files. In the examples of this chapter, we will place the definitions usually next to the code that uses them, to make them more easily readable and executable.

The `namespace` tag attaches a widget to a unique XML namespace. The `name` attribute of the `element` tag names the widget and binds it to a widget in the web application with the same name and same namespace.

An `extends` attribute can specify an inheritance relationship between widgets. This means that a TDL widget, which extends another TDL widget, can use methods and properties already defined in the widget it extends. See the section on *inheritance* later in this chapter for more information.

When placing a widget on an application page, a developer would declare the appropriate namespace, include the widget definition file of the widget and all dependent files, and instantiate the widget as named in the TDL definition.

The following example instantiates a widget that has a widget name of `yourWidget` and belongs to a namespace named `http://www.squaringthecircles.com/squared`:

```
<script xmlns:xi="http://www.w3.org/2001/XInclude"
   xmlns:sq="http://www.squaringthecircles.com/squared"
   type="application/backbase+xml">
   <!-- You may have the definition of your widget in an
      external file. -->
   <xi:include href="yourWidgetDefinitionFile.xml" />
```

```
    <sq:yourWidget>
        <!--    the contents of your widget go here -->
    </sq:yourWidget>
</script>
```

We have seen now how you can make a basic TDL widget definition and how to make use of namespaces. So far, there is not much you can do with a widget definition like this because it has no content. This is our next task to look at.

The template, attribute, and resource tags

This section provides a description of two primary TDL tags that are children of the `element` tag:

- The `template` tag, which allows you to define static XHTML content for your widget.

- The `attribute` tag, which allows you to influence the appearance of the widget when it is coded in a page. Attributes can have `changer` and `mapper` as child tags. These allow you to specify behavior depending on the value of the attribute when it is set or changed.

We'll also look at the `resource` tag, which can be used as an example for the purpose of defining CSS style information together with your widget. You can also use other kinds of file resources as we will see later in this chapter.

These tags allow you to build static widgets that have no behavior of their own. Dynamic behavior will be enabled by using *event handlers* (see the upcoming section, *Widget event handling*). The sections following the event handling discussion will look at the features of the TDL language that allow you to build elements as objects, with state and behavior, and the tags that implement it.

Templates

The `template` tag defines the structure of the visualized content, or the content rendered in the client browser when the widget is instantiated.

The `template` tag has one attribute:

Attribute	Description
type	This attribute is required and can have the value text/javascript or application/xml.

The template content *must* be in the XHTML namespace.

 A frequently asked question is why templates cannot contain BTL or your own widgets. It was just not implemented that way. There are other ways of composing widgets into larger widgets that we will discuss later. See also the discussion at the end of this chapter.

A very basic template might create something simple, such as a label with a text input field. Here is a widget that has static text (HTML) in a template.

```
<d:namespace xmlns:d="http://www.backbase.com/2006/tdl"
  name="http://www.squaringthecircles.com/squared">
  <d:element name="yourInputWidget">
    <d:template type="application/xhtml+xml">
      <div>
        <label for="myInput">
          My Text Input Field:
        </label>
        <input id="myInput" name="myInput" />
      </div>
    </d:template>
  </d:element>
</d:namespace>
<div xmlns:sq="http://www.squaringthecircles.com/squared">
  <p>
    See the instantiated widget below:
  </p>
  <sq:yourInputWidget />
</div>
```

If you try this out, you will see that this is not a very interesting widget because its contents are static. Moreover, although you will not get an error message, there is a problem with this widget: it contains an `id` attribute in the `input` field that is needed for the `for` attribute in the `label`. This means that you should instantiate this widget only once on a page, to avoid duplicate IDs.

See the instantiated widget below:
My Text Input Field:

It is instructive to see what this widget will be like both in the model and in the view layer of the framework. You can see this in the Backbase debugger, an excellent tool that we will talk about a little bit more in the next chapter. You can start it by pressing the *Esc* key, or sometimes it starts unexpectedly, with an error message. Maybe you have seen it!

In the **Model** part, you only see the tag as coded in the example: `<sq:yourInputWidget>`:

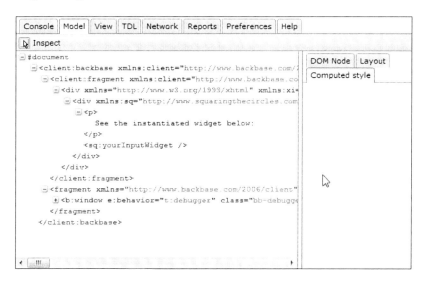

In the **View** part, you can see all the elements that were placed in the template. You can access them by referring to the `viewNode` of the widget:

The `template` element must contain a proper tree. The following example is invalid because it does not have a single root element.

```
<d:namespace xmlns:d="http://www.backbase.com/2006/tdl"
  name="http://www.squaringthecircles.com/squared">
  <d:element name="yourInputwidget">
      <d:template type="application/xml">
    <div>
       <label for="myInput1">My Text Input Field 1:
       </label>
       <input name="myInput1" id="myInput1" />
    </div>
    <div>
       <label for="myInput2">My Text Input Field 2:
       </label>
       <input name="myInput2" id="myInput2" />
    </div>
      </d:template>
    </d:element>
</d:namespace>
<div xmlns:sq="http://www.squaringthecircles.com/squared">
   <p>Can we instantiate the widget?</p>
   <sq:yourInputWidget />
</div>
```

If you try this one, you will get the following message:

```
TDL: Only one direct child element allowed in the
   "application/xhtml+xml" template.
```

Of course, you can easily fix the problem in this case by surrounding the content of the template with a `div`.

The content tag

Many UI widgets can have other widgets as children, for example, a `tabBox` can contain a set of `tab` elements and the XHTML `div` element can have almost any element as child. The place in the DOM tree where child elements are inserted is determined by the `content` tag that you can insert somewhere in a `template`.

The widget definition in the next example can have dynamic text and XHTML, inserted at the location of the `content` tag.

```
<d:namespace xmlns:d="http://www.backbase.com/2006/tdl"
  name="http://www.squaringthecircles.com/squared">
  <d:element name="yellowNote">
    <d:template type="application/xhtml+xml">
```

```
            <div xmlns="http://www.w3.org/1999/xhtml"
                class="sq-yellowNote">
                <d:content />
            </div>
        </d:template>
    </d:element>
</d:namespace>
```

On your instance page, you can add content as a child of your defined widget, for example, as follows:

```
<div xmlns:sq="http://www.squaringthecircles.com/squared">
    <sq:yellowNote>
        There is just some text here.
    </sq:yellowNote>
    <sq:yellowNote>
        Read the <strong>Backbase book</strong>.
        Read the <strong>Backbase book</strong>.
        Read the <strong>Backbase book</strong>.
    </sq:yellowNote>
    <sq:yellowNote>
        Here is a list:
        <ul>
            <li>item 1</li>
            <li>item 2</li>
        </ul>
    </sq:yellowNote>
</div>
```

This code will show on your page as in the figure below:

Note that you can use XHTML tags to be inserted as text in the note. These will be appropriately formatted in the output.

What did we achieve by defining this widget? At first sight, this is just a `div` with some specific style information that turns a `div` into a yellow rectangle with a gray border.

However, if an organization uses many yellow notes in its web applications, then having a widget like this will help to ensure consistency. It is also easier to guess from an element with the name `yellowNote` than from a `div` element about what it is supposed to look like on the page.

What we had in mind when designing the `yellowNote` widget was to offer the possibility to paste sticky notes on a photo to explain parts of it, like you can do for photos on the well-known **Flickr** site at `http://www.flickr.com`. Later in this chapter, you will gradually see more capabilities added to our `yellowNote` widget.

By the way, the style looks like this:

```
.sq-yellowNote {
    padding: 2px 2px 2px 5px;
    border: 1px solid gray;
    background-color: #ffff99;
    width: 100px;
    margin: 5px;
    font-size: 10px;
    font-family: cursive;
    color: navy;
    float: left;
}
```

Note that the CSS class name was carefully chosen as: *prefix - dash - element name*, which conforms to the class name rules that BTL uses.

Templates with JavaScript

By setting the value of the `type` attribute to `text/javascript`, you can use JavaScript to generate your XHTML template structure, as in the example below:

```
<d:namespace xmlns:d="http://www.backbase.com/2006/tdl"
  name="http://www.squaringthecircles.com/squared">
  <d:element name="yourWidget">
    <d:template type="text/javascript">
      var oRoot = document.createElement('div');
      bb.command.setStyle(oRoot,{'background-color':'cyan',
        'padding':'10px'});
      var oGate = document.createElement('div');
      bb.html.setStyle(oGate,'background-color', 'yellow');
      oGate.style.padding='10px';
      oRoot.appendChild(oGate);
      return [oRoot, oGate];
    </d:template>
  </d:element>
</d:namespace>
```

In this code, we create a `div` tag (`oRoot`) with a cyan background and padding. Then, we create another `div` tag (`oGate`) with a yellow background and padding. We attach the `oGate` to `oRoot` as child.

On purpose, we have used three different ways to set a CSS style attribute using JavaScript:

- The first one is the JavaScript equivalent to the `<c:setStyle>`:

```
bb.command.setStyle(oRoot,{'background-color':'cyan',
    'padding':'10px'});
```

  The advantage is that you can set several style attributes in one command.

- The second one shields you from browser incompatibilities:

```
bb.html.setStyle(oGate,'background-color', 'yellow');
```

  For the style attributes, only opacity will cause a problem.

- The third one directly accesses the view object:

```
oGate.style.padding='10px';
```

You can code style attributes in the last way if you are sure that the attribute will work the same across browsers.

 The return type of the JavaScript template function is an array with two elements. The first element is intended to be the *root* tag of the returned XML structure. The second element is intended to be used as a base to attach further elements to.

In our example, further elements will be attached to `oGate`.

When we create a nested structure of `yourWidget` widgets, the `div`s will be shown inside each other because each following widget is attached to `oGate`:

```
<div xmlns:sq="http://www.squaringthecircles.com/squared">
    <sq:yourWidget>ABC
      <sq:yourWidget>DEF
         <sq:yourWidget>HIJ
         </sq:yourWidget>
      </sq:yourWidget>
    </sq:yourWidget>
</div>
```

Assume that in the example, the return statement would have read:

```
return [oRoot, oRoot];
```

In that case, the oRoot object would have been used to attach further elements, instead of oGate.

The snapshots of the running example show the difference in results. Here's the snapshot of the root attached to oGate:

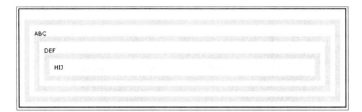

The next screenshot shows root attached to oRoot:

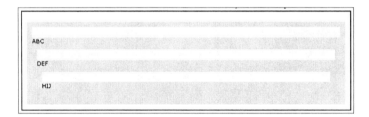

We conclude our discussion of templates by making several remarks:

- Place a content tag always as the only child of an XHTML tag, in most cases, a div.
- A template with JavaScript contents should always have a return statement, with the root node and the view gate as arguments.
- The view gate as specified in a template with JavaScript content has the same function as placing a content tag in an XHTML template.
- The Client Runtime produces a set of view nodes when it processes a template. This means that the content of a template can only reside in the XHTML namespace. As said previously, you cannot include BTL elements or elements from other namespaces in a template definition.

In the next part of this section, we will introduce the attribute element, which allows us to customize the appearance of a widget.

Attributes

Attributes help you to customize the visual appearance of a widget. An attribute is similar, but not the same as a property. We will explain this better in the *Defining Classes with TDL* section.

The `attribute` tag allows you to define an attribute for a TDL widget definition. You should create an attribute when you would like your widget to have certain characteristics that can be defined by the application developer when he/she puts the widget on the application page. Attribute values are always typed as string. The `attribute` tag can have these attributes:

Attribute	Description
default	Default value to be set in case no attribute value is provided.
name	Name of the attribute. This attribute is required.
namespace	Namespace for the attribute. Default attribute namespace is `null` (attribute not specified).
onchange	Script to be executed when the attribute value is changed.
onmap	Script to be executed when the element to which the attribute belongs is instantiated or when the attribute value is changed.

We will show the use of attributes in the next section.

Positioned yellow notes

Continuing with the *yellow note example*, we decided that yellow notes should be capable of being posted at any place in the browser window. Therefore, we will change the style of the `yellowNote` widget to include `position:absolute`, and we will add two attributes: `posx` and `posy`. The attributes will indicate where the widget will be put.

The example shows how to define these attributes. Because the `posx` and `posy` attributes need to have a value, they are given the default value `0`.

```
<d:namespace xmlns:d="http://www.backbase.com/2006/tdl"
  name="http://www.squaringthecircles.com/squared">
  <d:element name="yellowNote">
     <d:attribute name="posx" default="0"/>
     <d:attribute name="posy" default="0"/>
         <!-- ... the template goes here -->
  </d:element>
</d:namespace>
```

When you instantiate a widget on your application page, you can use the name of the attribute, in our example `posx` and so on, just like any other attribute in a BTL or XHTML widget. Here is a positioned yellow note:

```
<sq:yellowNote posx="160px" posy="80px">
    This is a positioned yellow note.
</sq:yellowNote>
```

Shortly, we will look into how we can do something with these attributes to see a yellow note on our page that is positioned. But first we show the methods that you can use to get and set attributes interactively:

In JavaScript, you can get or set the value of an attribute using the `getAttribute` or `setAttribute` methods respectively.

```
this.getAttribute('color');
this.setAttribute('color', 'yellow');
```

The `getAttribute` method returns the attribute value, while the `setAttribute` method allows you to set the attribute value.

Changers and mappers

We had no means yet to reflect attribute values onto some style attribute or do something else with them. **Changers** and **mappers** come to our rescue here.

The intention of our example is that if we set the `posx` attribute in the `yellowNote` widget to some value, the style attribute `left` of our widget should be set to the same value. The `posy` attribute value should be set as the `top` value of the style attribute. In other words, setting the attribute causes a *side effect*, which maps the attribute values to a position.

You can cause these side effects to occur by using either a `changer` or a `mapper`. This means that the `attribute` element can have `changer` and `mapper` as child tags. Code inside these child tags will be executed when the `setAttribute` method is called.

 The difference between a `mapper` and a `changer` is that the `mapper` is invoked when the widget is *instantiated* and the `changer` is not.

In the following snippet, the `posx` and `posy` values are used to set the position of the yellow note.

```
<d:attribute name="posx" default="0">
    <d:mapper type="text/javascript">
```

```
           bb.html.setStyle(this.viewNode, 'left', value);
       </d:mapper>
   </d:attribute>
   <d:attribute name="posy" default="0">
       <d:mapper type="text/javascript">
           bb.html.setStyle(this.viewNode, 'top', value);
       </d:mapper>
   </d:attribute>
```

The `mapper` code gets hold of the view node. We need this view node to set a `style` attribute, such as `left` and `top` in the example.

 `this` generally refers to the current context, which in this case is the object representing the instantiated widget and which is placed on the controller layer.

Here is a picture of what our page will look like with positioned notes. We *forgot* to position one yellow note, therefore, it appears at the top left of the page because the default values of the `posx` and `posy` attributes are both `0`.

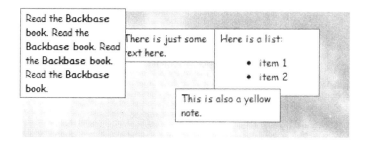

As mentioned, a `changer` is very similar to a `mapper`, except that the `changer` is not called when the widget is instantiated. Here's a not so useful example that just shows how it works:

```
   <d:attribute name="width">
       <d:changer type="text/javascript">
           alert(name + ' attribute changed to ' + value);
       </d:changer>
   </d:attribute>
```

Note the use of `name` and `value` in the previous examples. These are variables that are available within the body of an attribute or property so that you can easily work with the attribute/property name and value.

As a final example about attributes, we show that you can also create a `changer` or `mapper` as an attribute of the `attribute` tag itself:

```
<d:attribute name="width" onchange="alert('attribute value
    changed');" onmap="this.viewNode.style.width = value;" />
```

If the text of the JavaScript code you want to execute is very short, then this is a handy option.

Resources

Widgets may need custom styling or special functionality. In your TDL widget definition, you can specify a list of resources that must be included when the definition is loaded. These resources can be XML, CSS stylesheet files, JavaScript libraries, or image files. When you use an image resource, the file will preload to the browser cache. This can help to increase application performance.

The `resource` tag in your TDL widget definition allows you to specify a single resource to be included when the element definition is processed by the Client Runtime. Within the `resource` element, you must specify a source location and a value for the `type` attribute that describes the media type, for example `text/javascript`, `text/css`, or `image/jpg`. You can also specify the resource inline.

 The path to the included resource file is relative to the location of the file that includes it.

We will show a few examples of using resources. First, the inclusion of style information in the *yellow notes* example, and next, a rather complicated example using XSLT.

The yellow notes example using resources

We never told you how we included the style information for the yellow notes. Instead of a `style` tag, which would have been separate from the widget definition, we used a `resource` tag as follows:

```
<d:namespace
  name="http://www.squaringthecircles.com/squared">
  <d:resource type="text/css">
   .sq-yellowNote { /* the style definition goes here */ }
  </d:resource>
  <d:element name="yellowNote">
     <!-- The element definition goes here -->
  </d:element>
</d:namespace>
```

The `resource` tag allows you to define resources at the best place in your application. In our example, the style information should be with the element definition of the yellow notes widget, because it is specific for this widget. If you need a global resource from a file, CSS for example, then the `resource` tag can ensure that the resource is indeed available.

Named resources

You can also name your resources and define them inline if you wish. You can retrieve your resource later by adding the `name` attribute to the `resource` tag.

The following example defines two named resources: an XML file and a stylesheet to transform this XML with. The resource is retrieved within the template and the result of the transformation is XHTML that is processed by the browser.

```
<d:tdl xmlns:d="http://www.backbase.com/2006/tdl">
    <d:namespace
        name="http://www.squaringthecircles.com/squared">
        <d:element name="myBookList">
            <d:resource name="myXSL" type="application/xslt+xml">
                <xsl:stylesheet xmlns:xsl=
            "http://www.w3.org/1999/XSL/Transform" version="1.0">
                    <xsl:output method="html" />
                    <xsl:template match="/">
                        <div>   Book Title:
                            <ul>
                                <xsl:for-each select="books/book">
                                    <li>
                                        <xsl:value-of select="title" />
                                    </li>
                                </xsl:for-each>
                            </ul>
                        </div>
                    </xsl:template>
                </xsl:stylesheet>
            </d:resource>
            <d:resource name="myBooks"
                src="data/bookdata.xml" type="application/xml" />
            <d:template type="text/javascript">
            <![CDATA[
                var books = bb.getResource(this, 'myBooks');
                var oStylesheet = bb.getResource(this, 'myXSL');
                var oTransformedData =
                oStylesheet.transformToFragment(books, document);
                return [oTransformedData.firstChild, null];
```

```
        ]]>
        </d:template>
      </d:element>
    </d:namespace>
</d:tdl>
<!-- put the booklist on a page -->
<div xmlns:sq=  "http://www.squaringthecircles.com/squared"
id="book-list">
    <sq:myBookList />
  </div>
```

This example is interesting not only because of its use of named resources, but also because of its use of a stylesheet to generate the template. As input for the stylesheet, we need XML data, for example:

```
<books>
    <book sale="true">
        <title>book1</title>
        <price>$8.99</price>
    </book>
    <book sale="false">
        <title>book2</title>
        <price>$8.99</price>
    </book>
    <book sale="false">
        <title>book3</title>
        <price>$8.99</price>
    </book>
</books>
```

And this is the result:

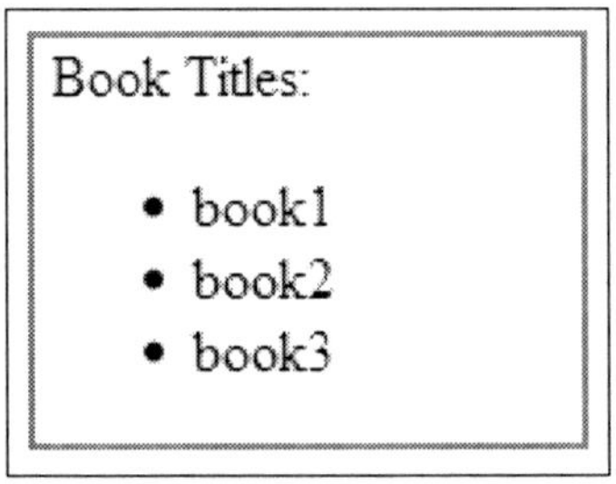

Book Titles:

- book1
- book2
- book3

In a real application, you would provide the data from a remote data source, as we explained in Chapter 5, when talking about data binding, instead of a fixed set of data like we used here.

This concludes our section about simple TDL elements. We have seen that with the three elements described (`template`, `attribute`, and `resource`) we can already build quite flexible widgets. In the next section, we will make our widgets dynamic by adding the capability to handle events.

Widget event handling

Events, such as mouse clicks or DOM mutation events can be handled for TDL widgets in a way very similar to that of XEL handlers attached to widget instances on a page. The handlers specified for TDL widget definitions will be there for *every instance* of that widget. Any XEL event handler that may be specified on a specific widget will be called before any handler defined in TDL. The TDL event handlers reside in the TDL namespace instead of the XEL namespace.

Event handlers allow you to respond to events that occur on a widget. Code within the handler is executed when the specified event type is triggered.

The handler tag

The `handler` tag describes an event that you want to handle for the widget and what functionality to execute when that event is triggered. The `handler` tag has these attributes:

Attribute	Description
defaultAction	Allows you to control the event flow. It defines the propagation behavior on a single node (`cancel`, `perform`).
event	The name of event to which the handler will listen. Once the event is fired within its context, the event handler will execute code within the handler.
match	Allows for adjusting the handler's target, so that it will only be processed when the rule specified matches on an element in the element view space.
phase	Specifies when the handler will be activated by the desired event. By setting the phase attribute to capture, the event will be handled during the capturing phase. Otherwise, the event will be handled during the bubbling or target phase.
propagate	Allows you to control the event flow. It defines the propagation behavior when bubbling or capturing. When set to `stop`, the event propagation will stop after the event is handled. By default, it is set to `continue`.
type	Mime type of the script.

If you look at the list of attributes above, you will recognize that this list is identical to the list of attributes you can use for an XEL event handler, except for the `match` attribute. This attribute makes it possible to have a complex tree of view nodes for one single controller node, while an event can be targeted at only one of the view nodes.

The following example shows how to use `handler` to perform some logic when the user clicks on an element:

```
<d: element name="myWidget">
   <!-- element definition -->
   <d:handler event="click" type="text/javascript">
      var sTagName = this.getProperty('tagName');
      alert('You clicked on element: ' + sTagName);
   </d:handler>
</d:element>
```

The `handler` tag applies to the controller; therefore, the event will be handled when, on the application page, the user performs the specified event on the widget. When you want to attach an event to a particular XHTML element inside your template, you can use `match` by pointing it to a class name on this XHTML element.

When an event is triggered on an element in a template, you might want to know which view node inside the template triggered the event. For this purpose, you can use the `viewTarget` attribute of the `event` object.

Updatable yellow notes

In the next example, we expand the *yellow note* widgets to include two handlers. The idea is that it would be nice to be able to update a yellow note. It should work as follows:

- When you click on a yellow note, a `textarea` will appear that contains the text of the yellow note
- You can update the text
- When you click with your mouse outside the area of the yellow note, the `textarea` is made invisible and the changed text replaces the text in the yellow note

First, we'll make a change to the template, to include a `textarea`. The attributes and their `mappers` stay unchanged.

```
<d:template type="application/xhtml+xml">
   <div xmlns="http://www.w3.org/1999/xhtml"
      class="sq-yellowNote">
```

```
            <div class="sq-yellowNote-div"
               style="height: 100%; width: 100%">
               <d:content />
            </div>
            <textarea class="sq-yellowNote-text"
              style="display: none">
               new text...
            </textarea>
         </div>
      </d:template>
```

There are some points you should note:

- We added a `textarea` that is initially hidden to the template.

- There is also an extra `div` that holds the initial content.

- Both the `div` and the `textarea` have a CSS class added. For the `div`, the class is only used to find it, and for the `textarea`, some formatting is needed:

```
.sq-yellowNote-text {
   font-size: 10px;
   margin-right: 2px;
   width: 90px;
   height: 60px;
}
```

We want to start editing when you click with your mouse on the `div` with class `sq-yellowNote-div`. Therefore, we add the following event handler:

```
<d:handler event="click" type="text/javascript"
   match=".sq-yellowNote-div">
   var sContent = event.currentView.innerHTML;
   var oText = bb.selector.query(this.viewNode,
     '.sq-yellowNote-text');
   oText.value = sContent;
   bb.command.show(oText);
   bb.command.hide(event.currentView);
</d:handler>
```

As you can see, the event handler handles the `click` event and the `match` attribute is used to identify the yellow note `div` element. Therefore, the event will only be activated if you click within the `sq-yellowNote-div`.

The event handler code first retrieves the content of the `sq-yellowNote-div`, and then, it finds the `textarea` with the class `sq-yellowNote-text`. It makes use of the `bb.selector.query` method, which is a handy alternative to the following line:

```
var oText = this.viewNode.
  getElementsByClassName('sq-yellowNote-text')[0];
```

Next, the text from the `div` is copied into the `textarea`, which is made visible while the `div` is hidden. The picture below shows what a yellow note will look like when being edited.

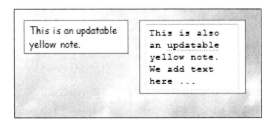

When you are done editing, the process should be reversed: the text in the `textarea` should be copied back into the `div` and the `textarea` should be hidden again.

We have chosen the `blur` event to signal the end of the editing. This means that if you click outside the yellow note, the event will be triggered. Here is the code:

```
<d:handler event="blur" type="text/javascript"
   match=".sq-yellowNote-text">
   var sContent = event.currentView.value;
   var oDiv = bb.selector.query(this.viewNode,
     '.sq-yellowNote-div');
   oDiv.innerHTML = sContent;
   bb.command.show(oDiv);
   bb.command.hide(event.currentView);
</d:handler>
```

Event handlers in TDL are always in addition to the previously defined event handlers in a parent object; they cannot be overridden in an inherited object. You will rarely have a good reason to overwrite a `handler` defined in a parent element. If this does come up, you should place the handler body in a method (we will look at the methods shortly). Methods can be overwritten, so, you will be changing the functionality of the event handler by altering the body of the method.

It is possible to specify additional event handlers for a single event.

We have taken an important step in making a TDL widget dynamic. Although it is theoretically possible to put all code for the event processing in event handlers, the TDL as a language provides us with many object-oriented facilities to enable good program design principles to be applied.

Widgets as objects

In the introductory sections of this chapter, we have already discussed TDL as an object-oriented language. We will now look at the TDL elements involved in more detail.

Defining classes with TDL

You already know how to create a TDL class definition: this is done by defining an element with the name `element`, where the `name` attribute is the name of the class.

All the elements that define the state and behavior of a TDL class are defined using child tags of the `element` tag.

In TDL, you use `property` elements to the define the state of an object. We have seen the `attribute` element that may seem similar to a `property`. However, attributes and properties are not the same:

Attributes	Properties
An attribute is always of type string and its value can be set like any XHTML attribute when placing the widget on a page.	Properties can be of any type, including of type `object`.
Attributes can be retrieved by using the `getAttribute` method.	Properties can be retrieved by using the `getProperty` method.
The value of a property can be set by using the `setProperty` method.	Attributes can be set by using the `setAttribute` method.
As child elements to an attribute, a `changer` and a `mapper` can be defined. The processing defined in these elements can cause side effects such as setting classes on the view of the widget.	`getter` and `setter` elements can be defined as child elements of property. Any desired side effect can be achieved by using these.

The behavior of a TDL object is coded within one or more `method` elements. As in any object-oriented language, a method has a name and a body. Optionally it has arguments. You will see all about it in the section on methods.

Inheritance

For many, an integral concept of object-orientation is *inheritance*, where objects may inherit the behavior of one or more other objects. We will explain the details of how you can implement and use inheritance in TDL later in this chapter, for example, we will see that we can inherit from other classes by using the `extends` attribute.

Creating and destructing TDL objects is done using the appropriately named `construct` and `destruct` elements. Note that `destruct` is almost never needed.

Composition

In the purest object-oriented languages, everything is an object. Actually, Java is not one of them and neither is TDL. In TDL, the inside of an elementary object is a structure of XHTML elements, augmented with CSS and JavaScript. Because this kind of object cannot contain BTL or other TDL objects, this poses the problem of how to apply the second integral concept of object-orientation:

> *Building larger objects out of smaller ones composition.*

Apparently, TDL was not really built to allow this. On the other hand, it is very well possible to compose a set of objects into larger ones, *not* using templates but using the `constructor` method, similar to how you would construct composite objects in Java.

We will show you how to do it in the *Composite widgets* section.

The element tag

Although we used the `element` tag in all examples in this chapter because it is the fundamental tag for defining widgets using TDL, we did not list its attributes yet. Here they are:

Attribute	Description
abstract	Boolean value, indicating whether the declaration is abstract. Abstract elements cannot be instantiated. They can only be used by derived elements in inheritance chains.
extends	Space-separated list of extended elements. Names must be fully qualified.
implements	Space-separated list of implemented interfaces. Names must be fully qualified.
name	Name of the element.

The direct child tags of the element tag can be: `attribute`, `constructor`, `destructor`, `handler`, `method`, `property`, `resource`, and `template`. We have seen the ones that allow us to define static elements already and also the event `handler` tag. The others will be described now.

Properties

Like attributes, properties are characteristics of a widget that indicate its state, such as `width` or `selectedIndex`. The attributes that you can specify on a `property` tag are:

Attribute	Description
name	Name of the property.
onget	Script to be executed when the property value is retrieved.
onset	Script to be executed when the property value is set.
type	Data type of the property.

The value of a property can be used to determine the shape of a widget or to perform particular operations. However, attributes and properties are different in several respects, as we already pointed out.

The `getProperty`/`setProperty` API functions retrieve or set a property value. The syntax for getting and setting properties is very similar to the getting and setting of attributes, as the following code snippet shows:

```
this.getProperty('selectedIndex');
this.setProperty('selectedIndex', 2);
```

Before we explain how to add properties to your own widgets, we show some examples of how you can get or set properties in BTL widgets. Both examples show a navBox that is opened and closed programmatically in a button click handler. The first example uses JavaScript in the click handler to get and set the `open` attribute of the navBox.

Let's show the navBox first:

```
<b:navBox width="300px" id="mynavbox" label="Open and Close">
    The open state of this navBox can be toggled by pressing
    the button above.

</b:navBox>
```

And here's a button that opens or closes the `navBox` with every click:

```
<b:button id="button1">
   Click me to toggle the open state of the navBox below
   <e:handler event="click" type="text/javascript">
      var navbox = bb.document.getElementById('mynavbox');
      navbox.setProperty
         ('open', !navbox.getProperty('open'));
   </e:handler>
</b:button>
```

Alternatively, you can use the XEL language as in the following example:

```
<b:button id="button1">
   Click me to toggle the open state of the navBox below
   <e:handler event="click" type="application/xml">
      <e:set with="id('mynavbox')" property="open"
         select="not(property::open)" />
   </e:handler>
</b:button>
```

The code snippet uses the `with` attribute because a different context from the one where the click occurred is needed.

Depending on your preference and your familiarity with JavaScript, you may favor the declarative XEL style or the procedural JavaScript style, where it should be noted that using JavaScript may result in a slightly better performance.

Knowing how to access an existing property, we are turning our attention to defining new ones in the next section.

Property definition

Similar to attributes, you can define properties as children of an element named `element`.

Here's the standard syntax of the TDL property element:

```
<d:namespace xmlns:d="http://www.backbase.com/2006/tdl"
   name="http://www.squaringthecircles.com/squared">
   <d:element name="yourWidget">
      <!-- ... -->
      <d:property name="yourProperty" />
   </d:element>
</d:namespace>
```

The syntax for retrieving or updating property values is different from what you have seen for attributes. There are no `mappers` and `changers` as for attributes, but only `setter` elements. While there are no side effects that you can implement when retrieving an attribute, you can use a `getter` to do so for a property.

Property getters

When you code `getProperty()` or `setProperty()`, these functions not only return or set property values, but also trigger property `getters` and `setters`. In TDL, the `getter` and `setter` tags can be placed as children of your `property` to establish additional script performed when the corresponding function is called. You can use `getter`, for example, to ensure that the correct value is returned even if the property has no value.

 When you use a `getter`, the standard behavior is no longer applied. This means that you must retrieve the value of the property involved and then return it.

Please note that the name of the property is available in a variable called `name` while `value` will hold its value. You can retrieve the value of a property in this way also:

```
var value = this._._nameOfYourProperty;
```

The Client Runtime stores the properties of an element in an internal object with the name _. This is done to improve the performance of some browsers:

```
<d:namespace xmlns:d="http://www.backbase.com/2006/tdl"
    name="http://www.squaringthecircles.com/squared">
    <d:element name="trafficLight">
        <!-- ... -->
      <d:property name="state">
         <d:getter type="text/javascript">
            var value = this._._state;
            alert(name ' = ' + value);
            return value;
         </d:getter>
      </d:property>
        <!-- ... -->
    </d:element>
</d:namespace>
```

As with the `template` element or any element that can contain executable logic, `getters` and `setters` need to define a value for the `type` attribute. This type states whether the `getter`/`setter` will be an XEL snippet or JavaScript.

Property setters

The body of the `setter` element establishes additional functionality that is executed when the `setProperty` function is called. The `setter` tag can be used to execute side effects to the change of the property value such as raising events, performing validation, throwing errors, and calling other functions.

In this example, when the `selectedIndex` property value is set, we alert the value of the selected index:

```
<d:namespace xmlns:d="http://www.backbase.com/2006/tdl"
    name="http://www.squaringthecircles.com/squared">
    <d:element name="yourWidget">
        <!-- ... -->
        <d:property name="selectedIndex">
            <d:setter type="text/javascript">
                alert('Property ' + name + ' is: ' + value);
                this._._selectedIndex = value;
            </d:setter>
        </d:property>
        <!-- ... -->
    </d:element>
</d:namespace>
```

To create a default value for a property, set the value in the constructor of the widget (using the `constructor` tag). Another way that is frequently used for BTL widgets is defining an attribute, often with the same name as the property that has a default value and a `mapper`. The `mapper` allows you to map the attribute to the property when the widget is built.

The next section describes a bit more concrete example of using attributes, mappers, and properties.

A web lamp example

Here is an example of a *lamp* widget. It has a background image that will let it look like (part of) a traffic light. There are two attributes, one that can define the color of the lamp and a second one that sets its initial state, "on" or "off".

We also define a property for the lamp, with the name `lampOn`. Why? The state of the lamp should really be a Boolean value indicating whether the lamp is on or off. Now that we have properties at our disposal, we can also ensure that the lamp is always in an allowed state.

Below, you can see the code for the *lamp* definition. The on/off state is kept in a property.

```
<d:tdl xmlns:d="http://www.backbase.com/2006/tdl">
    <d:namespace
        xmlns:sq="http://www.squaringthecircles.com/squared"
        name="http://www.squaringthecircles.com/squared">
    <d:resource type="text/css">
        .lamp {width: 31px; height: 31px;
            background-image: url('media/light.gif');
            border: solid black 1px;
        }
    </d:resource>
    <d:element name="lamp">
        <d:attribute name="color" default="white" />
        <d:attribute name="state" default="off">
            <d:mapper type="text/javascript">
                if (this.getAttribute('state') == 'on')
                    this.setProperty('lampOn', true);
                else
                    this.setProperty('lampOn', false);
            </d:mapper>
        </d:attribute>
        <d:property name="lampOn" type="boolean">
            <d:setter type="text/javascript">
                var oLight = this.viewNode;
                var sOffColor = '#463E3F';
                var sOnColor = this.getAttribute('color');
                if (value)
                    bb.html.setStyle(oLight,
                        'background-color', sOnColor);
                else
                    bb.html.setStyle(oLight,
                        'background-color', sOffColor);
                // set the property value!
                this._._lampOn = value;
            </d:setter>
        </d:property>
        <d:template type="application/xhtml+xml">
            <div class="lamp" />
```

```
            </d:template>
        </d:element>
      </d:namespace>
    </d:tdl>
```

Looking at the code, you can see that there is `<d:property>` and with the name `lampOn`, while we used the `mapper` code of the `state` attribute to give the `lampOn` property its initial value. Further, a property needs to have a type, therefore, we added `type="boolean"`.

Important to note is the last line we added to the `setter` code of the `lampOn` property. Since this `setter` code overrides the standard `setter` behavior, we need to make the change to the property explicitly.

We define a button to click the new *lamp* on or off. A click event handler is used to set the `state` attribute.

```
<div xmlns:sq="http://www.squaringthecircles.com/squared">
    <sq:lamp id="lamp1" color="yellow" />
    <button>
        <e:handler event="DOMActivate" type="text/javascript">
        var lamp = bb.document.getElementById('lamp1');
        lamp.setProperty('lampOn',
            !lamp.getProperty('lampOn'));
        </e:handler>
          Lamp Switch
    </button>
</div>
```

Note that the lamp appears initially with a yellow background because the `state` attribute is `on` by default.

Methods

A *method* usually consists of a sequence of statements to perform an action. A method can have set of input parameters to influence those actions, and possibly an output value can be returned.

In TDL, the `method` tag is used to define a method that will be executed as either XEL or JavaScript depending on the `type` in the `body` tag. A `method` element has one attribute:

Attribute	Description
name	Name of the attribute. This attribute is required.

A `method` element can have two child elements: `argument` and `body`. The `argument` tag describes the argument(s) that can be used to invoke the method, while the contents of the `body` tag provide the logic.

The argument tag

It declares an argument to be used in a method. The `argument` tag can have these attributes:

Attribute	Description
`default`	The default value of the argument to be used when no argument value is provided.
`name`	The name of the argument.
`required`	Specifies if the argument is required.
`type`	Data type of the property.

The value of the argument is available in the body element of the method as a variable with a name equal to the `name` attribute of the argument and a value equal to the value of the `value` attribute.

The body tag

The `body` tag declares the body of a method.

Attribute	Description
`type`	Mime type of the script, generally either `application/xml` or `text/javascript`.

The script content of the body element is executed when the method is called.

It is time for an example!

Sliding thumbnails

In the previous chapter, we were talking about adding animation to the C3D sample travel blog application. We showed a picture, but nothing of the code because it was not really usable in an application yet. We are now going to change that by defining two TDL widgets, which will make it easy to embed a set of pictures dynamically into an application when needed.

In the *Explorer* example, there was a JavaScript function called slide(). In a real production web application, it is not a good idea to have global functions like this, because you could have name clashes when using JavaScript libraries from others, and you could have a configuration problem to make sure that the right function is loaded at the right time.

We solve these problems here by encapsulating the slide() function as the method in an imageScrollContainer widget. We also wanted a vertical scrolling of the images instead of the horizontal scrolling used in the *Explorer* example. Actually, we would like the ability to do both, and this could be a further extension of the widget later.

Here is the layout of the widget:

```
<d:element name="imageScrollContainer">
    <d:template type="application/xhtml+xml">
        <div>
            <div class="imageScroll-btnBlock">
                <button class="btnUp">
                    <img src="media/go-up.gif" alt="Slide up" />
                </button>
                <button class="btnDown">
                    <img src="media/go-down.gif" alt="Slide down"/>
                </button>
            </div>
            <div xmlns="http://www.w3.org/1999/xhtml"
                class="sq-imageScroll-clipRegion">
                <div class="sq-imageScroll-container"
                    style="left:0px; top:0px;">
                    <d:content />
                </div>
            </div>
        </div>
    </d:template>
    <d:method name="slide">
        <!-- the content of the slide() method goes here -->
    </d:method>
</d:element>
```

As you can see, we have put the buttons right into the widget itself. We needed to use button widgets instead of b:button widgets because the latter are not allowed in a template. In this case, it does not make a difference, but if you had wanted to use a b:slider (for example), then you would need to find another way to build this widget.

The `slide` method looks like this:

```
<d:method name="slide">
   <d:argument name="oDirect" required="true" />
   <d:argument name="iPxPerSec" required="true" />
   <d:body type="text/javascript">
      var oAnimationInfo = {
      attributeName: "top",
         fill: "freeze"
      }
      var oContainer = bb.selector.query(this.viewNode,
         '.sq-imageScroll-container');
      var deltaHeight = oContainer.offsetHeight -
        oContainer.parentNode.offsetHeight;
      var hstart = parseInt(oContainer.style.top);
      var distance;
      if(oDirect == "up") {
         distance = deltaHeight - Math.abs(hstart);
         stop = -deltaHeight;
      }
      else {
         distance = Math.abs(hstart);
         stop = 0;
      }
      if(distance != 0) {
         oAnimationInfo.dur =
            (Math.round(100*distance/iPxPerSec)/100) + "s";
         oAnimationInfo.values = hstart +"px;" + stop + "px";
      var callback = function() {
         animationRef = null;
      }
      animationRef = bb.smil.animate(oContainer,
         oAnimationInfo, callback);
      }
      else {
         animationRef = null;
      }
   </d:body>
</d:method>
```

You can compare this code with the code we provided for the previous chapter in the `bookApps/animation/imageScroll.html` file (as a copy of the Explorer example code), and you will see that it is the same, apart from the change in direction we made. Also, the method finds the `sq-imageScroll-container` element, not by finding an `id` but instead by looking for a CSS selector. This allows us to have multiple `imageScrollContainer` widgets on one page.

In order for the widget to operate properly, we need a few event handlers:

```
<d:handler event="mousedown" match=".btnUp" type="text/javascript">
    this.slide('up', 400);
</d:handler>
<d:handler event="mouseup" match=".btnUp" type="text/javascript">
    if(animationRef != null) {
        bb.smil.stop(animationRef);
        animationRef = null;
    }
</d:handler>
<d:handler event="mousedown" match=".btnDown" type="text/javascript">
    this.slide('down', 400);
</d:handler>
<d:handler event="mouseup" match=".btnDown" type="text/javascript">
    if(animationRef != null) {
        bb.smil.stop(animationRef);
        animationRef = null;
    }
</d:handler>
```

The major remarkable thing for these event handlers is the use of the `match` attribute. This attribute allows us to have an event handler for the widget that applies to a specific element within the template of that widget. You need to be able to target this element as a CSS selector. We used the CSS classes defined on the buttons for this purpose.

Also, note the calls to the `slide()` method in the `mousedown` and `mouseup` event handlers.

We defined another widget: `sq:thumbnail`, to contain an image. Here, this widget is used only to make sure that the images are uniformly styled. Later, we can add event handlers to this widget to pop up a larger version of the photo, together with any yellow sticky notes that may have been defined for that image.

The code to display a list of images could be:

```
<sq:imageScrollContainer>
    <sq:thumbnail src="media/P1010862.JPG" />
```

```
    <sq:thumbnail src="media/P1010938.JPG" />
     <!-- more images ... -->
    <sq:thumbnail src="media/P1010991.JPG" />
</sq:imageScrollContainer>
```

When we integrate this widget into the C3D application, it will look like this:

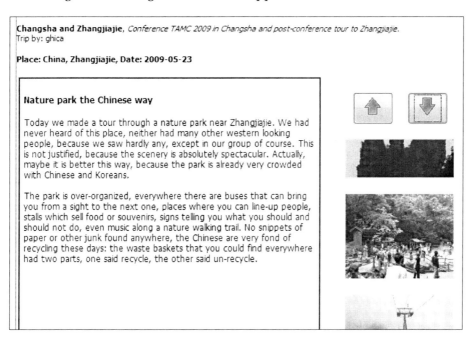

We will need to do a little more work to properly integrate the showing of thumbnails with a trip entry. The neatest way to show the photos would be to make the `imageScrollContainer` widget data bound. We have explained how to do that in Chapter 5.

Let's have one other example that we can use later to extend our *lamp* example. Earlier, we defined a button that, when clicked, would set the lamp *on* if it was *off* and the other way around. The code in the event handler needed to set a property in the lamp. In fact, this is not very desirable because you need to know the inner structure of the widget. A good rule is:

> *Use attributes to set the initial state of a widget and use methods to change the state of an object.*

We are defining a simple method for the lamp called `switchLamp`:

```
<d:method name="switchLamp">
   <d:body type="text/javascript">
      this.setProperty('lampOn', !this.getProperty('lampOn'));
   </d:body>
</d:method>
```

The lamp and the button that switches the lamp can now be coded as:

```
<sq:lamp id="lamp1" color="yellow" />
<button>
   <e:handler event="DOMActivate" type="text/javascript">
      bb.document.getElementById('lamp1').switchLamp();
   </e:handler>
   Lamp Switch
</button>
```

Constructors and destructors

The `constructor` tag in TDL provides execution instructions for what happens when a widget is instantiated. There is also a `destructor` element representing a method that is called when a widget is destructed.

Constructor elements have a single attribute, `type`, which describes the type of script code used to define the constructor. In fact, `constructor` is a special method that is invoked at a specific point in time, when the widget is constructed. In every other respect, constructors are just methods.

While the `template` tag builds the structural content of the widget, the `constructor` tag adds logic to the widget once it is built. The constructor is the last thing that is executed when the element is created, just before the `DOMNodeInsertedIntoDocument` event is fired.

The following example initializes a property value in the constructor:

```
<d:constructor type="text/javascript">
   bb.setProperty(this, "selectedIndex", 1);
</d:constructor>
```

Because constructors are just methods, it is possible to do a lot more in a constructor than setting a property or the color of your widget. By using a `c:create` or `c:load` command in a constructor, you can build complex objects without the constraints that a `template` imposes on the contents.

Opinions differ on the question of whether you should actually use the constructor in this way (see the discussion at the end of this chapter). The main problem is that all objects built using a Backbase command in a constructor are visible in the controller layer and therefore, lack the encapsulation and information hiding that you expect from a proper object. This would allow developers to manipulate widgets from the outside in undesirable ways.

However, if you refrain from doing nasty things and stay a good citizen in the DOM world, then the constructor allows you to build powerful widgets that are more scalable and maintainable than with any JavaScript-based framework.

We will give an example of how composition could work in the next section.

Composite widgets

The main motivation for using classes and objects when developing an application is the possibility to manage the complexity of your code. You can build larger chunks of code into an object and you are able to address this larger chunk of code via an API that hides the inner complexity of the object. Object-oriented languages allow larger objects to be built from smaller objects by composition, such as *Lego(R) blocks*. Although, you have to be careful when you do object composition with TDL; as we just explained, it can work very well.

Compose a pedestrian light

A pedestrian light has only two lamps. If you know how to make this one, you can also make a regular traffic light that has usually three lamps, or a light with five lamps, or a string of Christmas lamps, lit randomly.

The complete pedestrian light definition is as follows:

```
<d:tdl xmlns:d="http://www.backbase.com/2006/tdl">
   <d:namespace
      xmlns:sq="http://www.squaringthecircles.com/squared"
      name="http://www.squaringthecircles.com/squared">
   <d:uses element="lamp"
      src="data/tdl_lamp_definition.xml" />
   <d:element name="pedestrianLight">
      <d:property name="redLamp" type="object" />
      <d:property name="greenLamp" type="object" />
      <d:constructor type="application/xml">
         <c:create destination=".">
           <sq:lamp color="red" state="on" />
           <sq:lamp color="green" />
         </c:create>
```

```
                <e:set property="redLamp"
                    select="sq:lamp[@color = 'red']" />
                <e:set property="greenLamp"
                    select="sq:lamp[@color = 'green']" />
            </d:constructor>
            <d:method name="toggle">
                <d:body type="text/javascript">
                    this.getProperty('redLamp').switchLamp();
                    this.getProperty('greenLamp').switchLamp();
                </d:body>
            </d:method>
            <d:template type="application/xhtml+xml">
                <div>
                    <d:content />
                </div>
            </d:template>
        </d:element>
    </d:namespace>
</d:tdl>
```

If you look at the `constructor` method, you will see that it creates a green lamp that is *off* and a red lamp that is *on*. We have also added properties to save a reference to the red and the green lamp. The constructor has two `e:set` instructions to set these references. The reference itself is found as an XPath expression.

Note that the `template` of the `pedestrianLight` widget contains a `content` tag. This is needed because we want to add new nodes to the view structure of the widget in its constructor. The `c:create` in the constructor adds the elements it creates to the *view gate* of its destination. The `content` tag provides us with the proper view gate.

For some of you, it may be more straightforward to write the constructor code in JavaScript instead of XEL. On one hand, in XEL it is easier to see which nodes are constructed, on the other, the setting of the property values is more complicated. What the constructor looks like when written in JavaScript is shown below:

```
<d:constructor type="text/javascript">
<![CDATA[
    var oLamp = bb.document.createElementNS
        ('http://www.squaringthecircles.com/squared', 'lamp');
    oLamp.setAttribute('color', 'red');
    // keep the red lamp in a property
    this.setProperty('redLamp', oLamp);
    this.appendChild(oLamp); // build the lamp
    // switch the lamp on
    oLamp.setProperty('lampOn', true);
```

```
oLamp = bb.document.createElementNS
    ('http://www.squaringthecircles.com/squared', 'lamp');
oLamp.setAttribute('color', 'green');
// keep the green lamp in a property
this.setProperty('greenLamp', oLamp);
this.appendChild(oLamp); // build the lamp
oLamp.setProperty('lampOn', false); // switch the lamp off
]]>
</d:constructor>
```

To define the complete behavior of the pedestrian light, we need a method, switchLamp, to switch from red to green and back. You can see the code in the previous example. Once defined, we can control the lamp with a button like this:

```
<div xmlns:sq="http://www.squaringthecircles.com/squared">
    <sq:pedestrianLight id="ped1" />
    <button>
        <e:handler event="DOMActivate" type="text/javascript">
            var oLight = bb.document.getElementById('ped1');
            oLight.toggle();
        </e:handler>
         Click me to switch the pedestrian light!
    </button>
</div>
```

This is what it looks like (you have to imagine the colors in a black and white printed book):

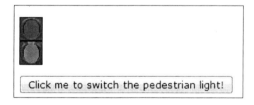

We can understand that you consider the traffic light example not very practical, except for illustrating how widget composition works. Therefore, we will now look at how you could simplify building forms.

Order form building blocks

We are going to show how you can encapsulate form elements into a widget that allows the code on the application page to be much clearer and shorter, and which allows us to add new fields to the form easily.

The inputElement widget that we will develop is an example of a widget that needs to be built using a constructor method and that *cannot* be built using a template. This is because the form uses Backbase form validation and because the validation functionality is part of the *forms* namespace; we use the bf prefix. This can only be built in the controller layer, while templates are restricted to building widgets in the view layer.

Before you start developing widgets like this, you should ask yourself a few questions:

- How often will I use the resulting widget? If used only once, then the development costs will not be compensated by ease of development later.

- Does the widget help to ensure a consistent look and feel for my web page? Proper use of widgets can help to achieve consistency.

- Is the content of the widget related to the user interface or to the application domain? If this is application domain content, you may consider writing a server component instead of a client-side widget.

- Building a widget at runtime takes some overhead. The performance of your application has to be weighed against its robustness and the productivity of your developers.

Here is a form with shipping information for an order. Some fields are required and therefore, an error message should be displayed when it is not filled in on submit. The form in the picture is already partially filled in to show what happens when partial information is submitted. Note that the row of the input information smoothly expands when an error message is displayed. You can see this in the next screenshot:

Roughly, for each row in the form you would need to write code like this:

```
<div class="row">
   <div class="lspan">
      <label for="name">Name:</label>
   </div>
   <input class="inputText" type="text"
      name="name" id="name" bf:required="true"
      bf:messagesRef="id('required_field')" />
   <span> * </span>
   <bf:messages id="required_field">
      <bf:message event="invalid"
         class="errorMessage" facet="required">
         <div>This field is required</div>
      </bf:message>
   </bf:messages>
</div>
```

If you look at the form, you see that for each input element, there are three parts, a `label`, `input`, and a `bf:messages` part. Together, they are put in a `div`. The variable elements in the code are the `label` value, the values of the `name` and `id` attributes, and whether the field is required to be filled in.

To accommodate the variability of the name of the input field and the text of the label, we define an element with attributes `name` and `label`. The `id` should always be the same as the `name` on the input field; therefore, we define it that way in the widget. We need a third attribute to indicate whether a value is required when the form is submitted. With this in mind, the basic widget definition looks like this:

```
<d:tdl>
   <d:namespace
      name="http://www.squaringthecircles.com/squared">
      <d:element name="inputElement">
         <d:attribute name="name" required="true" />
         <d:attribute name="label" />
         <d:attribute name="required" default="true" />
          <!--the constructor, methods, and template go here-->
      </d:element>
   </d:namespace>
</d:tdl>
```

Points to note are:

- The `name` attribute is always required. This is needed to be able to construct valid code.

- The `label` attribute is optional. If not specified, then the same value that the `name` attribute has will be used.

- The `required` attribute is optional too. It has a default value of `true`. This was done considering that most fields cannot be left empty.

Let's take a look at the template. It is not very interesting, except for the presence of the `content` element, which must be there because it functions as the `viewGate`, which allows child elements to be added to the widget. If you are defining a composite widget in a constructor, you *always* need to *include* a template as shown below:

```
<d:template type="application/xhtml+xml">
    <div class="row">
        <content />
    </div>
</d:template>
```

Constructing the `sq:inputElement` is a two-step process: first the new nodes are appended, for the `label` element, the `input` element, and if `required="true"`, the form validation nodes. The second step is to adapt the attributes of the nodes to the values as specified in the attributes of the `sq:inputElement`. This is done in three methods that are successively called.

```
<d:constructor type="application/xml">
    <e:choose>
        <e:when test="@required='true'">
            <c:create destination=".">
                <div class="lspan">
                    <label for="name" />
                </div>
                <input class="inputText"
                    type="text" name="name" bf:required="true"
                    bf:messagesRef="../bf:messages[1]" />
                <span> * </span>
                <bf:messages>
                    <bf:message event="invalid"
                        class="errorMessage" facet="required">
                        <div>This field is required</div>
                    </bf:message>
                </bf:messages>
            </c:create>
```

```
        </e:when>
        <e:otherwise>
          <c:create destination=".">
            <div class="lspan">
              <label for="name" />
            </div>
            <span> </span>
            <input class="inputText" type="text" name="name"/>
          </c:create>
        </e:otherwise>
      </e:choose>
      <e:call method="setNames" ndest="./input[1]" />
      <e:call method="setLabel" ldest="./*/label[1]" />
      <e:call method="addRowOdd" />
    </d:constructor>
```

The first method, setNames, sets the name and id attributes in the input that is addressed in the argument. The argument is specified as an XPath expression, to make it possible to target the nodes just built, without having to build IDs for each.

The second method is similar, but operates on the label element. As mentioned, the value of the name attribute is used if the label attribute was not specified.

The third method, addRowOdd, is a method that allows you to *zebrafy* the form, coloring the elements light blue or white in an alternating way. It does this by finding the previous sibling of the current sq:inputElement. If that node does not have the class rowOdd specified, it will be added to the current element.

```
    <d:method name="setNames">
      <d:argument name="ndest" />
      <d:body type="text/javascript">
        var sName= this.getAttribute('name');
        ndest.setAttribute('name', sName);
        ndest.setAttribute('id', sName);
      </d:body>
    </d:method>
    <d:method name="setLabel">
      <d:argument name="ldest" />
      <d:body type="text/javascript">
        var sName = this.getAttribute('name');
        var sLabel = this.getAttribute('label');
        ldest.setAttribute('for', sName);
        if (sLabel == '') sLabel = sName + ':';
        else sLabel = sLabel + ':';
        var oText = bb.document.createTextNode(sLabel);
```

```
         ldest.appendChild(oText);
      </d:body>
   </d:method>
   <d:method name="addRowOdd">
      <d:body type="text/javascript">
      <![CDATA[
         oSib = this.viewNode.previousSibling;
         if (oSib != null) {
            if (!bb.html.hasClass(oSib, 'rowOdd'))
               bb.html.addClass(this.viewNode, 'rowOdd');
         }
      ]]>
      </d:body>
   </d:method>
```

We would like to make a few more remarks:

- In the new form, the country field is a normal input field instead of the drop-down list or suggest box you would expect. You can just insert these if you like in the old way or you could define a similar widget for a drop-down list to encapsulate it in the same way.

- Similarly, you may want to perform other checks, such as a check for a valid email address and so on. This will complicate the design of your widget, but may further enhance the robustness of your applications and productivity of the developers.

- You could combine several input widgets together to build a *name and address* information form that can then be used in all your web applications to give them a consistent look and feel.

- If, at some point, your UI designers change their mind about how the form should look, all you have to do is change the CSS in the resource tag, and everywhere where the widgets are used will show the new look. Of course, this is the idea behind CSS in the first place, but in practice, this is really hard to keep consistent. We must confess that for this widget the CSS naming conventions used are not like we said it should be earlier, but even this is easier to correct because of the resource tag we used.

- If you change the order of the fields or add a new field, the alternate coloring of the rows would be automatically adjusted.

Finally, all the code you need to write to show this form when you use the widget we just developed is this:

```
<fieldset title="Shipping Information" id="checkOut">
    <legend>Shipping Information</legend>
    <sq:inputElement name="Name" />
    <sq:inputElement name="Surname" />
    <sq:inputElement name="birthDate"
        label="Date of Birth" required="false" />
    <sq:inputElement name="Address" />
    <sq:inputElement name="postalCode"
        label="Postal Code/Zip" />
    <sq:inputElement name="City" />
    <sq:inputElement name="Country" />
    <sq:inputElement name="eMail" label="E-mail" />
</fieldset>
<div class="row">
    <p>Fields marked with * are required.</p>
    <button type="submit">Order the T-shirt</button>
</div>
```

We hope you agree that this 15 line code is much clearer than the eight times longer code that you would need otherwise.

This concludes the discussion of constructing widgets from other widgets using composition. In the next section, we will look at what we can achieve by building new elements from old ones and inheriting their features.

Inheritance

Inheritance is a common concept in object-oriented languages. The idea behind inheritance is that one class (called a subclass, child class, or derived class) inherits the behavior of another class (also called the superclass, parent class, extended class, or base class). For example, you may create a superclass called animal. The animal superclass will contain general characteristics, such as hair or legs. The subclass might be mammal or reptile. Then, you might create a subclass of mammal that is even more specific, such as cat or human. The subclass inherits all the characteristics of the superclass, but then extends that class by adding more attributes and methods or by refining existing methods.

One of the main advantages of inheritance is that you can reuse code. Without inheritance, you would have to include all the attributes and methods of the mammal class in every specific mammal subclass.

In the case of Backbase Tag Definition Language, element, interface, behavior, and document definitions are like classes, and they, too, can inherit from each other. For example, in our BTL widgets, you might see that the skinned tabBox inherits from the base tabBoxBase abstract tag, which, in turn, inherits from the abstract element. This means that when employing the tabBox widget, you have access to all the methods and properties from not only the skinned tabBox, but also tabBoxBase and element.

In TDL, you can specify inheritance by using the extends attribute of the element tag. You can also specify if a class is an abstract class by setting the abstract attribute of the element tag to true. An abstract widget cannot be instantiated on an application page.

The next code snippet shows the definition of tabBoxBase. You will not be allowed to write <b:tabBoxBase/> on your application page because the widget is defined as abstract.

```
<d:tdl xmlns:d="http://www.backbase.com/2006/tdl"
  xmlns:b="http://www.backbase.com/2006/btl">
    <d:namespace name="http://www.backbase.com/2006/btl">
        <d:element name="tabBoxBase"
          extends="b:cardStack" abstract="true">
          <!-- ... -->
        </d:element>
    </d:namespace>
</d:tdl>
```

 All elements derive from the DOM element object. Therefore, elements that do not have an extends attribute derive directly from the DOM element object. Elements that *do* have an extends attribute will extend from the DOM element object via a chain of extended classes, where ultimately, some parent element will not have an extends attribute.

You might be surprised that in the example above, the tabBoxBase element is abstract. However, if you think about reusable design, it is a good idea to create a widget that provides only functionality and not visualization. That way, you can extend this widget to provide customized visual characteristics. If you want to have more visualization, you can create two visual classes that extend the functional, non-visual superclass. In BTL, this is used to provide a system and a chameleon skin, each having different characteristics. A skin represents a consistent look and feel of a set of UI widgets.

Note that items in the extends attribute contain a prefix. The extends attribute only accepts fully qualified names. This means that you must specify not only the class you would like to inherit, but also the prefix of the namespace in which the inherited class is defined. If no prefix is specified, the default namespace is used. This structure allows you to inherit from classes in different namespaces.

Inheritance is powerful because you can reuse information from superclasses. What makes it more powerful is that if necessary, you can override information from the superclass. All you need to do is write a method with the same name in the subclass, and that method will be the one used by the instantiated object. However, if you are trying to extend the functionality of the superclass method, meaning that you would like to use the superclass method and add functionality to it, you can use the callSuper method.

In the previous section, you saw reuse by composition. The question arises when to use composition and when to use inheritance. A good way to find an answer is to ask the **is-a** or **has-a** question.

For example:

- A pedestrian light *is a* traffic light, therefore we can inherit pedestrianLight from trafficLight.

- A **lamp** *is not* a traffic light, but a traffic light *contains* (*has*) one or more lamps. Therefore, we should compose a traffic light from one or more lamps.

- A **car** has wheels; therefore, I should compose a car of wheels, doors, and so on. We cannot inherit car from wheel.

TDL also supports multiple inheritance. Multiple inheritance means that a subclass can inherit from multiple superclasses. For example, you might have a visualElement and a dropDown. You may want to make a comboBox that inherits characteristics from both. To use multiple inheritance, you use a space-separated list as a value of the extends attribute. To inherit from a visualElement and a dropDown, your TDL tag definition might look like this:

```
<d:tdl xmlns:d="http://www.backbase.com/2006/tdl">
    <d:namespace name="http://www.backbase.com/2006/btl">
        <d:element name="comboBox"
            extends="b:visualElement b:dropDown">
            <!-- ... -->
        </d:element>
    </d:namespace>
</d:tdl>
```

Actually, the inheritance situation for the comboBox widget is more complicated; we just want to give you an idea of what it looks like.

 With multiple inheritance, inheritance is processed from right to left. This means that the leftmost inherited element will be processed last.

By inheriting from multiple classes, you have access to the elements of both classes, thus reusing classes and not duplicating code.

Yellow notes using inheritance

In addition to being allowed to update yellow notes, we would also like to be able to drag a yellow note to an appropriate place on top of a picture. In this way, we could use the yellow notes to mark interesting spots on a picture in the C3D travel blog web application.

The yellow notes are fine as they are; therefore, we would like to add the drag-and-drop behavior while defining a new widget, stickyYellowNote, and extending yellowNote to be able to use what we already have developed.

In addition to an example of inheritance, we'll also see some coding tricks you should be aware of.

In the previous chapter, we showed that you can add drag-and-drop behavior by extending b:drag. We will use this feature too.

Here is the skeleton definition of the sq:stickyYellowNote element:

```
<d:element name="stickyYellowNote"
    extends="b:drag sq:yellowNote">
    <d:attribute name="useDragClass" default="true" />
     <!-- the element definition goes here -->
</d:element>
```

The attribute useDragClass is there to allow us to use only part of the widget as drag handle. See the previous chapter for a description of the drag behavior attributes.

We chose to add btl-dragMove as class to the div that represents the drag handle, which means that the drag mode is *move*, because we would like to be able to drop the yellow note anywhere on the image, where it should stay put.

We cannot use the note as defined earlier for dragging because as soon as you click on it, the editing will start and a white text area is shown. Therefore, we decided to add an area at the top of the note that you can use as a drag handle. See the following picture for an idea of what this looks like:

We could add the element that functions as a drag handle using a constructor in the stickyYellowNote element, like this:

```
<d:constructor>
    <c:create destination="." mode="firstChild">
        <div class="sq-yellowNote-header btl-dragMove">
        >>   </div>
    </c:create>
</d:constructor>
```

This will work fine, but if you try this out and open a debugger to look at a stickyYellowNote element, you will see that the result is a kind of half-baked widget: some of it is hidden in the template and part of it is visible in the model.

```
<sq:stickyYellowNote>
    <div class="sq-yellowNote-header btl-dragMove">
        >>
    </div>
    This is a picture of HongKong, viewed from the P
</sq:stickyYellowNote>
```

This is clearly not desirable. It is much better to extend the template. To understand how this works, you should realize that a template is just a method on the TDL element; therefore, we can call it using callSuper in the inherited element, and then add nodes to it, like this:

```
<d:template type="text/javascript">
    var aTempl = this.callSuper('__template');
    var oRoot = document.createElement('div');
    bb.command.addClass(oRoot,
      'sq-yellowNote-header btl-dragMove');
```

```
        bb.command.setText(oRoot,'>>','replaceChildren');
        var oFirst = aTempl[0].childNodes[0];
        aTempl[0].insertBefore(oRoot, oFirst);
        var oDiv = bb.selector.query(this.viewNode,
          '.sq-yellowNote-div');
        bb.html.disableUserSelect(oDiv);
        bb.html.disableUserSelect(oRoot);
        return aTempl;
    </d:template>
```

The last thing that we do to complete the widget definition for sticky yellow notes is adding an event handler that fires when the dragging ends. For now, its content is just an alert, showing where you dropped the note. You could use this as a starting point to send information to the server and save it in a database, because you would like the yellow notes to appear at the same place with the same content when you reopen the image to where they are attached.

```
    <d:handler event="dragEnd" type="text/javascript">
        var oNote = event.currentView;
        alert('posx="' + bb.html.getStyle(oNote, 'left')
            + '" posy="' + bb.html.getStyle(oNote, 'top') +'"');
    </d:handler>
```

The element that we discuss in the next and last part of this section is `interface`. It can be used to develop robust widgets when other widgets inheriting from it should comply with a certain interface.

Interfaces

An *interface* is a way to define attributes, properties, and methods that must be explicitly declared on elements that implement the interface. It is defined at the same level as an `element`, and must be a child of the `namespace` widget in a TDL document. An interface does not contain any functionality; it merely defines what must be implemented. Primarily, interfaces are a convenient way to help developers enforce the consistency of their API. If a widget implements an interface and does not explicitly state what is declared in the interface, the Client Runtime will throw an error. The larger the project, developer team, and inheritance structure, the more important interfaces become.

To define an interface in TDL, use the `interface` element:

```
    <d:tdl xmlns:d="http://www.backbase.com/2006/tdl">
      <d:namespace
        name="http://www.squaringthecircles.com/squared">
        <!-- ... -->
```

```
<d:interface name="iYourInterface">
    <d:property name="selectedIndex" />
    <d:attribute name="width" />
    <d:method name="blur" />
</d:interface>
 <!-- ... -->
</d:namespace>
</d:tdl>
```

 Interfaces can also be extended by using the `extends` attribute.

In the above code snippet, the `iYourInterface` interface defines a property, attribute, and method that must be explicitly declared by implementing elements. Here's how you would implement this interface in your element:

```
<d:tdl xmlns:d="http://www.backbase.com/2006/tdl"
    xmlns:sq="http://www.squaringthecircles.com/squared">
    <d:namespace
      name="http://www.squaringthecircles.com/squared">
      <d:element name="yourWidget"
          implements="sq:iYourInterface">
        <!--    Implement all properties, attributes,
            and methods defined in the interface -->
      </d:element>
    </d:namespace>
</d:tdl>
```

You can implement multiple interfaces with a space-separated list in the `implements` attribute value.

Extending BTL

We have already seen several examples of extending BTL elements. Most notable are the data-bound widgets we made from existing elements such as `b:dataComboBox`, and the extension of `b:drag` to add drag-and-drop behavior.

Another thing you may want to do is build your own skin instead of the ones that are provided by Backbase. In this case, you'll want to find the `base` tag of the widget you are skinning. For example, to create a skinned `accordion` widget, your widget would inherit from `accordionBase`.

The Backbase framework also provides a base widget class called `element`. This class contains commonly used properties and methods for all UI widgets. As a result, if you want to create your own UI widget that is not derived from an already existing UI widget, you can inherit from `element`.

Behaviors

In some cases, you may want to create functionality that is modular and not tied to a specific widget. For this, you can use a behavior. These behaviors provide a generic behavioral model but not a visual component. Examples of behaviors are the *resize* and *drag-and-drop* functionality.

Behaviors provide advanced functionality to a widget, and generally, can be used with any supported markup language. The *resize* behavior, for example, can be applied both to BTL and XHTML widgets.

 By default, the `behavior` attribute, which you use to add behaviors to a widget, resides in the XEL namespace, while Backbase-defined behaviors are bound to the BTL namespace.

The `behavior` tag can have the following attributes:

Attribute	Description
extends	Space-separated list of extended behaviors. Names must be fully qualified.
implements	Space-separated list of implemented interfaces. Names must be fully qualified.
name	The name of the behavior. You must use the value of this attribute when adding a behavior to an element.

You create a behavioral class in TDL using the `behavior` tag. Behaviors exist within a namespace. So, the parent namespace determines the namespace of the behavior. Like elements, behaviors can contain attributes, methods, properties, and handlers, but no template, constructor, or destructor. Here's a basic behavior definition:

```
<d:namespace xmlns:d="http://www.backbase.com/2006/tdl"
   name="http://www.squaringthecircles.com/squared">
   <d:behavior name="yourBehavior">
      <!-- ... -->
   </d:behavior>
</d:namespace>
```

Behavior example

Assume that you would like to create a very special RSS reader, which can handle feeds from Amazon™. These can be about books, electronics, music, or toys and either the bestsellers or the new releases are shown.

We are not going to show a complete RSS reader. Although, with some XSLT, we would be able to define a crude one; it is not possible to define it without the help of a server-side script or by doing some `iframe` tricks. It you try to load an RSS feed from Amazon or any other feed that is not in the same domain as your client application, you will see a message like this:

```
GENERIC: Javascript error: "XMLHttpRequest.open failed,
  (cross-domain / bad method)"
```

We have a simple link on our page, which, when clicked, opens a new browser window from the URL as composed from the combination of comboboxes. You could expand it with server-side scripting to format the result in better ways. It is outside the scope of this example here.

If you try the example in a Firefox or IE browser, you will actually see a rendering of the RSS with pictures and nice formatting. First, we show how the example could be used:

```
<div xmlns:sq="http://www.squaringthecircles.com/squared">
   <b:comboBox id="topChoice" readonly="true"
       filter="true" e:behavior="sq:changeContext">
      <b:comboBoxOption>TopSeller</b:comboBoxOption>
      <b:comboBoxOption>NewRelease</b:comboBoxOption>
   </b:comboBox>
   <b:comboBox id="choiceList" readonly="false"
       filter="true" e:behavior="sq:changeContext">
      <b:comboBoxOption>electronics</b:comboBoxOption>
      <b:comboBoxOption>books</b:comboBoxOption>
      <b:comboBoxOption>music</b:comboBoxOption>
      <b:comboBoxOption>dvd</b:comboBoxOption>
      <b:comboBoxOption>toys</b:comboBoxOption>
   </b:comboBox>
    <!--  give the href an initial value, so that it can be
      clicked without changing the comboboxes -->
      <a id="amazon-link"
        href="http://rss.amazon.com/TopSeller/cat/books/">
         Click here!
      </a>
</div>
```

Next, we show what it could look like. The arrow points to a part of a new window that will open up:

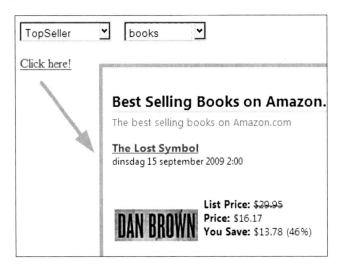

Why is a behavior a nice choice for this application? This is because the setting of a value in one comboBox triggers the setting of the value in the link based on the values in both. The code for the handler in each combobox would be exactly the same and therefore, it is better to separate the handler functionality from each combobox and implement it as a behavior. Here is the definition of the behavior:

```
<d:namespace xmlns:d="http://www.backbase.com/2006/tdl"
    xmlns:e="http://www.backbase.com/2006/xel"
    name="http://www.squaringthecircles.com/squared">
<d:behavior name="changeContext">
    <d:handler event="change">
        <e:variable name="cList"
            select="id('choiceList')/property::value" />
            <!-- make sure cList actually has a value -->
        <e:if test="$cList = ''">
            <e:set property="selectedIndex"
                with="id('choiceList')" select="0" />
            <e:variable name="cList"
                select="id('choiceList')/property::value" />
        </e:if>
        <e:variable name="tChoice"
            select="id('topChoice')/property::value" />
        <e:set property="href" with="id('amazon-link')"
            select="concat('http://rss.amazon.com/',
            $tChoice, '/cat/', $cList, '/')" />
```

```
    <!-- for example:
        http://rss.amazon.com/TopSeller/cat/books/ -->
    </d:handler>
  </d:behavior>
</d:namespace>
```

As you can see, the code in the click event handler of the behavior makes sure that the `choiceList` combobox actually has a value because it is initially empty. If empty, the handler sets a value. The link is targeted with an XPath expression to set the proper value in the `href` attribute. It you subsequently click on the link, the right page will be opened.

Uses

The `uses` tag is designed to automatically include files when a certain element, interface, behavior, or attribute is used. This could be when instantiating an element in your document, or when inheriting from one in a TDL definition. For example, say you want to create a new element called `myElm`. This element implements the interface `iInput` that is defined in a file called `iInput.xml`. In order to automatically load this file when the `iInput` interface is implemented, you must include its definition with the `uses` tag.

```
<d:namespace xmlns:d="http://www.backbase.com/2006/tdl"
    xmlns:sq="http://www.squaringthecircles.com/squared"
    name="http://www.squaringthecircles.com/squared">
    <d:uses interface="iInput" src="iInput.xml" />
    <d:uses element="inheritedTag" src="extrafile.xml" />
    <d:uses behavior="specialBehavior" src="extrafile.xml" />
    <d:element name="myTag" implements="sq:iInput" />
</d:namespace>
```

 The `uses` tag is only for file loading. To ensure that your element definition inherits from a base element or interface, you will also need to use the `extends` or `implements` attribute on the `element` tag or apply the behavior to the element.

There are quite a few details and attributes you can specify to control the way files are loaded when using the `uses` tag. You can find this information in the *Backbase API Reference*.

The limits of creating UI components

We have left this discussion as the last part in this chapter because you can now better understand some of the concerns that you need to be aware of when developing widgets using TDL.

The Tag Definition Language is designed and implemented to build UI components composed of XHTML elements, JavaScript, and CSS only. These components are encapsulated on the view layer, while at the controller layer you only see the custom tags that you have created using TDL. We have seen how this works by looking at screenshots of the Backbase debugger.

One side of the discussion is that you should *not* use TDL for purposes it was not designed for. Moreover, UI components should be small and have little behavior.

The other side of the discussion is that it is very tempting to use TDL for building larger and complex UI widgets. It means a new and revolutionary way to build web applications. With care and constraint, it is possible, therefore, why not?

TDL as a macro language

The example of using TDL to define widgets as building blocks for forms explained earlier in this chapter, is an example of using TDL as a macro language. The main purpose of defining the building blocks is to save you from writing a lot of repetitive code. If you take the trouble to just write the code, then the resulting XHTML elements would be in the Backbase area and therefore, in the controller layer. There would be no encapsulation in this case; using the TDL building blocks just improves modularity, which can never be wrong. Another example of using TDL this way are the menu item links used in the BTL and command function example exercises introduced in Chapters 2 and 3.

TDL as an object-oriented language

We discussed earlier in this chapter that TDL is a pure *object-oriented* language. Because of this, it has two main features for application construction: **inheritance** and **composition**.

Clearly, you can build larger objects by inheriting features of other objects. In TDL, you can even inherit multiple features as we had seen for the BTL widgets. For example, a `calendar` widget inherits from `focusableElement`, `dimensionElement`, and more.

There are limits to using inheritance. For example, if you build a car, it will be composed of smaller objects such as doors and wheels. A car does not inherit from wheels because a car *is not* a wheel but a composition. A car also has its composite behavior.

If you want to build larger components, you *must* use composition—if your UI component wants to have a chance to be maintainable and extensible.

The desirability of building larger UI components in your environment cannot be decided by us. On one hand, all the architects of large business applications will tell you that object composition is the basis of good application design: divide and conquer, build small simple parts and compose them into larger and more complex parts. Many design patterns use both inheritance and composition. On the other hand, the requirements at the client-side of a web application may be different.

If you are using TDL in a compositional way, the resulting component will work perfectly OK. However, there is a problem with encapsulation as we already mentioned. Composed widgets are visible in the controller layer and there is only one global DOM tree built. This allows malicious or stupid developers to trip up the component definitions by traversing the DOM tree from the outside and destroying it.

Squaring the circles

The not so technically inclined developers will appreciate that TDL allows you to put JavaScript back to the place where it came from: JavaScript is a very handy tool to implement small pieces of logic, the circles of JavaScript being squared by the square brackets of XML.

We are not claiming that you cannot do large scale application development with JavaScript. You certainly can. We are claiming that there is a mismatch between the declarative nature of XHTML and the procedural nature of JavaScript.

TDL allows you to define tag libraries on the client, just like JSP allows you to define tag libraries on the server, which makes this mismatch manageable.

Namespaces

Despite the hazards of using composition, if you really would like to restrict yourself to building UI components using what is allowed in a `template` only, elements in the XHTML namespace, there are some major things that you cannot do and that are part of the attractiveness of the Backbase framework.

Fundamentally, widgets built in other namespaces than the XHTML namespace, such as BTL or the forms `bf` namespace belong in the controller layer, because that is what the controller layer is for: an abstraction of the view elements, to provide you with widgets with more functionality, and to shield you from browser quirks.

The behaviors functionality that the Backbase framework offers is functionality that is defined outside the XHTML namespace and that is attached to elements in the controller layer, but not in the view layer. This includes drag-and-drop behavior. Earlier, we showed an example where the whole widget could be dragged—the sticky yellow notes. The dragging handle was not the whole widget, but only the top part. We could still use the event handlers on the whole widget because of the targeting that you can do with the `match` attribute.

However, if you want to make a UI component out of another example, the iPhone-like switch we showed in the previous chapter, you might not be so lucky. The thing that is dragged, a red rectangle, is embedded in the switch, but because it is dragged, it must be visible in the controller layer. Therefore, composition by building the widget in a constructor using a `create` command instead of a template to create the elements in the widget, is unavoidable, albeit only simple XHTML elements are needed. In the code provided with this book, there is an example where you can see the `switch` as TDL element.

Actually, it seems to be possible to attach drag-and-drop behavior to view nodes in a really sneaky way by creating loose controller nodes. We think tricks like this should be avoided at all cost!

Conclusion

The verdict is not out yet and maybe there should not be one. Of course, it is your choice to use the TDL in any way you like.

Summary

In this chapter, we gave a lot of detail about the Tag Definition Language, the most interesting and unique feature of the Backbase framework. We showed that you can build powerful UI components using TDL, which promises new ways of doing web application development, but also that some of the possible uses are controversial.

Some of the examples we used could be building blocks for the *C3D travel blog application*—the *sticky yellow notes* that you can attach to photos and the *sliding thumbnails* that you can use to show photos next to the text of a trip entry.

8
Widget Wrap-up

In the previous chapters we explained details about many BTL widgets. Still we are missing a set of widgets that might prove to be handy when developing a web application:

- **Action and menu widgets**: `button`, `contextMenu`, `menuBar`, `toolBar`, `menuPopUp`, and `pager`. For some widgets in this category there also exist data-bound versions: `dataContextMenu` and `dataMenu`. The action widgets perform an action/function when clicked. The menu widgets select menu items.

- **Window and dialogs**: `window`, `modal`, `taskBar`, and `windowArea`. These widgets open a window or dialog on top of the main browser window.

- **Multimedia**: `applet` and `flash`. These widgets embed multimedia files.

There is also a set of **command functions** that we did not cover yet: `alert`, `bookmark`, and `trace`.

In this chapter, we will complete the description of BTL widgets and the Command Functions by describing these categories.

Here is a detailed list:

- Action and menu widgets
- Data-bound menus
- Windows and dialogs
- Multimedia widgets
- An example with menus and windows
- Miscellaneous commands: `trace`, `alert`, and `bookmark`

Action and menu widgets

Action and menu widgets allow users to interact with a web application using elements that match the overall style of the application. Something happens when you click on an action or menu widget. Usually, you will wrap the functionality that you want performed when the user clicks on the widget in a `click` event handler.

button

The BTL `button` widget represents generic button functionality. When the user clicks on the button, an action is performed. You must implement the action in an event handler. Here's a screenshot showing the `button` widget:

 `button` inherits from `focusableElement`, `containerElement`, `dimensionElement`, and `positionElement`. `button` does not have local attributes or methods.

Look back to Chapter 2 to see the inheritance structure of the BTL widgets and the attributes that are supported by the parent classes of `button`.

The button is enabled by default. Set the `disabled` attribute to `true` to make the button disabled. The following example has an **Enabled** and a **Disabled** button, both with an event handler that will be activated when clicked. For the **Enabled** button, you will see an alert when you click on the button. When you click on the **Disabled** button, nothing will happen. Here's the code for the `button` widget:

```
<b:button id="enabledSubmit">
   <e:handler event="click" type="text/javascript">
      alert('This button is enabled.');
   </e:handler>
   Enabled
</b:button>
<b:button id="disabledSubmit" disabled="true">
   <e:handler event="click" type="text/javascript">
      alert('This button is disabled.');
   </e:handler>
   Disabled
</b:button>
```

contextMenu

The `contextMenu` is a menu that becomes visible when the user executes a right-click on a particular widget. Once visible, the user can select an item from that menu or navigate to a submenu by holding the mouse over a menu item. This is shown in the following screenshot:

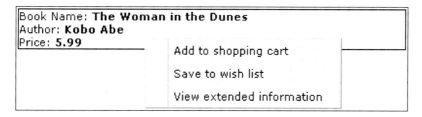

 `contextMenu` inherits directly from `element`.

`contextMenu` has one attribute:

Attribute	Description
menuPopUp	XPath query to the `menuPopUp` element (an element extending `menuPopUpBase`) that will be opened when the `contextMenu` is triggered. The evaluation of this query is done in `DOMNodeInsertedIntoDocument` event handler, which means that only elements before this element in the document order are accessible.

There are two ways to add a `contextMenu` to your application. In the first case, you add a `contextMenu` element as a child of the element that should trigger the `contextMenu`.

In the second case, you create the `contextMenu` in the same way as a child of the triggering element. However, this time you place your `menuPopUp` inline in the `contextMenu`.

Warning: It is not possible to support `contextMenu` properly in the Opera browser, as it does not allow the browser context menu to be disabled.

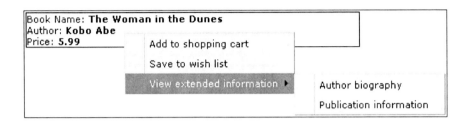

In the next example, the `contextMenu` uses XPath in the `menuPopUp` attribute to find the `menuPopUp`. Right-click in the bordered book description to see the pop up.

```
<div style="border:1px solid black; width:400px;">
    Book Name:<strong>The Woman in the Dunes</strong>
    <br />Author:<strong>Kobo Abe</strong>
    <br />Price:<strong>5.99</strong>
    <b:contextMenu menuPopUp="id('menubar_context')" />
</div>
<b:menuPopUp id="menubar_context">
    <b:menuPopUpItem label="Add to shopping cart" />
    <b:menuPopUpItem label="Save to wish list" />
    <b:menuPopUpItem label="View extended information" />
</b:menuPopUp>
```

In the next example, the `menuPopUp` is located as a child of the `contextMenu`, so the `menuPopUp` attribute is not needed on the `contextMenu`. Right-click in the bordered book description to see the pop up.

```
<div style="border:1px solid black; width:400px;">
    Book Name:
    <strong>
        The Woman in the Dunes
    </strong>
    <br />Author:<strong>Kobo Abe</strong>
    <br />Price:<strong>5.99</strong>
    <b:contextMenu>
        <b:menuPopUp id="menubar_context">
            <b:menuPopUpItem label="Add to shopping cart" />
            <b:menuPopUpItem label="Save to wish list" />
            <b:menuPopUpItem label="View extended information" />
        </b:menuPopUp>
    </b:contextMenu>
</div>
```

Next, we look at an example of a nested `menuPopUp`. Right-click in the bordered book description to see the pop up.

```
<div style="border:1px solid black; width:400px;">
   Book Name:
   <strong>The Woman in the Dunes</strong>
   <br />Author:<strong>Kobo Abe</strong>
   <br />Price:<strong>5.99</strong>
   <b:contextMenu>
      <b:menuPopUp>
         <b:menuPopUpItem label="Add to shopping cart" />
         <b:menuPopUpItem label="Save to wish list" />
         <b:menuPopUpItem label="View extended information">
            <b:menuPopUp id="submenu">
               <b:menuPopUpItem label="Author biography" />
               <b:menuPopUpItem
                  label="Publication information" />
            </b:menuPopUp>
         </b:menuPopUpItem>
      </b:menuPopUp>
   </b:contextMenu>
</div>
```

menuBar

The `menuBar` is displayed as a horizontal bar with menu items. When the user clicks on one of the menu items, either a developer-defined command such as `Print` can be executed, or the `menuBar` can display a vertically-aligned submenu. `menuBar` commands can be logically organized by using child elements: `menuBarItem` and `menuBarSeparator`.

  `menuBar` inherits from `dimensionElement` and `positionElement`. `menuBar` does not have local attributes, but it has `menuItems` and `selectedMenuItem` as properties.

The keyboard can be used to navigate through the `menuBar`:

Key	Description
Right	Selects the `menuBarItem` on the right of the selected `menuBarItem` and opens the `menuPopUp` of the `menuBarItem`. If the selection is on a `menuPopUpItem` with a `menuPopUp` inside, it will open the `menuPopUp` and select its first `menuPopUpItem`. When there is no `menuPopUp` inside, the selection in the `menuBar` will be moved to the right. When there is no `menuBarItem` on the right of the selected `menuBarItem`, the leftmost `menuBarItem` will be selected.
Left	Selects the `menuBarItem` on the left of the selected `menuBarItem` and opens the `menuPopUp` of the `menuBarItem`. If the selection is inside a `menuPopUp` with a `menuPopUp` ancestor, the `menuPopUp` with the selection is closed and navigation will continue for the first ancestor `menuPopUp`. When there is no `menuPopUp` ancestor, the selection in the `menuBar` will be moved to the left. When there is no `menuBarItem` on the left of the selected `menuBarItem`, the rightmost `menuBarItem` will be selected.
Up	Opens the `menuPopUp` of a `menuBarItem` if it is not already open and selects the bottom `menuPopUpItem`. When a `menuPopUp` is already open, the selection is moved to the `menuPopUpItem` above the currently selected `menuPopUpItem`. When there is no `menuPopUpItem` above the currently selected `menuPopUpItem`, the selection is moved to the bottom `menuPopUpItem`.
Down	Opens the `menuPopUp` of a `menuBarItem` if it is not already open and selects the top `menuPopUpItem`. When a `menuPopUp` is already open, the selection is moved to the `menuPopUpItem` below the currently selected `menuPopUpItem`. When there is no `menuPopUpItem` below the currently selected `menuPopUpItem`, the selection is moved to the top `menuPopUpItem`.
Enter	Opens the `menuPopUp` of a `menuBarItem` if it is not already open and selects the top `menuPopUpItem`. When a `menuPopUp` is already open, a `DOMActivate` event is dispatched when a `menuPopUpItem` without a `menuPopUp` is selected. When the selected `menuPopUpItem` contains a `menuPopUp`, the `menuPopUp` will be opened and its top `menuPopUpItem` will be selected.
Escape	Deactivates the `menuBar` when no `menuPopUp` is open. When `menuPopUps` are open, the `menuPopUp` that is lowest in the hierarchy is closed and navigation will continue for the first ancestor `menuPopUp` or `menuBar`.
Home	Selects the top `menuPopUpItem` of the open `menuPopUp` that is lowest in the hierarchy.
End	Selects the bottom `menuPopUpItem` of the open `menuPopUp` that is lowest in the hierarchy.

The next example shows a `menuBar` with inline `menuBarItem` elements and a `menuBarSeparator`:

```
<b:menuBar width="130px">
    <b:menuBarItem label="File">
        <b:menuPopUp>
            <b:menuPopUpItem label="Open" />
            <b:menuPopUpItem label="Save" />
            <b:menuPopUpSeparator />
            <b:menuPopUpItem label="Export">
                <b:menuPopUp>
                    <b:menuPopUpItem label="To gif..." />
                    <b:menuPopUpItem label="To png..." />
                </b:menuPopUp>
            </b:menuPopUpItem>
            <b:menuPopUpSeparator />
            <b:menuPopUpItem label="Save As..." />
        </b:menuPopUp>
    </b:menuBarItem>
    <b:menuBarSeparator />
    <b:menuBarItem label="Edit">
        <b:menuPopUp>
            <b:menuPopUpItem label="Cut" />
            <b:menuPopUpItem label="Copy" />
            <b:menuPopUpItem label="Paste" />
        </b:menuPopUp>
    </b:menuBarItem>
    <b:menuBarItem label="View">
        <b:menuPopUp>
            <b:menuPopUpItem label="Toolbar" />
            <b:menuPopUpItem label="Content" />
            <b:menuPopUpSeparator />
            <b:menuPopUpItem label="Windows" />
            <b:menuPopUpItem label="Errors" />
        </b:menuPopUp>
    </b:menuBarItem>
</b:menuBar>
```

menuPopUp

This is a pop-up menu that can be used inside a `contextMenu`, `menuBarItem`, or `menuPopUpItem`. It can also be used without the `contextMenu` element. In that case, the `menuPopUp` can be opened by adding a handler for the `contextmenu` event to an application. The handler should call the `open` method of the `menuPopUp`.

toolBar

The `toolBar` widget displays a horizontal command menu. When the user clicks on an item in the `toolBar`, a command is triggered. There are a number of child widgets, such as `toolBarItem`, `toolBarButton`, `toolBarSwitch`, and `toolBarSeparator`, which you can use to organize the commands.

 `toolBar` inherits from `disableElement`, `dimensionElement`, and `positionElement`. `toolBar` does not have local attributes or methods.

The `toolBar` widget is great for creating a desktop-like command bar. If you want to combine commands and submenus, you should use a `menuBar` widget.

In combination with drag-and-drop functionality, you can make the `toolBar` movable.

You can add many different types of items in your `toolBar`. The `toolBarItem` widget allows you to nest any other widget, allowing you to use a `calendar` or a radio button group. The `toolBarButton` gives you a generic button to provide extra functionality, such as `print`. The `toolBarSwitch` widget gives you a button you can toggle, such as the `bold/italics/underline` on/off functionality in text editors. Finally, the `toolBarSeparator` provides a vertical line that lets you logically organize your `toolBar` widgets.

The following `toolBar` is composed of multiple `toolBarButton` widgets:

```
<b:toolBar width="400px">
    <b:toolBarButton>
        <img alt="" style="height:16px; width:26px;"
            src="media/send.gif" />
        Send
    </b:toolBarButton>
    <b:toolBarButton>
```

```
    <img alt="" style="height:16px; width:20px;"
        src="media/compose.gif" />
    Compose
</b:toolBarButton>
<b:toolBarSeparator />
<b:toolBarButton>
    <img alt="" style="height:16px; width:19px;"
        src="media/erase.gif" />
    Erase
</b:toolBarButton>
</b:toolBar>
```

In the next example, the `toolBar` has a `toolBarItem`, a `toolBarSwitch`, a `toolBarButton`, and a `toolBarSeparator`. This `toolBar` can be dragged anywhere in the application.

```
<b:toolBar e:behavior="b:drag" dragBehavior="move">
    <b:toolBarItem>
        <select size="1">
            <option>High Resolution</option>
            <option>Low Resolution</option>
            <option>No Resolution</option>
        </select>
    </b:toolBarItem>
    <b:toolBarSeparator />
    <b:toolBarButton>
        <img alt="" style="height:16px; width:26px;"
            src="media/send.gif" />
    </b:toolBarButton>
    <b:toolBarSwitch active="true">
        Bold
    </b:toolBarSwitch>
</b:toolBar>
```

pager

The `pager` widget provides a visual means to navigate through data sets or information. A `pager` will most often be used in conjunction with a `dataGrid`. In Chapter 5, we have seen several examples of this. This is a screenshot of the `pager` widget:

Title	Director	Genre
Apocalypse Now	Francis Ford Coppola	War
Red Eye	Wes Craven	Thriller
Sin City	Robert Rodriguez	Action
The Shawshank Redemption	Frank Darabont	Drama
Lost in translation	Sofia Coppola	Drama
Star Wars	George Lucas	Adventur

≪ ◁   Page [2] of 3   ▷ ≫

pager inherits from `dimensionElement` and `positionElement`.

The `pager` has one attribute:

Attribute	Description
for	XPath query to the pageable widget to which the `pager` must connect.

When you click on one of the navigation buttons or type in the input field in the `pager`, the data set automatically updates to show the desired data rows. The `pagerBar` widget functions as a container and graphical border for the `pager`. Simply by connecting the `pager` to a data widget with the `for` attribute, the pager provides built-in functionality for page navigation. Values of the `page` attribute of the `pagerButton` element allow you to provide buttons for first, last, previous, and next functionality. Additionally, the `pagerJumper` widget provides extended navigational functionality; instead of navigating to a page through a list of numbered page links, the `pagerJumper` allows you to type in a page number. Pressing *Enter* navigates you directly to that page.

The pager widget provides advanced navigation possibilities for data widgets or other data sets, such as an image viewer that could have multiple blocks of information. It is a great way to provide navigation through rows of data sets without doing any extra programming. You can have more than one pager that refer to the same data widget. For example, you might want to place pager widgets above and below a dataGrid.

The following example shows a standard pager with First, Last, Previous, and Next buttons (specified by values of the pagerButton attribute) as well as a list of numbered links (as specified by the pagerNumbers widget):

```
<b:pagerBar width="260px">
   <b:pager for="id('myListGrid')" width="250px">
      <b:pagerButton type="First" />
      <b:pagerButton type="Previous" />
      <b:pagerSeparator />
      <b:pagerNumbers numbers="5" />
      <b:pagerSeparator />
      <b:pagerButton type="Next" />
      <b:pagerButton type="Last" />
   </b:pager>
</b:pagerBar>
```

Next, the example replaces the list of standard links with a pagerJumper, which allows you to type in a page number to which to navigate. The for attribute connects the pager to a data widget as shown in the following code:

```
<b:pagerBar width="260px">
   <b:pager for="id('myListGrid')" width="250px">
      <b:pagerButton type="First" />
      <b:pagerButton type="Previous" />
      <b:pagerSeparator />
       <b:pagerJumper />
      <b:pagerSeparator />
      <b:pagerButton type="Next" />
      <b:pagerButton type="Last" />
   </b:pager>
</b:pagerBar>
```

Data-bound menus

In addition to `contextMenu` and `menuBar`, where you should add menu items statically, there are also a data-bound versions of these widgets, `dataContextMenu` and `dataMenu`, where the menu items can be loaded dynamically.

The dataSource for a menu

As for all data-bound widgets, `dataContextMenu` and `dataMenu` need to have a `dataSource` associated to them. Some fields in the data source have a special meaning:

Field	Description
identifier	Unique identifier for the record
name	Label of the menu item
icon	Icon for the menu item (optional)
hasSubmenu	A boolean value that indicates whether the menu has a submenu. Default is `false`.
separator	A boolean value that indicates whether the menu is a separator. Default is `false`.
open	A boolean value that indicates whether the menu is opened or not. Default is `false`.
submenu	A pointer to a child menu of a menu item, if it has one.

The menuActivate event

When a data-bound menu item is clicked upon, the `menuActivate` event is fired. This event has a special property, `detail`, which allows you to find out which data item in the `dataSource` is activated. See the next section for an example.

dataContextMenu

The `dataContextMenu` widget is very similar to the `contextMenu` widget. It becomes visible when the user executes a right-click on a particular widget. Once visible, the user can select an item from that menu or navigate to a submenu by holding the mouse over a menu item.

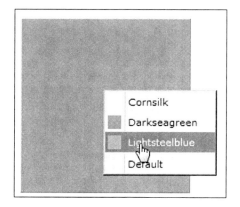

This is an example of a `dataContextMenu`:

```
<b:dataSource name="dataContextMenu" e:behavior="b:localData"
  recordSelect="item">
  <b:dataSchema>
    <b:dataField name="name" />
    <b:dataField name="icon" select="@icon" />
    <b:dataField name="hasSubmenu" select="@hasSubmenu" />
    <b:dataField name="separator" select="@separator" />
    <b:dataField name="open" select="@open" />
    <b:dataField name="submenu"
      dataSchema="_self" select="submenu/item" />
    <b:dataField name="color" select="@color" />
  </b:dataSchema>
  <b:dataContainer xmlns="">
    <menu>
      <item icon="media/patch_cornsilk.gif"
        color="#FFF8DC">
        <name>Cornsilk</name>
      </item>
      <item icon="media/patch_darkseagreen.gif"
        color="#8FBC8F">
        <name>Darkseagreen</name>
      </item>
      <item icon="media/patch_lightsteelblue.gif"
        color="#B0C4DE">
        <name>Lightsteelblue</name>
      </item>
      <item separator="true" />
      <item color="">
        <name>Default</name>
      </item>
```

```
          </menu>
      </b:dataContainer>
  </b:dataSource>
  <b:box width="200px" height="200px">
      <b:dataContextMenu dataSource="dataContextMenu">
          <e:handler event="menuActivate" type="text/javascript">
              var oDataSource = this.getProperty('dataSource');
              var sColor = btl.dataSource.getValue(oDataSource,
                  event.detail, 'color');
              this.getProperty('parentNode').
                  setAttribute('backgroundColor', sColor);
          </e:handler>
      </b:dataContextMenu>
  </b:box>
```

The interesting part in this piece of code is the event handler for the `menuActivate`
event. There is a property in the `dataContextMenu` that holds a reference to the
`dataSource`. This reference is retrieved and used to find the new color that is
required. Within the `dataSource`, the current record is found by using the
`event.detail` property of the event.

dataMenu

The `dataMenu` widget looks the same as the `menuBar` widget. It is displayed as a
horizontal bar with menu items. When the user clicks on one of the menu items,
either a developer-defined command can be executed or the `dataMenu` can display
a submenu.

This example shows a `dataMenu`:

```
<b:dataSource name="dataMenu" e:behavior="b:localData"
  recordSelect="item">
  <b:dataSchema>
      <b:dataField name="name" />
      <b:dataField name="icon" select="@icon" />
      <b:dataField name="hasSubmenu" select="@hasSubmenu" />
      <b:dataField name="separator" select="@separator" />
      <b:dataField name="open" select="@open" />
      <b:dataField name="submenu" dataSchema="_self"
          select="submenu/item" />
  </b:dataSchema>
  <b:dataContainer>
      <xi:include href="data/dataMenu.xml" />
  </b:dataContainer>
</b:dataSource>
<b:dataMenu dataSource="dataMenu" />
```

To understand the example fully, we show part of the XML file that contains the menu definition:

```
<menu>
  <item hasSubmenu="true">
    <name>File</name>
    <submenu>
      <item icon="media/icons/table.png">
        <name>File</name>
      </item>
      <item icon="media/icons/table_save.png">
        <name>Save</name>
      </item>
      <item separator="true" />
      <item hasSubmenu="true"
        icon="media/icons/table_go.png">
        <name>Export</name>
        <submenu>
          <item>
            <name>To gif...</name>
          </item>
          <item>
            <name>To png...</name>
          </item>
          <!-- more items -->
        </submenu>
      </item>
      <!-- more items -->
    </submenu>
  </item>
  <!-- more items -->
</menu>
```

Windows and dialogs

Windows and dialogs can display content that is disconnected from the main browser window. Unlike a JavaScript pop-up window where in fact a completely new browser window is created, the Backbase framework window and dialog widgets stay on top of the browser window and cannot be moved outside.

The `window` widget is a draggable, resizable container that fully supports maximize, minimize, restore, and close functionality. When used in combination with the `windowArea` and `taskBar`, the user can seamlessly navigate between multiple windows as easily as when using a standard desktop application.

The modal dialog is most commonly used to present (or request) important information to (from) the user while preventing interaction with the rest of the page or application.

window

The window widget represents a resizable window that floats above your application. It can be closed by clicking on the closeButton widget in the top right of the header.

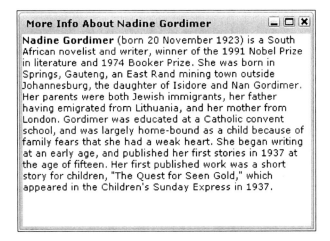

 window inherits from dimensionElement, positionElement, labelImplementorElement, iconElement, and containerElement.

The window widget has these specific attributes:

Attribute	Description
buttons	Enables or disables buttons in the window. If set to none, no buttons will be available.
mode	Specifies whether the window is embedded in the interface. inline embeds the window in your interface, while float detaches the window from the interface.
open	Set to open to open/expand the element by default.

window uses both drag-and-drop and resize behaviors, so it can be moved and resized by the user. The value of the label attribute becomes the window header, while any children of the window widget are displayed in the body of the window. The window will by default start in the top left of your application. However, by setting the mode attribute to inline, the window will be initially located at that point in the application.

The window is open by default. You can change the open attribute to a value of false to have the window closed by default.

This example shows a BTL window at work:

```
<b:window label="More Info About Nadine Gordimer" id="window"
  height="250px" position="relative">
  <strong>Nadine Gordimer</strong>
  (born 20 November 1923) is a South African novelist and writer,
  winner of the 1991 Nobel Prize in literature and 1974 Booker
  Prize.
  Her first published work was a short story for children, "The
  Quest for Seen Gold," which appeared in the Children's Sunday
  Express in 1937.
</b:window>
```

windowArea

The windowArea widget functions as a container for window widgets. It is used in combination with a taskBar widget, where the taskBar becomes a window manager for window widgets that are children of the windowArea.

The windowArea widget is required when you have multiple window widgets that you want to manage with a taskBar. It also helps communicate between window widgets.

In the next example, there is a windowArea that contains windows. The taskBar provides easy navigation between the windows. The windows cannot move beyond the boundaries of the windowArea.

```
<b:windowArea height="400px">
  <b:window label="Window 1" top="40px" left="20px"
    padding="5px">
    <p>Content of Window 1</p>
  </b:window>
  <b:window label="Window 2" top="60px" left="40px"
    padding="5px">
    <p>Content of Window 2</p>
```

```
      </b:window>
      <b:window label="Window 3" top="80px" left="60px"
        padding="5px">
          <p>Content of Window 3</p>
      </b:window>
      <b:taskBar orientation="top" />
    </b:windowArea>
```

See the picture in the next section, *taskbar*, for an impression of how the `windowArea` and the `taskBar` function together.

taskbar

The `taskBar` widget is used in combination with a `windowArea`. It helps to manage multiple `window` widgets by creating tabs at the bottom of the screen for each open window. This allows you to make a window active (in the foreground) by clicking on the correct tab. Similarly, if you minimize one of the windows, you can open it again by clicking on its tab in the `taskBar`. The text shown in the tab is the same as the header label of the `window`. Here's the screenshot of a `taskbar` widget used in combination with a `windowArea`:

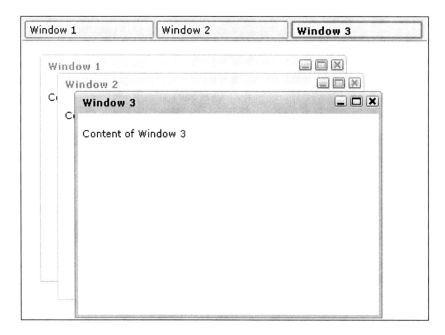

The `taskBar` widget should be used when you have multiple `window` widgets available in your application and you would like an easy way to navigate between them.

When you have multiple windows that need to be connected to your `taskBar`, your `taskBar` and all connected `window` widgets must be children of the `windowArea` widget.

modal

The `modal` widget displays a modal window as shown in the following screenshot:

The `modal` is a pop-up window that contains displayed information, most often a warning message.

 `modal` inherits from `containerElement`, `dimensionElement`, and `positionElement`. It also inherits `drag` behavior.

The `modal` widget has the following attributes:

Attribute	Description
center	Boolean value to indicate if the modal is centered automatically.
dragConstraint	dragConstraint defines an element that serves as a boundary for the dragged element. The dragged elements cannot go into this element or beyond it (if it is a parent). The value is a valid XPath expression. If the expression selects more than one node, only the first node is used.
for	XPath expression indicating which element will have its content blocked. The application programmer must set the targeted element with an offset.
open	Set to open to open/expand the element by default.

When the `modal` is open, the user cannot interact with another part of the application that you specify. They can interact with the content window, but the rest of the specified part of the application is covered in a gray window. Users can close the `modal` by clicking on the **x** icon in the top right of the `modal` window, or the application developer can build custom functionality (for example, using buttons) that offer the user a choice of options. You can use the `width` and `height` attributes to determine the size of the content area of the `modal`, while the `center` attribute allows the content area to be centered in the application, rather than being located at the place that it is initially rendered.

The parts of the application that are accessible when the `modal` is open is determined by the location of the `modal` and the use of the `for` attribute. When the `modal` is the first child of the `script` tag, the `modal` renders the rest of the application unavailable. However, if you use the `for` attribute, you can target an element that can be blocked. This is useful when you want to block one part of an application, but still allow users to interact with the rest of the application.

By default, the `open` attribute of the `modal` is set to a value of `false`, which means the `modal` is invisible. Generally speaking, the display of the `modal` is triggered by user interaction.

This example shows a BTL modal at work:

```
<b:modal label="Warning!" id="myModalWin" center="true" width="300px"
  height="100px">
  <div>
     You must click the OK button before you can re-access
     the application.
  </div>
  <div>
     <button>
        OK
        <e:handler event="click" type="text/javascript">
           var oModal = bb.document.getElementById('myModalWin');
           oModal.setAttribute('open', 'false');
        </e:handler>
     </button>
  </div>
</b:modal>
<button>
   Open modal
   <e:handler event="click">
      <c:setAttribute with="id('myModalWin')" name="open"
         select="'true'" />
   </e:handler>
</button>
```

Multimedia widgets

Certain multimedia technologies, such as Flash movies or Java applets can be embedded in browsers. However, it can sometimes be a bit complex to set up. BTL aims to make it easier to use those technologies and offers one interface for all browsers.

applet

An `applet` widget allows you to insert a Java applet in your application. Behind the scenes, we translate the `applet` widget into either an `object` for Microsoft Internet Explorer or an `embed` for the Firefox browser. The `appletParam` widget allows you to set parameters for your `applet`.

In the example below, a Java applet is loaded and given some parameters to show a bar chart. The `align="right"` attribute will cause the applet to be displayed at the right within its container. The BTL widgets allow you to use styling attributes like `width`, `height`, and `align` to make styling of specific elements easier.

```
<b:applet width="250px" height="100px" align="right">
   <b:appletParam name="code" value="BarChart.class" />
   <b:appletParam name="codebase" value="media" />
   <b:appletParam name="title" value="Performance" />
   <b:appletParam name="orientation" value="horizontal" />
   <b:appletParam name="columns" value="3" />
   <b:appletParam name="c1_label" value="Q1" />
   <b:appletParam name="c1_color" value="blue" />
   <b:appletParam name="c1" value="10" />
   <b:appletParam name="c2_label" value="Q2" />
   <b:appletParam name="c2_color" value="red" />
   <b:appletParam name="c2" value="20" />
   <b:appletParam name="c3_label" value="Q3" />
   <b:appletParam name="c3_color" value="green" />
   <b:appletParam name="c3" value="5" />
</b:applet>
```

Here is a picture of this applet:

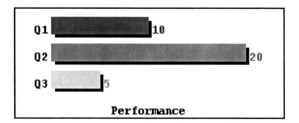

flash

The flash widget allows you to embed an Adobe Flash movie in your application. Enter a relative path as the value of the src attribute to point to the location of your Flash movie.

The flash widget bypasses the "activate control" message in Microsoft Internet Explorer 6 and 7.

You can specify the dimensions of the Flash movie using the width and height attributes. The src attribute is required.

The example shows how to insert a Flash movie:

```
<b:flash width="550px" height="350px" src="media/backbase.swf" />
```

An example with menus and windows

After having seen the isolated examples for the windows and menus, it is maybe not so clear how we can tie these things together to form the basis of an application. Just to show that this can be rather simple, we create a page on which you can place windows in random order, by choosing them from a menu. Let's make it clear with a screenshot:

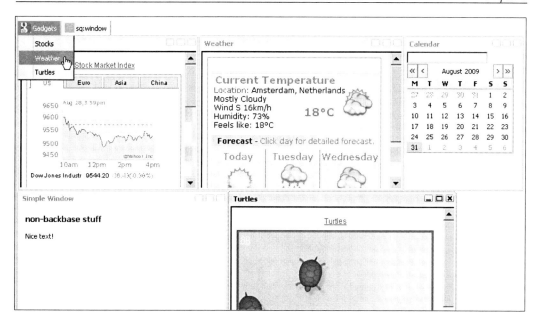

The source code for this example can be found in `bookApps/sqLittleWindows`.

The web application page consists of two parts: a *menu* and a *window area*. We created some simple windows that can be placed in the window area by choosing one of the menu options. There are two types of windows: windows that contain a Google gadget and windows that contain handcrafted items. The Google gadgets were rather randomly chosen from the vast supply at `http://www.google.com/ig/directory?synd=open&cat=all`. These gadgets must be placed in an `iframe` within the window to work. The other windows just contain some text or some BTL widgets.

The `index.html` page contains nothing special; therefore, we do not show it here. The page includes `app.xml`, which is the starting point for the application. This file has only two interesting lines of code:

```
<sq:windowMenu windowArea="myWindowArea"
   menuData="resources/data/mydatamenu.xml" />
<b:windowArea id="myWindowArea" overflow="auto" />
```

We do not need to explain what the purpose of the `b:windowArea` is, because you have seen this widget in the previous sections in this chapter. But what about `sq:windowMenu`? The `sq:windowMenu` widget hides all complexity of the *sqLittleWindows* mini application. From the name you can guess that it is the menu for the `b:windowArea`, and also that it is a custom widget we created using TDL.

`sq:windowMenu` extends `b:dataMenu`; therefore, there must be an XML file that defines what the structure of the menu is. This is what the `menuData` attribute of `sq:windowMenu` is for. Indeed there is a file called `mydatamenu.xml` that looks like this:

```xml
<menu>
    <item icon="resources/media/googleg.gif" hasSubmenu="true">
        <name>Gadgets</name>
        <submenu>
            <item url="myWindows/mystocks.xml" width="300px">
                <name>Stocks</name>
            </item>
            <item url="myWindows/myWeather.xml" width="340px">
                <name>Weather</name>
            </item>
            <item url="myWindows/myturtles.xml" width="380px">
                <name>Turtles</name>
            </item>
        </submenu>
    </item>
    <item separator="true" />
    <item icon="resources/media/patch_lightsteelblue.gif"
      hasSubmenu="true">
        <name>sq:window</name>
        <submenu>
            <item url="myWindows/simple.xml">
                <name>Simple Window</name>
            </item>
            <item url="myWindows/calendar.xml" width="200px">
                <name>Calendar</name>
            </item>
        </submenu>
    </item>
    <item separator="true" />
</menu>
```

The contents as shown above look very much like what we have seen before to define a `dataMenu`. What may attract your attention are the `url` and `width` attributes on the `item` tag. We will use these later when handling the `menuActivate` event to load the proper window into the `windowArea`.

The `dataSource` needs to be adjusted accordingly:

```xml
<b:dataSource name="menuData" e:behavior="b:remoteData"
  recordSelect="item" url="resources/data/mydatamenu.xml">
  <b:dataSchema>
```

```
            <b:dataField name="name" />
            <b:dataField name="icon" select="@icon" />
            <b:dataField name="hasSubmenu" select="@hasSubmenu" />
            <b:dataField name="separator" select="@separator" />
            <b:dataField name="open" select="@open" />
            <b:dataField name="url" select="@url" />
            <b:dataField name="width" select="@width" />
            <b:dataField name="submenu" dataSchema="_self"
               select="submenu/item" />
        </b:dataSchema>
    </b:dataSource>
```

As you can see, we have added specific `dataField` elements to cover `url` and `width`.

Let's take a look at the definition of the `sq:windowMenu` now. It has three parts:

- A `constructor` where the `dataSource` will be created
- A `template` that is needed to append the `dataSource` nodes to
- A `menuActivate` event handler, where the window selected from the menu will be loaded into the `windowArea`

Here is the skeleton for `sq:windowMenu`:

```
<d:namespace name="http://www.squaringthecircles.com/squared">
    <d:element name="windowMenu" extends="b:dataMenu">
        <d:attribute name="windowArea" default="myWindowArea" />
        <d:attribute name="menuData" />
        <d:constructor type="text/javascript">
            <!-- the constructor code goes here -->
        </d:constructor>
        <d:template type="application/xml">
            <div>
                <d:content />
            </div>
        </d:template>
        <d:handler event="menuActivate" type="text/javascript">
            <!-- handler code goes here -->
        </d:handler>
    </d:element>
</d:namespace>
```

The `constructor` does not look very straightforward. If you look at it, it is just a string with the XML for the `dataSource`, where its `url` attribute is filled in by concatenating the `menuData` attribute value of the `sq:windowMenu`. This string is then taken by `bb.command.create` to create a set of nodes that is appended to the `sq:windowMenu` widget.

It would have been clearer if we would have been able to put the XML of the `dataSource` within `c:create` tags in the `constructor`. This would work fine if we did not have the requirement that the name of the file containing the menu definitions should be variable and therefore, we wanted to have an attribute where you could specify it. Somehow setting the attribute interferes with the `c:create` XEL processing, therefore, we decided to use straight JavaScript.

The JavaScript string that we built must contain namespace declarations as appropriate.

This is the code for the `constructor`:

```
<d:namespace name="http://www.squaringthecircles.com/squared">
   <d:element name="windowMenu" extends="b:dataMenu">
      <!-- attributes go here -->
      <d:constructor type="text/javascript"><![CDATA[
var sCstr = '<b:dataSource
  xmlns:b="http://www.backbase.com/2006/btl" ';
sCstr += ' xmlns="http://www.w3.org/1999/xhtml"
  xmlns:e="http://www.backbase.com/2006/xel" ';
sCstr += ' e:behavior="b:remoteData" recordSelect="item" ';
sCstr += ' url="' + this.getAttribute('menuData') + '">';
sCstr += ' <b:dataSchema>';
sCstr += ' <b:dataField name="name" />';
sCstr += ' <b:dataField name="icon" select="@icon" />';
sCstr += ' <b:dataField name="hasSubmenu"';
sCstr += '        select="@hasSubmenu" />';
sCstr += ' <b:dataField name="separator"';
sCstr += '        select="@separator" />';
sCstr += ' <b:dataField name="open" select="@open" />';
sCstr += ' <b:dataField name="url" select="@url" />';
sCstr += ' <b:dataField name="width" select="@width" />';
sCstr += ' <b:dataField name="submenu" dataSchema="_self"';
sCstr += ' select="submenu/item" />';
sCstr += ' </b:dataSchema>';
sCstr += ' </b:dataSource>';
bb.command.create(sCstr, this,'replaceChildren');
      ]]></d:constructor>
  <!-- the template and menuActivate event handler go here -->
   </d:element>
</d:namespace>
```

We agree that the code is not pretty. It would be better to construct the nodes by using `createElement` commands, but then it would be harder to see what is going on. If you look at the string we are building in the constructor, you will see that it is an exact copy of the code for the `dataSource` we showed earlier.

Finally, here's the code for the `menuActivate` event handler:

```
<d:namespace name="http://www.squaringthecircles.com/squared">
   <d:element name="windowMenu" extends="b:dataMenu">
     <!--    attributes, template and constructor go here -->
       <d:handler event="menuActivate" type="text/javascript">
          var oDataSource = this.getProperty('dataSource');
          var sUrl = btl.dataSource.getValue(oDataSource,
             event.detail, 'url');
          var sWidth = btl.dataSource.getValue(oDataSource,
             event.detail, 'width');
          if (sUrl) {
             var sName = btl.dataSource.getValue(oDataSource,
                event.detail, 'name');
             var sId = this.getAttribute('windowArea');
             var oWinArea = bb.document.getElementById(sId);
             var oMyWin = bb.document.createElementNS
                ('http://www.backbase.com/2006/btl', 'window');
             oMyWin.setAttribute('label', sName);
             if (sWidth) oMyWin.setAttribute('width', sWidth);
             oMyWin.setAttribute('overflow', 'hidden');
             oWinArea.appendChild(oMyWin);
             // load the window contents
             bb.command.load(sUrl,'GET',null,null,oMyWin);
             bb.command.tile(oWinArea,
                true, false, '1px', '1px');
          }
       </d:handler>
    </d:element>
</d:namespace>
```

What does the event handler do? First, it retrieves the value for the `url` and the `width` of the menu option selected. These represent the `url` and the `width` of the window to be loaded. You can set the width, but not the height of the window, because we want to arrange the windows neatly into rows within the `windowArea`.

After creating a `window`, its attributes are set, and the name of the menu option becomes the `label` of the window.

The `window` is appended to the `windowArea` and the window contents are loaded according to the `url` given. Finally, the `windowArea` is tiled to arrange the windows into rows.

Let's look at an example of loading a window containing the *stocks* gadget. The value of the `url` attribute is in this case `myWindows/mystocks.xml`. If you look in this file, it contains:

```
<iframe xmlns="http://www.w3.org/1999/xhtml"
   height="100%" width="100%"
   src="../googlegadgets/stocks.html">
</iframe>
```

The `iframe` has a `url` where the code that we retrieved for the gadget is stored. You can find it in `stocks.html`. The line of code below should really be all on one line:

```
<script src="http://www.gmodules.com/ig/ifr?
  url=http://hosting.gmodules.com/ig/gadgets/
  file/114860707221226021925/stock-tab-index-
  publish.xml&synd=open&w=250&h=470& title=Stock+Market+Index
  &border=%23ffffff%7C3px%2C1px+solid+%23999999& output=js">
</script>
```

Is the sq:windowMenu widget useful?

As the widget is now, there are some restrictions to it:

- You can drag-and-drop a window, but if you retile the `windowArea`, the window will go back to where it came from. If you want to prevent this, you could either disable drag-and-drop or you could write your own tiling routine, which is not a trivial task.

- If you close a window, it leaves a hole in the tiling, which you could try to repair of course. You should also destroy the window to remove all its resources properly.

- Some windows may not like to be displayed twice. For our examples this is not a problem because they do not contain any `id` values. Still, this is something to watch out for.

The usefulness of the `sq:windowMenu` widget depends on the way you are going to deploy your web application and on the structure of your development team. If your team is really small and consists of expert JavaScript developers, and you make this kind of application only once, then it would be better to just place the code that we folded into a widget now, straight onto your page.

Otherwise, you may reap the advantages of being able to specify the menu layout separately in a file, and of allowing your UI designers to put a `sq:windowMenu` on the page without worrying about the `dataSource` widgets and the `dataField` elements that it should contain.

If you ever add new function to the `sq:windowMenu`, such as custom tiling, this will be available to all instances of the widget everywhere in your application.

Miscellaneous commands

This category contains, as the name suggests, some commands that we did not know how to place in another category: `trace`, `alert`, and `bookmark`.

trace

Adds the specified message to the event log. The context (either the current context or a context defined by the XEL `with` element/attribute) is automatically added to the message.

The `trace` command supports the `select` and `with` attributes.

Logs a message and places it in the console. Here's the code for `trace` command:

```
<div>
    Log a message to the console for debugging...
    <e:handler event="click">
        <c:trace select="'My Debug Message'" />
    </e:handler>
</div>
```

The next screenshot shows what happens when you click on the text:

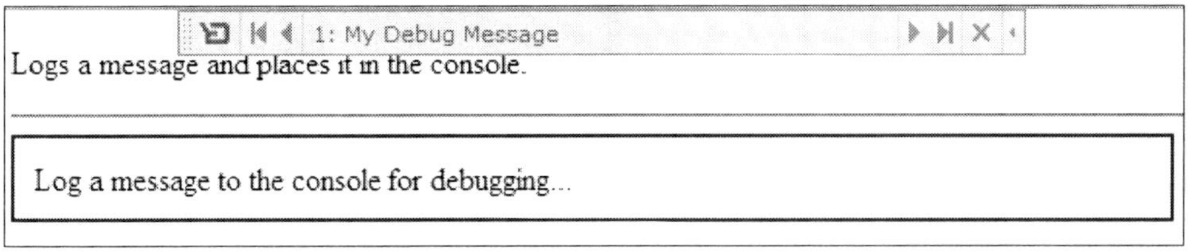

alert

Alert requires no introduction. You have seen so many already!

It raises an `alert` box with the text as specified by the `select` attribute. Let's look at the following code:

```
<div>
   Click for Command Alert (string) - returns "alert text"
   <e:handler event="click">
      <c:alert select="'alert text'" />
   </e:handler>
</div>
```

You can use an alert like the following for debugging:

```
<div>
   Click for Command Alert (node) - returns "object"
   <e:handler event="click">
      <c:alert select="id('cmd_object')" />
   </e:handler>
</div>
<div id="cmd_object" style="border: solid;">
   Alert with this div
</div>
```

bookmark

Adds a state to the browser which can be activated by pressing the **Back/Forward** buttons, thus enabling history and bookmarking for AJAX applications.

The `bookmark` command can have two attributes:

Attribute	Description
name	The string label to be used as bookmark identifier. When this parameter is omitted, a random string is created.
title	The title associated with the bookmark (to be displayed in the browser navigation history).

In the following example, the state of a `tabBox` is added to the browser history. Whenever a `tab` is selected, the URL is updated to reflect the current selection. To do this, once `bb.command.bookmark` is used, once `c:bookmark`, and twice `bb.history.add` is used. They all have the same functionality. A handler is added to the `tabBox` (when the tabBox is added to the page) that will listen to the history event. When the user navigates through the history, the `tabBox` is restored to match the selected `tab` when the state was added to the history.

```
<b:tabBox>
    <e:handler event="DOMNodeInsertedIntoDocument"
        type="text/javascript">
        <![CDATA[
        //Add the handler for history actions!
        var oTabbox = this;
        //Function used for restoring the tabbox
        function bookmarkTabbox(sTab){
            //It's a tabselect
            if(sTab.indexOf('tab') == 0){
                var iTab = sTab.charAt(3);
                oTabbox.setProperty('selectedIndex', iTab-1);
                return true;
            }
            return false;
        }
        //Add the tabbox update to the history event
        bb.document.addEventListener('history',
            function(event) {
                bookmarkTabbox(event.bookmark);
            }, false);
        //Restore the initial state
        if (!bookmarkTabbox(bb.history.current)) {
            //add the first tab because there will be
            //no select event for it
            bb.command.bookmark('tab1', 'Tab 1');
        }
        ]]>
    </e:handler>
    <b:tab label="Tab 1">Tab 1
        <e:handler event="select">
         <!-- Add the action to history -->
            <c:bookmark name="tab1" title="Tab 1" />
        </e:handler>
    </b:tab>
    <b:tab label="Tab 2">Tab 2
        <e:handler event="select" type="text/javascript">
            //Add the action to history
            bb.history.add('tab2', 'Tab 2');
        </e:handler>
    </b:tab>
    <b:tab label="Tab 3">Tab 3
        <e:handler event="select" type="text/javascript">
            //Add the action to history
```

```
        bb.history.add('tab3', 'Tab 3');
    </e:handler>
  </b:tab>
</b:tabBox>
```

It is a bit hard to visualize this example with a picture. You should try it out using the BTL Example Exerciser. What you will see is that the URL in the browser is adapted each time you click on another tab. The browser history will be updated and when the history event is triggered, the proper tab will be made active in the `history` event handler.

Summary

By reaching the end of this chapter you have seen almost all, BTL widgets and command functions. The ones you have not seen are seldom used, deprecated, or otherwise not advisable to use. To make it easier to find a specific widget, you can find the category to which it belongs in Chapter 2. An overview of the command functions can be found in Chapter 3.

You can find an example of a `tree` widget in the BTL Exerciser sample application; we just did not have space in Chapter 5 to describe it. The `treeGrid` was omitted from the book because the `plusDataGrid` we developed in Chapter 5 is a better alternative.

We did not formally describe the CSS-related commands. However, you can find many examples throughout the book using them. There are also specific examples in the Command Exerciser sample application.

In the next chapter, we will look at the Backbase debugger, provide some optimization tips, and discuss deployment of your Backbase application.

Debugging, Optimization, and Deployment

Sometimes, something goes wrong when you test a newly developed application. How can you figure out where the problem is? In this chapter, we give some tips specifically adapted to development using the Backbase framework.

When everything works, it is a good idea to look at your application again from a different standpoint, instead of just checking whether it functions correctly. We will discuss some ways by which you can make your application perform faster and more robustly.

Next, it is time to think about deploying your web application on a web server. We will have some points on this subject too.

Part of the information in this chapter may be found almost literally in the online documentation for the Backbase framework. We are repeating the text here in an adapted and abbreviated form because we think it is handy to have all the information you need to effectively develop a client web application in one place, in this book. In addition, some of this documentation is hard to find if you do not know where to look. We will also tell you where it is.

This chapter covers the following topics in detail:

- Debugging and the Backbase debugger with the various tabs you can see
- Application optimization, focusing on YSlow
- The TDL Optimizer and the options it offers
- Deployment of your client web application on a server

Debugging

Whether you do development using Extreme Programming and a test-first approach or whether you develop with the old fashioned waterfall method, there will be moments when your web application does not react in the way you expect or does not look like the designers said it should. You'll need tools and ingenuity to figure out what is wrong.

Probably still the best toolset for web developers to help them with the task of debugging their application is a combination of the Firefox browser with the *Firebug* and *Web Developer* plugins. They allow you to inspect and change almost anything on your page when you are testing your application. Within Firebug, you can see exactly what was sent and received between browser and server, set breakpoints, and so on. We have shown you some examples of Firebug usage in the earlier chapters.

Here is a list of the frequent problems that we encountered ourselves or that we saw in the forum on the Backbase developer network (`http://bdn.backbase.com`):

- Debugging a web application using the Backbase framework is no different from debugging any other web application using JavaScript. You can use the same tools and the same tricks.

- Old fashioned, well-placed JavaScript `alert` statements sometimes help to find the cause of a problem more quickly than any other way.

- Using XHTML has its challenges; some browsers punish you for forgetting end tags or for inserting *funny* characters by not displaying anything. Firebug can sometimes help to find out where the cause is by inspecting the reply sent from the server.

- Another cause for not seeing any output is sending `text/html` instead of `application/xml` as **Content-type** from the server. This happens to us more often than you would expect!

- Although the Backbase framework can shield you from browser incompatibilities, the JavaScript you write or the CSS you use can still show differences across browsers. You must test your work at least in Chrome, Firefox, MSIE, Opera, and Safari, unless you can prescribe to your users which browser to use.

- If you have *performance* problems instead of functional ones, the **Console** log and **Net** tab of Firebug can help because they show time in milliseconds for every file loaded.

- Make it work, make it right, make it fast (Kent Beck, the inventor of Extreme Programming, said this). Fast is last. We will talk much more about performance later in this chapter.

The Backbase debugger

The Backbase debugger has functionality that resembles the Firebug plugin of the Mozilla Firefox browser, with the advantage that it will work with all browsers supported by the Backbase framework.

The details of what you can do with the debugger are explained here: http://bdn.backbase.com/client/examples/debugger.

Overview

When you are running the Backbase development version (as opposed to the optimized version, which we will talk about later), the debugger is always present in the background. When something goes wrong, such as a JavaScript error occurs, or the XML you are trying to load is invalid, then the debugger will pop up with one bar containing an error message. If you click on this bar, a window will open in which you can search for details.

You can also make the debugger appear on demand, by pressing the *Esc* key. This can be useful if you want to take a look at the structure of a widget or at the CSS used. You have seen examples of this in Chapter 7 when we looked at the model and view structure of the widgets we developed.

The information/error bar

Below you see a typical picture that could appear when something goes wrong.

Press the *Esc* key to toggle the visibility of the bar. A gray Backbase icon will appear. If you click on the small right arrow, the bar will expand. When an error occurs, the information/error bar will open automatically. You can click on the icon or the bar to open the debugger window:

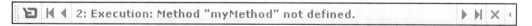

The error bar is rather intuitive; you will probably not need any help with it. Just note that you can move the bar around by dragging the Backbase icon. Note also that the messages are numbered. You can step back and forth to see the status of your application at the time when the message was issued.

The debugger window

The debugger window shows a set of tabs when it is opened:

- **Console**: Shows details about error messages and source text of failing JavaScript if applicable. It logs messages written by the `bb.console` function.

- **Model**: Provides an interactive overview of the application's model space.

- **View**: Provides an interactive overview of the view space.

- **TDL**: Provides an interactive overview of defined namespaces and classes.

- **Network**: Provides an I/O inspector of all `XMLHttpRequests`.

- **Reports**: Provides system information and a summary of the elements in both the **Model** and the **View** space.

- **Preferences**: Provides various settings, for example, when the debugger window should be opened.

- **Help**: Provides basic help on how to use the debugger.

At the bottom of the debugger window you'll see **>>>**. You can type commands here. This line will be visible with every tab that you have open. The output of the command will differ depending on the tab that is active.

For example, if we had a simple `accordion` on our page and selected an `accordionItem` in the **Model** tab, then typing `bb.console.log(this)` in the command area and clicking **Run** will result in `b:accordionItem` as console output.

Now, if we go over to the **View** tab, you will see that a `div` with `class="btl-accordionItem"` is selected. Typing the same `bb.console.log(this)` in the command area will now show: `div.btl-accordionItem`.

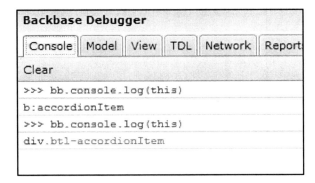

Console tab

Let's look at a realistic scenario that often happens to us:

```
2: XInclude: Failed loading resource from
   "http://snippetviewer/snippetViewer/testcases/btl_accordion.xml".
```

Usually, this means that you forgot to code a *namespace declaration*. To make sure, you can open the debugger window, click on the blue `sourceText` link and see this in the console window:

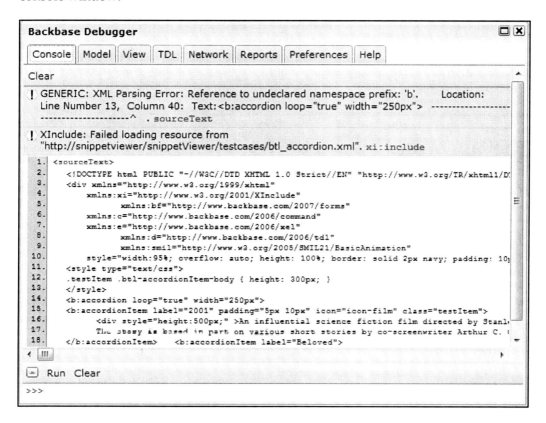

When debugging TDL widgets, it can be really useful to see the source text of a failing method, or when debugging server scripts, you should see what the script sent back.

We have seen the `bb.console` command above. Here are a few examples of what you can do with it. The complete list can be found in the online documentation.

If you are familiar with the Firebug tool, you will see that this command is very similar to the `console` command in Firebug, with the obvious difference that the Backbase debugger commands also work in other browsers, such as Internet Explorer. The methods available on the `bb.console` object are designed to match the Console API as used in the Firebug tool for the Firefox browser.

Methods	Description
`bb.console.error(object [, object, ...])`	Writes a message to the console with the visual "error" icon and color coding.
`bb.console.assert(expression [, object, ...])`	Tests whether an expression is true. If not, it will write a message to the console and throw an exception.
`bb.console.dir(object)`	Prints an interactive listing of all properties of the object.

The Model and View tabs

In Chapter 7, we have already shown you an example of the **Model** and **View** tabs when we discussed the model and view layers of the Backbase framework. Below are some more examples that should make clear that there is a lot of information to be found in the debugger that can help you when developing widgets and web applications. A practical feature is that you can find a node by first clicking the **Inspect** button, and then clicking on the element in your browser window that you want to find. Then, the corresponding model or view node (depending on the tab you activated) will be selected. On the right-hand side, you can find all the information about the DOM tree and the CSS layout.

The picture below shows a part of the Model DOM tree:

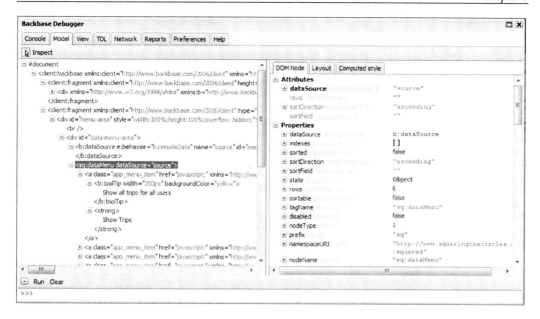

The next picture has the same application code, but now the **View** part is shown:

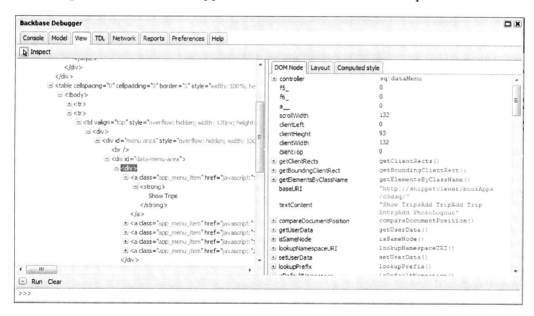

The HTML DOM (View) nodes are available for inspection and you can get detailed information about the layout of the component and its style.

TDL tab

In this tab, you can inspect the complete namespace and class structure as defined in TDL for all namespaces that are defined in your page. You can find a class by drilling down the namespaces and classes. The following is a picture of what the TDL tab window looks like:

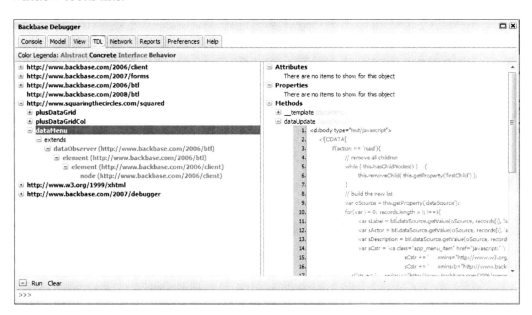

On the right side of the screen, there is an overview of the different attributes, properties, and methods of the class.

Network tab

In this tab, you can inspect the XMLHttpRequests occurring in the application. You can see:

XMLHttpRequests	Description
Request Headers	The headers sent to the server on request
Request Body	The body (data) sent to the server on request
Response Headers	The headers sent from the server when returning the request
Response Body	The response text of the request returned by the server

You can also see the size of the files that were loaded and how long it took in milliseconds.

Reports tab

In this tab, you can see statistics about your application.

Preferences tab

Here, you can set debugger preferences as shown in the next screenshot:

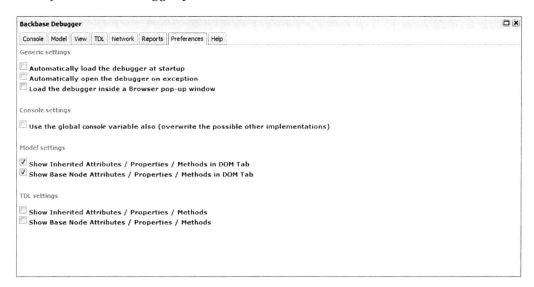

Help tab

This tab provides instructions for using the debugger.

Application optimization

With optimization, we mean optimization for performance from the perspective of the user of your web application. Performance should be looked at **last** as we said earlier in this chapter. This is because optimizations in an application are always needed in a different area than where you thought they would be needed at the start of your development process. Looking at performance as the last activity of course does not mean that you should do stupid things during development, such as including long database queries in your web application.

You can find a wealth of information on the Web about making your applications faster. However, we base the discussion in the following sections on this site: http://developer.yahoo.com/performance/.

This site has a list of 34 points that you should look at when trying to optimize your site, subdivided into seven categories: Content, Server, Cookie, CSS, Javascript, Images, and Mobile. We will look at the first six of these categories, not to repeat information that is already well described on the site, but to add specific points to be aware of concerning the Backbase framework. The seventh category, Mobile, is interesting but out of the scope for this book.

 One more point before we start discussing optimizing the content of your page: Install **YSlow**!

As it says on the Yahoo developer site:

> *YSlow analyzes web pages and suggests ways to improve their performance based on a set of rules for high performance web pages. YSlow is a Firefox add-on integrated with the Firebug web development tool.*

This tool checks for each of the rules and gives recommendations for improvement.

The following is a picture of using YSlow with the C3D travel blog application. As a result, apparently, we need to do something about **compression** and **minifying** both CSS and JavaScript.

Optimizing content

Optimizing the content of your web page involves the following points:

- Making fewer HTTP requests
- Reducing DNS lookups
- Avoiding redirects
- Making AJAX cacheable
- Post-loading components
- Preloading components
- Reducing the number of DOM elements
- Splitting components across domains
- Minimizing the number of iframes
- Preventing 404 errors

If you have only a limited amount of time to do the optimization of your application and you have to make a choice of what to do, then, look at the items here that help optimize the **content** of the pages in your web application because they will have the greatest effect.

We pick out four points here to discuss in more detail: *Making fewer HTTP requests, Making AJAX cacheable, Post- or preloading components*, and *Reducing the number of DOM elements*.

Making fewer HTTP requests

Balancing the number of HTTP requests against the file size of the components you load seems to be the *number one* activity that can help to speed up the loading of your web pages. If you've ever taken a look at the **Console** and **Net** tabs of Firebug, you would have seen that multiple requests are issued to the server: in the case of the startup window of the C3D travel blog sample application, it amounts to around 30 requests, while nothing special happens on that page. Particularly in the **Net** tab of Firebug, you can evaluate what types of requests were sent, how long it took to receive a reply, and so on.

The bindings in the Backbase framework (the TDL definitions for the BTL widgets) are split up in many small files to allow lazy loading of what you need. For good performance, the granularity of these building blocks is too high. It would, therefore, be advantageous to combine these files into larger chunks based on what you actually use in your application.

To help you with this rather complex task, there is a tool available, the *TDL Optimizer*, that can combine files together and also compress and minify the contents by taking out whitespace and comments. The TDL Optimizer is discussed later in this chapter. Be sure though, that your files do not become too long because this will adversely affect performance and some browsers cannot cope with very large files.

Another way to minimize the number of HTTP requests is to combine images. This can be done using CSS sprites. It involves combining background images into one and by using `background-image` and `background-position` in CSS, you can display the right part of the image. This technique is used for many of the BTL background images.

Making AJAX cacheable

We assume you know how to add Expires or Cache-Control Headers. This should be applied not only to components of complete pages, but also to AJAX responses. Also, think of compressing and minifying responses.

It may not have been obvious to you that it is also possible to cache **data** responses. Look into the YSlow documentation for an example of how this could be done.

Post- or preloading components

The old wisdom about user interaction response times says that a user who is looking at his/her browser window may be willing to wait three seconds for a page to be loaded or a reply to be received. If it takes longer, most users will become increasingly annoyed.

This is especially important when the initial page of your application is loaded. Therefore, you should try to load as few components as possible initially. For a Backbase application, there are a few rules of thumb:

- Try to put static content or content that uses HTML only outside of Backbase areas. Note that you can still dynamically change content outside Backbase areas using `bb.command.load`.

- Make Backbase areas initially empty wherever possible. Fill these areas using an `onload` event handler; this'll cause them to be filled after the rest of the page is loaded.

- If you have large chunks of standard XHTML within a Backbase area, escape these blocks using `b:xhtml`.

- If you are using the TDL Optimizer or hand-crafted combinations of widget definitions, combine only those files that are absolutely required on the first page.

Sometimes, it is impossible to keep response times below the three-second threshold and in that situation, you need to do something to keep the user busy. An often-used trick is to display a *busy* image. Alternatively, you could display extra textual information or a short Flash movie. Be careful not to hide the bad design behind a busy image.

Preloading can be useful if you can predict that a user will need some component or data and that you can utilize the idle time of the browser-server connection.

Reducing the number of DOM elements

A while ago, we read an article of someone who was trying to use an earlier version of the Backbase framework and who was complaining that his application slowed down considerably when the number of DOM nodes were above 12,000. We thought this was insane: when you can request new data using AJAX dynamically, why would you try to squeeze 12,000 nodes in a page, while you would be able to see only a part of it?

Nevertheless, the new `dataGrid` BTL component in the Backbase framework was specifically designed to be able to handle thousands of nodes. Despite this, the `dataGrid` will perform better when you serve it one page at a time from a remote data source, instead of feeding it with a flood of nodes!

Because of the double-layer approach of the Backbase framework architecture, there are sometimes three nodes instead of one, for the *controller*, the *model*, and the *view*. Therefore, it is extra helpful for speed of processing when you keep the DOM nodes at a minimum.

Maybe, surprisingly, defining and using TDL components helps to minimize the model DOM tree because this tree will only contain the nodes for the tags you defined, as we have seen in Chapter 7. To minimize the number of view nodes, the usual rules apply as detailed in the YSlow documentation.

Optimizing the server

Optimizing the server that is hosting your web application involves the following points:

* Use a Content Delivery Network
* Add an Expires or a Cache-Control Header
* Gzip components (Compression)
* Configure ETags
* Flush the buffer early
* Use GET for AJAX requests

Using a *Content Delivery Network* involves deploying your application on a number of distributed servers, serving static content from a location near the user. This seems to improve performance more than distributing the server processing, which would involve complicated synchronization issues.

Adding an Expires or a Cache-Control Header can be very useful to enable the server to cache components and therefore avoiding HTTP requests. However, you should be careful with dynamic components or new releases of your application, because the browser could try to use old versions of these components, which may cause problems.

Compression

Compression will make files smaller. Of course, it takes time to compress and decompress files before and after they are sent over the network, but the gain in shorter transmission time offsets this extra processing easily. Therefore, compression makes your application perform faster and results in shorter response times.

Browsers automatically decompress zipped files, but on the server side you must usually do something, such as configuring the server in the right way. Here are some tips.

Both Apache Httpd Server 2.0 and 1.3 support server-side compression, which means that you do not have to compress your files yourself.

To enable compression on Apache Httpd Server 2.0, you must load the `mod_deflate` module in your `httpd.conf` configuration file. `mod_deflate` adds a filter to Gzip the content. You can allow the compression of all web files by using the `SetOutputFilter` directive, or you can specify file types with the `AddOutputFilterByType`. Refer to the Apache Httpd Server 2.0 documentation (`http://httpd.apache.org/docs/2.0/`) for more information.

Apache Httpd Server 1.3 uses the `mod_gzip` module rather than the `mod_deflate` module for compression. Refer to the `mod_gzip` home page for more information: `http://sourceforge.net/projects/mod-gzip/`.

Microsoft Internet Information Server 6 includes a native compression system that can be configured to compress both static content and dynamic content. Microsoft Internet Information Server 6 also caches the compressed information in a directory, which helps improve performance by eliminating the need to compress already-compressed content.

To enable HTTP compression in Microsoft Internet Information Server 6, open the website's property page to edit the global properties for the site. Navigate to the **Service** tab and configure the **HTTP Compression** section.

IIS version 5.x does not have native support for compression. There are third-party commercial plugins available, but it is also possible to compress the files manually using Gzip and have an ASP page to check for compression support on the client browser.

If you cannot or do not want to use the Apache Httpd Server server-side compression modules, you can also use PHP. When using PHP, you must compress the files yourself using a utility such as Gzip. The next step is to create a PHP script that checks to see if the client can accept compressed files. If it can, then you can send the manually compressed files to the client. If not, you should send the uncompressed files.

Using *Etags* is more flexible than using expiration dates. However, if you do not know what you are doing, it is better to remove them, for example by adding `FileETag none` to the Apache configuration file.

Flushing the buffer early

Although the piece of advice given for this item is not specific to Backbase applications and applies to using PHP on the server, if you do use PHP, this is an easy thing to do. Use the `flush()` function right after the head of the page, to enable the browser to start rendering the page earlier.

Using GET for AJAX requests

It seems that browsers implement POST as a two-step process. POST is often used instead of GET to avoid long URLs that may contain sensitive data, but as you do not see the URL when using an AJAX request and GET requests are mostly easier to construct in a Backbase application, it is better to avoid POST if you are not sending, but retrieving data.

Optimizing cookies

Optimizing cookies involves *reducing cookie size* and *using cookie-free domains for components*.

From a Backbase framework point of view, there is nothing specific about reducing cookie size.

Regarding using cookie-free domains, which is useful for hosting static and public content: it would theoretically be possible to put the images used for styling Backbase components into a different domain, however, this is probably not worth the effort.

Optimizing JavaScript and CSS

For CSS, we should look at these points:

- Put stylesheets at the top
- Avoid CSS expressions
- Choose `<link>` over `@import`
- Avoid filters

When considering optimizing JavaScript, you should look at the following list. Some of the points also apply to CSS:

- Put scripts at the bottom
- Make JavaScript and CSS external
- Minify JavaScript and CSS
- Remove duplicate scripts
- Minimize DOM access
- Develop smart event handlers

We do not need to discuss CSS Expressions, `@import`, and filters here, but for the placement of CSS and JavaScript, there are some considerations with respect to Backbase.

Placing JavaScript code at the end of the page and CSS at the top

Having your application's JavaScript code at the bottom of a page makes the page load faster because execution of scripts will block parallel downloads.

This is not always possible when using the Backbase framework because it is necessary to have the libraries and widget definitions loaded before they are used. Therefore, your options in this respect are not many. One trick to consider is to keep the Backbase areas empty when the page is initially loaded and then fill these areas when the loading is completed.

 The inclusion of the Backbase `boot.js` file should still be inside the `head` element of the page.

With CSS, it is exactly the other way around. When CSS is placed at the top of the page, it *appears* to be loading faster because the browser will be able to progressively render the elements on the page.

Backbase widgets usually contain their own CSS that is loaded using `resource` tags when the widget is loaded. This is OK because when a widget is not used, its CSS is not loaded and processed unnecessarily.

Minify JavaScript and CSS

You can improve application load times by decreasing the number of bytes sent to the client. Minifying JavaScript and CSS involves removing whitespace and comments. The following are some examples of regular expressions that you could use to remove these unwanted items. It is also possible and probably preferable to use the TDL Optimizer tool for this purpose. We will talk about this tool in a later section of this chapter.

To remove items such as whitespaces and comments, you can use XSLT or you can use regular expressions to strip files. These regular expressions can be included in an Apache Ant build process, or you can run a find/replace on your files:

- Remove CSS comments (simple):

  `\/\*[\s\S]*?\*\/`

- Remove CSS comments (advanced):

  `^\/\*[\s\S]*?\*\/\s*`

- Remove empty lines:

  `^[\r\n]+`

- Remove tabs:

  `^[\t]+`

- Remove CSS comments, tabs, whitespaces, and carriage returns (please note that this is a single line regular expression):

  ```
  (^\/\*[\s\S]*?\*\/\s*|\/\*[\s\S]*?\*\/|^\s+|(?<=:)[ ]+|(?<=\{)\s+\
  s+|\s+(?=\}))|
  (?<=;)[\r\n]+|(?<=,)[\r\n]+)|\t
  ```

 Although these expressions were tested by Backbase, there is no guarantee they'll work in your situation.

Removing duplicate scripts

Loading the same JavaScript script twice is certainly not a good idea. If you are using Backbase widgets only to contain JavaScript, this should not happen. If you are loading a Backbase function twice, you will see a warning.

Minimizing DOM access

Minimizing DOM access can be achieved in a Backbase environment by using properties to keep references to DOM nodes that you need to access. Using composite widgets defined in TDL can also help to abstract from the DOM tree. However, you must be aware of the other drawbacks of using these as outlined in Chapter 7.

Developing smart event handlers

The trick for *developing smart event handlers* seems to be to attach the event handlers not to many lowest items in a component, but to a container that can accept the events. The Backbase event handlers have `event.target` objects that make it easier to find the element that actually caused the event.

Optimizing images

Optimizing the images you are using in your web application involves these points:

- Optimize images
- Optimize CSS sprites
- Don't scale images in HTML
- Make `favicon.ico` small and cacheable

There is nothing specific for a Backbase application here. Nevertheless, there is some sound advice on the YSlow website. Please check out the *ImageMagick* tool at: `http://www.imagemagick.org`, if you did not do so already, to help with identifying and solving image problems.

One last point on optimization in general (or actually two):

Good enough is good enough. Do not over optimize your application, instead, spend your efforts on functional improvements.

Make your optimizations repeatable and document what you did. You will have to redo many optimizations, such as minifying code, for every release of your application.

The TDL Optimizer

In the Backbase framework package, you can find a special utility program, the TDL Optimizer. Look in the `tools` folder to find a `tdlOptimizer` subfolder. A detailed documentation is also located there. Here, we give a practical overview.

What does the TDL Optimizer do and why would you want to use such a utility?

A problem with JavaScript frameworks and libraries like the Backbase framework is that the JavaScript code must be loaded each time a new page is loaded into the browser. The libraries consist of many large files and not only the size of the files, but more than that, the number of files may make the initial loading of a page slow.

One way of limiting the number of files that are loaded is by loading files only on demand. While this helps, you will see when you use the Firebug tool in the Firefox browser that still a large number of files are loaded.

What you can do to bring the number of files down, is to combine the files that are needed for an application into larger ones. You can minimize file sizes by taking out comments and whitespace, and by compressing the files.

Creating a configuration file for the optimizer

To create a configuration file for the optimizer, perform the following steps:

1. Boot up the application.
2. Make note of the bindings that are loaded at startup (but not at runtime). For Firefox, you can use Firebug's Net watcher tool. For IE, you can use Fiddler.
3. As an alternative, you can use the Backbase Debugger tool, and select the TDL tab to see which bindings and widgets are being used by your Backbase application.
4. Create a configuration file for the optimizer with `xi:include` statements to the tags that you need.
5. Make sure the application still works correctly when using the configuration file you just created, by replacing the `<xi:include src="/Backbase/4_4_1/bindings/config.xml"/>` declaration in your HTML file with an `xi:include` of the newly created configuration file.

Running the TDL Optimizer

You must set the JAVA_HOME environment variable before running this program. To run the TDL Optimizer, simply execute the `tdlOptimizer.bat` or `tdlOptimizer.sh` file, specifying at least the first two arguments defined below:

- `-i` or `--inputFile`—the path to the input file.

- `-o` or `--outputFile`—the path to the output file.

- `-dco` or `--disableCssOptimization`—turns off CSS optimization.

- `-djo` or `--disableJavascriptOptimization`—turns off JavaScript optimization and obfuscation.

- `-djob` or `--disableJavascriptObfuscation`—turns off obfuscation of local JavaScript variables.

- `-iu` or `--ignoreUses`—ignores `d:uses` everywhere, so that no `d:uses` will be resolved.

- `-iiu` or `--ignoreInputUses`—ignores `d:uses` in the input file. This option has no effect if `--ignoreUses` is also specified, in which case no `d:uses` will be resolved.

- `-r` or `--relocate`—overrides the optimized (output) `xml:base` setting. This is useful when invoking the TDL Optimizer from a build script because the location of the bindings files will probably be different when the application is deployed.

- `-p` or `--pretty`—if present, the output file will be properly formatted and indented for best readability (but non-optimal performance).

- `-h` or `--help`—prints a help screen explaining command line syntax.

Deploying the optimized bindings

Firefox browsers have a known issue with handling large XML files. Therefore, we recommend that you split your optimized files within your Backbase application if they are excessively large.

Simply replace the reference to your original configuration file with the generated optimized bindings file. Please note that you can keep some bindings to be resolved through the automated loading mechanism (`d:uses`). This way, you can balance the overhead between boot and runtime.

Deployment on a server

Deployment of your web application ultimately means copying the sources or compiled versions of what you developed on a publicly accessible server, together with the Backbase framework package.

If you have a large organization that is developing the web application, there are probably dedicated people who know all about installation and deployment on a web server. If you are in a small group, deploying on a hosted service, you probably do not have many options of customizing the server to your needs. In this section, there are some general points that will apply.

A vast majority of web applications are deployed on a server running some version of Unix and using an Apache web server. If you are using Java Servlets or JavaServer Pages, you will have additional configuration concerns, such as installing Tomcat or some other server supporting Java. You will need to know details of the specific server you are dealing with, which is outside the scope of this book.

A source of detailed information is the *Production Deployment Guide* of the Backbase Client Framework. There is also a *Deployment Guide* for the JSF or the Struts editions of the framework that has more information about deploying in a Java environment. You can find this documentation on the developer network of Backbase, `http://bdn.backbase.com/`.

The Production Deployment Guide can be confusing because it has a lot of seemingly duplicate information. It repeats the story for every kind of web server you may be interested in. Because we assume that most of you will be interested in using Apache as a web server, we made *one* story concentrating on Apache.

Here, we are covering some general points that specifically apply to deploying the Backbase framework and the code that you have developed with it:

- **Install** — the quickest way to deploy the Backbase framework is to copy the files into the server's `DocumentRoot`. This is the default directory from which a server serves documents and requires no additional configuration.

- **Defining Aliases** — if you want a server to serve documents from locations other than the `DocumentRoot`, you have to set up aliases using the Alias directive for the Apache server or by defining Virtual Directories for the Microsoft Internet Information Server to point to these locations.

- **Compression** — compressing the Client Runtime JavaScript files allows quicker downloading of the Backbase framework to the client. We already discussed compression earlier in this chapter when we were talking about application optimization.

Install

A server has a default directory, also called `DocumentRoot` for an Apache web server, from which it serves your documents. The quickest way to put a Backbase framework application into a production environment is to place the Client Runtime, bindings files, and the application itself into this directory.

The place where you can find the `DocumentRoot` can vary depending on the operating system and type of web server you are using. For an Apache server, its location is specified in the `http.conf` file.

For example, in a default Apache Httpd Server Windows installation, the `DocumentRoot` is `C:\Program Files\Apache Group\Apache2\htdocs`, while Linux uses the directory `/var/www/html` as the server `DocumentRoot`.

Here is what you need to do, assuming that you are using version 4.4.1:

1. Copy the `backbase/4_4_1_optimized` directory to the server's `DocumentRoot`. If you are using a hosted service, you will probably have access using the FTP protocol to copy files onto your server.

2. You can, of course, copy the `backbase/4_4_1_optimized` directory anywhere inside your `DocumentRoot` (or an aliased location). The key point is that your application startup page(s) (any file that points to the Client Runtime JavaScript file) has the correct relative pathway.

3. Rename the `backbase/4_4_1_optimized` directory to `backbase/4_4_1`.

4. Adjust the permissions and the ownership of the Backbase directory and the files and directories below it to make sure that the user under whom the server is running can access them.

5. Move your application to a location of your choice in the `DocumentRoot` directory.

6. Each startup page of a Backbase framework application loads a Client Runtime initialization file named `boot.js`:

```
<head>
<title>Startup Page</title>
<script type="text/javascript"
  src="../backbase/4_4_1/engine/boot.js">
</script>
</head>
```

7. We have talked about initialization of files at length in Chapter 1. Ensure that the relative pathway named as the value of the `src` attribute correctly points to the location of the `boot.js`. The `boot.js` file is located in `backbase/4_4_1/engine`.

8. Test your application.

Installation in a Java environment

For use in a Java environment, there are WAR files available, both a development and an optimized version. Look into the Java Technologies documentation of the Backbase framework for more information.

Defining alias locations

If you want a server to serve documents from locations other than the DocumentRoot, use the Alias directive to allow manipulation and control of a URL, as requests arrive at the server.

In the following example, we are assuming that you are using an Apache Httpd Server. The Alias directive is used to map a URL to filesystem paths. This allows for content that is not directly under the DocumentRoot to be served as part of the web document tree. It allows you to cleanly separate the Backbase framework installation directory from your projects' directory and the server directory.

We use the following settings/locations to show you how to create an alias:

* The backbase/4_4_1 directory (that contains the Client Runtime and bindings files) is placed at the root of the /usr/local/ directory
* There is a /usr/local/myApps directory that will contain your applications

Naturally, if you have set up your environment differently, you will need to make the necessary path adjustments.

Use the following steps to create an alias:

1. Adjust the permissions and the ownership of the Backbase directory and the files and directories below it to make sure that the user of the server can access them.
2. Locate the server configuration file httpd.conf.
3. Open the httpd.conf file in an editor.
4. In the aliases section, add the aliases and the directory directives to enable your web server to locate your Backbase Framework Client Runtime installation and project directory:

```
Alias /myapps /usr/local/www/data/myApps
Alias /Backbase /usr/local/backbase/4_4_1
<Directory /usr/local/www/data/myApps>
Options Indexes MultiViews
AllowOverride None
Order allow,deny
```

```
Allow from all
</Directory>
<Directory /usr/local/backbase/4_4_1>
Options Indexes MultiViews
AllowOverride None
Order allow,deny
Allow from all
</Directory>
```

5. Restart Apache.

6. Test your application.

Summary

This was a short chapter to give you some hints for debugging, optimization, and deployment of your application.

We have seen that the Backbase tool set, especially the *debugger*, has an advantage over other tools because they work with all browsers. In addition, the Backbase debugger allows you to inspect your Backbase application structure and all custom built widgets easily.

Using the guidelines set forth by the YSlow tool, we described what you can do to optimize a Backbase web application.

Deploying the Backbase framework libraries is not very different from deploying other JavaScript libraries. Optimization and tuning of the JavaScript in your application follows the same rules as before.

Deploying the TDL bindings can be optimized using the TDL Optimizer if needed. Using the optimized versions of the bindings delivered with the Backbase package may be already sufficient.

In the next chapter, we will make a comparison of the Backbase framework with some other frameworks.

10
Framework Comparison

It does not matter whether you opened this chapter after having read the major part of the book or whether you ended up here out of curiosity while looking through the table of contents; you are probably curious to know how the Backbase AJAX framework compares to the other similar frameworks.

We will start the chapter with an attempt to classify the multiple solutions used today to build interactive websites and client-side applications. By doing a drill-down, we will approach the category to which we believe the Backbase AJAX framework belongs and from which the candidates for a more detailed comparison will be picked up. To make a fair comparison, we will eliminate any server-side frameworks, client-side libraries, and application frameworks—this is why you won't see GWT, JSF, jQuery, or PureMVC in the final comparison.

 The libraries and frameworks mentioned in this comparison are very briefly described at the end of this chapter.

Also, at the end of this chapter (but before the framework reference overview), there is a section about integrating other frameworks with Backbase.

This chapter discusses the following topics in detail:

- Toolkit classification
- Backbase comparison to similar products
- Techniques of integrating third-party widgets into Backbase
- References to the mentioned libraries and frameworks

The landscape of client-side technologies

Since 2005, when the term *AJAX* was invented, many JavaScript libraries and tools have popped up. In fact, there have been several tools earlier to aid DHTML development, which can be seen as predecessors for the AJAX tools and libraries. One of these is the earlier version of the *Backbase framework*, and another example is *Bindows*.

Some of those libraries survived the AJAX technology hype and grew into a solid base for many RIA projects and services, whereas some vanished. Libraries that survived have gone through a series of transformations and refactoring phases as well as marketing repositioning attempts. By now, there are hundreds of libraries, frameworks, and other tools, and it is not easy at all to find your way in this abundance and make the right choice.

Before we get to the actual comparison of the Backbase AJAX framework against similar solutions, we should look around to see how the canvas of relevant technologies is laid out. So, let's first go through the tree of technologies until we end up in a group where Backbase resides.

 We mentioned earlier in this book that there were a number of other versions of the Backbase framework, all Java-related, such as a JSF Edition. These products are currently supported only for existing customers and not available for new development. Therefore, they are not included in this comparison. Of course, it is still possible to easily use Java with the Backbase Client Framework!

Server-side and client-side

Until recently, we thought of web applications as websites being created and run on a web server somewhere on the Internet. The server-side application was entirely responsible for the page generation: it checked for authorization, retrieved data from data sources, and generated static web pages filled in with the data.

With time, server output in HTML became enhanced with scripts running on the client-side, but the page generation and the business logic between user interactions was still processed on the server-side. To aid such rather complex development, several technologies and frameworks are available, for example, **GWT**, **ASP.NET MVC**, and **ZK**.

Today, web applications development has radically changed; the frontend of the application is moving to the client-side, the web browser. Both application logic and UI generation are moving with it. This is exactly where client-side toolkits come into play.

Let's proceed with those and ignore the server-dependent frameworks in the rest of this chapter. See the end of this chapter for more information on the frameworks mentioned earlier in this section.

Client-side libraries and frameworks

Most of JavaScript toolkits position themselves today as *frameworks*, although they called themselves *libraries* earlier. Some may really have evolved into a framework, whereas others are still, libraries.

In reality, it is not easy to differentiate between the two types of software: libraries and frameworks.

- The common understanding of a library concludes that a library is designed to execute a well-defined task, for example, a library can decode data or, in the case of a JavaScript toolkit, it can simplify DOM traversal. As a library is designed to execute a certain task or a couple of tasks, it is usually not extensible in nature.

- A software framework usually has wider scope. Eventually, it could be composed of several libraries. A framework, opposite to what a library does, allows and sometimes even requires extensions. A JavaScript framework often provides means to create widgets; it enables its own event's flow and provides well-designed APIs to those widgets.

Is it important to know whether a certain JavaScript toolkit is a library or a framework? We believe, yes, it is important.

In practice, you will see that a library is often used to fine-tune web pages, while a framework is used to build true client-side applications. For example, the *Script.aculo.us* library provides great visual effects that can be used to improve web page appearance and interaction, while the framework *qooxdoo* can hardly be used for that purpose; it is only suitable for building an application.

Being categorized as a library does not decrease the quality or capabilities of a toolkit. Instead, it properly positions software so that a right choice can be made based on the purpose of using it. *jQuery*, *MooTools*, *Prototype.js*, and *Script.aculo.us* are all JavaScript libraries, and they are great at what they had been designed for: enhancing web pages without changing much in the overall development process.

We will not include the JavaScript libraries mentioned in this section further in our comparison.

Flash, Silverlight, and JavaScript-based frameworks

For the sake of completeness of the technology comparison, it may also be interesting to check out how some AJAX frameworks stand compared to plugin-based solutions, such as, Flash or Silverlight.

Both Flash and Silverlight employ XML for application layout, MXML and XAML respectively.

Both Flash and Silverlight have a way to extend their component base by implementing custom tags in custom namespaces, something that the Backbase AJAX framework also offers.

Both platforms, similar to some JavaScript-based frameworks, implement the *Document Object Model*, which enables document access and event flow, although Silverlight provides a custom, lighter version of the DOM API. *Styling* is not done with CSS, in either Flash or Silverlight.

The plugin-based solutions such as Flash and Silverlight are both great choices for building Rich Internet Applications that run on a desktop. They are not usable for mobile devices because these plugins do not run on them.

Client-side GUI framework and application framework

There is another category of frameworks that we would like to exclude from our comparison: the **application frameworks**. Examples of such a framework are **Cappuccino**, **SproutCore**, and **PureMVC**.

PureMVC is, as the name suggests, a framework that is there to help you implement the MVC part of your application.

To position Cappuccino, we quote here some text from their website, which sums up very nicely what it is trying to achieve:

> *Cappuccino is not designed for building web sites, or making existing sites more "dynamic". We think these goals are too far removed from those of application development to be served well by a single framework. Projects like Prototype and jQuery are excellent at those tasks, but they are forced by their nature to make compromises which render them ineffective at application development.*

On the other end of the existing frameworks are technologies like SproutCore. While SproutCore set out with similar goals to Cappuccino, it takes a distinctly different approach. It still relies on HTML, CSS, JavaScript, Prototype, and an entirely new and unique set of APIs. It also requires special development software and a compilation step.

The Backbase AJAX framework is not an application framework; rather it is a *GUI framework*. For smaller to medium-sized applications, you do not need an application framework, as long as you structure your application correctly. For larger applications, you could consider developing your own client MVC support, or try to integrate with a framework like PureMVC.

Backbase and other client-side GUI frameworks

In our knock-out competition, we have progressed now to a state where we have a set of JavaScript frameworks that are comparable in functionality to what the Backbase offers. For the comparison below, we selected: *Bindows, Dojo, Ext JS, Javeline, qooxdoo,* and *YUI.* Let's now take a deeper look at the most relevant characteristics of those toolkits and see how Backbase compares. We will consider the programming model, the widget set, component models, data binding, support for standards, performance, internationalization, and long-term viability.

We start with an overview table. Detailed descriptions follow in the next sections.

	Backbase	Bindows	Dojo	Ext JS	Javeline	qooxdoo	YUI
Programming model	XML/JS	XML/JS	JS/JS	JS/JS	XML/JS	JS/JS	JS/JS
Widget library	Yes	Yes	Yes	Yes	Yes	Yes	Yes
Component model	Binding Language	Binding Language	Dijit plugin	Plugin	Binding Language	Javascript	--
Data Binding	field set	data set	data set	data set	field set	data set	data set
Cross-browser support	Yes	Yes	Yes	Yes	Yes	Yes	Yes
Internationalization	+/-	++	++	+	-	++	++

As you can see, this comparison table is not too useful because it merely shows what these frameworks have in common. We left out performance in this table because there is no easy way to compare these frameworks quantitatively and we do not know about any benchmark tests.

Programming model

The programming model varies between frameworks. It is a matter of developer preference to see which model he/she is more comfortable with. To help you find your own preference, we included a section at the end of this chapter to compare an Ext JS example with the same example in Backbase. We also use this example to show you how you can integrate other frameworks into Backbase if desired.

There are two different approaches used:

- XML for UI layout and JavaScript for UI logic
- JavaScript both for UI layout and for UI logic

In the first group, we have advanced toolkits such as Backbase, Bindows, and Javeline; in the second group, there are Dojo, Ext JS, qooxdoo, and YUI. The toolkits in the first group make use of XML as a way to layout the application UI and they provide a DOM or a DOM-like interface to it.

The toolkits in the second group produce widgets in a different way. They also provide other ways to register widget event handlers.

The major benefit of using XML for UI layout is better separation of the three concerns: UI, logic, and style. Just using different syntaxes for those areas forces better understanding of how to organize code; it also enables programming practices that were used for designing native HTML pages that have been proved to work well. Such a separation comes with a price: a framework might need some more time to process the XML initially. However, in practice, this does not seem to lead to significant degradation.

Using JavaScript both for UI layout and logic may lead to, as it is known "spaghetti-code", where at some point it becomes rather complex to maintain the application source base. A major problem is that often the look and feel of a page is hidden away in JavaScript source files. If they are included in the HTML page, it will make the code incomprehensible to most graphical web designers.

Widgets

Every framework in our comparison has a great variety of UI widgets. There are comboboxes, tab boxes, date pickers, grids, and so on. It is vital that widgets in a framework follow common design principles so that the developer would be able to start using one, without the necessity to dig in first into documentation.

The widgets are often grouped into the following categories:

- Layout widgets
- User input widgets
- Grid widgets
- Windowing widgets
- Others

In the Backbase AJAX framework, the widgets fall into similar categories, which is accidental, but rather because of the inheritance chains they follow. For example, all user input widgets have `disabled` and `value` attributes, and all layout widgets have `margin` and `padding` attributes.

Component model

The ability to create new components or extend existing ones helps hiding widget-specific logic and presentation issues away from the application logic. A reusable component can be instantiated several times inheriting all logic its class has defined.

Backbase has a great technology for defining and extending UI widgets, the Tag Definition Language (TDL), as you have seen in Chapter 7. TDL is a core concept in the Backbase methodology because it is used to build its own GUI library of widgets.

The other toolkits are all (except YUI) enabled to build components, some in similar and others in different ways. For example, *Dojo* is working on building a solid plugin system to create components, while Ext JS has provided this earlier. A model for creating components is not applicable to YUI, as YUI is rather a collection of disconnected widgets.

Data binding

Data binding is an essential mechanism for building more complex applications as you have seen in Chapter 5. The toolkits that provide data binding have all *data set* bindings, to bind sets of data to lists and grids. Javeline and Backbase also allow finer granularity field bindings.

Standards support

Talking about standards, support for our set of JavaScript toolkits is tough. It is well known that browsers don't support well-established standards, so why would some framework aim to do so? And what standards can a framework support?

Most JavaScript frameworks support standards exactly for the reason that *browsers* do **not** support them: to allow developers to create applications that work cross-browser or that can use new standards not available in any browser yet.

The Backbase APIs have been greatly inspired by the DOM and XBL (XML Binding Language, see `http://www.w3.org/TR/xbl/`) standards. In browsers, the implementations for the DOM and for XBL are either very inconsistent or missing. As there is awareness of these standards among web developers and because there is evidence that browsers are striving to implement those eventually, application logic written today against the Backbase AJAX framework will pretty much work in future browsers natively or it will be easier to migrate it when these standards become available.

Internationalization

Open source AJAX frameworks such as Dojo, YUI, or qooxdoo have done a great job implementing aspects of internationalization. Their widgets can be easily adjusted to use different date or time formats for example.

The Backbase framework has some functionality for date formatting in its `calendar` widget, but further internationalization support is currently absent. Internationalization is on the radar of the Backbase development team and we expect that better support will be available at some point in time.

Performance

Performance considerations have always been of high importance when choosing an AJAX framework.

A major problem for many frameworks is the occurrence of memory leaks causing performance to degrade over time. At Backbase, performance is watched closely by running nightly performance tests and thus tracking the changes in the framework, and spotting potential memory leaks.

Performance can be adversely impacted by the necessity to do additional interpretation or compilation of the framework-specific code. The extra model and controller layers in the Backbase framework certainly require extra time. The gain in the level of abstraction you can use for your development and the shorter development times that should result are in the long run more important than the raw performance impact. History shows that eventually better optimizers and better hardware will offset the slower performance. After all, nobody would consider these days to program an application in Assembler language anymore.

Web browsers recently made a great leap in the struggle for the rendering speed. In fact, they have come to a point that the difference in performance of different frameworks became rather slight.

Long-term viability

The long-term existence of any software product depends on many factors other than its technical merits. Company strategy and profitability of a product are essential for the survival of closed source or company-owned products like the Backbase framework, Bindows, or Javeline.

Also, many open source products can only survive because of support by large companies: Microsoft supports jQuery, and the Apache web server or the Eclipse IDE would not exist today without considerable grants from IBM.

If we just look at the technical side of things, we believe that the Backbase AJAX framework has longer term viability because it tries to preserve the application programming model that exists in a browser rather than creating a new one.

The Backbase Core implements DOM APIs that you know from the browser, and these APIs will stay. XML as a technology for UI layout is well proven for HTML. Although it has not been given enough attention in the development community, XML-based markup for the UI of web applications will exist in a foreseeable future because, for UI designers , an XML-based language is much more manageable than a conventional programming language such as JavaScript.

Similar to Flash making use of MXML or Silverlight making use of XAML, the Backbase XML languages simplify interface creation while providing great separation between UI, logic, and style.

Conclusion

We did not try to convince you that the Backbase framework is the best framework by telling you that it has more widgets than its competition or something else. We did tell you however, where to find the competition and what features you can expect from a framework like the Backbase framework. We hope that it is now easier for you to decide for yourself what you want or need from a JavaScript toolkit and how Backbase can fit into your requirements.

To make this story a bit more practical, we have an example in the next section for comparing programming styles and integration of other frameworks within the Backbase framework.

An integration example

We are going to discuss an example of integrating a data grid widget as it is offered by the *Ext JS* framework, into the Backbase framework.

We have a dual purpose for this:

- Firstly, it will give you a feel for what it is like to program using a framework that employs JavaScript exclusively
- Secondly, we show that it is fairly easy to incorporate functionality that is offered by another framework or library, if for some reason you prefer that over what is offered by Backbase or if it offers something additional

In the next chapter, we will show another integration example, using *Google maps* in our C3D sample application.

To start, we are going to display a data grid with XML data. In this case, the data is a list of trips from our sample application, using the Backbase framework. We have seen this example before in Chapter 5, therefore, please look back to see the contents of XML file we will use. For clarity, we show the code for the `dataGrid` here:

```
<b:dataGrid width="100%" e:behavior="b:dataGridSortOneColumn"
    sortDirection="descending" sortField="startDate">
    <b:dataGridCol dataField="name" width="150px">
    name</b:dataGridCol>
    <b:dataGridCol dataField="description" width="250px">
    description</b:dataGridCol>
```

```
    <b:dataGridCol dataField="startDate" width="90px">
    start date</b:dataGridCol>
    <b:dataGridCol dataField="endDate" width="90px">
    end date</b:dataGridCol>
    <b:dataSource e:behavior="b:localData"
       dataType="application/xml"
       requestType="application/xml">
       <b:dataContainer>
           <xi:include href="data/tripdata.xml" />
       </b:dataContainer>
    </b:dataSource>
  </b:dataGrid>
```

Of course, we have to embed this file into an HTML page, which we assume that you know how to do, however, we discussed this in detail in Chapter 1.

So far, nothing new. But we know that Ext JS offers a very nice data grid and let's assume now that we would like to use the Ext JS grid in our application instead of the Backbase dataGrid.

Our first question is what the example would look like, *without* using the Backbase framework:

```
<html>
    <head>
        <title>XML Grid Example</title>
        <link rel="stylesheet" type="text/css"
           href="ext/ext-all.css" />
        <script type="text/javascript" src="ext/ext-base.js">
        </script>
        <script type="text/javascript" src="ext/ext-all.js">
        </script>
        <link rel="stylesheet" type="text/css"
           href="ext/grid-examples.css" />
        <link rel="stylesheet" type="text/css"
           href="ext/examples.css" />
         <!--     The javascript for the example -->
        <script type="text/javascript" src="tripdata-grid.js">
        </script>
    </head>
    <body>
        <h1>XML Grid Example</h1>
        <p>
           The data in the grid is loaded from tripdata.xml
        </p>
        <div id="tripdata-grid"></div>
    </body>
</html>
```

We hear you say :"*Huh!* Where is my grid?" We just see a `div` that suggests holding the `div` because of the value of the `id` attribute.

In the previous sections, we have claimed a few times that declarative code using XML markup is preferable over a pure JavaScript approach, and here you see why.

Compare this with the grid we coded for the pure Backbase solution and then decide for yourself. We do not want to pick on Ext JS in particular because all pure JavaScript libraries and frameworks are like this.

Some call this *unobtrusive JavaScript* and will tell you it is a virtue!

To know what is going on, we need to look at the JavaScript file in `tripdata-grid.js`:

```
Ext.onReady(function(){
    // create the Data Store
    var store = new Ext.data.Store({
        // load using HTTP
        url: 'data/tripdata.xml',
        // the return will be XML, so let's set up a reader
        reader: new Ext.data.XmlReader({
            // records will have an "Item" tag
            record: 'record',
            id: 'id',
            totalRecords: '@totalRecords'
        }, [
            // set up the fields mapping into the xml doc
            // The first needs mapping, the others are very basic
            'name', 'description', 'startDate', 'endDate',
        ])
    });
    // create the grid
    var grid = new Ext.grid.GridPanel({
        store: store,
        columns: [
            {header: "Name", width: 200, dataIndex: 'name',
                sortable: true},
            {header: "Description", width: 400,
                dataIndex: 'description', sortable: true},
            {header: "Start Date", width: 80,
                dataIndex: 'startDate', sortable: true},
            {header: "End Date", width: 80, dataIndex: 'endDate',
                sortable: true}
        ],
        renderTo:'tripdata-grid',
```

```
        width:780,
        height:160
    });
    store.load();
});
```

If you study this piece of JavaScript, you will probably understand how the grid is coded. You can see that similar concepts are used as for a `dataGrid` in the Backbase framework. There is a data source called `Ext.data.Store` with `fields`, there is an `Ext.data.XmlReader` that reads and maps the data like a data container in the Backbase framework, and there is a grid with columns, here it's called `Ext.grid.GridPanel`, where the columns are embedded as anonymous objects.

Here is a picture of what the grid looks like when the example is executed:

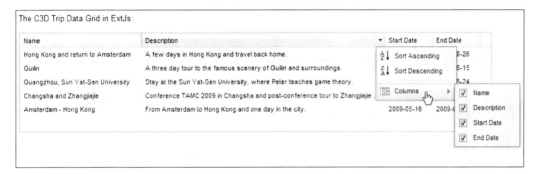

Another problem with this kind of JavaScript coding is that everything, the name of the XML file, the names of the columns, and the `div` where the grid is rendered is hard coded. If we want to use the grid in a different situation, the best we can do is cut and paste this code and adapt it to the new situation. For our example, we have already done this, using the original example and changing it to suit our trip data.

What if you have five grids in your application? Do you still know from the `id` of the `div` which is which? And what particular mappings to XML fields you were using or column sorting, and so on? Or which JavaScript file contains the code to fill the grid? You would have to open up the JavaScript files to find out.

To improve on the situation, you could try to generalize the data grid functionality and encapsulate it into a parameterized function. You could embed the JavaScript code in `script` tags right where the `div` is that contains the grid. Within a short time, your HTML page will become cluttered with intangible JavaScript and your UI designers will probably not be very happy.

There is nothing technically wrong with putting any JavaScript in your Backbase application, although it is probably necessary to keep grid code like this outside the Backbase areas. But, there is an alternative: use the TDL markup language of the Backbase framework. We are going to encapsulate the Ext JS grid into a Backbase widget.

From the description above, you would've guessed that we need four elements for our grid example. We will call them `grid`, `gridCol`, `dataStore`, and `field`. Further more, we thought it was a good idea to place the widgets in their own namespace: `http://www.extjs.com/ext30`.

The code that you need to put into a Backbase application for an Ext JS grid, after you have done the integration, looks like this:

```
<ext:grid xmlns:ext="http://www.extjs.com/ext30" width="780">
   <ext:dataStore url="data/tripdata.xml">
      <ext:field name="name" />
      <ext:field name="description" />
      <ext:field name="startDate" />
      <ext:field name="endDate" />
   </ext:dataStore>
   <ext:gridCol header="Name" width="200" dataIndex="name"
      sortable="true" />
   <ext:gridCol header="Description" width="400"
      dataIndex="description" sortable="true" />
   <ext:gridCol header="Start Date" width="80"
      dataIndex="startDate" sortable="true" />
   <ext:gridCol header="End Date" width="80"
      dataIndex="endDate" sortable="true" />
</ext:grid>
```

We hope you agree that this code is similar to the code we made for the pure Backbase example, except for the names of the widgets and the attributes used. We could have made them more similar to the Backbase equivalents, but we have chosen to define names closer to the names used in the pure Ext JS example.

Now that you have seen what the final result is, it will be easier to understand the definition in TDL for the grid itself:

- The grid needs to have two attributes to hold the size of the grid: width and height.

- The template of the grid element needs to be a div that can be used to attach the Ext JS grid to. Using this div to put the grid, we do not need the external div with a specific id.

```
<d:element name="grid">
    <d:attribute name="width" default="500" />
    <d:attribute name="height" default="160" />
    <d:template type="application/xhtml+xml">
        <div xmlns="http://www.w3.org/1999/xhtml">
            <d:content />
        </div>
    </d:template>
    <d:handler event="DOMNodeInsertedIntoDocument"
      type="text/javascript">
        // The rendering of the div takes place here.
    </d:handler>
</d:element>
```

If you look at the JavaScript code for the example (tripdata-grid.js), you will see that the grid is rendered after the page is loaded, using Ext.onReady(function(){...}. We mimic this behavior by using the DOMNodeInsertedIntoDocument event. Here is the code for the event handler:

```
<d:handler event="DOMNodeInsertedIntoDocument"
    type="text/javascript">
    // get the store
    var oStoreEl =
      this.getElementsByTagNameNS('http://www.extjs.com/ext30',
        'dataStore')[0];
    var store = oStoreEl.getStore();
    // create the grid columns
    var aColElements =
      this.getElementsByTagNameNS ('http://www.extjs.com/ext30',
      'gridCol');
    var aCols = new Array();
    for (var i=0; i < aColElements.length ; i++) {
      aCols[i] = {
          header: aColElements[i].getAttribute('header'),
          width: parseFloat(aColElements[i].getAttribute('width')),
```

```
            dataIndex: aColElements[i].getAttribute('dataIndex'),
            sortable: (aColElements[i].getAttribute('sortable') ==
               'true')? true : false
        };
    }
    // create the grid
    var grid = new Ext.grid.GridPanel({
        store: store,
        columns: aCols,
        renderTo: this.viewGate,
        width: parseFloat(this.getAttribute('width')),
        height: parseFloat(this.getAttribute('height'))
    });
    store.load();
</d:handler>
```

The code in the DOMNodeInsertedIntoDocument event handler is essentially a copy of the original example code. Look carefully at the following though:

- The dataStore widget is created by placing the widget as a nested element within the grid element. All we need to do is find it, using this.getElementsByTagNameNS('http://www.extjs.com/ext30', 'dataStore')[0].

- The Ext JS dataStore object is created by calling the getStore() method on the dataStore element. Be careful to make the distinction between the Ext JS data.Store object that we get returned from the getStore() method and the Backbase dataStore that is returned by the getElementsByTagNameNS function.

- In a very similar way as finding the data store, we find a set of gridCol elements. The anonymous column elements in the array that we will need to create the grid are created using the attributes provided in the gridCol elements.

- Next, the grid itself, a new Ext.grid.GridPanel object is created, which has the store object and the column array we created before as arguments. The width and the height are taken from the width and height attributes, which have a default value, therefore, you will always see a grid, even if it does not have the proper size.

- Note in particular the renderTo attribute, which specifies this.viewGate, indicating that the grid will be rendered as child of the view node of the widget. This is exactly what we want because the grid will be shown where the grid widget is placed, and no extra div with a specific id is needed.

The gridCol widget is very simple: just a set of attributes. This is all we need to build the columns array.

```
<d:element name="gridCol">
   <d:attribute name="header" />
   <d:attribute name="width" />
   <d:attribute name="dataIndex" />
   <d:attribute name="sortable" />
</d:element>
```

We have seen something about the `dataStore` widget already. However, we would still like to point out a few things in the `getStore()` method:

- The `field` elements contained in the `dataStore` are found in a similar way as the `gridCol` elements in the `grid`.

- The data to be inserted in the grid is retrieved by an AJAX call from the server by the XML reader. The `url` used is an attribute for the `dataStore` widget.

- The reader needs to know a few things, like how many records there are in the file, what tag it should look for, and what is the ID in each record. This is very similar to what is needed in the Backbase case, and our XML file already contains the necessary information. We need to define attributes on the `dataStore` widget to provide these values. We gave them handy defaults because we know that our XML files always look the same, except for the record contents of course.

```
<d:element name="dataStore">
   <d:attribute name="url" />
   <d:attribute name="record" default="record" />
   <d:attribute name="id" default="id" />
   <d:attribute name="totalRecords" default="totalRecords" />
   <d:method name="getStore">
      <d:body type="text/javascript">
         var aFields =
         this.getElementsByTagNameNS('http://www.extjs.com/ext30',
         'field');
         var aStoreFields = new Array();
         for (var i=0; i < aFields.length ; i++) {
            aStoreFields[i] =
              aFields[i].getAttribute('name');
         }
         var store = new Ext.data.Store({
            // load using HTTP
            url: this.getAttribute('url'),
            // the return will be XML, so let's set up a reader
            reader: new Ext.data.XmlReader({
```

```
                        // records will have a "record" tag
                        record: this.getAttribute('record'),
                        id: this.getAttribute('id'),
                        totalRecords: '@' + this.getAttribute('totalRecords')
                        }, aStoreFields )
                });
                return store;
            </d:body>
        </d:method>
    </d:element>
```

The `field` element is very simple. It just has one attribute specifying its name. In fact, we could have made this element a bit more interesting by allowing mappings of the `xml` tags to grid fields to take place. We did not need it here; therefore, we decided to keep it simple.

```
<d:element name="field">
    <d:attribute name="name" />
</d:element>
```

You already saw what the code to place our example grid on the page looks like. The HTML page needs to contain a link to all the Ext JS scripts in its head part, except the `tripdate-grid.js` script because its logic is now captured in the set of widgets we just defined.

One more remark: we found it quite difficult to assemble the required CSS and images. We think the way Backbase handles this (keeping all CSS and images together with the widget definitions) is much more manageable, although it may have a small adverse effect on performance.

The picture shown earlier was actually a picture of running the Backbase version of the Ext JS grid example; the output is identical for both.

You saw that it is indeed not difficult to encapsulate Ext JS widgets into Backbase widgets. There is no general rule to how you can do this encapsulation. To start, you can take a look at the `Ext.onReady(function(){...}` or similar code that many framework plugins use to start rendering their widgets. Just fold this code into the `DOMNodeInsertedIntoDocument` event handler of your new widget, and you have a working start to continue with, in a refactoring process.

AJAX toolkit reference

Here is an alphabetical, short description of the libraries and frameworks mentioned in this chapter. Some of the descriptions are directly taken from the website where the library or framework is hosted and therefore, may sound a bit subjective. We provide a link to the website of each of the toolkits, to allow you to find out more.

ASP.NET AJAX

ASP.NET AJAX is the free Microsoft AJAX framework for building highly interactive and responsive web applications that work across all popular browsers. The ASP.NET AJAX framework includes server-side ASP.NET AJAX, client-side ASP.NET AJAX, the AJAX Control Toolkit, and the jQuery library. ASP.NET AJAX enables developers to choose their preferred method of AJAX development, whether it is server-side programming, client-side programming, or a combination of both.

Obviously, ASP.NET AJAX depends on a Microsoft server environment, but Microsoft makes it possible to use the AJAX Library on any site by offering a Content Delivery Network where an ASP.NET AJAX application can link to. Remarkable is also the standard inclusion of the *jQuery* library into ASP.NET AJAX.

Reference: `http://www.asp.net/ajax/`.

Bindows

Bindows is an object-oriented platform for developing AJAX applications. With Bindows, you can generate web applications with the exact look and feel of Windows applications.

Bindows applications require no end-user downloads: it has a true zero-footprint (no Java, Flash, plug-ins, or ActiveX are used).

The Bindows framework is based on Dynamic HTML and the programming language used is Application Description Files (ADF), which is executed at the client's end as JavaScript.

The framework follows the Swing programming and DOM models. Class names start with "Bi", that is BiObject, BiRadioButton, and so on. The name Bindows comes from a combination of Business Intelligence (BI) and windows, BI being one of the interests of the company MB Technologies, responsible in creating the framework.

Reference: `http://www.bindows.net/`.

Cappuccino

Cappuccino is an open source framework that makes it easy to build desktop-caliber applications that run in a web browser.

Cappuccino is built on top of standard web technologies like JavaScript, and it implements most of the familiar APIs from GNUstep and Apple's Cocoa frameworks. When you program in Cappuccino, you don't need to concern yourself with the complexities of traditional web technologies like HTML, CSS, or even the DOM.

Cappuccino was implemented using a new programming language called Objective-J, which is modeled after Objective-C and built entirely on top of JavaScript.

Reference: `http://cappuccino.org`.

Ext JS

Like Backbase, **Ext JS** is developed commercially and has both open source (GNU GPL v3) and commercial licensing options. It is primarily a widget-based framework, although it seems to provide the essential cross-browser utilities, including a powerful element selection mechanism.

Ext JS is backed up by subscription-based support services, professional training, and consulting. One of the strengths of the framework is the cosmetic appeal of the widgets, which is complimented by extensive use of animation (that is, open/ close effects for windows and tree branches). Grid support is also impressive and includes XML and JSON data binding, editing, row-based grouping, enhancement (conversion of an HTML table to an interactive grid component), and filtering.

Compared with Backbase, the syntax can be more complex, as JavaScript is used exclusively.

Reference: Ext JS (`http://extjs.com`).

The Dojo toolkit

Dojo is an open source framework that has been in development for approximately four years. The latest release (1.3.2) consists of three distinct components: Dojo core, Dijit, and DojoX. The core file is relatively lightweight (less than 30k gzipped) and provides a comprehensive set of cross-browser utilities including DOM manipulation, normalized event handling, and basic animation. The second component (Dijit) is a widget library consisting of relatively common widgets including button, menu, panel layouts, progress bar, rich text editor, slider, and tree. The final component (DojoX) consists of a wide range of extensions at varying levels of readiness. For example, charting support is available as an extension, but the online demos do not work in IE7. The intention is that widgets will be moved from DojoX to Dijit as and when they reach the appropriate level of quality.

Widgets can be added to a document either using a declarative model or JavaScript. The declarative model makes use of HTML with the class or custom `dojoType` attributes used to identify widgets. When the document is parsed, elements having a class or `dojoType` attribute referencing a known widget will be replaced with the relevant HTML. When creating a widget programmatically using JavaScript, a constructor for the desired widget must be used. For example, calling `new dijit.ProgressBar()` with appropriate parameters will create a progress bar widget.

In Dojo, widgets consist of three files: an HTML file that defines the component structure, a CSS file for styling, and a JavaScript file for implementing control logic. However, the general architecture seems significantly less powerful and harder to use than the Backbase approach.

Reference: `http://www.dojotoolkit.org`.

Google Web Toolkit

With **Google Web Toolkit** (**GWT**), you write your AJAX frontend in the Java programming language, which GWT then cross-compiles into optimized JavaScript that automatically works across all major browsers. During development, you can iterate quickly in the same "edit-refresh-view" cycle you're accustomed to with JavaScript.

Reference: Google Web Toolkit (`http://code.google.com/webtoolkit`).

Javeline

Javeline Platform is an application development framework (also called a library, or toolkit) aimed at developers for building applications that run via web browsers, but look and feel like conventional desktop applications.

Javeline seems to have a very similar philosophy of development as Backbase. It uses JML (Javeline Markup Language) with a `j:` prefix, to code web applications. There are extensive MVC facilities built in, but there does not seem to be a custom component building facility.

Reference: `http://www.javeline.com`.

jQuery

jQuery is a concise but complete AJAX library. Although the core is small, the plugins contain all of the necessary parts. The relationship between jQuery and jQuery UI is similar to the one between Prototype and Script.aculo.us, where jQuery contains the basic AJAX functions and jQuery UI contains behaviors like drag-and-drop and widgets like an `accordion` and `slider`.

One advantage of jQuery is its powerful multi-selector, which makes finding an element easy. The syntax looks similar to CSS selector and it adds many more filters, such as content, attribute, and forms. Another advantage is its big plugin community. It has over 300 different plugins to choose from. You can find cutting edge UI-like fisheye or carousel view, as well as functional plugins for event propagation. These plugins are specific to certain purposes and are maintained by the community.

On the down side, the plugin community requires a lot of time to maintain and update these plugins.

Reference: jQuery (`http://jquery.com`).

MooTools

MooTools is a compact, modular, object-oriented JavaScript framework designed for the intermediate to advanced JavaScript developer.

Mootools seems to be rather limited in scope; it has animation and event handling, but just a limited set of available *plugins*: Accordion, slider, and sortables.

Reference: `http://mootools.net`.

Prototype and Script.aculo.us

These two libraries are most often mentioned in one sentence. There are other libraries that are based on the Prototype library, but Script.aculo.us is certainly the best known.

Prototype

Prototype is more like a basic AJAX tool that allows you to extend from it and make your own AJAX library (like Script.aculo.us).

One advantage of Prototype is that it is very generic and focuses on JavaScript and DOM data manipulation. Because it is one of the first AJAX frameworks, Prototype has many JavaScript add-on functions that allow you to take advantage of other language features, such as inheritance, complicated data structure (hash table), and array manipulation.

On the other hand, Prototype delegates fancy layout functions, such as animation, charting, drag-and-drop, or resize, to Script.aculo.us. Also, it does not have its own widgets library.

Reference: Prototype (`www.prototypejs.org`).

Script.aculo.us

Script.aculo.us is based on Prototype, so it inherits all Prototype functions.

Script.aculo.us has over 20 types of high quality animation effects. Another advantage is that the cores are modulated, so that you can easily pick the core that you need. For example, if you do not need drag-and-drop functionality in the project, you can simply exclude the `dragdrop.js` file.

A drawback of Script.aculo.us is that it focuses too much on animation rather than creating more useful widgets and demos. For example, it does not have form validation and data binding services.

Reference: Script.aculo.us (`http://script.aculo.us/`).

PureMVC

PureMVC is a lightweight framework for creating applications based upon the classic Model-View-Controller concept.

Based upon proven design patterns, this free, open source framework, which was originally implemented in the ActionScript 3 language for use with Adobe Flex, Flash, and AIR, has been ported to many development platforms among which is JavaScript.

Reference: `http://puremvc.org`.

qooxdoo

qooxdoo is a comprehensive and innovative framework for creating RIAs. Leveraging object-oriented JavaScript allows developers to build impressive cross-browser applications. No HTML, CSS, or DOM knowledge is needed.

qooxdoo has a comprehensive set of widgets. Using JavaScript and no HTML makes it orthogonal in development philosophy to Backbase. This seems to be squares circled instead of circles squared.

Reference: `http://qooxdoo.org`.

SproutCore

This is an HTML5 Application Framework for building rich cloud applications running in any modern web browser without plugins.

Reference: `http://www.sproutcore.com`.

The Yahoo User Interface (YUI) library

The **Yahoo User Interface** (YUI) library consists of five distinct elements: a set of CSS files designed to ensure that interfaces look the same in different browsers, the core engine, which includes normalized DOM and Event utilities, and the global YAHOO object, a utility module that provides support for features like animation and drag-and-drop, widgets, and developer tools.

Reference: YUI (`http://developer.yahoo.com/yui`).

ZK

ZK is an open source AJAX web application framework, written in Java that enables creation of rich graphical user interfaces for web applications with no JavaScript and little programming knowledge.

The core of ZK consists of an AJAX-based event-driven mechanism, over 123 XUL and 83 XHTML-based components, and a markup language for designing user interfaces. Programmers design their application pages in feature-rich XUL/XHTML components, and manipulate them upon events triggered by end user's activity. It is similar to the programming model found in desktop GUI-based applications.

ZK takes the so-called server-centric approach that the content synchronization of components and the event pipelining between clients and servers are automatically done by the engine and AJAX plumbing codes are completely transparent to web application developers. Therefore, the end users get the similar engaged interactivity and responsiveness as a desktop application, while programmers' development retains a similar simplicity to that of desktop applications.

In addition to component-based programming in a manner similar to Swing, ZK supports a markup language for rich user interface definition called ZUML.

Reference: `http://www.zkoss.org/`.

Summary

In this rather theoretical chapter, we have shown you a way to look at the various JavaScript frameworks available and how to categorize them.

As a result of our comparison, we showed some benefits of using the Backbase framework:

- XML-based UI layout technology

- Standards-based APIs

- Extensibility: TDL is a powerful and object-oriented mechanism to create new components

- Server agnostic framework, although products exist for the Java environment specifically

- Longer term viability: Technologies enabled in Backbase are more likely to stay for longer

There are some points to watch out for concerning the Backbase framework:

- XML-based resources (such as TDL bindings) cannot be served from a third domain

- Application markup is hardly accessible for Internet crawlers

- Does not fit traditional website creation, which actually is also a benefit

We illustrated the difference in coding style for a pure JavaScript framework as opposed to the Backbase framework using XML for UI layout. We also illustrated how easy it is to integrate other frameworks into the Backbase framework.

In order to enable you to explore all the frameworks mentioned, we included references and a short description.

11
The Square Web Application

In this last chapter we will try to integrate what we have discussed in this book and we will formulate the concept of a *square web application*. We will then apply this knowledge and take a last look at our C3D travel blog application. Before we finish the chapter we need to discuss a few subjects that can badly interfere with our goal to develop a square web application, such as how to handle legacy applications. We end this chapter and therefore this book, with a wink: a square puzzle, which we hope will spark discussion by way of an example, on how client web applications can be best developed.

Until we all walk through 3D holograms to interact with the Web, the flat, rectangular browser window will be our main way to view the Web.

This means that everything you see in the browser is confined to rectangles within its window, often laid out in intricate ways and sometimes rectangles can overlap. Each rectangle within the browser window can have an autonomous existence, its contents can be replaced using AJAX communication with a server, or a rectangle can be added, copied, moved, or deleted anywhere within the browser window. Even though there is lots of freedom within the browser window, the web application cannot step outside and interact with your PC, such as accessing files in your file system, except for storing some cookies.

In this chapter we will talk about the *square* web application, a web application that fits well in square browser windows. Do not confuse this with *Web Squared* (See: http://assets.en.oreilly.com/1/event/28/web2009_websquared-whitepaper.pdf). This is an entirely different concept, where Tim O'Reilly talks about taking Web 2.0 one step further.

We should recognize that it is not difficult to interact with the Web in ways other than via a browser or where a browser accepts inputs that are very different from the click of a button. In the last year, the so-called *Augmented Reality* (AR) applications are popping up, especially for mobile phones like the iPhone and for mobile operating systems like the Android, where the camera view is mixed with extra information or virtual objects. We just read about a new AR language called Augmented Reality Markup Language (ARML), which suggests that an XML-based approach like the Backbase framework uses can be extended effectively into new web realms.

For now, there are still too many websites with awkward interfaces where pages start shaking each time we press a button. There are still too many web applications that would need to be rewritten if they should allow input from other servers or if they should integrate external information.

A square web application on the other hand is flexible and fluid. So, what is it? Let's define it in the next section.

Here is a list of topics that we will cover in this last chapter:

- The nine features of a square web application: No global JavaScript, data-bound widgets where possible, no complex HTML generation at the server, send only XML from server to client, make the layout modular, use MVC throughout, the client is the view, the controller is at the server, and no business logic at the client.
- Complete the C3D travel blog sample application (make it work, make it right, and make it fast): Handle image upload, add a Google map, initial page loading, optimization of the client, and server-side issues.
- Usability aspects: Legacy integration, progressive enhancement, internationalization, and accessibility.
- What will the future bring?
- A square puzzle example.

What is a square web application?

In the very beginning of this book we said something along these lines: would it not be nice if...

- You would have an extensive library of UI widgets that could be used in the same way as HTML?
- You could extend HTML with new widgets and components in any way you like?

- You could use AJAX almost transparently?
- You could bind data retrieved from the server in flexible ways to any widget, in particular data grids?

We explained in this book that the Backbase framework allows you to develop applications answering these questions with a resounding "yes". A *square* web application is a *single page application* that uses BTL, TDL, XHTML, CSS, and data-bound widgets, **and nothing else**.

That may sound obvious at first, but it actually isn't. You can use the Backbase framework in any way you wish, also for traditional multi-page applications, with just a few BTL widgets, or with JavaScript all across the page. The framework may be slow if you try to do so because of the overhead involved in loading the library for each page. However, if you are trying to transform a classical web application to a modern Rich Internet Application (RIA), this may be a good approach. We will talk a little bit more about this later in this chapter.

It is indeed rather hard to square your application! It will be very tempting to just quickly create a JavaScript function to handle user interaction, instead of considering to develop a behavior or a new widget using TDL. If you are starting a new application by squaring your application from the start, meaning you plan to have only XML on your page, that may make design and communication with your web designers a lot easier, because you will be able to use traditional page layout tools effectively and if your designers know HTML, they will have a feel for what the result will be.

Below we show a kind of checklist, which we will expand in the next sections. When we look at the client application, we would like to see the following:

- There will be no global JavaScript functions
- Make widgets data bound where possible
- There will be no server code that generates XHTML
- All data content will be sent as XML from the server to the client
- The layout and styling of the page should be easily adaptable

Here are some points that apply to the total application architecture:

- Design according to the MVC design pattern
- The client application is the *view*
- The *controller* is at the server
- The *model* is at the server

We think that these are the most important aspects of creating a square web application, where the encapsulated JavaScript requirement is by far the most important one, followed by the use of a Model-View-Controller architecture.

No global JavaScript functions

There will be no global JavaScript functions. Does this sound like too strict of a requirement? Would it not be nice to define some JavaScript functions to do some generic UI handling? Well, yes, but if you think more about what you are trying to achieve, it will probably be just as easy to define a behavior as explained in Chapter 7, *Creating UI Components*. Or, even better, maybe you can create a new widget, as explained in the same chapter.

Any global function that you define has the chance to conflict with functions from another library that you may want to integrate. If you use only widgets, behaviors, or XEL event handlers to contain JavaScript code, this will force all JavaScript code to be properly namespaced.

By encapsulating JavaScript code in widgets or behaviors, they become objects and are consequently easier to maintain, manage, and extend.

By using the Backbase lazy loading facilities, the JavaScript code loaded into the browser can be minimized. Contrast this with loading every JavaScript file that you can find within your enterprise, out of fear that you may need some function, which is hidden deep into your page.

Make widgets data bound

Make widgets data bound wherever possible. This will diminish the need for generating pages containing data at the server, such as generating tables together with their content.

Another way data-bound widgets can be used is exemplified by the data-driven menu system we made for the C3D travel blog. You will see it described later in this chapter. In this case, it allows you to take away any awareness about authorizations from the client because items that a user cannot click are not sent back from the server.

A data-driven approach could also be used to support multiple languages: the client asks for a template in a certain language.

Do not generate HTML at the server

There will be no server code that generates XHTML beyond templates with simple variable replacement. Loops should be avoided in the server templates.

If you remember our discussion in Chapter 4, *Client-Server Communication and Forms*, about *scriptlets* which were somehow associated to professional wrestling, then you will understand why you should not generate complex HTML in complex scripts.

Send only XML data from server to client

All data content will be sent as XML from the server to the client. It seems that XML is more secure than the obvious alternative: JSON. With XML, it is possible to define schemas for XML and in this way XML data structures can be made very robust.

Make the layout modular

The layout and styling of the page should be easily adaptable without changes to the server code.

This does not need further explanation. We followed this rule in our web applications by including all real content in the main page through `include` statements, either a static PHP `include`, or a static XInclude, or a dynamic `load` command.

Use MVC throughout

Design the total structure of the web application according to the MVC design pattern. We have described this in Chapter 4.

In our comparison with other frameworks in Chapter 10, we briefly discussed the MVC approach you could take for the client application itself. There is a lot more that could be said about this, which unfortunately falls outside the scope of this book.

The client is the view

The client application is the *view* of the total web application. Ideally, the view is very loosely coupled with the model, which would make it possible to exchange the server technology used with another one, with minimal effort. For example, exchange JSP with PHP.

Place the controller at the server

The *controller* of the application should be positioned at the server because it is the gateway to the model business processes and guards its security.

No business logic at the client

The client application should **never** contain *model* processes, for security reasons. However, it is possible to have a snapshot of model processes to enhance the user experience. The obvious example is validity checking in forms.

By now we gave you a lot of points that you may look at to achieve a square application, an application where all JavaScript is encapsulated within XML tags. A last but not the least point is: *Don't be dogmatic!* If you are trying to transform an old application or a conservative development team, be patient. It is more important that your application functions in the right way at every step than that it is squared, as long as you do not lose sight of your final goal.

In the next sections, we are going to complete some parts of our C3D travel blog sample application. In the *C3D: make it right* section, we will try to square an important part of this application: the *menu structure*.

Complete the C3D example

Throughout the book we have illustrated the subjects we were discussing with code for the C3D sample application, a simple travel blog. This is our last chance in this book to add functionality to it and also explain it to you. We will show you a few more things we implemented.

Like in a real development project, we changed our mind about the design of our application several times. Also, because you have more knowledge about the Backbase framework now, it is possible to use more of its advanced facilities.

We will look at the C3D application in the spirit of what we have explained in Chapter 9 about *make it work, make it right, and make it fast*. There is still a need to add functionality to make the C3D application work and be usable. We need to refactor the web application to make it more easily extensible and to improve its performance. Finally, we need to deploy the application on a real website.

C3D: make it work

There are a number of items still on our list that need to be done to make the C3D travel blog usable. We describe two of these here:

- The upload form for a photo
- Displaying a Google map with a trip entry

To make it really work, there is also work to be done at the server-side. For example, we need to do image handling to resize images that are too large and to allow thumbnails to be generated.

The photo upload form

The first item we are going to look at is the form that allows us to upload a photo. We are showing here some details because the implementation of this form posed some unexpected challenges. Here is the form:

The dataComboBoxes

A challenge is the presence of two dataComboBox elements, where the value of the second one depends on the value of the first one because you would not like to allow trip entries in the second dataComboBox to be chosen that do not belong to the trip chosen in the first dataComboBox.

We have encountered the dataComboBox in Chapter 5, *Data-bound Widgets*. We need to make updates to it now to support updating the list of dataComboBoxOption elements.

We start with showing how the comboboxes are used. Here is the code for the first dataComboBox:

```
<sq:dataComboBox name="tripId" width="200px"
    valueSelect="*[1]" optionSelect="*[2]"
    bf:required="true"
    bf:messagesRef="../../td/bf:messages[1]">
    <b:dataSource e:behavior="b:remoteData"
        url="cntrl.php?req=tripdataforuser"
        dataType="application/xml"
        requestType="application/xml" />
    <e:handler event="change" type="text/javascript">
        var oEntryComboDS = bb.document.getElementById('trip-entries');
        var sURL = oEntryComboDS.getAttribute('urlbase');
        oEntryComboDS.setAttribute('url',sURL + '&tripId=' +
            this.getProperty('value'));
        oEntryComboDS.refresh();
    </e:handler>
</sq:dataComboBox>(select a trip)
```

We gave the `dataSource` of second `dataComboBox` an id in order to be able to address it from the first one. It would have been better to construct an XPATH expression to find the second combobox, but for now it works.

When a choice is made for the trips, the event handler for the `change` event will fire. In the event handler, we retrieve the URL as found for the `dataSource` of the trip entries, and the `dataSource` is then refreshed. Note that we coded a `urlbase` attribute instead of a `url` attribute because if we changed our mind about the selection in the first combobox, we would construct a wrong URL if we used the already changed `url` attribute.

The last line in the event handler causes the second `dataComboBox` to refresh itself. Because of this, we need to make a change to the code for the `dataComboBox` widget, otherwise the new `dataComboBoxOption` elements would be appended to the previous list. We add the following lines of code at the start of the `dataUpdate` method:

```
// remove all comboboxOptions children
var aChildren = this.getElementsByTagNameNS(btl.namespaceURI,
    'comboBoxOption');
for (i = aChildren.length, i > -1 ; i-- ) {
    this.removeChild( aChildren[i] );
}
```

Here's the second `dataComboBox`. Just notice the id for the data source in it and the `urlbase` attribute:

```
<sq:dataComboBox name="entryId" width="200px"
    valueSelect="*[1]" optionSelect="*[3]"
    bf:required="true"
    bf:messagesRef="../../td/bf:messages[1]">
```

```
    <b:dataSource e:behavior="b:remoteData" id="trip-entries"
        urlbase="cntrl.php?req=tripentrydata"
        dataType="application/xml"
        requestType="application/xml" />
</sq:dataComboBox>(select a trip entry)
```

With these updates it is now possible to show only the trip entries that belong to a certain trip.

Handling the image upload

Another challenge in handling this form is the upload of the image. We have talked about the `fileInput` widget in Chapter 4, but we conveniently skipped how you could synchronize the uploading of the file with the submission of the rest of the form. To start, we put some tricky stuff in the image upload form:

```
<input type="hidden"
    value="<?php $dvar = time(); echo $dvar;?>"
    name="uploadFormId" />
<bf:fileInput action="fileUpload.php" name="myFile">
    <e:handler event="load" type="application/javascript">
        document.getElementById('myFileDiv').innerHTML =
            bb.getProperty(this,
            'responseHTML').documentElement.innerHTML;
    </e:handler>
    <bf:fileInputParameter name="uploadId"
      value="<?php echo $dvar;?>" />
</bf:fileInput>
```

The `bf:fileInput` will be used to create an iframe that is used to upload the image. The trick is to send the same, but otherwise unique value with both the form and the iframe. The hidden input field value will be sent together with the form, and the `bf:fileInputParameter` will go with the iframe. Thanks to PHP, we can generate the same value for both. To make it unique, we use a timestamp as the value. It is created in the hidden input field.

There will be two requests to the server, the controller (`cntrl.php`) will be called with an `insert` request and `fileUpload.php` will be called to process the image upload.

The final result of the upload should be a row in the `c3d_photo` table, with information about the image as entered in the form. Because we do not know what will arrive first, we also store the timestamp we sent with both the form and the iframe, as `uploadId` in the table. In both scripts, we will check first whether a row with the `uploadId` already exists. If yes, we will update the existing row with the additional information. Otherwise, we will create a new row.

Add a Google map

Would it not be nice if we could show on a map where on earth each trip entry was situated? Using the Google Maps API, this is not difficult to do at all. In this section, we will construct a simple widget defined in TDL that can display a small map centered at a location with the help of a geocoder. We will use the new version 3 of the Google Maps API, which has the great advantage that you no longer need an API key to use it. Apparently, there is still functionality missing in this version that is available in version 2, but for our application we do not need it.

To start our integration of Google Maps, we look at an example. We found one that covers our functional need: display a map using a string that describes a place on earth. You can find it here: http://gmaps-samples-v3.googlecode.com/svn/trunk/geocoder/getlatlng.html

We show the code for the script below, so that you can understand how we do the integration:

```
var geocoder;
var map;
function initialize() {
    geocoder = new google.maps.Geocoder();
    var latlng = new google.maps.LatLng(-34.397, 150.644);
    var myOptions = {
        zoom: 8,
        center: latlng,
        mapTypeId: google.maps.MapTypeId.ROADMAP
    }
    map = new google.maps.Map(document.getElementById("map_canvas"),
        myOptions);
}
function codeAddress() {
    var address = document.getElementById("address").value;
    if (geocoder) {
        geocoder.geocode( { 'address': address},
            function(results, status) {
                if (status == google.maps.GeocoderStatus.OK) {
                    map.setCenter(results[0].geometry.location);
                    var marker = new google.maps.Marker({
                    map: map,
                    position: results[0].geometry.location
                    });
                } else {
                    alert("Geocode was not successful" +
                        "for the following reason: "
                        + status);
                }
            }
```

```
        });
    }
}
```

The `initialize()` function will be called at the `onload` event of the page. This function initializes the map with a default location. The `codeAddress()` function is called when a button is clicked. The value in the address input field is then taken to find the new map location.

To allow the map to fit in our application we will need to integrate the Maps API into the Backbase framework. Here is how we do it:

1. Add the library to `index.php`. This means adding the following code to the `<head>` section of the page:

    ```
    <script type="text/javascript"
        src="http://maps.google.com/maps/api/js?sensor=false">
    </script>
    ```

2. Define a new namespace. We have chosen `http://maps.google.com/v3` with prefix `gm`. We could have decided to add our `map` widget to the `sq` namespace, but we thought "Maybe we can grow this widget into a more general package for Google Maps". For now, the widget is rather specific to the C3D application.

3. Create a bindings directory and files. We need to put our definition for the `map` widget at the proper place; therefore, we defined the `resources/bindings/maps.google.com.v3` directory, which contains a `map.xml` file. We also update `squared.xml` in the `resources/bindings` directory to include our new widget:

    ```
    <d:namespace name="http://maps.google.com/v3"
        xml:base="maps.google.com.v3/">
        <d:uses element="map" src="map.xml" />
    </d:namespace>
    ```

4. Create a `map` element.

5. Put the widget in the `tripEntry` template. Note the namespace declaration in the `div`. It is needed because the standard generation of a response does not include it. We do not want to include it there because it is used only once.

    ```
    <div xmlns:gm="http://maps.google.com/v3"
        style="padding:5px">
        <!-- template showing trip entry title and place-->
        <gm:map place="<?php echo $place; ?>" />
        <!-- template showing trip entry text -->
    </div>
    ```

Let's show the skeleton code for the widget now:

```
<d:element name="map">
    <d:property name="geocoder" />
    <d:property name="map" />
    <d:template type="application/xml">
        <div style="margin-top: 20px; margin-bottom: 20px;
            width: 360px; height: 150px;
            border: solid 1px green;">
            <d:content />
        </div>
    </d:template>
    <d:handler event="DOMNodeInsertedIntoDocument"
        type="text/javascript">
        this.initialize();
        this.codeAddress(this.getAttribute('place'));
    </d:handler>
    <d:method name="initialize">
        <d:body type="text/javascript">
        // the code for the initialize method goes here
        </d:body>
    </d:method>
    <d:method name="codeAddress">
        <d:argument name="address" />
        <d:body type="text/javascript">
        // the code for the codeAddress method goes here
        </d:body>
    </d:method>
</d:element>
```

The code for the `initialize` method is as follows:

```
<d:method name="initialize">
    <d:body type="text/javascript">
        var geocoder = new google.maps.Geocoder();
        var latlng =
            new google.maps.LatLng(52.3737671, 4.8909347);
        var myOptions = {
            zoom: 5,
            center: latlng,
            mapTypeId: google.maps.MapTypeId.ROADMAP
        }
        var map =
            new google.maps.Map(this.viewGate, myOptions);
        this.setProperty('geocoder', geocoder);
        this.setProperty('map', map);
```

```
        </d:body>
    </d:method>
```

In essence, this is the same code as in the original `initialize()` function. We use properties to save the values of the `geocoder` and `map` variables because we need these later when the `codeAddress()` function is called. Here's the code for the `codeAddress` function:

```
<d:method name="codeAddress">
    <d:argument name="address" />
    <d:body type="text/javascript">
        var geocoder = this.getProperty('geocoder');
        var map = this.getProperty('map');
        if (geocoder) {
            geocoder.geocode(
                { 'address': address},
                    function(results, status) {
                        if (status == google.maps.GeocoderStatus.OK) {
                            map.setCenter(results[0].geometry.location);
                            var marker = new google.maps.Marker({
                                map: map,
                                position: results[0].geometry.location
                            });
                        } else {
                            alert("Geocode was not " +
                                "successful for the following reason:"
                                + status);
                        }
                    });
        }
    </d:body>
</d:method>
```

Except for the loading of property values into variables, the code is the same as for the demo example. Actually, we could have folded the methods into one because we have only one location to geocode. However, we think that the way we did the integration has more possibilities for expanding it later into a mapping layer for the Backbase framework.

For now, the widget does what it needs to do—it works. In addition, by using a widget instead of embedded JavaScript, we think that the `tripEntry` template kept its clarity, while it is clear that we used a Google map.

Finally, we show a picture of what the showing of the trip entry now looks like.

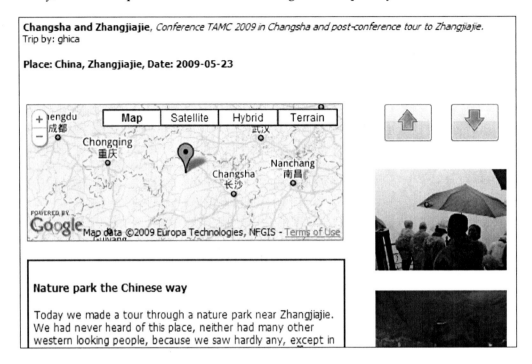

We are aware that there are more things that need to be done to make the C3D sample application usable. In particular, as said, the handling of images needs to be developed further.

C3D: make it right

When developing the code as we have shown in the previous chapters, we were constrained sometimes because we could not use functionality that we had not discussed yet. We also found problems in the end result of the application as developed so far:

- We ended up having quite a bit of PHP code generating HTML. This makes our web application more dependent on PHP than it should be, and it is more difficult for web designers to see what the page will look like when the application is used.

- We would like to add other types of users, such as an *admin* user. With the current structure it would be difficult to display the right menu options for each user.

- We would like to be able to easily add new menu options. The actions for each menu option should be more loosely coupled.
- The *controller* (cntrl.php) became rather messy.

The application was therefore not complying with our own standards. When looking at all the PHP code that crept in generating XHTML and Backbase code, we saw that the biggest problem was the *menu system*. Therefore, we decided to overhaul it.

We already have a database table listing the users of our C3D application and their passwords. We are going to add the authorizations each user has for using menu items. Because we would like to have a flexible authorization structure, we also need a table relating authorizations and menu item actions.

Here is a database model for three new tables and how they relate to the c3d_user table:

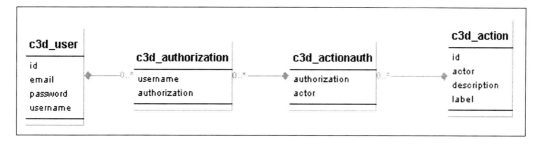

And here is what we have in the c3d_action table right now:

id	actor	description	label
1	showTrips	Show all trips for all users	Show Trips
2	addTrip	Add a new trip description	Add Trip
3	addEntry	Add a new entry for a trip	Add Trip Entry
4	addPhoto	Add a photo for a trip entry	Add Photo
5	login	Login into the C3D Travel Blog	Login
6	logout	Logout	Logout

The values in actor column are symbolic for the actions that are called when the user clicks on a menu item. The real actions are determined by the *controller*. The label is what is shown in the menu. It would be possible to extend the menu system for use in multiple languages, by having a table with label values in another language, keyed by the actor. The id column is there to allow sorting of the menu items, which are then displayed in this order in the menu. The real unique value should be the actor value.

For each actor, we need to specify the authorizations a user needs to call the action:

authorization	actor
public	showTrips
restricted	addTrip
restricted	addEntry
restricted	addPhoto
restricted	logout
public	login
restricted	insert

You may wonder why the `insert` action is in the list of actors here and not in the list of menu actions. This is because `insert` is an action that is caused by submitting a form to add a new trip, new trip entry, or to upload a photo. Any action that causes communication with the server must have an entry in this list.

There is also a `c3d_authorization` table, which lists authorizations for each user. A user can have more than one authorization and each actor could be activated through multiple authorizations with this model. This means that we have a very flexible authorization structure now. How do we implement the menu widgets and the PHP backend for our new menu system?

We replace the PHP function found in setup.php that built the initial menu in `index.php`, with XML code, which you can find in `menu.xml`:

```
<b:dataSource e:behavior="b:remoteData" name="source"
    id="menu-source" url="cntrl.php?req=dataMenu"
    dataType="application/xml" requestType="application/xml">
</b:dataSource>
<sq:dataMenu dataSource="source" />
<div id="menu-action">
</div>
```

As you might guess, the `dataSource` enables us to fetch the right menu information from the server. We should never keep information about user authorizations at the client, and by fetching the menu items dynamically, this is not necessary. There is also an `sq:dataMenu` widget that refers to the `dataSource`. We are going to explore this widget further now.

Actually, if you look into resources/bindings/www.squaringthecircles.com/ dataMenu.xml, you will find two widgets, dataMenu and dataMenuItem. You have seen this pattern several times before, where there is a data-bound widget that contains a list of items created dynamically, using the information from a dataSource. Let's look at the code of dataMenu:

```
<d:element name="dataMenu" extends="b:dataObserver">
    <!--    The dataUpdate method goes here -->
    <d:template type="application/xhtml+xml">
        <div>
            <d:content />
        </div>
    </d:template>
</d:element>
```

Please note that the name of this widget is the same as a BTL widget. This does not matter because we placed our widget in our own namespace. Next, here is the code for the dataUpdate method, which we need for all data-bound widgets:

```
<d:method name="dataUpdate">
    <d:argument name="action" />
    <d:argument name="records" />
    <d:body type="text/javascript">
    <![CDATA[
        if(action == 'read'){
        // remove all children
        while ( this.hasChildNodes() ) {
            this.removeChild( this.getProperty('firstChild') );
        }
        // build the new list
        var oSource = this.getProperty('dataSource');
        for(var i = 0; records.length > i; i++){
            var sLabel =
                btl.dataSource.getValue(oSource,
                records[i], 'label');
            var sActor =
                btl.dataSource.getValue(oSource,
                records[i], 'actor');
            var sDescription =
            btl.dataSource.getValue(oSource,
            records[i], 'description');
            var oItem =
              bb.document.createElementNS(
              'http://www.squaringthecircles.com/squared',
              'dataMenuItem');
            oItem.buildItem(sActor, sLabel, sDescription);
```

```
                this.appendChild(oItem);
            }
        }
    ]]>
    </d:body>
</d:method>
```

As you can see, the `dataUpdate` method removes all children, which is necessary when the menu is renewed, after a login, for example. Then, the method loops through all records returned by the remote `dataSource` and creates `dataMenuItem` elements, which are filled by calling the `buildItem` on them. The `dataMenuItem` element looks as follows:

```
<d:element name="dataMenuItem">
    <d:template type="application/xhtml+xml">
        <div>
            <d:content />
        </div>
    </d:template>
    <d:method name="buildItem">
        <d:argument name="actor" />
        <d:argument name="label" />
        <d:argument name="description" />
        <d:body type="text/javascript">
            var sCstr = '<a class="app_menu_item" href="javascript:" ';
            sCstr += ' xmlns="http://www.w3.org/1999/xhtml"';
            sCstr += ' xmlns:b="http://www.backbase.com/2006/btl"';
            sCstr += ' xmlns:c="http://www.backbase.com/2006/command"';
            sCstr += ' xmlns:e="http://www.backbase.com/2006/xel"';
            sCstr += ' xmlns:xi="http://www.w3.org/2001/XInclude" >';
            sCstr += ' <b:toolTip width="200px" ' +
                'backgroundColor="yellow">';
            sCstr += description;
            sCstr += ' </b:toolTip>';
            sCstr += ' <strong>' + label + '</strong>';
            sCstr += ' <e:handler event="click">';
            sCstr += ' <c:load url="cntrl.php?req=menuItem&amp;actor=' +
                actor + '"';
            sCstr += ' destination="."';
            sCstr += ' mode="appendChild" />';
            sCstr += ' </e:handler>';
            sCstr += ' </a>';
            bb.command.create(sCstr, this, 'appendChild');
        </d:body>
    </d:method>
</d:element>
```

A string is built-in JavaScript containing the XML for an a (anchor) element with a tool tip and an event handler, which causes the actor to be activated when the user clicks on the menu item.

We are not proud of this code because we do not like this type of string handling. But it works. When tried to create these elements with XEL, it was rather difficult to fold in variable information, like we need to do here. We have seen this problem before in our examples. Maybe this is a candidate for the next round of refactoring.

The menu system we built now has no support for nested menus. This will not be difficult to add, when we need it in the future.

This was an example of refactoring that we could do. Of course, there are many more things that could be refactored and we did some more that we will not describe here. In line with good refactoring principles, be careful not to try to make your application perfect. Good enough is good enough.

C3D: make it fast

As we have argued in Chapter 9, *Debugging, Optimization, and Deployment*, performance optimizations are best done when your application is almost ready to be deployed because only then you can truly determine where the bottlenecks are.

We have already looked at performance a little bit when we deployed the first prototype of the C3D travel blog on our website; see the discussion about the application page layout in the *Page Layout* section of Chapter 4.

Initial page loading

A major concern was the time it took to load the main page of the application. To summarize what we did about it: we replaced the panelSet with a classical HTML table for the basic layout of the page and we replaced XInclude to include the content with a PHP include to avoid an extra HTTP request. As a result the main page is not server language agnostic anymore. This is a price to pay for better performance.

Optimizing client runtime processing

If the script tag encloses the bulk of the application code in the content part of the C3D application, it may seem that the performance gain will be minimal after the first loading of the page. You can still try to minimize this overhead by using the BTL escape tags b:xhtml and b:xml. We described these in Chapter 2, *User Interface Development*.

There may also be functional reasons to put part of your page in non-Backbase controlled areas. If you are loading HTML from an external source, you may not know for sure that this code is proper XHTML. By placing the code outside the Backbase area or within escape tags, you minimize the chance for parsing errors that cause your page to stay blank.

Server-side issues

There are two types of issues we can look at: the server-side *programming issues* and the server-side *configuration issues*.

As far as programming issues are concerned, the most likely cause of bad performance is slow queries. The database system you are using will undoubtedly have tools to help you find these bad queries. For example, MySQL has a slow query log that you could turn on and examine.

Other items we should look at are configuration issues, such as, whether the server really is sending compressed pages to the client. It turns out that the hosting provider where our C3D application resides does not send compressed files, or actually, it did not send CSS and JavaScript files in a compressed form.

After some experimentation, we found that the following line in our .htaccess file on the server had the desired effect on YSlow to grade us with an **A** for the item *Compress components with Gzip*:

```
AddOutputFilterByType DEFLATE text/html text/plain text/xml
    text/css application/x-javascript
```

Additional things you can do are: use the *optimized* version of the Backbase framework, use the TDL Optimizer and study the **YSlow** statistics and the **Firebug** loading times to see if there are spikes in performance. Basically, those things we discussed in Chapter 9.

Remember though that we made a performance trade-off by encapsulating JavaScript and CSS locally within XML tags because the gain of effective development must weigh heavier than the slight performance gain we could expect by really placing all CSS at the top and all JavaScript at the bottom.

You can see the result of our deployment work at:
http://www.squaringthecircles.com.

After this intermezzo with a final look at our C3D travel blog sample application, we should look at some aspects of web application development that are not always compatible with our ideas of a squared application.

Usability aspects

So far, we took a technical approach to the development of a web application. We tried to convince you that if you would follow the principles of developing a square web application and had a UI designer who would make things look nice, then you would have a *good* web application. There are, however, other aspects that have to be taken into account. We name a few:

- The integration of legacy web pages or web applications
- Internationalization aspects
- Accessibility aspects

Legacy integration

The implementation of AJAX web applications can range from simply creating an AJAX page using an existing HTML page with an added BTL widget to creating an AJAX application with desktop-like behavior. This range of web applications allows you the possibility to stage a gradual transition of an existing Multi-page Interface infrastructure, thereby mitigating risk and leveraging existing Multi-page Interface investments. For these reasons, a gradual transition to an AJAX web application will often be the preferred choice. The following list describes the various scenarios in more detail:

- **Enhance parts of existing web pages**: You may want to keep the existing Multi-page Interface application, but you also want to spice up the application by adding rich UI widgets, such as a `calendar` or `contextMenu`. By creating pages with BTL or custom defined widgets, the developer increases the usability of the application without changing the web application architecture.

- **Build a complete Single Page Interface AJAX application**: This scenario is typical if you intend to migrate a fat server to a rich thin client, thereby transforming an entire server-centered architecture to an RIA. Another possibility is that you want to migrate a non web-based client/server application from a fat client to a web-based rich thin client. These represent alternatives to Swing, VB, or Oracle Forms, by essentially web-enabling fat client web applications.

- **Integrate AJAX applications within a Multi-page Interface infrastructure**: To reduce risk and leverage the investment in a Multi-page Interface application, you may opt either for an intermediate web application or for a gradual transition, whereby parts of an existing Multi-page Interface infrastructure are converted into AJAX applications, leaving the rest of their web presence intact. In this scenario, a series of smaller Single Page Interface applications can be created that integrate the dynamic asynchronous loading of content with their rich widgets. This makes applications such as dashboards, Internet banking, and administrative systems more responsive and consistent, without implementing a domain-wide AJAX web application.

- **Combining different AJAX frameworks**: If you have already adopted AJAX web application development, you may discover that a combination of features from different AJAX frameworks best satisfies your requirements. In this circumstance, it is important that the frameworks are sufficiently flexible to accommodate third-party components. The Backbase framework can support coexistence with third-party frameworks as you have seen in the previous chapter and earlier in this chapter.

Progressive enhancement

Wikipedia defines **progressive enhancement** as follows:

> *Progressive enhancement uses web technologies in a layered fashion that allows everyone to access the basic content and functionality of a web page, using any browser or Internet connection, while also providing those with better bandwidth or more advanced browser software an enhanced version of the page.*

If you have this requirement for your application, then it should function *without* AJAX and *without* JavaScript. To enable enhancements for users with more advanced browser facilities, you can develop your application using the somewhat exotic tags, importHTML and enhanceHTML, which we did not mention before. See the API Reference and the importHTML demo application to find more information on these tags.

It is obvious that you cannot build a full Rich Internet Application in the way we described in this book using only these two tags. And it certainly makes your application more difficult to maintain. You may have to make careful trade-offs when designing for progressive enhancement.

Internationalization and localization

Internationalization and localization involves the ability to support multiple languages in one application and displaying dates, times, and currencies in a format that is appropriate for the country or region the user resides in. We have told you earlier that the Backbase framework does not have much support for internationalization and localization, except some support for formatting `calendar` dates.

Actually, this is not quite true. In the Java environment, you could use *resource bundles* and there are several examples available on the Backbase developer network (`http://bdn.backbase.com`) that show how you could do this.

There is also an example in the *Backbase Explorer*, (`http://demo.backbase.com/explorer`) under the heading **Localization**, which shows right-to-left display of text and the use of Unicode for special fonts such as Japanese.

Many languages other than Java also support internationalization and localization, which you could use to make your web application support multiple languages.

Other options include using *data binding* extensively and return data for a data-bound widget depending on the locale of the user. For example, we could extend the menu-item tables in the C3D application to include columns containing translations in other languages of the label texts, and return these translated texts instead of the English ones if asked.

Accessibility

Of course accessibility is a worldwide concern; however, in the USA there is a law that addresses this need most clearly:

Section 508 of the United States Rehabilitation Act of 1973 is a law requiring that electronic and information technology developed, procured, used, or maintained by all agencies and departments of the Federal Government be accessible both to Federal employees with disabilities and to members of the public with disabilities. Section 508 applies to web applications as a series of regulations including usability for people that are visually impaired, such as alternative keyboard navigation.

Backbase User Interface widgets comply with Section 508 regulations as much as possible. The widgets meet the directives in the following ways:

- Partial focus implementation—implementation of the focus model allows full keyboard navigation
- Almost complete resize support—full resize support allows users to change the size of text and objects to meet their needs

What will the future bring?

If we all knew how to convince the world to use the best technology for a specific purpose, we would have peace on earth, have solved pollution, eradicated poverty, and all developers would be using the Backbase framework to build web applications.

While this is not true and because our crystal ball looking skills are not great, we need to find other ways to predict what will happen with the Web in general and the Backbase framework in particular.

Backbase as a company realized that the Backbase framework and all its competitors are *foundation* technologies. These technologies are becoming more and more like commodities that developers take for granted to be available freely.

This means that most frameworks and libraries are open source or have free community licenses. So does the Backbase framework. It has a free community license and the open source issue will be solved in due time. When, we don't know, but remember that it took the implementation of the Java language about ten years to become open source. The availability of the source of the Backbase framework will undoubtedly be sooner. This does not make a lot of difference for using the framework because it is free now and most of you would not be interested in reading or changing the source code anyway.

Despite the popular belief that open source projects are built by young professionals in their evening hours, for many projects that is not true. Apache and the Eclipse IDE were heavily funded by IBM; jQuery, being part of ASP.NET AJAX, will certainly receive money from Microsoft, and MySQL, now owned by Oracle, was made profitable by selling commercial licenses, giving paid support and organizing expensive courses.

Backbase has decided to fund the Client Framework by broadening the scope of the company. Backbase has used the framework to develop new *portal software*, a kind of iGoogle that companies can install on their own servers. This software has been very successfully marketed to some very large enterprises.

For the Backbase framework itself this is good news because the success of the portal software is dependent on the stability and functionality of the framework. It may be the case that the marketing attention of a small company like Backbase, will, for a while, be more focused on this new product.

A square puzzle

We are going to end this book with a puzzle and a challenge—both a real and a metaphorical *square* puzzle. *Real*, because it is square as you can see from the screenshot a few pages later. *Metaphorical*, because the code of the puzzle is a squared JavaScript using TDL to the max.

One of the authors thinks this is a good example of what can be achieved in a simple way using TDL. The other author thinks this example is a bridge too far in using component composition. Therefore, we entered this puzzle as a challenge for improvement and as a pun on the title of this chapter.

The example we are going to describe is an implementation of a puzzle you all know from childhood: the 15 square puzzle.

The puzzle has a 4 x 4 square board with 15 tiles on it, that are initially randomly placed and one square is left empty. By sliding a tile that is in a position adjacent to the empty square to the empty square position, you can rearrange the tiles, until the tiles are properly ordered from 1 to 15. A variation that you often see for children has a picture on the tiles, instead of numbers.

The **challenge** we would like to put forward is to ask you to develop a better implementation of the puzzle using pure JavaScript or your favorite framework (could be Backbase!), but no server-side code. Better looks of the puzzle are of course nice, but not the objective of this challenge. Drag-and-drop of the puzzle tiles should be supported and our implementation allows defining other sizes other than a 4 x 4 square, as added complexity.

To get a puzzle board on your page, you need to code this:

```
<sq:puzzleBoard />
```

Or, if you wanted a 3 x 10 puzzle board, you could code this:

```
<sq:puzzleBoard rows="3" columns="10" />
```

Looking at the object model for this puzzle, we recognize three classes: `puzzleBoard`, `puzzleSquare`, and `tile`. The `tile` is the thing that is actually dragged around, to an empty `puzzleSquare` from a neighboring `puzzleSquare`. Here is a picture of this model:

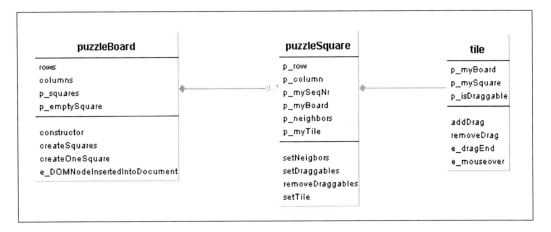

We prefixed properties with `p_` and events with `e_` to accommodate our little modeling tool.

Rather than showing you all 200 lines of code, we will explain how it works. We invite you to look for yourself in the sample code provided with the book.

- The `puzzleBoard` calculates how many tiles and squares there will be and determines a random sequence for the tiles, with a random position for the empty square. We should note here that half of the random sequences result in an insolvable puzzle where two tiles will always be in reverse order. With some extra calculation this can be avoided, but we did not bother to do so for this example.

- The `puzzleBoard` creates all the squares and for each square it sets the row, column, and sequence number. It asks each `puzzleSquare` to create a `tile` too. Each of these is a UI component in its own right, with appropriate behavior and defined as a widget in TDL. The `puzzleBoard` widget composes them together into the square puzzle.

- It is important to recognize that there are *only two interaction points* with the DOM in the whole implementation of the puzzle. The `puzzleBoard` creates an ordinary HTML table and appends in each cell a square as child. The `puzzleSquare` creates a `tile`, sets its properties, and adds it to itself as child. The interaction with the DOM during dragging and dropping of the tiles is done transparently by the framework.

- It is also important to note that dragging behavior and capabilities are dynamically added and removed. This makes it much easier to avoid tiles to be dragged that should not be movable. To achieve this, it is necessary to know the neighboring squares to an empty square, in order to make the tile on this square draggable and remove the possibility to drag others.

- Therefore, each `puzzleSquare` knows who its neighbors are, which is kept in an array of sequence numbers.

- When a `puzzleSquare` becomes empty, it will set its neighboring tiles as draggable and itself as a drag receiver:

```
<d:method name="setDraggables">
   <d:body type="text/javascript">
      var oNeighbors = this.getProperty('neighbors');
      var aSquares =
         this.getProperty('myBoard').getProperty('squares');
      for (var i=0; i < oNeighbors.length; i++) {
         oTile =
            aSquares[oNeighbors[i]].getProperty('myTile');
         oTile.addDrag();
      }
      // make me a receiver
      this.setAttributeNS
         ('http://www.backbase.com/2006/btl',
         'dragReceive', '*');
   </d:body>
</d:method>
```

- Here is the method on the `tile` to make itself draggable:

```
<d:method name="addDrag">
   <d:body type="text/javascript">
      bb.addBehavior(this,
         'http://www.backbase.com/2006/btl', 'drag');
      this.setProperty('isDraggable', true);
   </d:body>
</d:method>
```

- The `isDraggable` property is there to allow the `mouseover` event handler to change the cursor.

- The last interesting piece of code is the event handler for the dragEnd event. This event occurs when the tile is already dropped. To understand this event handler, remember that there is only one drag receiver, the empty square, and that only its neighboring tiles are draggable.

- The event handler removes all drag-and-drop capabilities from the previous empty square. This is the square that had the tile on top of it on which the event was fired. Then, it asks the new empty square to add drag-and-drop capabilities as we have seen above.

- Note again that this event handler does not access the DOM in any way, it just adapts the references to squares and tiles in the right way.

```
<d:handler event="dragEnd" type="application/javascript">
   oBoard = this.getProperty('myBoard');
   oSquare = oBoard.getProperty('emptySquare');
   oSquare.removeDraggables();
   oOldSquare = this.getProperty('mySquare');
   oBoard.setProperty('emptySquare', oOldSquare);
   this.setProperty('mySquare', oSquare);
   oSquare.setProperty('myTile', this);
   oOldSquare.setProperty('myTile', null);
   oOldSquare.setDraggables();
</d:handler>
```

Finally, here is a picture:

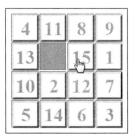

This completes the square puzzle example.

Summary

In this last chapter of this book, we gave you a summary of the design principles that apply to the development of a good web application using the Backbase Client Framework. We called a web application that is built using these principles **a square web application**, not to be confused with web squared, which is an extension of Web 2.0 ideas defined by Tim O'Reilly.

The main characteristic of a square application is that everything is XML. XHTML is considered just one markup language in one namespace that you can use in a web application, but there can be many others, such as BTL or XEL. You can create your own XML tags that encapsulate your own UI components in your own namespace using the object-oriented Tag Definition Language (TDL) that make the framework seamlessly and transparently extensible or adaptable to new requirements.

In the second part of this chapter, we tried to complete the C3D travel blog sample application. Of course *complete* is a relative concept, but the resulting application has the essential ingredients for a travel blog: trip entries categorized in trips, photos, and maps.

We completed the example using some guidelines presented in earlier chapter: *Make it work* using your best effort, but avoiding perfectionism. *Make it right*, which we demonstrated by refactoring the menu system of the application. *Make it fast* by looking at what is loaded initially, optimizing database queries, and so on.

In the third part of this chapter, we gave an overview, but no details of usability aspects such as legacy integration, progressive enhancement, internationalization, and accessibility.

In the last part of this chapter we tried to see a glimpse of the future and we presented a not-so-serious example, the square puzzle, pun intended.

Having read this book, you should be able now to develop your own client web applications. The book contains enough details to allow offline development, and enough pointers to online documentation should you need even more detail.

The online documentation offers practically no help with developing your web application as a whole. This book fills that void by also offering you design and development guidelines, with examples in PHP, but applicable to other server-side languages. The book also puts the various web technologies and standards like DOM, CSS, XHTML, and more in perspective and explains how the Backbase Client Framework fits into these.

BDN, the Backbase developer network, at `http://bdn.backbase.com` provides a discussion platform for further questions, comments, and ideas. We hope to see you there soon.

Index

XSLT 135

Y

yellow notes
  inheritance, using 328-330
YSlow 380
YUI library 418

Z

ZK 419

Thank you for buying
Backbase 4 RIA Development

Packt Open Source Project Royalties

When we sell a book written on an Open Source project, we pay a royalty directly to that project. Therefore by purchasing Backbase 4 RIA Development, Packt will have given some of the money received to the Backbase project.

In the long term, we see ourselves and you—customers and readers of our books—as part of the Open Source ecosystem, providing sustainable revenue for the projects we publish on. Our aim at Packt is to establish publishing royalties as an essential part of the service and support a business model that sustains Open Source.

If you're working with an Open Source project that you would like us to publish on, and subsequently pay royalties to, please get in touch with us.

Writing for Packt

We welcome all inquiries from people who are interested in authoring. Book proposals should be sent to author@packtpub.com. If your book idea is still at an early stage and you would like to discuss it first before writing a formal book proposal, contact us; one of our commissioning editors will get in touch with you.

We're not just looking for published authors; if you have strong technical skills but no writing experience, our experienced editors can help you develop a writing career, or simply get some additional reward for your expertise.

About Packt Publishing

Packt, pronounced 'packed', published its first book "Mastering phpMyAdmin for Effective MySQL Management" in April 2004 and subsequently continued to specialize in publishing highly focused books on specific technologies and solutions.

Our books and publications share the experiences of your fellow IT professionals in adapting and customizing today's systems, applications, and frameworks. Our solution-based books give you the knowledge and power to customize the software and technologies you're using to get the job done. Packt books are more specific and less general than the IT books you have seen in the past. Our unique business model allows us to bring you more focused information, giving you more of what you need to know, and less of what you don't.

Packt is a modern, yet unique publishing company, which focuses on producing quality, cutting-edge books for communities of developers, administrators, and newbies alike. For more information, please visit our website: www.PacktPub.com.

PUBLISHING

Learning jQuery 1.3

ISBN: 978-1-847196-70-5   Paperback: 444 pages

Better Interaction Design and Web Development with Simple JavaScript Techniques

1. An introduction to jQuery that requires minimal programming experience

2. Detailed solutions to specific client-side problems

3. For web designers to create interactive elements for their designs

Learning Ext JS

ISBN: 978-1-847195-14-2   Paperback: 324 pages

Build dynamic, desktop-style user interfaces for your data-driven web applications

1. Learn to build consistent, attractive web interfaces with the framework components.

2. Integrate your existing data and web services with Ext JS data support.

3. Enhance your JavaScript skills by using Ext's DOM and AJAX helpers.

Please check **www.PacktPub.com** for information on our titles

AJAX and PHP: Building Responsive Web Applications

ISBN: 978-1-904811-82-4   Paperback: 284 pages

Enhance the user experience of your PHP website using AJAX with this practical tutorial featuring detailed case studies

1. Build a solid foundation for your next generation of web applications

2. Use better JavaScript code to enable powerful web features

3. Leverage the power of PHP and MySQL to create powerful back-end functionality and make it work in harmony with the smart AJAX client

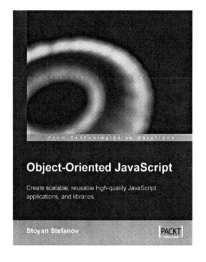

Object-Oriented JavaScript

ISBN: 978-1-847194-14-5   Paperback: 356 pages

Create scalable, reusable high-quality JavaScript applications and libraries

1. Learn to think in JavaScript, the language of the web browser

2. Object-oriented programming made accessible and understandable to web developers

3. Do it yourself: experiment with examples that can be used in your own scripts

Please check **www.PacktPub.com** for information on our titles

LaVergne, TN USA
16 December 2009
167130LV00003B/8/P